Women Writers At Work

The *Paris Review* Interviews

Edited by GEORGE PLIMPTON

Introduction by MARGARET ATWOOD

THE MODERN LIBRARY
NEW YORK

Modern Library Paperback Original

Copyright © 1998 by The Paris Review

All rights reserved under International and Pan-American Copyright
Conventions. Published in the United States by Random House, Inc.,
New York, and simultaneously in Canada by Random House of
Canada Limited, Toronto.

Modern Library is a registered trademark of Random House, Inc.

Library of Congress Cataloging-in-Publication Data is available
ISBN 0-679-77129-8

Modern Library website address:
www.randomhouse.com/modernlibrary
Printed in the United States of America

BVG 01

Acknowledgments

The editor thanks the interviewers and the following staff members of *The Paris Review* for their help in preparing this volume: Elizabeth Gaffney, Ben Howe and David Rosenthal.

Contents

Introduction

MARGARET ATWOOD

What is it about interviews that attracts us? Specifically, what is it about interviews with writers? Why should we pry? If a writer is august enough to be subject to interviews, we already have the books to read; shouldn't that be enough for us? (And the books must have been books we liked, because if we didn't, we presumably wouldn't be much interested in knowing anything about the person who has written them.)

Some of us are wary; even if we admire a book, we avoid an interview with its author. The writer is just the raw material, after all, and we prefer things cooked. Or perhaps we have a superstition about peeking: why ruin the memory of a night of magic by sneaking a look backstage, where the magician is wiping off the grimy makeup and the rabbits are born in hutches instead of, miraculously, out of silk hats? As Dorothy discovered in *The Wizard of Oz*, the fire that burns yet is not consumed may turn out to be—much to our disappointment—just a trick pulled by some wizened old fraud from Kansas. Some people may not be able to tell the dancer from the dance, but we think we can, and we prefer the dance.

Sometimes, on the other hand, we're greedy to know more. More of what? More of everything; more of anything; more of how and why, more of how-to. We would like to stand behind the interviewer and dictate the questions: what road did you travel on, and whom did you meet on the way, and who helped you across the river where the water was deepest? What other writers did you learn from, and does it matter what age, color, gender or nationality they were? (P. L. Travers's Mary Poppins as an avatar of the Great Mother in her Kali incarnation? Alarming, but just barely possible. Simone de Beauvoir influenced by *The Mill on the Floss*? After the first shock, it fits. . . .) Once upon a time you, too, were young, untried, unpublished; so how did you manage, against all odds—or against some odds, at least—to accomplish as much as you have? Do you think that what you do makes any difference, to your individual readers or to the world in general? Where did the books come from—what part of your life? Does the writing always flow, or do you struggle? Do you have to suffer to be an artist, and if so, how much, and what kind of suffering would you recommend? Should you use—*do* you use—a pencil, or a pen, or your finger dipped in blood? Are there any special foods? What kind of chair?

It is our illusion that by knowing the answers to these questions we will know the central, the hidden, the necessary thing; that a writer's power is to be found in the sum of such answers. It isn't, of course. An interview is also a performance, and although a performance can reveal much, its revelations are selective, and its omissions and concealments are often as instructive as its grand pronouncements. (In this collection, for instance, it's an education to watch Elizabeth Bishop evading the issues.) Sometimes a writer doesn't want to tell; sometimes a writer doesn't know; sometimes a writer has forgotten. But why should a writer tell all? Why should anyone? How *can* anyone? *All* is a giant subject. In the interview, we must largely settle for conversation instead.

Your next-door neighbor might give you some of the very same answers as the ones you'll find in this collection—with a pencil, on a bed, with a glass of sherry, and *yes* to the suffering—but that is the mystery; or, if you prefer, the lack of mystery. Writers are human beings; they too inhabit bodies, had childhoods, get through the day somehow, experience joy and fear and boredom, confront death. The rabbits they produce are only common rabbits, after all; it's the hat that's magic. And yet it is only a hat. This is what fuels our curiosity: the mix of the familiar, even the banal, and the radically inexplicable.

This volume is a revised version of the 1988 collection, *Women Writers at Work*, which was part of the *Paris Review*'s highly praised series of interviews with writers. Both that book and this one are a departure from the norm. Previous *Paris Review* collections mixed men and women, but *Women Writers at Work*, as its title suggests, is unisexual. That the editors have chosen to bring together fifteen writers as diverse as Dorothy Parker and Nadine Gordimer, P. L. Travers and Maya Angelou, Marianne Moore and Simone de Beauvoir, Toni Morrison and Katherine Anne Porter, over what, in some cases, would be their dead bodies, merely because they share a double-X chromosome, was the result of readers' requests. Why not a gathering of women writers? the editors were asked. Which is not quite the same thing as *why*.

To some the answer is self-evident: women writers belong together because they are different from men, and the writing they do is different as well and cannot be read with the same eyeglasses as those used for the reading of male writers. Nor can writing by women be read in the same way by men as it can by women, and vice versa. For many women, Heathcliff is a romantic hero; for many men, he's a posturing oaf they'd like to punch in the nose. *Paradise Lost* reads differently when viewed by the daughters of Eve, and with Milton's browbeaten secretarial daughters in mind; and so on down through the canon.

Such gender-polarized interpretations can reach beyond subject matter and point of view to encompass matters of structure and style: are women really more subjective? do their novels really end with questions? Gender-linked analysis may seek to explore attitudes toward language itself. Is there a distinct female *écriture*? Does the mother tongue really belong to mothers, or is it yet one more male-shaped institution bent, like foot-binding, on the deformation and hobbling of women? I have had it suggested to me, in all seriousness, that women ought not to write at all, since to do so is to dip one's hand, like Shakespeare's dyer, into a medium both sullied and sullying. (This suggestion was not made telepathically, but in spoken sentences, since, for polemicists as for writers themselves, the alternative to language is silence.)

Some years ago I was on a panel—that polygonal form of discourse so beloved of the democratic twentieth century—consisting entirely of women, including Jan Morris, who used to be James Morris, and Nayantara Sahgal of India. From the audience came the question "How do you feel about being on a panel of women?" We all prevaricated. Some of us protested that we had been on lots of panels that included men; others said that most panels were male, with a woman dotted here and there for decorative effect, like parsley. Jan Morris said that she was in the process of transcending gender and was aiming at becoming a horse, to which Nayantara Sahgal replied that she hoped it was an English horse, since in some other, poorer countries, horses were not treated very well. Which underlined, for all of us, that there are categories other than male or female worth considering.

I suppose we all should have said, "Why not?" Still, I was intrigued by our collective uneasiness. No woman writer wants to be overlooked and undervalued for being a woman; but few, it seems, wish to be defined solely by gender, or constrained by loyalties to it alone—an attitude that may puzzle, hurt or enrage those whose political priorities cause them to view writing as a tool, a means to an end, rather than as a vocation subject to a Muse who will desert you if you break trust with your calling. In the interview that begins this collection, Dorothy Parker articulates the dilemma:

> I'm a feminist and God knows I'm loyal to my sex, and you must remember that from my very early days, when this city was scarcely safe from buffaloes, I was in the struggle for equal rights for women. But when we paraded through the catcalls of men and when we chained ourselves to lamp posts to try to get our equality—dear child, we didn't foresee those female writers.

Male writers may suffer strains on their single-minded dedication to their art for reasons of class or race or nationality, but so far no male writer is likely to be asked to sit on a panel addressing itself to the special problems of a male writer, or be expected to support another writer simply because he happens to be a man. Such things are asked of women writers all the time, and it makes them jumpy.

Virginia Woolf may have been right about the androgynous nature of the artist, but she was right also about the differences in social situation these androgynous artists are certain to encounter. We may agree with Nadine Gordimer when she says, "By and large, I don't think it matters a damn what sex a writer is, so long as the work is that of a real *writer*," if what she means is that it *shouldn't* matter, in any true assessment of talent or accomplishment; but unfortunately it often has mattered, to other people. When Joyce Carol Oates is asked the "woman" question, phrased in her case as "What are the advantages of being a woman writer?" she makes a virtue of necessity:

Advantages! Too many to enumerate, probably. Since, being a woman, I can't be taken altogether seriously by the sort of male critics who rank writers 1, 2, 3 in the public press, I am free, I suppose, to do as I like.

Joan Didion is asked the same question in its negative form—"disadvantages" instead of "advantages"—and also focuses on social differences, social acceptance and role:

When I was starting to write—in the late fifties, early sixties—there was a kind of social tradition in which male novelists could operate. Hard drinkers, bad livers. Wives, wars, big fish, Africa, Paris, no second acts. A man who wrote novels had a role in the world, and he could play that role and do whatever he wanted behind it. A woman who wrote novels had no particular role. Women who wrote novels were quite often perceived as invalids. Carson McCullers, Jane Bowles. Flannery O'Connor of course. Novels by women tended to be described, even by their publishers, as sensitive. I'm not sure this is so true anymore, but it certainly was at the time, and I didn't much like it. I dealt with it the same way I deal with everything. I just tended my own garden, didn't pay much attention, behaved—I suppose—deviously.

I think of Marianne Moore, living decorously with her mother and her "dark" furniture, her height of social rebellion the courageous ignoring of the need for chaperons at Greenwich Village literary parties, and wonder how many male writers could have lived such a circumscribed life and survived the image.

Not least among perceived social differences is the difficulty women writers have experienced in being taken "altogether *seriously*" as legitimate artists. Ezra Pound, writing in the second decade of this century, spoke for many male authors and critics before and since: "I distrust the 'female artist.' . . . Not wildly anti-feminist we are yet to be convinced that any woman ever invented anything in the arts." Cognate with this view of writing as a male preserve has been the image of women writers as lightweight puffballs, neurotic freaks suffering from what Edna O'Brien has called "a double dose of masochism: the masochism of the woman and that of the artist," or, if approved of, as honorary men. Femininity and excellence, it seemed, were mutually exclusive. Thus Katherine Anne Porter:

> If there is such a thing as a man's mind and a woman's mind—and I'm sure there is—it isn't what most critics mean when they talk about the two. If I show wisdom, they say I have a masculine mind. If I am silly and irrelevant—and Edmund Wilson says I often am—why then, they say I have a typically feminine mind! . . . But I haven't ever found it unnatural to be a woman.

The interviewer responds with a question that is asked, in one form or another, not only of almost every woman included in this book, but of almost every woman writer ever interviewed: "But haven't you found that being a woman presented to you, as an artist, certain special problems?"

Katherine Anne Porter's reply—"I think that's very true and very right"—is by no means the only one possible. Some, such as Mary McCarthy, are clearly impatient with the question itself. McCarthy accepts some version of the "masculine" versus the "feminine" sensibility, but aligns herself firmly with the former.

> INTERVIEWER: What do you think of women writers, or do you think the category "woman writer" should not be made?
>
> MCCARTHY: Some women writers make it. I mean, there's a certain kind of woman writer who's a capital W, capital W. Virginia Woolf certainly was one, and Katherine Mansfield was one, and Elizabeth Bowen is one. Katherine Anne Porter? Don't think she really is—I mean, her writing is certainly very feminine, but I would say that there wasn't this "WW" business in Katherine Anne Porter. Who else? There's Eudora Welty, who's certainly not a "Woman Writer," though she's become one lately.

INTERVIEWER: *What is it that happens to make this change?*

MCCARTHY: *I think they become interested in décor. You notice the change in Elizabeth Bowen. Her early work is much more masculine. Her later work has much more drapery in it. . . . I was going to write a piece at some point about this called "Sense and Sensibility," dividing women writers into these two. I am for the ones who represent sense. . . .*

There is, still, a sort of trained-dog fascination with the idea of women writers—not that the thing is done well, but that it is done at all, by a creature that is not supposed to possess such capabilities. And so a biographer may well focus on the woman, on gossip and sexual detail and domestic arrangements and political involvement, to the exclusion of the artist. However, what these writers have in common is not their diverse responses to the category "woman writer," but their shared passion toward the category "writer."

This is true as well when that other "special" category, race, is tacked on. Neither the white women writers nor the black women writers in this book feel that they have to deny anything about themselves to gain entry into the category of writer; but none of them feel, either, that their other attributes should be allowed to obscure what it is they are focused on, what it is they have been called to do. For them, writing is not an offshoot; it is the one thing that includes all the other aspects of their lives. Thus Maya Angelou:

> *When I am writing, I am trying to find out who I am, who we are, what we're capable of, how we feel, how we lose and stand up, and go on from darkness into darkness. I'm trying for that. But I'm also trying for the language. I'm trying to see how it can really sound. I really love language. I love it for what it does for us, how it allows us to explain the pain and the glory, the nuances and the delicacies of our existence. And then it allows us to laugh, allows us to show wit. Real wit is shown in language. We need language.*

Reading through these interviews, I was struck again and again by the intensity of the writers' dedication: their commitment to craft, the informed admiration for the work of other writers from whom they have learned, the insistence on the importance of what has been done, and what can be done, through the art itself. Thus Toni Morrison:

> It is not possible for me to be unaware of the incredible violence, the willful ignorance, the hunger for other people's pain. . . . What makes me feel I belong here, out in this world, is not the teacher, not the mother, not the lover but what goes on in my mind when I am writing. Then I belong here, and then all of the things that are disparate and irreconcilable can be useful. I can do the traditional things that writers always say they do, which is to make order out of chaos. . . .

In no other art is the relationship of creation to creator so complex and personal and thus so potentially damaging to self-esteem: if you fail, you fail alone. The dancer realizes someone else's dance, the writer her own. The relationship of any writer toward a vocation so exacting in its specificity, so demanding of love and energy and time, so resistant to all efforts to define its essence or to categorize its best effects, is bound to be an edgy one, and in these conversations the edginess shows through. Some disclaim ego, remarkable in a collection of such strong, assertive, individual voices; others keep secrets; others fence with their considerable intelligence; others have recourse to mysticism; others protect themselves with wit. It would be a brave person who would try to stuff these wonderful and various talents into one tidy box labeled "WW," and accept that designation to be definitive. Despite the title of this book, the label should probably read, "WWAAW," Writers Who Are Also Women.

To write is a solitary and singular act; to do it superbly, as all of these writers have done, is a blessing. Despite everything that gets said about the suffering and panic and horror of being a writer, the final impression left by these remarkable voices is one of thankfulness, of humility in the face of what has been given. From Joyce Carol Oates, one of the youngest writers in this group:

> I take seriously Flaubert's statement that we must love one another in our art as the mystics love one another in God. By honoring one another's creation we honor something that deeply connects us all, and goes beyond us.

And from Dorothy Parker, one of the oldest:

> I want so much to write well, though I know I don't. . . . But during and at the end of my life, I will adore those who have.

WOMEN WRITERS AT WORK

MARIANNE MOORE

Marianne Moore was born on November 15, 1887, in Kirkwood, Missouri, a St. Louis suburb. Her father, an engineer who attempted to build a smokeless furnace, suffered a nervous breakdown after her birth and returned to his parents' home. The family never saw him again.

Moore's early youth was spent under the care of her maternal grandfather, a Presbyterian minister in Kirkwood. His death in 1894 prompted Moore's mother to take a teaching job at the Metzger Institute, a girls' school in Carlisle, Pennsylvania. Moore herself enrolled at Metzger and entered Bryn Mawr in 1906. Academically mediocre and often unhappy, Moore studied biology at Bryn Mawr and contributed poems to the literary magazine. After graduating in 1909 she returned to Carlisle, took secretarial courses at a local college, then taught until 1915 at the U.S. Industrial Indian School in Carlisle.

Moore's breakthrough came in 1918, the year two influential magazines, *Poetry* and the London-based *Egoist*, published her poems. Her work soon found its way to Ezra Pound, who began hailing her as one of the country's promising young poets.

In 1918 Moore moved with her mother to Greenwich Village, where she took a part-time job at the New York City library. *Poems,* her first collection, appeared in 1921. It was followed by *Observations,* winner of the prestigious *Dial* magazine award in 1925. That same year Moore became editor of the *Dial,* a position she held until the magazine folded in 1929.

Moore then moved with her mother to Brooklyn. Over the next forty years she produced a body of work that includes essays, translations and collections of verse. In 1951 she received the Bollingen and Pulitzer prizes, as well as the National Book Award, for *Collected Poems,* her ninth book. Other works include *The Pangolin and Other Verse* (1936), *What Are Years?* (1941), *Nevertheless* (1944), *Like a Bulwark* (1956) and *O to Be a Dragon* (1959). She died in New York on February 5, 1972.

MARIANNE MOORE

American poetry is a great literature, and it has come to its maturity only in the last seventy years; Walt Whitman and Emily Dickinson in the last century were rare examples of genius in a hostile environment. One decade gave America the major figures of our modern poetry: Wallace Stevens was born in 1879, and T. S. Eliot in 1888. To the ten years that these dates enclose belong H. D., Robinson Jeffers, John Crowe Ransom, William Carlos Williams, Ezra Pound, and Marianne Moore.

Marianne Moore began to publish during the First World War. She was printed and praised in Europe by the expatriates T. S. Eliot and Ezra Pound. In Chicago, Harriet Monroe's magazine Poetry, which provided the enduring showcase for the new poetry, published her too. But she was mainly a poet of New York, of the Greenwich Village group which created magazines called Others and Broom.

To visit Marianne Moore at her home in Brooklyn, you had to cross the Brooklyn Bridge, turn left at Myrtle Avenue, follow the elevated for a mile or two, and then turn right onto her street. It was pleasantly lined with a few trees, and Miss Moore's apartment was conveniently near a grocery store and the Presbyterian church that she attended.

The interview took place in November 1960, the day before the presiden-

RESCUE WITH YUL BRYNNER
(appointed by President Eisenhower, consultant
to the United Nations commission of Refugees,
(1959-1960)

with Dances Galanta by Zoltán Kodály
favorites of Budapest Symphony Orchestra
now refugee Symphonia Hungarica in Marl—
CBS;December 10, 1960

Head down low over the guitar,
he barely seemed to hum; ending "all come home";
did not smile;came by air;
did not have to come.
    The guitar's an event.
    Guests of honor is old. doesn't dance; can't smile.
    "Have a home?" a boy asks. "Shall we live in a tent?"
        "In a house", Yul answers. His neat cloth hat
has nothing like the glitter that reflected on the face
of milkweed-seed brown dominating a palas place
in those hells devoid of solace
where he is now. His deliberate pace
is a king's however, "You'll have plenty of space."
    "recital"? "concert is the word".—
in Marl Austria's Marl, by the Budapest Symphonia Symphony—
    displaced but not deterred—
listened to by me —
    detachedly then—
    like a frog or grasshopper that did not
    know it had missed the mower, a pigmy citizen;
        in any case, too slow a grower.
There were thirty million; there are thirteen still -
healthy to begin with, kept waiting till they're ill/
History judges. It certainly will
remember Winnipeg's incredible
conditions: "Ill;no p sponsor;and no kind of skill."
    Odd - a reporter with small guitar - a puzzle.
    Mysterious Yul did not come to dazzle.

Magic bird with multiple tongue -
five tongues - embarked on a crazy twelve-month tramp
or plod); he flew among
the damned, / found each camp
    where hope had slowly died.
    & came to end that sort of death;
Instead of did not feather himself,
    "Two small fishes and five loaves of bread.
    nourished seeds of dignity. All were fed,
He said, you may feel strange; not dressed the way they dress.
Nobody notices; you'll find some happiness.
No new "big fear"; no distress."
He can sing twinned with an enchantress —
elephant-borne fairy with blue sequinned-spangled dress -
    oried aloft by trunk, with star-tipped wand, Tamara,
    tru-er to the beat than Symphonia Hungarica.

A manuscript page from a poem by Marianne Moore.

tial election. The front door of Miss Moore's apartment opened onto a long narrow corridor. Rooms led off to the right, and at the end of the corridor was a large sitting room that overlooked the street. On top of a bookcase that ran the length of the corridor was a Nixon button.

Miss Moore and the interviewer sat in her sitting room, a microphone between them. Piles of books stood everywhere. On the walls hung a variety of paintings. One came from Mexico, a gift of Mabel Dodge; others were examples of the heavy, tea-colored oils that Americans hung in the years before 1914. The furniture was old-fashioned and dark.

Miss Moore spoke with an accustomed scrupulosity, and with a humor that her readers will recognize. When she ended a sentence with a phrase that was particularly telling, or even tart, she glanced quickly at the interviewer to see if he was amused, and then snickered gently. Later Miss Moore took the interviewer to an admirable lunch at a nearby restaurant. She decided not to wear her Nixon button because it clashed with her coat and hat.

INTERVIEWER: Miss Moore, I understand that you were born in St. Louis only about ten months before T. S. Eliot. Did your families know each other?

MOORE: No, we did not know the Eliots. We lived in Kirkwood, Missouri, where my grandfather was pastor of the First Presbyterian Church. T. S. Eliot's grandfather—Dr. William Eliot—was a Unitarian. We left when I was about seven, my grandfather having died in 1894, February 20. My grandfather, like Dr. Eliot, had attended ministerial meetings in St. Louis. Also, at stated intervals, various ministers met for luncheon. After one of these luncheons my grandfather said, "When Dr. William Eliot asks the blessing and says, 'and this we ask in the name of our Lord Jesus Christ,' he is Trinitarian enough for me." The Mary Institute, for girls, was endowed by him as a memorial to his daughter Mary, who had died.

INTERVIEWER: How old were you when you started to write poems?

MOORE: Well, let me see, in Bryn Mawr. I think I was eighteen when I entered Bryn Mawr. I was born in 1887, I entered college in 1906. Now, how old would I have been? Can you deduce my probable age?

INTERVIEWER: Eighteen or nineteen.

MOORE: I had no literary plans, but I was interested in the undergraduate monthly magazine, and to my surprise (I wrote one or two little things for it) the editors elected me to the board. It was my sophomore year—I am sure it was—and I stayed on, I believe. And then when I had left college I offered contributions (we weren't paid) to the *Lantern*, the alumnae magazine. But I didn't feel that my product was anything to shake the world.

INTERVIEWER: At what point did poetry become world-shaking for you?

MOORE: Never! I believe I was interested in painting then. At least I said so. I remember Mrs. Otis Skinner asking at commencement time, the year I was graduated, "What would you like to be?"

"A painter," I said.

"Well, I'm not surprised," Mrs. Skinner answered. I had something on that she liked, some kind of summer dress. She commended it—said, "I'm not at all surprised."

I like stories. I like fiction. And—this sounds rather pathetic, bizarre as well—I think verse perhaps was for me the next best thing to it. Didn't I write something one time, "Part of a Poem, Part of a Novel, Part of a Play"? I think I was all too truthful. I could visualize scenes, and deplored the fact that Henry James had to do it unchallenged. Now, if I couldn't write fiction, I'd like to write plays. To me the theater is the most pleasant, in fact my favorite, form of recreation.

INTERVIEWER: Do you go often?

MOORE: No. Never. Unless someone invites me. Lillian Hellman invited me to *Toys in the Attic*, and I am very happy that she did. I would have had no notion of the vitality of the thing, have lost sight of her skill as a writer if I hadn't seen the play; would like to go again. The accuracy of the vernacular! That's the kind of thing I am interested in, am always taking down little local expressions and accents. I think I should be in some philological operation or enterprise, am really much interested in dialect and intonations. I scarcely think of any that comes into my so-called poems at all.

INTERVIEWER: I wonder what Bryn Mawr meant for you as a poet. You write that most of your time there was spent in the biological laboratory. Did you like biology better than literature as a subject for study? Did the training possibly affect your poetry?

MOORE: I had hoped to make French and English my major studies, and took the required two-year English course—five hours a week—but was not able to elect a course until my junior year. I did not attain the requisite academic stand of eighty until that year. I then elected seventeenth-century imitative writing—Fuller, Hooker, Bacon, Bishop Andrews, and others. Lectures in French were in French, and I had had no spoken French.

Did laboratory studies affect my poetry? I am sure they did. I found the biology courses—minor, major, and histology—exhilarating. I thought, in fact, of studying medicine. Precision, economy of statement, logic employed to ends that are disinterested, drawing and identifying, liberate—at least have some bearing on—the imagination, it seems to me.

INTERVIEWER: Whom did you know in the literary world, before you came to New York? Did you know Bryher and H.D.?

MOORE: It's very hard to get these things seriatim. I met Bryher in 1921 in New York. H.D. was my classmate at Bryn Mawr. She was there, I think, only two years. She was a nonresident and I did not realize that she was interested in writing.

INTERVIEWER: Did you know Ezra Pound and William Carlos Williams through her? Didn't she know them at the University of Pennsylvania?

MOORE: Yes. She did. I didn't meet them. I had met no writers until 1916, when I visited New York, when a friend in Carlisle wanted me to accompany her.

INTERVIEWER: So you were isolated really from modern poetry until 1916?

MOORE: Yes.

INTERVIEWER: Was that your first trip to New York, when you went there for six days and decided that you wanted to live there?

MOORE: Oh, no. Several times my mother had taken my brother and me sightseeing and to shop; on the way to Boston, or Maine, and to Washington and Florida. My senior year in college in 1909, I visited Dr. Charles Spraguesmith's daughter, Hilda, at Christmastime in New York. And Louis Anspacher lectured in a very ornamental way at Cooper Union. There was plenty of music at Carnegie Hall, and I got a sense of what was going on in New York.

INTERVIEWER: And what was going on made you want to come back?

MOORE: It probably did, when Miss Cowdrey in Carlisle invited me to come with her for a week. It was the visit in 1916 that made me want to live there. I don't know what put it into her head to do it, or why she wasn't likely to have a better time without me. She was most skeptical of my venturing forth to bohemian parties. But I was fearless about that. In the first place, I didn't think anyone would try to harm me, but if they did I felt impervious. It never occurred to me that chaperons were important.

INTERVIEWER: Do you suppose that moving to New York, and the stimulation of the writers whom you found there, led you to write more poems than you would otherwise have written?

MOORE: I'm sure it did—seeing what others wrote, liking this or that. With me it's always some fortuity that traps me. I certainly never intended to write poetry. That never came into my head. And now, too, I think each time I write that it may be the last time; then I'm charmed by something and seem to have to say something. Everything I have written is the result of reading or of interest in people, I'm sure of that. I had no ambition to be a writer.

INTERVIEWER: Let me see. You taught at the Carlisle Indian School, after Bryn Mawr. Then after you moved to New York in 1918 you taught at a private school and worked in a library. Did these occupations have anything to do with you as a writer?

MOORE: I think they hardened my muscles considerably, my mental approach to things. Working as a librarian was a big help, a tremendous help. Miss Leonard of the Hudson Park branch of the New York Public Library opposite our house came to see me one day. I wasn't in, and she asked my mother did she think I would care to be on the staff, work in the library, because I was so fond of books and liked to talk about them to people. My mother said no, she thought not; the shoemaker's children never have shoes, I probably would feel if I joined the staff that I'd have no time to read. When I came home she told me, and I said, "Why, certainly. Ideal. I'll tell her. Only I couldn't work more than half a day." If I had worked all day and maybe evenings or overtime, like the mechanics, why, it would *not* have been ideal.

As a free service we were assigned books to review and I did like that. We didn't get paid but we had the chance to diagnose. I reveled in it. Somewhere I believe I have carbon copies of those "P-slip" summaries. They were the kind of things that brought the worst-best out. I was always wondering why they didn't honor me with an art book or medical book or even a history, or criticism. But no, it was fiction, silent-movie fiction.

INTERVIEWER: Did you travel at this time? Did you go to Europe at all?

MOORE: In 1911. My mother and I went to England for about two months, July and August probably. We went to Paris and we stayed on the left bank, in a pension in the rue Valette, where Calvin wrote his *Institutes,* I believe. Not far from the Panthéon and the Luxembourg Gardens. I have been much interested in Sylvia Beach's book—reading about Ezra Pound and his Paris days. Where was I and what was I doing? I think, with the objective, an evening stroll—it was one of the hottest summers the world has ever known, 1911—we walked along to 12, rue de l'Odéon, to see Sylvia Beach's shop. It wouldn't occur to me to say, "Here am I, I'm a writer, would you talk to me a while?" I had no feeling at all like that. I wanted to observe things. And we went to every museum in Paris, I think, except two.

INTERVIEWER: Have you been back since?

MOORE: Not to Paris. Only to England in 1935 or 1936. I like England.

INTERVIEWER: You have mostly stayed put in Brooklyn, then, since you moved here in 1929?

MOORE: Except for four trips to the West: Los Angeles, San Francisco, Puget Sound, and British Columbia. My mother and I went through the canal previously, to San Francisco, and by rail to Seattle.

INTERVIEWER: Have you missed the Dodgers here, since *they* went West?

MOORE: Very much, and I am told that they miss us.

INTERVIEWER: I am still interested in those early years in New York. William Carlos Williams, in his *Autobiography,* says that you were "a rafter holding up the superstructure of our uncompleted building," when he talks about the Greenwich Village group of writers. I guess these were people who contributed to *Others.*

MOORE: I never was a rafter holding up anyone! I have his *Autobiography* and took him to task for his misinformed statements about Robert McAlmon and Bryher. In my indignation I missed some things I ought to have seen.

INTERVIEWER: To what extent did the *Others* contributors form a group?

MOORE: We did foregather a little. Alfred Kreymborg was editor, and was married to Gertrude Lord at the time, one of the loveliest persons you could ever meet. And they had a little apartment somewhere in the village. There was considerable unanimity about the group.

INTERVIEWER: Someone called Alfred Kreymborg your American discoverer. Do you suppose this is true?

MOORE: It could be said, perhaps; he did all he could to promote me. Miss Monroe and the Aldingtons had asked me simultaneously to contribute to *Poetry* and the *Egoist* in 1917. Alfred Kreymborg was not inhibited. I was a little different from the others. He thought I might pass as a novelty, I guess.

INTERVIEWER: What was your reaction when H.D. and Bryher brought out your first collection, which they called *Poems*, in 1921 without your knowledge? Why had you delayed to do it yourself?

MOORE: To issue my slight product—conspicuously tentative—seemed to me premature. I disliked the term "poetry" for any but Chaucer's or Shakespeare's or Dante's. I do not now feel quite my original hostility to the word, since it is a convenient almost unavoidable term for the thing (although hardly for me—my observations, experiments in rhythm, or exercises in composition). What I write, as I have said before, could only be called poetry because there is no other category in which to put it. For the chivalry of the undertaking—issuing my verse for me in 1921, certainly in format choicer than the content—I am intensely grateful. Again, in 1925, it seemed to me not very self-interested of Faber and Faber, and simultaneously of the Macmillan Company, to propose a *Selected Poems* for me. Desultory occasional magazine publications seemed to me sufficient, conspicuous enough.

INTERVIEWER: Had you been sending poems to magazines before the *Egoist* printed your first poem?

MOORE: I must have. I have a little curio, a little wee book about two by three inches, or two and a half by three inches, in which I systematically entered everything sent out, when I got it back, if they took it, and how much I got for it. That lasted about a year, I think. I can't care as much as all that. I don't know that I submitted anything that wasn't extorted from me.

I have at present three onerous tasks, and each interferes with the others, and I don't know how I am going to write anything. If I get a promising idea I set it down, and it stays there. I don't make myself do anything with it. I've had several things in *The New Yorker*. And I said to them, "I might never write again," and not to expect me to. I never knew anyone who had a passion for words who had as much difficulty in saying things as I do and I very seldom say them in a manner I like. If I do it's because I don't know I'm trying. I've written several things for *The New Yorker*—and I did want to write *them*.

INTERVIEWER: When did you last write a poem?

MOORE: It appeared in August. What was it about? Oh . . . Carnegie Hall. You see, anything that really rouses me . . .

INTERVIEWER: How does a poem start for you?

MOORE: A felicitous phrase springs to mind—a word or two, say—simultaneous usually with some thought or object of equal attraction: "Its leaps should be *set*/to the flageo*let*"; "Katydidwing subdivided by *sun*/till the nettings are *legion*." I like light rhymes, inconspicuous rhymes and un-pompous conspicuous rhymes: Gilbert and Sullivan:

> Yet, when the danger's near,
> We manage to appear
> As insensible to fear
> As anybody here.

I have a passion for rhythm and accent, so blundered into versifying. Considering the stanza the unit, I came to hazard hyphens at the end of the line, but found that readers are distracted from the content by hyphens, so I try not to use them. My interest in La Fontaine originated entirely independent of content. I then fell prey to that surgical kind of courtesy of his.

I fear that appearances are worshiped throughout France
Whereas pre-eminence perchance
Merely means a pushing person.

I like the unaccented syllable and accented near-rhyme:

By love and his blindness
Possibly a service was done,
Let lovers say. A lonely man has no criterion.

INTERVIEWER: What in your reading or your background led you to write the way you do write? Was imagism a help to you?

MOORE: No. I wondered why anyone would adopt the term.

INTERVIEWER: The descriptiveness of your poems has nothing to do with them, you think?

MOORE: No; I really don't. I was rather sorry to be a pariah, or at least that I had no connection with anything. But I *did* feel gratitude to *Others*.

INTERVIEWER: Where do you think your style of writing came from? Was it a gradual accumulation, out of your character? Or does it have literary antecedents?

MOORE: Not so far as I know. Ezra Pound said, "Someone has been reading Laforgue, and French authors." Well, sad to say, I had not read any of them until fairly recently. Retroactively I see that Francis Jammes' titles and treatment are a good deal like my own. I seem almost a plagiarist.

INTERVIEWER: And the extensive use of quotations?

MOORE: I was just trying to be honorable and not to steal things. I've always felt that if a thing had been said in the *best* way, how can you say it better? If I wanted to say something and somebody had said it ideally, then I'd take it but give the person credit for it. That's all there is to it. If you are charmed by an author, I think it's a very strange and invalid imagination that doesn't long to share it. Somebody else should read it, don't you think?

INTERVIEWER: Did any prose stylists help you in finding your poetic style? Elizabeth Bishop mentions Poe's prose in connection with your writing, and you have always made people think of Henry James.

MOORE: Prose stylists, very much. Dr. Johnson on Richard Savage: "He was in two months illegitimated by the Parliament, and disowned by his mother, doomed to poverty and obscurity, and launched upon the ocean of life only that he might be swallowed by its quicksands, or dashed upon its rocks. . . . It was his peculiar happiness that he scarcely ever found a stranger whom he did not leave a friend; but it must likewise be added, that he had not often a friend long without obliging him to become a stranger." Or Edmund Burke on the colonies: "You can shear a wolf; but will he comply?" Or Sir Thomas Browne: "States are not governed by Ergotisms." He calls a bee "that industrious flie," and his home his "hive." His manner is a kind of erudition-proof sweetness. Or Sir Francis Bacon: "Civil War is like the heat of fever; a foreign war is like the heat of exercise." Or Cellini: "I had by me a dog black as a mulberry. . . . I swelled up in my rage like an asp." Or Caesar's *Commentaries*, and Xenophon's *Cynegeticus:* the gusto and interest in every detail! In Henry James it is the essays and letters especially that affect me. In Ezra Pound, *The Spirit of Romance:* his definiteness, his indigenously unmistakable accent. Charles Norman says in his biography of Ezra Pound that he said to a poet, "Nothing, *nothing*, that you couldn't in some circumstance, under stress of some emotion, *actually say.*" And Ezra said of Shakespeare and Dante, "Here we are with the masters; of neither can we say, 'He is the greater'; of each we must say, 'He is unexcelled.'"

INTERVIEWER: Do you have in your own work any favorites and unfavorites?

MOORE: Indeed, I do. I think the most difficult thing for me is to be satisfactorily lucid, yet have enough implication in it to suit myself. That's a problem. And I don't approve of my "enigmas," or as somebody said, "the not ungreen grass." I said to my mother one time, "How did you ever permit me to let this be printed?" And she said, "You didn't ask my advice."

INTERVIEWER: One time I heard you give a reading, and I think you said that you didn't like "In Distrust of Merits," which is one of your most popular poems.

MOORE: I do like it; it is sincere but I wouldn't call it a poem. It's truthful; it is testimony—to the fact that war is intolerable, and unjust.

INTERVIEWER: How can you call it not a poem, on what basis?

MOORE: Haphazard; as form, what has it? It is just a protest—disjointed, exclamatory. Emotion overpowered me. First this thought and then that.

INTERVIEWER: Your mother said that you hadn't asked her advice. Did you ever? Do you go for criticism to your family or friends?

MOORE: Well, not friends, but my brother if I get a chance. When my mother said "You didn't ask my advice" must have been years ago, because when I wrote "A Face," I had written something first about "the adder and the child with a bowl of porridge," and she said, "It won't do." "All right," I said, "but I have to produce something." Cyril Connolly had asked me for something for *Horizon.* So I wrote "A Face." That is one of the few things I ever set down that didn't give me any trouble. She said, "I like it." I remember that.

Then, much before that, I wrote "The Buffalo." I thought it would probably outrage a number of persons because it had to me a kind of pleasing jerky progress. I thought, "Well, if it seems bad my brother will tell me, and if it has a point he'll detect it." And he said, with considerable gusto, "It takes my fancy." I was happy as could be.

INTERVIEWER: Did you ever suppress anything because of family objections?

MOORE: Yes, "the adder and the child with a bowl of porridge." I never even wanted to improve it. You know, Mr. Saintsbury said that Andrew Lang wanted him to contribute something on Poe, and he did, and Lang returned it. Mr. Saintsbury said, "Once a thing has been rejected, I would not offer it to the most different of editors." That shocked me. I have offered a thing, submitted it thirty-five times. Not simultaneously, of course.

INTERVIEWER: A poem?

MOORE: Yes. I am very tenacious.

INTERVIEWER: Do people ever ask you to write poems for them?

MOORE: Continually. Everything from on the death of a dog to a little item for an album.

INTERVIEWER: Do you ever write them?

MOORE: Oh, perhaps; usually quote something. Once when I was in the library we gave a party for Miss Leonard, and I wrote a line or two of doggerel about a bouquet of violets we gave her. It has no life or point. It was meant well but didn't amount to anything. Then in college, I had a sonnet as an assignment. The epitome of weakness.

INTERVIEWER: I'm interested in asking about the principles, and the methods, of your way of writing. What is the rationale behind syllabic verse? How does it differ from free verse in which the line length is controlled visually but not arithmetically?

MOORE: It never occurred to me that what I wrote was something to define. I am governed by the pull of the sentence as the pull of a fabric is governed by gravity. I like the end-stopped line and dislike the reversed order of words; like symmetry.

INTERVIEWER: How do you plan the shape of your stanzas? I am thinking of the poems, usually syllabic, which employ a repeated stanza form. Do you ever experiment with shapes before you write, by drawing lines on a page?

MOORE: Never, I never "plan" a stanza. Words cluster like chromosomes, determining the procedure. I may influence an arrangement or thin it, then try to have successive stanzas identical with the first. Spontaneous initial originality—say, impetus—seems difficult to reproduce consciously later. As Stravinsky said about pitch, "If I transpose it for some reason, I am in danger of losing the freshness of first contact and will have difficulty in recapturing its attractiveness."

No, I never "draw lines." I make a rhyme conspicuous, to me at a glance, by underlining with red, blue or other pencil—as many colors as I have rhymes to differentiate. However, if the phrases recur in too incoherent an architecture—as print—I notice that the words as a tune do not sound right. I may start a piece, find it obstructive, lack a way out, and not complete the thing for a year, or years, am thrifty. I salvage anything promising and set it down in a small notebook.

INTERVIEWER: I wonder if the act of translating La Fontaine's *Fables* helped you as a writer.

MOORE: Indeed it did. It was the best help I've ever had. I suffered frustration. I'm so naïve, so docile, I *tend* to take anybody's word for anything the person says, even in matters of art. The publisher who had commissioned the *Fables* died. I had no publisher. Well, I struggled on for a time and it didn't go very well. I thought, I'd better ask if they don't want to terminate the contract; then I could offer it elsewhere. I thought Macmillan, who took an interest in me, might like it. *Might.* The editor in charge of translations said, "Well, I studied French at Cornell, took a degree in French, I love French, and . . . well, I think you'd better put it away for a while." "How long?" I said. "About ten years; besides, it will hurt your own work. You won't write so well afterward."

"Oh," I said, "that's one reason I was undertaking it; I thought it would train me and give me momentum." Much dejected, I asked, "What is wrong? Have I not a good ear? Are the meanings not sound?"

"Well, there are conflicts," the editor reiterated, as it seemed to me, countless times. I don't know yet what they are or were. (A little "editorial.")

I said, "Don't write me an extenuating letter, please. Just send back the material in the envelope I put with it." I had submitted it in January and this was May. I had had a kind of uneasy hope that all would be well; meanwhile had volumes, hours and years of work yet to do and might as well go on and do it, I had thought. The ultimatum was devastating.

At the same time Monroe Engel of the Viking Press wrote to me and said that he had supposed I had a commitment for my *Fables*, but if I hadn't would I let the Viking Press see them? I feel an everlasting gratitude to him.

However, I said, "I can't offer you something which somebody else thinks isn't fit to print. I would have to have someone to stabilize it and guarantee that the meanings are sound."

Mr. Engel said, "Who do you think could do that? Whom would you like?"

I said, "Harry Levin," because he had written a cogent, very shrewd review of Edna St. Vincent Millay's and George Dillon's translation of Baudelaire. I admired its finesse.

Mr. Engel said, "I'll ask him. But you won't hear for a long time. He's very busy. And how much do you think we ought to offer him?"

"Well," I said, "not less than ten dollars a Book; there would be no incentive in undertaking the bother of it, if it weren't twenty."

He said, "That would reduce your royalties too much on an advance."

I said, "I don't want an advance, wouldn't even consider one."

And then Harry Levin said, quite soon, that he would be glad to do it as a "refreshment against the chores of the term," but of course he would accept no remuneration. It was a very dubious refreshment, let me tell you. (He is precise, and not abusive, and did not "resign.")

INTERVIEWER: I've been asking you about your poems, which is of course what interests me most. But you were editor of *The Dial*, too, and I want to ask you a few things about that. You were editor from 1925 until it ended in 1929, I think. How did you first come to be associated with it?

MOORE: Let me see. I think I took the initiative. I sent the editors a couple of things and they sent them back. And Lola Ridge had a party—she had a large apartment on a ground floor somewhere—and John Reed and Marsden Hartley, who was very confident with the brush, and Scofield Thayer, editor of *The Dial*, were there. And much to my disgust, we were induced each to read something we had written. And Scofield Thayer said of my piece, "Would you send that to us at *The Dial*?"

"I did send it," I said.

And he said, "Well, send it again." That is how it began, I think. Then he said, one time, "I'd like you to meet my partner, Sibley Watson," and invited me to tea at 152 West Thirteenth Street. I was impressed. Dr. Watson is rare. He said nothing, but what he did say was striking and the significance would creep over you because unanticipated. And they asked me to join the staff, at *The Dial*.

INTERVIEWER: I have just been looking at that magazine, the years when you edited it. It's an incredible magazine.

MOORE: *The Dial*? There *were* good things in it, weren't there?

INTERVIEWER: Yes. It combined George Saintsbury and Ezra Pound in the same issue. How do you account for it? What made it so good?

MOORE: Lack of fear, for one thing. We didn't care what other people said. I never knew a magazine that was so self-propulsive. Everybody liked what he was doing, and when we made grievous mistakes we were sorry but we laughed over them.

INTERVIEWER: Louise Bogan said that *The Dial* made clear "the obvious division between American avant-garde and American conventional writing." Do you think this kind of division continues or has continued? Was this in any way a deliberate policy?

MOORE: I think that individuality was the great thing. We were not conforming to anything. We certainly didn't have a policy, except I remember hearing the word "intensity" very often. A thing must have "intensity." That seemed to be the criterion.

The thing applied to it, I think, that should apply to your own writing. As George Grosz said, at that last meeting he attended at the National Institute, "How did I come to be an artist? Endless curiosity, observation, research—and a great amount of joy in the thing." It was a matter of taking a liking to things. Things that were in accordance with your taste. I think that was it. And we didn't care how unhomogeneous they might seem. Didn't Aristotle say that it is the mark of a poet to see resemblances between apparently incongruous things? There was any amount of attraction about it.

INTERVIEWER: Do you think there is anything in the change of literary life in America that would make *The Dial* different if it existed today under the same editors? Were there any special conditions in the twenties that made the literary life of America different?

MOORE: I think it is always about the same.

INTERVIEWER: I wonder, if it had survived into the thirties, if it might have made that rather dry literary decade a little better.

MOORE: I think so. Because we weren't in captivity to anything.

INTERVIEWER: Was it just finances that made it stop?

MOORE: No, it wasn't the Depression. Conditions changed. Scofield Thayer had a nervous breakdown, and he didn't come to meetings. Dr. Watson was interested in photography—was studying medicine; is a doctor of medicine, and lived in Rochester. I was alone. I didn't know that Rochester was about a night's journey away, and I would say to Dr. Watson, "Couldn't you come in for a make-up meeting, or send us these manuscripts and say what you think of them?" I may, as usual, have exaggerated my enslavement and my preoccupation with tasks—writing letters and reading manuscripts. Originally I had said I would come if I didn't have to write letters and didn't have to see contributors. And presently I was doing both. I think it was largely chivalry—the decision to discontinue the magazine—because I didn't have time for work of my own.

INTERVIEWER: I wonder how you worked as an editor. Hart Crane complains, in one of his letters, that you rearranged "The Wine Menagerie" and changed the title. Do you feel that you were justified? Did you ask for revisions from many poets?

MOORE: No. We had an inflexible rule: do not ask changes of so much as a comma. Accept it or reject it. But in that instance I felt that in compassion I should disregard the rule. Hart Crane complains of me? Well, I complain of *him.* He liked *The Dial* and we liked him—friends, and with certain tastes in common. He was in dire need of money. It seemed careless not to so much as ask if he might like to make some changes ("like" in quotations). His gratitude was ardent and later his repudiation of it commensurate—he perhaps being in both instances under a disability with which I was not familiar. (Penalizing us for compassion?) I say "us," and should say "me." Really I am not used to having people in that bemused state. He was so *anxious* to have us take that thing, and so *delighted.* "Well, if you would modify it a little," I said, "we would like it better." I never attended "their" wild parties, as Lachaise once said. It was lawless of me to suggest changes; I disobeyed.

INTERVIEWER: Have you had editors suggest changes to you? Changes in your own poems, I mean?

MOORE: No, but my ardor to be helped being sincere, I sometimes *induce* assistance: the *Times,* the *Herald Tribune, The New Yorker,* have a number of times had to patch and piece me out. If you have a genius of an editor, you are blessed: e.g., T. S. Eliot and Ezra Pound, Harry Levin and others; Irita Van Doren and Miss Belle Rosenbaum.

Have I found "help" helpful? I certainly have; and in three instances when I was at *The Dial,* I hazarded suggestions the results of which were to me drama. Excoriated by Herman George Scheffauer for offering to suggest a verbal change or two in his translation of Thomas Mann's *Disorder and Early Sorrow,* I must have posted the suggestions before I was able to withdraw them. In any case, his joyous subsequent retraction of abuse, and his pleasure in the narrative, were not unwelcome. Gilbert Seldes strongly commended me for excisions proposed by me in his "Jonathan Edwards" (for *The Dial*); and I have not ceased to marvel at the overrating by Mark Van Doren of editorial conscience on my reverting (after an interval) to keeping some final lines I had wished he would omit. (Verse! but not a sonnet.)

We should try to judge the work of others by the most that it is, and our own, if not by the least that it is, take the least into consideration. I feel that I would not be worth a button if not grateful to be preserved from myself, and informed if what I have written is not to the point. I think we should feel free, like

La Fontaine's captious critic, to say, if asked, "Your phrases are too long, and the content is not good. Break up the type and put it in the font." As Kenneth Burke says in *Counter-Statement:* "[Great] artists feel as opportunity what others feel as a menace. This ability does not, I believe, derive from exceptional strength, it probably arises purely from professional interest the artist may take in his difficulties."

Lew Sarett says, in the *Poetry Society Bulletin,* we ask of a poet: Does this mean something? Does the poet say what he has to say and in his own manner? Does it stir the reader?

Shouldn't we replace vanity with honesty, as Robert Frost recommends? Annoyances abound. We should not find them lethal—a baffled printer's emendations for instance (my "elephant with frog-colored skin" instead of "fog-colored skin," and "the power of the invisible is the invisible," instead of "the power of the visible is the invisible") sounding like a parody on my meticulousness; a "glasshopper" instead of a "grasshopper."

INTERVIEWER: Editing *The Dial* must have acquainted you with the writers of the day whom you did not know already. Had you known Hart Crane earlier?

MOORE: Yes, I did. You remember *Broom?* Toward the beginning of that magazine, in 1921, Lola Ridge was very hospitable, and she invited to a party—previous to my work on *The Dial*—Kay Boyle and her husband, a French soldier, and Hart Crane, Elinor Wylie and some others. I took a great liking to Hart Crane. We talked about French bindings, and he was diffident and modest and seemed to have so much intuition, such a feel for things, for books—really a bibliophile—that I took special interest in him. And Dr. Watson and Scofield Thayer liked him—felt that he was one of our talents, that he couldn't fit himself into an IBM position to find a livelihood; that we ought to, whenever we could, take anything he sent us.

I know a cousin of his, Joe Nowak, who is rather proud of

him. He lives here in Brooklyn, and is* at the Dry Dock Savings Bank and used to work in antiques. Joe was very convinced of Hart's sincerity and his innate love of all that I have specified. Anyhow, *The Bridge* is a grand theme. Here and there I think he could have firmed it up. A writer is unfair to himself when he is unable to be hard on himself.

INTERVIEWER: Did Crane have anything to do with *Others?*

MOORE: *Others* antedated *Broom. Others* was Alfred Kreymborg and Skipwith Cannéll, Wallace Stevens, William Carlos Williams. Wallace Stevens—odd; I nearly met him a dozen times before I did meet him in 1941 at Mount Holyoke, at the college's *Entretiens de Pontigny* of which Professor Gustav Cohen was chairman. Wallace Stevens was Henry Church's favorite American poet. Mr. Church had published him and some others, and me, in *Mésure,* in Paris. Raymond Queneau translated us.

During the French program at Mount Holyoke one afternoon Wallace Stevens had a discourse, the one about Goethe dancing, on a packet boat in black wool stockings. My mother and I were there; and I gave a reading with commentary. Henry Church had an astoundingly beautiful Panama hat—a sort of pork-pie with a wide brim, a little like Bernard Berenson's hats. I have never seen as fine a weave, and he had a pepper-and-salt shawl which he draped about himself. This lecture was on the lawn.

Wallace Stevens was extremely friendly. We should have had a tape recorder on that occasion, for at lunch they seated us all at a kind of refectory table and a girl kept asking him questions such as, "Mr. Stevens, have you read the—*Four—Quartets?*"

"Of course, but I can't read much of Eliot or I wouldn't have any individuality of my own."

INTERVIEWER: Do you read new poetry now? Do you try to keep up?

*Was; killed; his car run into by a reckless driver in April 1961.—M.M.

MOORE: I am always seeing it—am sent some every day. Some, good. But it does interfere with my work. I can't get much done. Yet I would be a monster if I tossed everything away without looking at it; I write more notes, letters, cards in an hour than is sane.

Although everyone is penalized by being quoted inexactly, I wonder if there is anybody alive whose remarks are so often paraphrased as mine—printed as verbatim. It is really martyr-dom. In his book *Ezra Pound*, Charles Norman was very scrupulous. He got several things exactly right. The first time I met Ezra Pound, when he came here to see my mother and me, I said that Henry Eliot seemed to me more nearly the artist than anyone I had ever met. "Now, now," said Ezra. "Be careful." Maybe that isn't exact, but he quotes it just the way I said it.

INTERVIEWER: Do you mean Henry Ware Eliot, T. S. Eliot's brother?

MOORE: Yes. After the Henry Eliots moved from Chicago to New York to—is it Sixty-eighth Street? It's the street on which Hunter College is—to an apartment there, they invited me to dinner, I should think at T. S. Eliot's suggestion, and I took to them immediately. I felt as if I'd known them a great while. It was some time before I felt that way about T. S. Eliot.

About inaccuracies—when I went to see Ezra Pound at St. Elizabeths, about the third time I went, the official who es-corted me to the grounds said, "Good of you to come to see him," and I said, "Good? You have no idea how much he has done for me, and others." This pertains to an early rather than final visit.

I was not in the habit of asking experts or anybody else to help me with things that I was doing, unless it was a librarian or someone whose business it was to help applicants; or a teacher. But I was desperate when Macmillan declined my *Fa-*

bles. I had worked about four years on them and sent Ezra Pound several—although I hesitated. I didn't like to bother him. He had enough trouble without that; but finally I said, "Would you have time to tell me if the rhythms grate on you? Is my ear not good?"

INTERVIEWER: He replied?

MOORE: Yes, said, "The least touch of merit upsets these blighters."

INTERVIEWER: When you first read Pound in 1916, did you recognize him as one of the great ones?

MOORE: Surely did. *The Spirit of Romance.* I don't think anybody could read that book and feel that a flounderer was writing.

INTERVIEWER: What about the early poems?

MOORE: Yes. They seemed a little didactic, but I liked them.

INTERVIEWER: I wanted to ask you a few questions about poetry in general. Somewhere you have said that originality is a by-product of sincerity. You often use moral terms in your criticism. Is the necessary morality specifically literary, a moral use of words, or is it larger? In what way must a man be good if he is to write good poems?

MOORE: If emotion is strong enough, the words are unambiguous. Someone asked Robert Frost (is that right?) if he was selective. He said, "Call it passionate preference." Must a man be good to write good poems? The villains in Shakespeare are not illiterate, are they? But rectitude *has* a ring that is implicative, I would say. And with *no* integrity, a man is not likely to write the kind of book I read.

INTERVIEWER: Eliot, in his introduction to your *Selected Poems,* talks about your function as poet relative to the living language, as he calls it. Do you agree that this is a function of a poet? How does the poetry have the effect on the living language? What's the mechanics of it?

MOORE: You accept certain modes of saying a thing. Or

strongly repudiate things. You do something of your own, you modify, invent a variant or revive a root meaning. Any doubt about that?

INTERVIEWER: I want to ask you a question about your correspondence with the Ford Motor Company, those letters that were printed in *The New Yorker.* They were looking for a name for the car they eventually called the Edsel, and they asked you to think of a name that would make people admire the car—

MOORE: Elegance and grace, they said it would have—

INTERVIEWER: ". . . some visceral feeling of elegance, fleetness, advanced features and design. A name, in short, that flashes a dramatically desirable picture in people's minds."

MOORE: Really?

INTERVIEWER: That's what they said, in their first letter to you. I was thinking about this in connection with my question about language. Do you remember Pound's talk about expression and meaning? He says that when expression and meaning are far apart, the culture is in a bad way. I was wondering if this request doesn't ask you to remove expression a bit further from meaning.

MOORE: No, I don't think so. At least, to exposit the irresistibleness of the car. I got deep in motors and turbines and recessed wheels. No. That seemed to me a very worthy pursuit. I was more interested in the mechanics. I am interested in mechanisms, mechanics in general. And I enjoyed the assignment, for all that it was abortive. Dr. Pick at Marquette University procured a young demonstrator of the Edsel to call for me in a black one, to convey me to the auditorium. Nothing was wrong with that Edsel! I thought it was a very handsome car. It came out the wrong year.

INTERVIEWER: Another thing: in your criticism you make frequent analogies between the poet and the scientist. Do you think this analogy is helpful to the modern poet? Most people would consider the comparison a paradox, and assume that the poet and the scientist are opposed.

MOORE: Do the poet and scientist not work analogously? Both are willing to waste effort. To be hard on himself is one of the main strengths of each. Each is attentive to clues, each must narrow the choice, must strive for precision. As George Grosz says, "In art there is no place for gossip and but a small place for the satirist." The objective is fertile procedure. Is it not? Jacob Bronowski says in *The Saturday Evening Post* that science is not a mere collection of discoveries, but that science is the process of discovering. In any case it's not established once and for all; it's evolving.

INTERVIEWER: One last question. I was intrigued when you wrote that "America has in Wallace Stevens at least one artist whom professionalism will not demolish." What sort of literary professionalism did you have in mind? And do you find this a feature of America still?

MOORE: Yes. I think that writers sometimes lose verve and pugnacity, and he never would say "frame of reference" or "I wouldn't know." A question I am often asked is: "What work can I find that will enable me to spend my whole time writing?" Charles Ives, the composer, says, "You cannot set art off in a corner and hope for it to have vitality, reality, and substance. The fabric weaves itself whole. My work in music helped my business and my work in business helped my music." I am like Charles Ives. I guess Lawrence Durrell and Henry Miller would not agree with me.

INTERVIEWER: But how does professionalism make a writer lose his verve and pugnacity?

MOORE: Money may have something to do with it, and being regarded as a pundit; Wallace Stevens was really very much annoyed at being cataloged, categorized, and compelled to be scientific about what he was doing—to give satisfaction, to answer the teachers. He wouldn't do that. I think the same of William

Carlos Williams. I think he wouldn't make so much of the great American language if he were plausible; and tractable. That's the beauty of it; he is willing to be reckless; if you can't be that, what's the point of the whole thing?

—DONALD HALL

1960

KATHERINE ANNE PORTER

Katherine Anne Porter was born May 15, 1890, in Indian Creek, Texas. She spent her early youth in Texas and Louisiana, and received her education from small convent schools in that area. She began writing, she once said, almost as soon as she could put words on paper. "I did not choose this vocation, and if I had any say in the matter, I would not have chosen it . . . yet for this vocation I was and am willing to live and die, and I consider very few other things of the slightest importance."

Supporting herself by book reviewing, political articles, hack writing, and editing, she worked continually at her own stories, although she did not publish until she was in her thirties. Her first collection of short stories, *Flowering Judas*, appeared in 1930 and earned her an immediate reputation. In 1931 she was awarded a Guggenheim Fellowship and went abroad to study and write—in Berlin, Basel and Madrid.

When she returned to America she received a Book-of-the-Month Club Fellowship and, in 1938, another Guggenheim grant. In 1949 Porter was given an honorary doctorate in literature from the Woman's College of the University of North Carolina. She was a vice president of the National Institute of

Arts and Letters, a fellow in the Library of Congress, and in 1952 was the only woman writer in the United States delegation to the Cultural Exposition in Paris sponsored by the Congress for Cultural Freedom.

Her published work includes *Hacienda* (1934), *Noon Wine* (1937), *Pale Horse, Pale Rider* (1939), *The Leaning Tower and Other Stories* (1944), *The Days Before* (essays, 1952), *Ship of Fools* (1962), and *Collected Stories* (1965), which won both the Pulitzer Prize and the National Book Award. In 1970 an augmented version of her *Collected Essays and Occasional Writings* was published. She died in 1980.

417 Ship of Fools

or ~~some~~ greeting for any one. She sat there alone reading stale magazines until
the luncheon bugle sounded. The exact vision of the Baumgartner's faces ~~would not leave~~,
would not leave her. It was plain they too had ~~and~~ some sort of shabby little incident
during the night— no matter what. Mrs. Treadwell did not even wish to guess what it
might have been, but that sad dull display of high manners after they had behaved
no doubt disgracefully to each other and their child— ~~trying~~ to prove ~~so truth~~ that
they were not so base as they had caused each other to seem. That dreadful little
door-holding, bowing scene had meant to say You can see, can't you, that in another
time or place, or another society, I might have been very different, much better than
you have ever seen me? Mrs. Treadwell leaned back and closed her eyes. What they
were saying to each other was only Love me, love me in spite of all! Whether or not
I love you, whether I am fit to love, whether you are able to love, even if there
is no such thing as love, Love me!

A small deep wandering sensation of disgust, self-distaste came with these
straying thoughts. She remembered as in a dream again her despairs, her long
weeping, her incurable grief over the failure of love or what she had been told was
love, and the ruin of her hopes— what hopes? she could not remember— and what had
it been but the childish refusal to admit an accept on some terms or other the
difference between what one had hoped was true and what one discovers to be the
~~mere force of The human Condition?~~ She had been hurt, she had recovered, and what had it all
been but a foolish piece of romantic carelessness? She stood up to take a deep
breath and walk around the stuffy room. All morning long she had been trying in
the back of her mind to piece together exactly what had happened last night to her,
and what she had done. The scene with that young officer was clear enough. She remembered Herr Baumgartner hanging over the rail looking sick. Lizzi delivered to
her hands later, when she had been amusing herself painting her face; and then—

No good putting it off any longer. She could not find her gilded sandals when
she was putting her things in order. There were small random bloodspots on the
lower front of her night gown. And as she walked, she remembered, and stopped clutching
a chairback feeling faint; walked again, then left the room and set out to look
for Jenny Brown. She should know everything about it, being the "girl" of that
rather self-absorbed young man, Denny cabin mate... Mrs. Treadwell remembered very
well what had happened, what she had done; she wanted a few particulars of the dosage
she had done, and above all to learn whether her enemy had recognized her.

Jenny Brown was reading the bulletin board. A ragged-edged imitation of an ancient
proclamation announced" The victims of last night's violence and bloodshed are rest-
ing quietly. The suspected criminals are under surveillance, not yet apprehended,
~~but formally disclosures that several interesting personages is expected;"~~
but an early disclosure of several interesting identities is expected.
Signed Los Camelots de la Cucaracha.

A Katherine Anne Porter manuscript page.

KATHERINE ANNE PORTER

he Victorian house in which Katherine Anne Porter lived was narrow and white, reached by an iron-railed stairway curving up from the shady brick-walked Georgetown street. The parlor to which a maid admitted the caller was an elegant mélange of several aspects of the past, both American and European. Dim and cool after the midsummer glare, the high-ceilinged room was dominated by a bottle-green settee from the period of Napoleon III. Outside the alcove of windows there was a rustle of wind through ginkgo trees, then a hush.

Finally, a voice in the upper hallway: its tone that of someone talking to a bird, or coquetting with an old beau—light and feathery, with a slight flutter. A few moments later, moving as lightly as her voice, Miss Porter hurried through the wide doorway, unexpectedly modern in a soft green suit of woven Italian silk. Small and elegant, she explained her tardiness, related an anecdote from the morning's mail, offered a minted ice tea, and speculated aloud on where we might best conduct our conversation.

She decided on the dining room, a quiet, austere place overlooking the small enclosed garden. Here the aspect was a different one. "I want to live in a world capital or the howling wilderness," she said once, and did. The drawing room was filled with pieces that had once been part of the house on the rue Notre-

Dame des Champs; this one was bright with Mexican folk art—whistles and toy animals collected during a recent tour for the Department of State— against simpler, heavier pieces of furniture. The round table at which we sat was of Vermont marble, mottled and colored like milk glass, on a wrought- iron base of her own design. There was a sixteenth-century cupboard from Avila, and a refectory table of the early Renaissance from a convent in Fiesole. Here we settled the tape recorder, under an image of the great god Horus.

We tried to make a beginning. She was an experienced lecturer, familiar with microphone and tape recorder, but now she was to talk about herself as well as her work, the link between, and the inexorable winding of the tape from one spool to the other acted almost as a hypnotic. Finally we turned it off and talked for a while of other things, more frivolous and more autobiographical, hoping to surprise an easier revelation. . . .

INTERVIEWER: You were saying that you had never intended to make a career of writing.

PORTER: I've never made a career of anything, you know, not even of writing. I started out with nothing in the world but a kind of passion, a driving desire. I don't know where it came from, and I don't know why—or why I have been so stubborn about it that nothing could deflect me. But this thing between me and my writing is the strongest bond I have ever had— stronger than any bond or any engagement with any human being or with any other work I've ever done. I really started writing when I was six or seven years old. But I had such a mul- tiplicity of half-talents, too: I wanted to dance, I wanted to play the piano, I sang, I drew. It wasn't really dabbling—I was inves- tigating everything, experimenting in everything. And then, for one thing, there weren't very many amusements in those days. If you wanted music, you had to play the piano and sing your- self. Oh, we saw all the great things that came during the sea- son, but after all, there would only be a dozen or so of those occasions a year. The rest of the time we depended upon our own resources: our own music and books. All the old houses that I knew when I was a child were full of books, bought generation after generation by members of the family. Everyone was literate as a matter of course. Nobody told you to read this or not to read that. It was there to read, and we read.

INTERVIEWER: Which books influenced you most?

PORTER: That's hard to say, because I grew up in a sort of mélange. I was reading Shakespeare's sonnets when I was thirteen years old, and I'm perfectly certain that they made the most profound impression upon me of anything I ever read. For a time I knew the whole sequence by heart; now I can only remember two or three of them. That was the turning point of my life, when I read the Shakespeare sonnets, and then all at one blow, all of Dante—in that great big book illustrated by Gustave Doré. The plays I saw on the stage, but I don't remember reading them with any interest at all. Oh, and I read all kinds of poetry—Homer, Ronsard, all the old French poets in translation. We also had a very good library of—well, you might say secular philosophers. I was incredibly influenced by Montaigne when I was very young. And one day when I was about fourteen, my father led me up to a great big line of books and said, "Why don't you read this? It'll knock some of the nonsense out of you!" It happened to be the entire set of Voltaire's philosophical dictionary with notes by Smollett. And I plowed through it; it took me about five years.

And of course we read all the eighteenth-century novelists, though Jane Austen, like Turgenev, didn't really engage me until I was quite mature. I read them both when I was very young, but I was grown up before I really took them in. And I discovered for myself *Wuthering Heights;* I think I read that book every year of my life for fifteen years. I simply adored it. Henry James and Thomas Hardy were really my introduction to modern literature; Grandmother didn't much approve of it. She thought Dickens might do, but she was a little against Mr. Thackeray;

she thought he was too trivial. So that was as far as I got into the modern world until I left home!

INTERVIEWER: Don't you think this background—the comparative isolation of Southern rural life and the atmosphere of literary interest—helped to shape you as a writer?

PORTER: I think it's something in the blood. We've always had great letter writers, readers, great storytellers in our family. I've listened all my life to articulate people. They were all great storytellers, and every story had shape and meaning and point.

INTERVIEWER: Were any of them known as writers?

PORTER: Well, there was my sixth or seventh cousin once removed, poor William Sidney. O. Henry, you know. He was my father's second cousin—I don't know what that makes him to me. And he was more known in the family for being a bank robber. He worked in a bank, you know, and he just didn't seem to find a talent for making money; no Porter ever did. But he had a wife who was dying of TB and he couldn't keep up with the doctor's bills. So he took a pitiful little sum—oh, about three hundred and fifty dollars—and ran away when he was accused. But he came back, because his wife was dying, and went to prison. And there was Horace Porter, who spent his whole eight years as ambassador to France looking for the bones of John Paul Jones. And when he found them, and brought them back, he wrote a book about them.

INTERVIEWER: It seems to me that your work is pervaded by a sense of history. Is that part of the family legacy?

PORTER: We were brought up with a sense of our own history, you know. My mother's family came to this country in 1648 and went to the John Randolph territory of Virginia. And one of my great-great-grandfathers was Jonathan Boone, the brother of Daniel. On my father's side I'm descended from Colonel Andrew Porter, whose father came to Montgomery County, Pennsylvania, in 1720. He was one of the circle of George Washington during the Revolution, a friend of

Lafayette, and one of the founders of the Society of the Cincinnati—oh, he really took it seriously!—and when he died in 1809—well, just a few years before that he was offered the post of secretary of war, but he declined. We were never very ambitious people. We never had a president, though we had two governors and some in the army and the navy. I suppose we did have a desire to excel but not to push our way to higher places. We thought we'd *already* arrived!

INTERVIEWER: The "we" of family is very strong, isn't it? I remember that you once wrote of the ties of blood as the "absolute point of all departure and return." And the central character in many of your stories is defined, is defining herself often, in relation to a family organization. Even the measure of time is human—expressed in terms of the very old and the very young, and how much of human experience they have absorbed.

PORTER: Yes, but it wasn't a conscious made-up affair, you know. In those days you belonged together, you lived together, because you were a family. The head of our house was a grandmother, an old matriarch, you know, and a really lovely and beautiful woman, a good soul, and so she didn't do us any harm. But the point is that we did live like that, with Grandmother's friends, all reverend old gentlemen with frock coats, and old ladies with jet breastplates. Then there were the younger people, the beautiful girls and the handsome young boys, who were all ahead of me; when I was a little girl, eight or nine years old, they were eighteen to twenty-two, and they represented all glamour, all beauty, all joy and freedom to me. Then there was my own age, and then there were the babies. And the servants, the Negroes. We simply lived that way; to have four generations in one house, under one roof, there was nothing unusual about that. That was just my experience, and this is just the way I've reacted to it. Many other people didn't react, who were brought up in very much the same way.

I remember when I was very young, my older sister wanted to buy some old furniture. It was in Louisiana, and she had just been married. And I went with her to a wonderful old house in the country where we'd been told there was a very old gentleman who probably had some things to sell. His wife had died, and he was living there alone. So we went to this lovely old house, and, sure enough, there was this lonely beautiful old man, eighty-seven or -eight, surrounded by devoted Negro servants. But his wife was dead and his children were married and gone. He said, yes, he had a few things he wanted to sell. So he showed us through the house. And finally he opened a door, and showed us a bedroom with a beautiful four-poster bed, with a wonderful satin coverlet: the most wonderful, classical-looking bed you ever saw. And my sister said, "Oh, that's what I want." And he said, "Oh, madame, that is my marriage bed. That is the bed that my wife brought with her as a bride. We slept together in that bed for nearly sixty years. All our children were born there. Oh," he said, "I shall die in that bed, and then they can dispose of it as they like."

I remember that I felt a little suffocated and frightened. I felt a little trapped. But why? Only because I understood that. I was brought up in that. And I was at the age of rebellion then, and it really scared me. But I look back on it now and think how perfectly wonderful, what a tremendously beautiful life it was. Everything in it had meaning.

INTERVIEWER: But it seems to me that your work suggests someone who was searching for new—perhaps broader—meanings . . . that while you've retained the South of your childhood as a point of reference, you've ranged far from that environment itself. You seem to have felt little of the peculiarly Southern preoccupation with racial guilt and the death of the old agrarian life.

PORTER: I'm a Southerner by tradition and inheritance, and I have a very profound feeling for the South. And, of course, I belong to the guilt-ridden white-pillar crowd myself, but it just didn't rub off on me. Maybe I'm just not Jewish enough, or Puritan enough, to feel that the sins of the father are visited on the third and fourth generations. Or maybe it's because of my European influences—in Texas and Louisiana. The Europeans didn't have slaves themselves as late as my family did, but they *still* thought slavery was quite natural. . . . But, you know, I was always restless, always a roving spirit. When I was a little child I was always running away. I never got very far, but they were always having to come and fetch me. Once when I was about six, my father came to get me somewhere I'd gone, and he told me later he'd asked me, "Why are you so restless? Why can't you stay here with us?" and I said to him, "I want to go and see the world. I want to know the world like the palm of my hand."

INTERVIEWER: And at sixteen you made it final.

PORTER: At sixteen I ran away from New Orleans and got married. And at twenty-one I bolted again, went to Chicago, got a newspaper job, and went into the movies.

INTERVIEWER: The movies?

PORTER: The newspaper sent me over to the old S. and A. movie studio to do a story. But I got into the wrong line, and then was too timid to get out. "Right over this way, Little Boy Blue," the man said, and I found myself in a courtroom scene with Francis X. Bushman. I was horrified by what had happened to me, but they paid me five dollars for that first day's work, so I stayed on. It was about a week before I remembered what I had been sent to do; and when I went back to the newspaper they gave me eighteen dollars for my week's nonwork and fired me!

I stayed on for six months—I finally got to nearly ten dollars a day—until one day they came in and said, "We're moving to the coast." "Well, I'm not," I said. "Don't you want to be a movie actress?" "Oh, no!" I said. "Well, be a fool!" they said, and they left. That was 1914 and world war had broken out, so in September I went home.

INTERVIEWER: And then?

PORTER: Oh, I sang old Scottish ballads in costume—I made it myself—all around Texas and Louisiana. And then I was supposed to have TB, and spent about six weeks in a sanitarium. It was just bronchitis, but I was in Denver, so I got a newspaper job.

INTERVIEWER: I remember that you once warned me to avoid that at all costs—to get a job "hashing" in a restaurant in preference.

PORTER: Anything, anything at all. I did it for a year and that is what confirmed for me that it wasn't doing me any good. After that I always took little dull jobs that didn't take my mind and wouldn't take all of my time, and that, on the other hand, paid me just enough to subsist. I think I've only spent about ten percent of my energies on writing. The other ninety percent went to keeping my head above water.

And I think that's all wrong. Even Saint Teresa said, "I can pray better when I'm comfortable," and she refused to wear her haircloth shirt or starve herself. I don't think living in cellars and starving is any better for an artist than it is for anybody else; the only thing is that sometimes the artist has to take it, because it is the only possible way of salvation, if you'll forgive that old-fashioned word. So I took it rather instinctively. I was inexperienced in the world, and likewise I hadn't been trained to do anything, you know, so I took all kinds of laborious jobs. But, you know, I think I could probably have written better if I'd been a little more comfortable.

INTERVIEWER: Then you were writing all this time?

PORTER: All this time I was writing, writing no matter what else I was doing; no matter what I *thought* I was doing, in fact. I was living almost as instinctively as a little animal, but I realize now that all that time a part of me was getting ready to be an artist. That my mind was working even when I didn't know it, and didn't care if it was working or not. It is my firm belief that all our lives we are preparing to be somebody or something, even if we don't do it consciously. And the time comes one morning when you wake up and find that you have become irrevocably what you were preparing all this time to be. Lord, that could be a sticky moment, if you had been doing the wrong things, something against your grain. And, mind you, I know that can happen. I have no patience with this dreadful idea that whatever you have in you has to come out, that you can't suppress true talent. People *can* be destroyed; they can be bent, distorted and completely crippled. To say that you can't destroy yourself is just as foolish as to say of a young man killed in war at twenty-one or twenty-two that that was his fate, that he wasn't going to have anything anyhow.

I have a very firm belief that the life of no man can be explained in terms of his experiences, of what has happened to him, because in spite of all the poetry, all the philosophy to the contrary, we are not really masters of our fate. We don't really direct our lives unaided and unobstructed. Our being is subject to all the chances of life. There are so many things we are capable of, that we could be or do. The potentialities are so great that we never, any of us, are more than one-fourth fulfilled. Except that there may be one powerful motivating force that simply carries you along, and I think that was true of me. . . . When I was a very little girl I wrote a letter to my sister saying I wanted glory. I don't know quite what I meant by that now, but it was something different from fame or success or wealth. I know that I wanted to be a good writer, a good artist.

INTERVIEWER: But weren't there certain specific events that crystallized that desire for you—something comparable to the experience of Miranda in *Pale Horse, Pale Rider?*

PORTER: Yes, that was the plague of influenza, at the end of the First World War, in which I almost died. It just simply divided my life, cut across it like that. So that everything before that was just getting ready, and after that I was in some strange way altered, ready. It took me a long time to go out and live in the world again. I was really "alienated," in the pure sense. It was, I think, the fact that I really had participated in death, that I knew what death was, and had almost experienced it. I had what the Christians call the "beatific vision," and the Greeks called the "happy day," the happy vision just before death. Now if you have had that, and survived it, come back from it, you are no longer like other people, and there's no use deceiving yourself that you are. But you see, I did: I made the mistake of thinking I was quite like anybody else, of trying to live like other people. It took me a long time to realize that that simply wasn't true, that I had my own needs and that I had to live like me.

INTERVIEWER: And that freed you?

PORTER: I just got up and bolted. I went running off on that wild escapade to Mexico, where I attended, you might say, and assisted at, in my own modest way, a revolution.

INTERVIEWER: That was the Obregón Revolution of 1921?

PORTER: Yes—though actually I went to Mexico to study the Aztec and Mayan art designs. I had been in New York, and was getting ready to go to Europe. Now, New York was full of Mexican artists at that time, all talking about the renaissance, as they called it, in Mexico. And they said, "Don't go to Europe, go to Mexico. That's where the exciting things are going to happen." And they were right! I ran smack into the Obregón Revolution, and had, in the midst of it, the most marvelous, natural, spontaneous experience of my life. It was a terribly exciting time. It was alive, but death was in it. But nobody seemed to think of that: life was in it, too.

INTERVIEWER: What do you think are the best conditions for a writer, then? Something like your Mexican experience, or—

PORTER: Oh, I can't say what they are. It would be such an individual matter. Everyone needs something different. . . . But what I find most dreadful among the young artists is this tendency toward middle-classness—this idea that they have to get married and have lots of children and live just like everybody else, you know? Now, I am all for human life, and I am all for marriage and children and all that sort of thing, but quite often you can't have that and do what you were supposed to do, too. Art is a vocation, as much as anything in this world. For the real artist, it is the most natural thing in the world, not as necessary as air and water, perhaps, but as food and water. But we really do lead almost a monastic life, you know; to follow it you very often have to give up something.

INTERVIEWER: But for the unproven artist that is a very great act of faith.

PORTER: It *is* an act of faith. But one of the marks of a gift is to have the courage of it. If they haven't got the courage, it's just too bad. They'll fail, just as people with lack of courage in other vocations and walks of life fail. Courage is the first essential.

INTERVIEWER: In choosing a pattern of life compatible with the vocation?

PORTER: The thing is not to follow a pattern. Follow your own pattern of feeling and thought. The thing is to accept your own life and not try to live someone else's life. Look, the thumbprint is not like any other, and the thumbprint is what you must go by.

INTERVIEWER: In the current vernacular, then, you think it's necessary for an artist to be a "loner"—not to belong to any literary movement?

PORTER: I've never belonged to any group or huddle of any kind. You cannot be an artist and work collectively. Even the fact that I went to Mexico when everybody else was going to Europe—I went to Mexico because I felt I had business there.

And there I found friends and ideas that were sympathetic to me. That was my entire milieu. I don't think anyone even knew I was a writer. I didn't show my work to anybody or talk about it, because—well, no one was particularly interested in that. It was a time of revolution, and I was running with almost pure revolutionaries!

INTERVIEWER: And you think that was a more wholesome environment for a writer than, say, the milieu of the expatriated artist in Europe at the same time?

PORTER: Well, I know it was good for me. I would have been completely smothered—completely disgusted and revolted—by the goings-on in Europe. Even now when I think of the twenties and the legend that has grown up about them, I think it was a horrible time: shallow and trivial and silly. The remarkable thing is that anybody survived in such an atmosphere—in a place where they could call F. Scott Fitzgerald a great writer!

INTERVIEWER: You don't agree?

PORTER: Of course I don't agree. I couldn't read him then and I can't read him now. There was just one passage in a book called *Tender Is the Night*—I read that and thought, "Now I will read this again," because I couldn't be sure. Not only didn't I like his writing, but I didn't like the people he wrote about. I thought they weren't worth thinking about, and I still think so. It seems to me that your human beings have to have some kind of meaning. I just can't be interested in those perfectly stupid meaningless lives. And I don't like the same thing going on now—the way the artist simply will not face up to the final reckoning of things.

INTERVIEWER: In a philosophical sense?

PORTER: I'm thinking of it now in just the artistic sense—in the sense of an artist facing up to his own end meanings. I suppose I shouldn't be mentioning names, but I read a story some time ago, I think it was in *The Paris Review*, called "The

McCabes."* Now I think William Styron is an extremely gifted man: he's very ripe and lush and with a kind of Niagara Falls of energy, and a kind of power. But he depends so on violence and a kind of exaggerated heat—at least it looks like heat, but just turns out to be summer lightning. Because there is nothing in the world more meaningless than that whole escapade of this man going off and winding up in the gutter. You sit back and think, Well, let's see, where are we now? All right, it's possible that that's just what Styron meant—the whole wicked point-lessness of things. But I tell you, nothing is pointless, and nothing is meaningless if the artist will face it. And it's his business to face it. He hasn't got the right to sidestep it like that. Human life itself may be almost pure chaos, but the work of the artist—the only thing he's good for—is to take these handfuls of confusion and disparate things, things that seem to be irreconcilable, and put them together in a frame to give them some kind of shape and meaning. Even if it's only his view of a meaning. That's what he's for—to give his view of life. Surely, we understand very little of what is happening to us at any given moment. But by remembering, comparing, waiting to know the consequences, we can sometimes see what an event really meant, what it was trying to teach us.

INTERVIEWER: You once said that every story begins with an ending, that until the end is known there is no story.

PORTER: That is where the artist begins to work: with the consequences of acts, not the acts themselves. Or the events. The event is important only as it affects your life and the lives of those around you. The reverberations, you might say, the overtones: that is where the artist works. In that sense it has sometimes taken me ten years to understand even a little of some important event that had happened to me. Oh, I could

---

*"The McCabes" was mistakenly not identified as a section from Styron's novel *Set This House on Fire*

have given a perfectly factual account of what had happened, but I didn't know what it meant until I knew the consequences. If I didn't know the ending of a story, I wouldn't begin. I always write my last lines, my last paragraph, my last page first, and then I go back and work towards it. I know where I'm going. I know what my goal is. And how I get there is God's grace.

INTERVIEWER: That's a very classical view of the work of art—that it must end in resolution.

PORTER: Any true work of art has got to give you the feeling of reconciliation—what the Greeks would call catharsis, the purification of your mind and imagination—through an ending that is endurable because it is right and true. Oh, not in any pawky individual idea of morality or some parochial idea of right and wrong. Sometimes the end is very tragic, because it needs to be. One of the most perfect and marvelous endings in literature—it raises my hair now—is the little boy at the end of *Wuthering Heights*, crying that he's afraid to go across the moor because there's a man and woman walking there.

And there are three novels that I reread with pleasure and delight—three almost perfect novels, if we're talking about form, you know. One is *A High Wind in Jamaica* by Richard Hughes, one is *A Passage to India* by E. M. Forster, and the other is *To the Lighthouse* by Virginia Woolf. Every one of them begins with an apparently insoluble problem, and every one of them works out of confusion into order. The material is all used so that you are going toward a goal. And that goal is the clearing up of disorder and confusion and wrong, to a logical and human end. I don't mean a happy ending, because after all at the end of *A High Wind in Jamaica* the pirates are all hanged and the children are all marked for life by their experience, but it comes out to an orderly end. The threads are all drawn up. I have had people object to Mr. Thompson's suicide at the end of *Noon Wine*, and I'd say, "All right, where was he going? Given what he was, his own situation, what else could he do?" Every once in a while when I see a character of mine just going towards perdition, I think, Stop, stop, you can always stop and choose, you know. But no, being what he was, he already *has* chosen, and he can't go back on it now. I suppose the first idea that man had was the idea of fate, of the servile will, of a deity who destroyed as he would, without regard for the creature. But I think the idea of free will was the second idea.

INTERVIEWER: Has a story never surprised you in the writing? A character suddenly taken a different turn?

PORTER: Well, in the vision of death at the end of "Flowering Judas" I knew the real ending—that she was not going to be able to face her life, what she'd done. And I knew that the vengeful spirit was going to come in a dream to tow her away into death, but I didn't know until I'd written it that she was going to wake up saying, "No!" and be afraid to go to sleep again.

INTERVIEWER: That was, in a fairly literal sense, a "true" story, wasn't it?

PORTER: The truth is, I have never written a story in my life that didn't have a very firm foundation in actual human experience—somebody else's experience quite often, but an experience that became my own by hearing the story, by witnessing the thing, by hearing just a word perhaps. It doesn't matter, it just takes a little—a tiny seed. Then it takes root, and it grows. It's an organic thing. That story had been on my mind for years, growing out of this one little thing that happened in Mexico. It was forming and forming in my mind, until one night I was quite desperate. People are always so sociable, and I'm sociable too, and if I live around friends . . . Well, they were insisting that I come and play bridge. But I was very firm, because I knew the time had come to write that story, and I had to write it.

INTERVIEWER: What was that "little thing" from which the story grew?

PORTER: Something I saw as I passed a window one evening. A girl I knew had asked me to come and sit with her, because a man was coming to see her, and she was a little afraid of him. And as I went through the courtyard, past the flowering judas tree, I glanced in the window and there she was sitting with an open book on her lap, and there was this great big fat man sitting beside her. Now Mary and I were friends, both American girls living in this revolutionary situation. She was teaching at an Indian school, and I was teaching dancing at a girls' technical school in Mexico City. And we were having a very strange time of it. I was more skeptical, and so I had already begun to look with a skeptical eye on a great many of the revolutionary leaders. Oh, the idea was all right, but a lot of men were misapplying it.

And when I looked through that window that evening, I saw something in Mary's face, something in her pose, something in the whole situation, that set up a commotion in my mind. Because until that moment I hadn't really understood that she was not able to take care of herself, because she was not able to face her own nature and was afraid of everything. I don't know why I saw it. I don't believe in intuition. When you get sudden flashes of perception, it is just the brain working faster than usual. But you've been getting ready to know it for a long time, and when it comes, you feel you've known it always.

INTERVIEWER: You speak of a story "forming" in your mind. Does it begin as a visual impression, growing to a narrative? Or how?

PORTER: All my senses were very keen; things came to me through my eyes, through all my pores. Everything hit me at once, you know. That makes it very difficult to describe just exactly what is happening. And then, I think the mind works in such a variety of ways. Sometimes an idea starts completely inarticulately. You're not thinking in images or words or—well, it's exactly like a dark cloud moving in your head. You keep wondering what will come out of this, and then it will dissolve itself into a set of—well, not images exactly, but really thoughts. You begin to think directly in words. Abstractly. Then the words transform themselves into images. By the time I write the story my people are up and alive and walking around and taking things into their own hands. They exist as independently inside my head as you do before me now. I have been criticized for not enough detail in describing my characters, and not enough furniture in the house. And the odd thing is that I see it all so clearly.

INTERVIEWER: What about the technical problems a story presents—its formal structure? How deliberate are you in matters of technique? For example, the use of the historical present in "Flowering Judas"?

PORTER: The first time someone said to me, "Why did you write 'Flowering Judas' in the historical present?" I thought for a moment and said, "Did I?" I'd never noticed it. Because I didn't *plan* to write it any way. A story forms in my mind and forms and forms, and when it's ready to go, I strike it down— it takes just the time I sit at the typewriter. I never think about form at all. In fact, I would say that I've never been interested in anything about writing after having learned, I hope, to write. That is, I mastered my craft as well as I could. There is a technique, there is a craft, and you have to learn it. Well, I did as well as I could with that, but now all in the world I am interested in is telling a story. I have something to tell you that I, for some reason, think is worth telling, and so I want to tell it as clearly and purely and simply as I can. But I had spent fifteen years at least learning to write. I practiced writing in every possible way that I could. I wrote a pastiche of other people, imitating Dr. Johnson and Laurence Sterne, and Petrarch's and Shakespeare's sonnets, and then I tried writing my own way. I spent fifteen years learning to trust myself: that's what it comes to. Just as a pianist runs his scales for ten years before he gives his concert: because when he gives that concert, he can't be thinking of his fingering or of his hands; he has to be thinking of his interpretation, of the music he's playing. He's thinking of what he's trying to communicate. And if he hasn't got his technique perfected by then, he needn't give the concert at all.

INTERVIEWER: From whom would you say you learned most during this period of apprenticeship?

PORTER: The person who influenced me most, the real revelation in my life as a writer—though I don't write in the least like him—was Laurence Sterne, in *Tristram Shandy*. Why? Because, you know, I loved the grand style, and he made it look easy. The others, the great ones, really frightened me; they were so grand and magnificent they overawed me completely. But Laurence Sterne—well, it was just exactly as if he said, "Oh, come on, do it this way. It's so easy." So I tried to do it that way, and that taught me something, that taught me more than anybody else had. Because Laurence Sterne is a most complex and subtle man.

INTERVIEWER: What about your contemporaries? Did any of them contribute significantly to your development as a writer?

PORTER: I don't think I learned very much from my contemporaries. To begin with, we were all such individuals, and we were all so argumentative and so bent on our own courses that although I got a kind of support and personal friendship from my contemporaries, I didn't get very much help. I didn't show my work to anybody. I didn't hand it around among my friends for criticism, because, well, it just didn't occur to me to do it. Just as I didn't even try to publish anything until quite late because I didn't think I was ready. I published my first story in 1923. That was "María Concepción," the first story I ever finished. I rewrote "María Concepción" fifteen or sixteen times.

That was a real battle, and I was thirty-three years old. I think it is the most curious lack of judgment to publish before you are ready. If there are echoes of other people in your work, you're not ready. If anybody has to help you rewrite your story, you're not ready. A story should be a finished work before it is shown. And after that, I will not allow anyone to change anything, and I will not change anything on anyone's advice. "Here is my story. It's a finished story. Take it or leave it!"

INTERVIEWER: You are frequently spoken of as a stylist. Do you think a style can be cultivated, or at least refined?

PORTER: I've been called a stylist until I really could tear my hair out. And I simply don't believe in style. The style is you. Oh, you can cultivate a style, I suppose, if you like. But I should say it remains a cultivated style. It remains artificial and imposed, and I don't think it deceives anyone. A cultivated style would be like a mask. Everybody knows it's a mask, and sooner or later you must show yourself—or at least, you show yourself as someone who could not afford to show himself, and so created something to hide behind. Style is the man. Aristotle said it first, as far as I know, and everybody has said it since, because it is one of those unarguable truths. You do not create a style. You work, and develop yourself; your style is an emanation from your own being. Symbolism is the same way. I never consciously took or adopted a symbol in my life. I certainly did not say, "This blooming tree upon which Judas is supposed to have hanged himself is going to be the center of my story." I named "Flowering Judas" after it was written, because when reading back over it I suddenly saw the whole symbolic plan and pattern of which I was totally unconscious while I was writing. There's a pox of symbolist theory going the rounds these days in American colleges in the writing courses. Miss Mary McCarthy, who is one of the wittiest and most acute and in some ways the worst-tempered woman in American letters, tells about a little girl who came to her with a story. Now Miss

McCarthy is an extremely good critic, and she found this to be a good story, and she told the girl that it was—that she considered it a finished work, and that she could with a clear conscience go on to something else. And the little girl said, "But Miss McCarthy, my writing teacher said, 'Yes, it's a good piece of work, but now we must go back and put in the symbols!'" I think that's an amusing story, and it makes my blood run cold.

INTERVIEWER: But certainly one's command of the language can be developed and refined?

PORTER: I love the purity of language. I keep cautioning my students and anyone who will listen to me not to use the jargon of trades, not to use scientific language, because they're going to be out of date the day after tomorrow. The scientists change their vocabulary, their jargon, every day. So do the doctors, and the politicians, and the theologians—every body, every profession, every trade changes its vocabulary all of the time. But there is a basic pure human speech that exists in every language. And that is the language of the poet and the writer. So many words that had good meanings once upon a time have come to have meanings almost evil—certainly shabby, certainly inaccurate. And "psychology" is one of them. It has been so abused. This awful way a whole segment, not a generation but too many of the young writers, have got so soaked in the Freudian and post-Freudian vocabulary that they can't speak—not only can't speak English, but they can't speak *any* human language anymore. You can't write about people out of textbooks, and you can't use a jargon. You have to speak clearly and simply and purely in a language that a six-year-old child can understand; and yet have the meanings and the overtones of language, and the implications, that appeal to the highest intelligence—that is, the highest intelligence that one is able to reach. I'm not sure that I'm able to appeal to the highest intelligence, but I'm willing to try.

INTERVIEWER: You speak of the necessity of writing out of

your own understanding rather than out of textbooks, and I'm sure any writer would agree. But what about the creation of masculine characters, then? Most women writers, even the best of them like George Eliot, have run aground there. What about you? Was Mr. Thompson, say, a more difficult imaginative problem than Miranda?

PORTER: I never did make a profession of understanding people, man or woman or child, and the only thing I know about people is exactly what I have learned from the people right next to me. I have always lived in my immediate circumstances, from day to day. And when men ask me how I know so much about men, I've got a simple answer: everything I know about men, I've learned from men. If there is such a thing as a man's mind and a woman's mind—and I'm sure there is—it isn't what most critics mean when they talk about the two. If I show wisdom, they say I have a masculine mind. If I am silly and irrelevant—and Edmund Wilson says I often am—why then, they say I have a typically feminine mind! (That's one thing about reaching my age: you can always quote the authorities about what you are.) But I haven't ever found it unnatural to be a woman.

INTERVIEWER: But haven't you found that being a woman presented to you, as an artist, certain special problems? It seems to me that a great deal of the upbringing of women encourages the dispersion of the self in many small bits, and that the practice of any kind of art demands a corraling and concentrating of that self and its always insufficient energies.

PORTER: I think that's very true and very right. You're brought up with the notion of feminine chastity and inaccessibility, yet with the curious idea of feminine availability in all spiritual ways, and in giving service to anyone who demands it. And I suppose that's why it has taken me twenty years to write this novel; it's been interrupted by just anyone who could jimmy his way into my life.

INTERVIEWER: Hemingway said once that a writer writes best when he's in love.

PORTER: I don't know whether you write better, but you feel so good you *think* you're writing better! And certainly love does create a rising of the spirit that makes everything you do seem easier and happier. But there must come a time when you no longer depend upon it, when the mind—not the will, really, either—takes over.

INTERVIEWER: In judging that the story is ready? You said a moment ago that the actual writing of a story is always done in a single spurt of energy—

PORTER: I always write a story in one sitting. I started "Flowering Judas" at seven P.M. and at one-thirty I was standing on a snowy windy corner putting it in the mailbox. And when I wrote my short novels, two of them, I just simply took the manuscript, packed a suitcase and departed to an inn in Georgetown, Pennsylvania, without leaving any forwarding address! Fourteen days later I had finished *Old Mortality* and *Noon Wine.*

INTERVIEWER: But the new novel *Ship of Fools* has been in the writing since 1942. The regime for writing this must have been a good deal different.

PORTER: Oh, it was. I went up and sat nearly three years in the country, and while I was writing it I worked every day, anywhere from three to five hours. Oh, it's true I used to do an awful lot of just sitting there thinking what comes next, because this is a great big unwieldy book with an enormous cast of characters—it's four hundred of my manuscript pages, and I can get four hundred and fifty words on a page. But all that time in Connecticut, I kept myself free for work: no telephone, no visitors—oh, I really lived like a hermit, everything but being fed through a grate! But it is, as Yeats said, a "solitary sedentary trade." And I did a lot of gardening, and cooked my own food, and listened to music, and of course I would read. I was really very happy. I can live a solitary life for months at a time, and it does me good, because I'm working. I just get up bright and early—sometimes at five o'clock—have my black coffee, and go to work.

INTERVIEWER: You work best in the morning, then?

PORTER: I work whenever I'm let. In the days when I was taken up with everything else, I used to do a day's work, or housework, or whatever I was doing, and then work at night. I worked when I could. But I prefer to get up very early in the morning and work. I don't want to speak to anybody or see anybody. Perfect silence. I work until the vein is out. There's something about the way you feel, you know when the well is dry, that you'll have to wait till tomorrow and it'll be full up again.

INTERVIEWER: The important thing, then, is to avoid any breaks or distractions while you're writing?

PORTER: To keep at a boiling point. So that I can get up in the morning with my mind still working where it was yesterday. Then I can stop in the middle of a paragraph and finish it the next day. I began writing *Ship of Fools* twenty years ago, and I've been away from it for several years at a time and stopped in the middle of a paragraph—but, you know, I can't tell where the crack is mended, and I hope nobody else can.

INTERVIEWER: You find no change in style, or in attitudes, over the years?

PORTER: It's astonishing how little I've changed: nothing in my point of view or my way of feeling. I'm going back now to finish some of the great many short stories that I have begun and not been able to finish for one reason or another. I've found one that I think I can finish. I have three versions of it: I started it in 1923, and it's based on an episode in my life that took place when I was twenty. Now here I am, seventy, and it's astonishing how much it's like me now. Oh, there are certain things, certain turns of sentence, certain phrases that I think I can sharpen and make more clear, more simple and direct, but my point of view, my being, is strangely unchanged. We change, of course, every day; we are not the same people who sat down at this table, yet there is a basic and innate being that is unchanged.

INTERVIEWER: *Ship of Fools* too is based upon an event that took place ten years or more before the first writing, isn't it? A sea voyage just before the beginning of the European war.

PORTER: It is the story of my first voyage to Europe in 1931. We embarked on an old German ship at Vera Cruz and we landed in Bremerhaven twenty-eight days later. It was a crowded ship, a great mixture of nationalities, religions, political beliefs—all that sort of thing. I don't think I spoke a half-dozen words to anybody. I just sat there and watched—not deliberately, though. I kept a diary in the form of a letter to a friend, and after I got home the friend sent it back. And, you know, it is astonishing what happened on that boat, and what happened in my mind afterwards. Because it is fiction now.

INTERVIEWER: The title—isn't it from a medieval emblem?—suggests that it might also be an allegory.

PORTER: It's just exactly what it seems to be. It's an allegory if you like, though I don't think much of the allegorical as a standard. It's a parable, if you like, of the ship of this world on its voyage to eternity.

INTERVIEWER: I remember your writing once—I think in the preface to "Flowering Judas"—of an effort to understand what you called the "majestic and terrible failure" of Western man. You were speaking then of the World War and what it signified of human folly. It seems to me that *Ship of Fools* properly belongs to that investigation of betrayal and self-delusion—

PORTER: Betrayal and treachery, but also self-betrayal and self-deception—the way that all human beings deceive themselves about the way they operate. . . . There seems to be a kind of order in the universe, in the movement of the stars and the turning of the earth and the changing of the seasons, and even in the cycle of human life. But human life itself is almost pure chaos. Everyone takes his stance, asserts his own rights and feelings, mistaking the motives of others, and his own. . . . Now, nobody knows the end of the life he's living, and neither do I. Don't forget I am a passenger on that ship; it's not the other people altogether who are the fools! We don't really know what is going to happen to us, and we don't know why. Quite often the best we can do is to keep our heads, and try to keep at least one line unbroken and unobstructed. Misunderstanding and separation are the natural conditions of man. We come together only at these prearranged meeting grounds; we were all passengers on that ship, yet at his destination, each one was alone.

INTERVIEWER: Did you find that the writing of *Ship of Fools* differed from the writing of shorter fiction?

PORTER: It's just a longer voyage, that's all. It was the question of keeping everything moving at once. There are about forty-five main characters, all taking part in each other's lives, and then there was a steerage of sugar workers, deportees. It was all a matter of deciding which should come first, in order to keep the harmonious moving forward. A novel is really like a symphony, you know, where instrument after instrument has to come in at its own time, and no other. I tried to write it as a short novel, you know, but it just wouldn't confine itself. I wrote notes and sketches. And finally I gave in. Oh, no, this is simply going to have to be a novel, I thought. That was a real horror. But it needed a book to contain its full movement: of the sea, and the ship on the sea, and the people going around the deck, and into the ship, and up from it. That whole movement, felt as one forward motion: I can feel it while I'm reading it. I didn't "intend" it, but it took hold of me.

INTERVIEWER: As writing itself, perhaps, "took hold" of · you—we began by your saying that you had never intended to be a professional anything, even a professional writer.

PORTER: I look upon literature as an art, and I practice it as an art. Of course, it is also a vocation, and a trade, and a profession, and all kinds of things; but first it's an art, and you should practice it as that, I think. I know a great many people disagree, and they are welcome to it. I think probably the important thing is to get your work done, in the way you can—and we all have our different and separate ways. But I look upon literature as an art, and I believe that if you misuse it or abuse it, it will leave you. It is not a thing that you can nail down and use as you want. You have to let it use you, too.

—BARBARA THOMPSON
1963

REBECCA WEST

Rebecca West was born Cicily Isabel Fairfield in County Kerry, Ireland, in December 1892. She changed her name to that of the heroine of Ibsen's play *Rosmersholm*, who is characterized by a passionate will. As "Rebecca West" she began in journalism and literary criticism, and continued to write throughout the traumatic years when she was alone bringing up her only child, Anthony Panther West, born to her and H. G. Wells in 1914. She published her first book in 1916 and her first novel, *The Return of the Soldier*, in 1918. She wrote novels throughout the twenties (*The Judge*, 1922; *Harriet Hume, A London Fantasy*, 1929), and in 1928 collected her criticism in *The Strange Necessity*. The subject of the title essay is the touchstone of Rebecca West's philosophy: the unquenchable need of human beings for art and literature. More essays followed in *Ending in Earnest: A Literary Log* (1931), in which, notably, she acclaimed the genius of D. H. Lawrence. Two years later she published her biographical masterwork, *St. Augustine*.

In the late thirties she traveled widely with her husband, Henry Maxwell Andrews, in the Balkans, and from these experiences she built her formidable analysis of the origins of

World War II, *Black Lamb and Grey Falcon* (1941), generally considered to be her finest book. The marked political and historical character of this work led naturally to *The New Meaning of Treason* (1947) and *A Train of Powder* (1955), West's matchless account of the Nuremberg trials.

Honored with the French Legion of Honor and an award from the Women's Press Club for Journalism, Dame Rebecca West was still writing book reviews up until her death on March 16, 1983.

REBECCA WEST

In Rebecca West's hallway hung a drawing of her by Wyndham Lewis done in the thirties, "before the ruin," as she put it. But her brown eyes remained brilliant and penetrating, her voice energetic, and her attention to all things acute. She was wearing a bright and patterned caftan when we first met, a loose blouse over trousers the second time. Cataracts meant she had two pairs of spectacles, on chains like necklaces; arthritis had made a stick necessary. Her hair was white and short; she wore beautiful rings. Her voice had kept some of the vowel sounds of the Edwardian period, and some of its turns of phrase: "I can't see someone or something" meant "I can't tolerate." She said words of foreign derivation, like "memoirs," with the accent of the parent language. We sat in her sitting room, a room filled with drawings and paintings with a wide bay window looking out on some of London's tall trees. Their leaves, which were turning when we met, almost brushed against the window panes.

INTERVIEWER: In your novel, *The Fountain Overflows*, you describe the poverty of the educated class very beautifully. Was that your background?

WEST: Oh, yes. I'll tell you what the position was. We had

Once moreuse it had died and been reborn.

Its rebirth, I calculated rapidly, was likely to be followed by an agonising existence. I knew at once, as everybody must who had any knowledge of international affairs what foreign powers had combined to kill this man. It appeared to me then, as I lay in bed in the nursing-home, inevitable that war must follow; and indeed it must have done, had not the Yugoslavian Government exercised an iron control over its population then and thereafter, and abstained from the smallest provocative action against its enemies. On that forbearance, which is indeed one of the most extraordinary feats of statesmanship performed in post-war Europe, I could not be expected to rely. So I saw myself widowed and childless which was another instance of the archaic outlook of the back of the mind; for in the next war we women will have hardly any reason to fear bereavement, as bombardment unpreceded by declaration of war will send us and our loved ones to the next world in the breathless unity of scrambled eggs. That thought did not then occur to me, so I rang for my nurse, and when she came I cried to her, 'Get me a telephone quickly' I must speak to my husband at once. A most terrible thing has happened. The King of Yugoslavia has been assassinated' 'Oh, dear!' she replied 'Did you know him?' 'No,' I said. 'Then why,' she said, 'do you think it is so terrible?'

Her words made me realise that the word 'idiot' comes from a Greek root meaning a private person. She was certainly intelligent in her work and was probably so in her personal life, but her unawareness of the bonds that linked her to strangers made her follow her fate in a darkness deep as that cast by malformed cells in the brain. It might be argued that she was happier so; but that is true only in the most limited sense. She would not be happy long. A population which does not know that the assassination of the King of Yugoslavia might precipitate a European war is a perpetual temptation to its governors; it will believe any lies, it can be seduced into supporting unnecessary wars and peace treaties that favour class interests. But it might be

_____

A manuscript page from Rebecca West's
Black Lamb and Grey Falcon

lots of pleasant furniture that had belonged to my father's family, none that had belonged to my mother's family, because they didn't die—the whole family all went on to their eighties, nineties—but we had furniture and we had masses of books, and we had a very good piano my mother played on. We were poor because my father's father died, when he and his three brothers were schoolboys. Their mother was a member of the Plymouth Brethren and a religious fanatic with a conscience that should have been held down and, you know, been eunuchized or castrated. She refused to keep on, to accept any longer, an annuity, which she was given by the royal family. And nobody knows why she was given it, and she found out the reason and she didn't approve of it, and she refused it, and they were poor forever after. The maddening thing was nobody ever knew why she said to Queen Victoria, "I cannot accept this allowance." It was hard on my father, who was in the army, because you needed money to be an officer. He was a ballistics expert. He did quite well in various things.

INTERVIEWER: He was a professional soldier?

WEST: No. Not all his life. He left the army after he got his captaincy. He went out to America and he ran a mine and wrote a certain amount, mostly on political science. He wrote well. He had a great mechanical mind and he drew very well. He did all sorts of things, and he'd had a fairly good training at Woolwich, a military academy. We were the children of his second marriage and he could no longer make much money. He went out to Africa and just got ill there. He came back and died in Liverpool when I was twelve or thirteen.

INTERVIEWER: Was he a remote and admirable figure, as the father is in *The Fountain Overflows*?

WEST: Oh, he wasn't so cracked as the father and he didn't sell furniture that didn't belong to him and all that sort of thing. That was rather a remembrance of another strange character.

INTERVIEWER: You've written very movingly, in several of your books, on how cruel natural death is, how it is the greatest hardship, as opposed to some of the more violent deaths that you've also written about. Was it a very traumatic experience for you, as a child, when you lost your father?

WEST: Oh, yes, it was terrible. . . . The whole of life was extremely uncomfortable for us at that time. We had really got into terrible financial straits, not through anybody's fault. My mother had had to work very hard, and though she was a very good pianist, she was out of the running by then, and when she realized that my father was old and wasn't going to be able to go on with things, she very nobly went and learned typewriting. Do you know people are always writing in the papers and saying that typists started in the last war, but they've been going on since the eighties and the nineties and 1900. Well, my mother did some typing for American evangelists called Torry and Alexander and she took over their music. They toured in England and my mother whacked the "Glory Song," a famous hymn—you still hear it whistled in the streets—out on the grand piano on the platform. It was a very noble thing to do. She wasn't well and she wasn't young, and then we came up to Scotland. My sister was studying medicine. My other sister had a scholarship at Cheltenham, which was rather useless to her; she was very brilliant indeed, and amusing as well.

INTERVIEWER: Which sister was that?

WEST: That's Winifred, who was more or less like Mary in *The Fountain Overflows.* Then there was myself, who had to go and try to get scholarships, which I usually did, at the local school. My mother ran a typing business, and I assisted her, which was amusing and which gave me a quickness of eye, which has been quite useful. She used to type manuscripts, particularly for the music faculty in Edinburgh. There was a German professor she'd known all her life. He used to send along pieces and I remember still with horror and amusement an enormous German book of his on program music with sentences like "If the hearer turns his attention to the flutes and the piccolos, surely there will come to his mind the dawn rising over the bronze horses of Venice." There is a lot of rather good idiom of writing I can summon up, if necessary, about music in the post-Wagnerian period, which was very, very lush.

INTERVIEWER: Were you brought up to play yourself?

WEST: I played, but not well. From an early age—but it was not detected for many, many years—I've had difficulty about hearing. Finally, I lost my hearing almost entirely in this ear. I got pneumonia in it, which I think is rather chic. Then I thought I'd got my hearing back slowly, but really I'd learned to lip-read and, it's an extraordinary thing, young people—if they lose their hearing young—learn lip-reading unconsciously, lots of them. It's quite common. I did that without knowing—when I got double cataracts, I suddenly found my hearing going and I said, "Goodness, I've gone deaf at the same time as my eyes are going wrong," but my aurist, who's a very nice man, said, "No, you haven't. Your lip-reading power is breaking down," which was very disappointing, but, on the other hand, I was amazed at the ingenuity of the human animal. It did strike me as an extraordinary thing.

INTERVIEWER: In your home, was the atmosphere for women very emancipated because you were left alone?

WEST: Oh, yes. We were left alone. We had an uncle, who was very preoccupied. He was president of the Royal Academy of Music, Sir Alexander MacKenzie, and he didn't really think anything of any woman but his wife. He was very thoughtless about his own daughter, who was an actress who acted very well in the early Chekhov plays. He treated her very inconsiderately and made her come back and nurse her mother and leave her husband in Paris, and the husband, after six years, lost heart and went off with someone else. We were very feminist altogether, and it was a very inspiring thing. Who is that man,

David Mitchell, who writes silly hysterical books about Christabel Pankhurst? What is he? Who is he?

INTERVIEWER: He's now writing a book about the Jesuits.

WEST: The Jesuits? How does he know about the Jesuits?

INTERVIEWER: You thought his book on Christabel was hysterical, did you?

WEST: Absolute rubbish and nonsense. He writes about how she went to Paris and how she didn't go down to the cafés and meet the young revolutionaries. But how on earth was she to find out where they were? Because, you see, the Bolshevik generation was not yet identifiable. How would she find out any of the people, who hadn't really made their mark? It was an obscure time in the history of revolution. It was a time when very remarkable people were coming up, but they weren't visible yet. She did know the people like Henri de Rochefort very well. Mitchell also says she took a flat and had a housekeeper, who was also a very good cook, and didn't that show great luxury? Well, if he'd asked anybody, he would have found that, in those days, you couldn't take a furnished flat or house in Paris, nor, so far as I know, in most parts of France, unless you took a servant, who was left by the owner. All the furnished houses I ever had in France, modest as they were, had somebody that I had to take with the house.

INTERVIEWER: But you yourself broke with the suffragette movement.

WEST: I was too young and unimportant for that to mean much. I admired them enormously, but all that business about venereal disease, which was supposed to be round every corner, seemed to me excessive. I wasn't in a position to judge, but it did seem a bit silly. [Christabel Pankhurst headed a chastity campaign for women.]

INTERVIEWER: Christabel, in her later phase, became the equivalent of a misogynist. She became very, what would the word be, misanthropic against men only, didn't she?

WEST: It wasn't quite that. She fell curiously into a sort of transatlantic form of mysticism, where there is a sort of repudiation of sex. Do you ever read anything about Thomas Lake Harris? He was an American mystic. Curious thing—you repudiated sex but you had a "counterpart," and you usually could get a counterpart by getting into bed with somebody else, with whom your relations were supposed to be chaste, but when you lay in his arms, you were really lying in the counterpart's arms, and . . . isn't it a convenient arrangement? That was one sort of pattern of American mysticism and dottyism. Christabel got caught up with that vagueness—though not with counterparts. If you read Harris's sermons—somebody took them down and I had a look at them—they were all very queer like that, disguised sexuality, but I wouldn't say the worse for that.

INTERVIEWER: You have written that there is a great difference between a male sensibility and a female sensibility, and you have a marvelous phrase for it in *Black Lamb and Grey Falcon.*

WEST: Idiots and lunatics. It's a perfectly good division. [The Greek root of "idiot" means "private person"; men "see the world as if by moonlight, which shows the outlines of every object but not the details indicative of their nature."] It seems to me in any assembly where you get people, who are male and female, in a crisis, the women are apt to get up and, with a big wave of the hand, say: "It's all very well talking about the defenses of the country, but there are thirty-six thousand houses in whatever—wherever they're living—that have no bathrooms. Surely it's more important to have clean children for the future." Silly stuff, when the enemy's at the gate. But men are just as silly. Even when there are no enemies at the gate, they won't attend to the bathrooms, because they say defense is more important. It's mental deficiency in both cases.

INTERVIEWER: But do you think it's innate or do you think it's produced by culture?

WEST: Oh, I really can't tell you that. It's awfully hard. You can't imagine what maleness and femaleness would be if you got back to them in pure laboratory state, can you? I suspect the political imbecility is very great on both sides.

I've never gone anywhere where the men have come up to my infantile expectations. I always have gone through life constantly being surprised by the extreme, marvelous qualities of a small minority of men. But I can't see the rest of them. They seem awful rubbish.

INTERVIEWER: In many of the political things that you've written, it would be impossible to tell that you were a woman, except that here and there you sometimes produce a comparison to do with a child or something, which may betray a certain feminine stance, but, in fact, you have overcome completely this division between idiot and lunatic. You're not an "idiot" at all. You don't think only of the personal angle.

WEST: I think that probably comes of isolation, that I grew up just as I was without much interference from social images except at my school.

INTERVIEWER: What were they at school?

WEST: We had large classes, which was an ineffable benefit, because the teachers really hadn't time to muck about with our characters. You see, the people who wanted to learn, sat and learned, and the people who didn't, didn't learn, but there was no time, you know, for bringing out the best in us, thank God. I had some magnificent teachers, actually, a Miss MacDonald, who taught me Latin irregular verbs.

INTERVIEWER: Did you have a classical training?

WEST: No, no. I had no Greek. They didn't teach any Greek for the reason that our school took on from a very early school, at which they had followed Madame de Maintenon's school at St. Cyr, where the children were taught Latin but not Greek. Why do you think I wasn't taught Greek?—Because Madame de Maintenon thought girls shouldn't learn Greek in case they fell into the toils of the heretical Eastern Orthodox Church, which is rather funny, considering we were all good girls at Edinburgh. Very curious bit of history, that.

INTERVIEWER: And this tradition reached as far as Scotland?

WEST: Well, you see, the man who was the begetter of our school had been to St. Cyr, and he just took the whole thing on.

INTERVIEWER: What did your mother expect you to be? What images did she set up for you?

WEST: There was a great idea that I should be an actress because a woman called Rosina Fillipi had seen me act in a play and she thought I was terribly good as a comedian, as a sort of low-comedy character, and she said, "If you come to the Royal Academy of Dramatic Art, I will look after you and you can get a job." I'm the only person I ever heard of who wanted to go on the stage not because I was stagestruck but it just seemed to be the thing to do. I loved the theater. I still love it, but I had no stagestruck feeling. I felt how nice if people would give me a part. I went to the Royal Academy of Art, where there was a man called Kenneth Barnes, who ran it, who had got his job because he was the brother of the Vanbrughs, Irene and Violet Vanbrugh, if that means anything to you. He couldn't understand what Rosina Fillipi had seen in me and he made me very uncomfortable. I didn't stay out the course.

INTERVIEWER: But you chose the name of a dramatic character—Rebecca West.

WEST: Yes. Not really for any profound reason. It was just to get a pseudonym.

INTERVIEWER: It really wasn't profound? You don't think unconsciously it was?

WEST: People have always been putting me down in any role that was convenient but it would not, I think, naturally have been my own idea. I've aroused hostility in an extraordinary lot of people. I've never known why. I don't think I'm formidable.

INTERVIEWER: I think that your hallmark is that you have always disliked people who wanted approval. You like the heterodox.

WEST: I should like to be approved of. Oh, yes. I blench. I hate being disapproved of. I've had rather a lot of it.

INTERVIEWER: And yet, in your writing, there is quite a strong strain of impatience with people who do things because society approves of it.

WEST: Oh, yes. I think I see what you mean. Oh, that's Scotch, I think, yes, Scotch, because . . . oh, yes, and it's also a bit of my mother and my father. My father was educated by Élisée and Eli Reclus, two famous French brothers, early geographers; my cracked grandmother, the religious maniac who refused the family fortune, had hired them because they were refugees in England; she thought that, as young Frenchmen in England, they must be Protestants who had escaped from the wicked Catholics' persecution. They were actually anarchists and they'd escaped, run away from France because they'd seized the town hall—I can't remember which town it was—in the course of an émeute against Louis Napoleon. They were very sweet. They said, when they found out the mistake, "Oh, well, we must be careful about teaching the children." They taught them awfully well. My father was a very, very well educated man, and so were all his brothers.

INTERVIEWER: What did you read at home as a child? Who were the early formative influences?

WEST: Oh, pretty well everything. We read a terrific lot of Shakespeare, which my mother knew by heart and so did my father . . . and a lot of George Borrow. Funny thing to read, but . . . really early Victorian England was quite familiar to me because of that. Oh, lots . . . I can't think. My mother and my sister, Winifred, who was much the cleverest of us, she read frightfully good poetry. She taught me a lot of poetry, which

I've all forgotten now, but you know, if I see the first line, I can go on.

INTERVIEWER: Would you acknowledge Conrad or anyone else as an influence on you?

WEST: Well, I longed, when I was young, to write as well as Mark Twain. It's beautiful stuff and I always liked him. If I wanted to write anything that attacked anybody, I used to have a look at his attack on Christian Science, which is beautifully written. He was a man of very great shrewdness. The earliest article on the Nazis, on Nazism, a sort of first foretaste, a prophetic view of the war, was an article by Mark Twain in *Harper's* in, I should think, the nineties. He went to listen to the Parliament in Vienna and he describes an awful row and what the point of view of Luger, the Lord Mayor, was, and the man called George Schwartz, I think, who started the first Nazi paper, and what it must all lead to. It's beautifully done. It's the very first notice that I've ever found of the Austrian Nazi Party, that started it all.

INTERVIEWER: What was your first conscious encounter with fascism?

WEST: A lot of boys, who stopped my sister and myself and took her hockey stick away from her. The thing was they weren't doing it as robbery but it was fun and good fellowship, and they were the boys together. That was the first. They were just street children. We had a brick wall and an alley behind it and we used to come up half the alley, if we were going into the house of some neighbors, and there these boys caught us in the alley and they took it away; but we fought them and screamed and shouted and got back the hockey stick.

INTERVIEWER: That was when?

WEST: That must have been—I was born in 1892—about 1903, or, no earlier than that, just in this century perhaps.

INTERVIEWER: Yes, so, before the First World War, you saw the seeds of fascism.

WEST: No, no. I just saw violence. There was the race thing and sacred Germanism and all that, but the enemy before the First World War you can't really compare with fascism. It was the imperialism of Germany and the supremacy of the army, but that isn't exactly fascism. I think you could say, there was more fascism, but of an intellectualized kind, in France. The crux of the Dreyfus case was that it didn't matter whether Dreyfus was guilty or not, you mustn't spoil the image of the army. That was more or less fascist.

INTERVIEWER: But do you feel, with your strong sense of justice and of pity, that our wars have remained as terrible, or do you feel that we have learned?

WEST: I don't know what *you've* learned. I'll tell you I think the Second World War was much more comfortable because in the First World War women's position was so terrible, because there you were, not in danger. Men were going out and getting killed for you and you'd much prefer they weren't. My father was always very tender about armies, having been a soldier. The awful feeling for a small professional army was that they were recruited from poor people who went out and got killed. That was, do you know, very disagreeable. There was a genuine humanitarian feeling of guilt about that in the first war. It was very curious, you see. There I sat on my balcony in Leigh-on-Sea and heard guns going in France. It was a most peculiar war. It was really better, in the Second World War, when the people at home got bombed. I found it a relief. You were taking your chance and you might be killed and you weren't in that pampered sort of unnatural state. I find the whole idea of a professional army very disgusting still. Lacking a normal life, they turn into scoundrels. As Wellington said, they're despised for being scoundrels and it's not their fault and they die like flies and have the worst discomforts.

INTERVIEWER: And yet a conspired army, as fought in Vietnam . . . You laugh?

WEST: Well, I can't help thinking that the whole of the Vietnam war was the blackest comedy that ever was, because it showed the way you can't teach humanity anything. We'd all learned in the rest of the world that you can't now go round and put out your hand and, across seas, exercise power; but the poor Americans had not learned that and they tried to do it. The remoteness of America from German attack had made them feel confident. They didn't really believe that anything could reach out and kill them. Americans are quite unconscious now that we look on them as just as much beaten as we are. They're quite unconscious of that. They always have talked of Vietnam as if by getting out they were surrendering the prospect of victory, as if they were being noble by renouncing the possibility of victory. But they couldn't have had a victory. They couldn't possibly have won.

INTERVIEWER: But when you say they're beaten as we are, in what way do you mean we are beaten?

WEST: Only as regards world power. We can't put our hands out and order things to happen a long way away. Oh, I think we're also beaten in other ways—in industry. I think the war between the public and the unions is very difficult and I don't see where its solution lies.

INTERVIEWER: Have you ever seen a society about which you really felt: Here is society that works for the benefit of its citizens without harming others?

WEST: No, I think the earth itself is slightly resistant to routine. You might come to a place which was favorable, because of a discovery of minerals that could be mined more easily, you know, "place mines," as they call the ones on the surface, and you'd think that was very nice and they would get on with it. Then round the corner you'd find there was a dispute about water rights. Humanity wasn't obviously a made-to-order thing. It's a continual struggle, isn't it?

INTERVIEWER: Have you ever been tempted at all to any religious belief?

WEST: Oh, yes. It all seems so damned silly and incomprehensible, there might as well be a silly and incomprehensible solution, don't you think? I'd be quite prepared for anything to happen, but not very respectfully, I think.

INTERVIEWER: I think you might stand up to God.

WEST: No, not exactly that, but I don't think there would be a God who would really demand it. If there is a God, I don't think He would demand that anybody bow down or stand up to Him. I have often a suspicion God is still trying to work things out and hasn't finished.

INTERVIEWER: Were your parents at all believing?

WEST: My mother was, in a sort of musical way, and I think my father accepted it as part of the structure, but didn't do anything. We always went to church and enjoyed it. I don't feel the slightest resistance to the Church except when it's a bad landlord or something like that. I don't see why people feel any écrasez l'infâme. I know much infâm-er things than religion, much more worthy of being écraséed.

INTERVIEWER: What can you remember as being a moment of great happiness?

WEST: Extremely few. I had a very unhappy time with H. G. Wells, because I was a victim of a sort of sadistic situation. Partly people disapproved of H. G. so much less than they did of me, and they were very horrible to me, and it was very hard. It was particularly hard later, people being horrid to me because I was living with H. G., when I was trying as hard as I could to leave him. It was really absurd, and now I think it's rather funny, but it wasn't funny at the time. Then I had a short time of happiness on my own and a time of happiness with my marriage [R. W. married Henry Andrews in 1930], but then my husband got ill, very ill. He had meningitis, this thing that's always struck at people near me, when he was young and then he got cerebral arteriosclerosis, and after years it came down on him. He was in a very unhappy state of illness for a good many years before he died, but we had a great many good years together. I was very happy.

INTERVIEWER: Have any of the men you've known helped you?

WEST: The men near you always hinder you because they always want you to do the traditional female things and they take a lot of time. My mother helped me to work because she always talked to me as if I were grown-up.

INTERVIEWER: Do you feel men did not want to help you as a writer?

WEST: Oh, yes! So many men hate you. When my husband was dying I had some very strange dialogues. People were very rude just because they'd heard I was a woman writer. That kind of rudeness is as bad as ever.

INTERVIEWER: Would it have been easier to have been a man?

WEST: It certainly would have been.

INTERVIEWER: Are there any advantages at all in being a woman and a writer?

WEST: None whatsoever. You could have a good time as a woman, but you'd have a much better time as a man. If in the course of some process, people turn up a card with a man's name on it and then a card with a woman's, they feel much softer towards the man, even though he might be a convicted criminal. They'd treat the man's card with greater tenderness.

INTERVIEWER: You don't think there's been an improvement?

WEST: Not very much.

INTERVIEWER: Everyone is still very curious about your love affair with H. G. Wells.

WEST: Why, I can't see why. It was a very long time ago, and it wasn't interesting. Why would I have brought it to an end if it had been interesting? It wasn't.

INTERVIEWER: What did your husband, Henry Andrews, do?

WEST: He was unfortunately put into a bank. He should have been an art historian. He got out of the bank in the end because he was too ill. He did a bit in the war where he was in the Ministry of Economic Warfare and very good. He was a delightfully funny man. He said very funny things, and he was very scholarly and he was very generous and he was very kind. There were all sorts of pleasant things about him.

INTERVIEWER: You could talk to him.

WEST: We talked a very great deal, but it's extraordinary the really tragic and dreadful things there are in marriage which are funny. I've never known anybody to write about this. My husband would insist on going and driving a car, and he'd never been a good driver. Like all bad drivers, he thought he was the best driver in the world and he couldn't drive at all at the end and it was terrible. I'm one of the few women who have been driven on the left side of a bus queue, on the *near* side of the pavement. It was awful. Well, that really made my life poisoned for years. All the time I never thought I would live to the end of the year. I thought he would be sure to kill me here or there. And he meant no harm.

INTERVIEWER: You weren't able to tell him this?

WEST: I told him and he wouldn't believe me. Two doctors said to me it could be so bad for his ego values, if he was not allowed to drive a car. Doctors tend to be chumps. I have had two or three marvelous doctors. I have a marvelous doctor now, who's very nice, very funny and very clever, but some of my worst enemies have been doctors, I can assure you.

INTERVIEWER: You have actually been quite ill yourself, haven't you?

WEST: Well, I had an attack of TB when I was a schoolgirl. Everybody did in those days. It simply meant that you got a shot of TB in your youth and you didn't get it later on. It was rather dramatic. What was awful was that I got it at the same time as my great friend, Flora Duncan, who was at school with me and whom I liked enormously; she died of it years afterwards in the most dreary way. She went with her aunt to stay in a hotel from which she was coming to lunch with me—this was just after I was married—and she pulled down the window and the bit where her left lung had gone thin started to hemorrhage; and she was dead in a few hours. They couldn't stop the hemorrhage. It has sometimes inconvenienced me, but as I've lived to be eighty-eight, I can't say I've really suffered very much from it. At the time it gave me a lot of time to read.

INTERVIEWER: When you look back on all the books that you've written, is there one that you like best?

WEST: Oh, no. They don't seem to me as good as they might be. But I really write to find out what I know about something and what is to be known about something. And I'm more or less experimental. I wish I could have written very much more, but to be absolutely frank, for twenty-five years, you see, I've had this disastrous personal trouble. You don't easily get over it if someone near to you is constantly attacking you in public. Do you know Anthony [West]?

INTERVIEWER: I've met him once. He's writing about Joan of Arc, he told me.

WEST: What on earth about Joan of Arc?

INTERVIEWER: He believes that she was a princess, a bastard princess.

WEST: Why? What an extraordinary idea.

INTERVIEWER: A lot of people do.

WEST: What! This is new to me. Who might she be?

INTERVIEWER: She's meant to be the result of an incestuous adulterous match, the queen and the queen's brother-in-law, Louis d'Orléans.

WEST: I wish he'd turn his mind to other problems than bastardy. Alas. He's writing about six books, he told me. But I wonder why this. Whose theory is this? I never heard of it.

INTERVIEWER: Oh, it's a very old one. It was produced in 1810 by Pierre Caze in a play. Instead of accepting that Joan of Arc was exciting for spiritual reasons, you say she was exciting because she was a royal princess—which is a practical solution.

WEST: Nonsense. Have you seen Princess Anne? Can you imagine, if she appeared and said, "Save England," or whatever, that it would work? What a wonderful idea.

INTERVIEWER: What are you working on now?

WEST: I've been looking at old photographs . . . Rangoon in the last century. Goodness, some are absolutely beautiful. It's funny how photographs were better in the past than they are now.

INTERVIEWER: Why are you looking at Rangoon?

WEST: In what I'm writing now, I'm describing my husband's mother's life. She went out to Rangoon and lived there in vast, great big rooms each the size of a gymnasium, and full of cluttered little tables.

INTERVIEWER: She was the wife of an official, was she?

WEST: No, she was the wife of a man who had a job in Wallace Export-Import. They exported Burmese teak and they imported machinery. I've got masses of photographs I have to give to the Institute of Machinery but I never get round to it, showing the machines, as they came in. They had the largest army of elephants ever. There are beautiful photographs in this book of things like a lot of elephants crossing a wide river in a sort of floating island. She was a lady of very mixed ancestry, my husband's mother, and after Rangoon, she came back to Hamburg. Her mother was a Miss Chapman, who was related to the Chapman family that T. E. Lawrence belonged to. They lived in Lancashire, and then she married a local alien, a member of the hereditary Teutonic Knights of Lithuania. She had various children in Lithuania, and then her daughter came to live in Hamburg and married Lewis Andrews, who was working in this firm in Rangoon, and ultimately became my mother-in-law.

INTERVIEWER: What are you writing about her?

WEST: It comes into my memoirs. Poor widow. She took her

son [Henry Andrews] out with her to Hamburg and kept him too long. It was 1914 and the war came. Eventually she was sent back to England, but he was sent into a camp. He was there all through the war, in Rubleden [the civilian POW camp at Spandau]. It was very sad. It did spoil his life, really. He was nineteen. It was very tough. But these young creatures were highly educated; he wrote quite clever letters to Romain Rolland.

INTERVIEWER: How far have you got with your memoirs?

WEST: I've nearly got my father and mother to the end of their respective careers. It's been supernatural, which is always encouraging. Do you know, my mother was always saying that the scenery in Australia was so extraordinarily beautiful, and my father did some very nice pictures of Australian landscapes. Suddenly, a man started sending me picture books of Australia. He said, "I've always liked your books, and I wanted to send these to you." So extraordinarily dead-on: pictures of what Australia was like when my parents were there in the last century.

INTERVIEWER: Are you taking only a section of your life in your memoirs?

WEST: Well, I hope to cover most of it, but still, I've only just begun it really and I must really get on with it. I haven't read anybody's memoirs for ages except Coulton's [medieval historian, author of *Five Centuries of Religion*], which I liked very much. He wrote a life called *Four Score.* Hated Catholics. When did you read him?

INTERVIEWER: I read him on the Virgin Mary.

WEST: You know, I don't really appreciate the Virgin Mary. She always looks so dull. I particularly hate Raphael, Raphael's Madonnas. They are awful, aren't they?

INTERVIEWER: Are you working on anything else?

WEST: I'm doing a book for Weidenfeld on the 1900s, but it's not a long book. I'm not approaching the 1900s chronologically. I've started by doing a lot with the paintings of Sargent, and with some beautiful photographs. But that period in America has been done and done and done, and it's hard to be fresh. They've really dealt with nostalgia too fiercely. I begin with the death of Gladstone in 1898, and more I cannot tell you.

INTERVIEWER: You have lots of paintings. Have you written about them?

WEST: To a certain extent, yes. My husband bought the ones over there, but these I bought. It was lovely that I could buy them when they were cheap. They didn't cost me very much, even the Bonnard, and I think that's the best picture that Dufy ever painted. I have a passion, too, for Carol Weight, the man who painted this one, because I think he paints the contours of the land so beautifully. And that's by Vuillard, the woman over there, Madame Marchand. She committed suicide in the war, alas. She was a Polish Jewess, a friend of Colette's and a lot of other people.

INTERVIEWER: You have a high opinion of Colette, don't you?

WEST: Yes. I didn't like her very much as a person and I think she was repetitive and I hate all her knowing nudges about men, but I think she was a good writer on the whole and she was very good on landscape. She did a wonderful book called *Trio.* She was really more egotistical than you could possibly imagine, and she was outside a lot of experiences in a most curious way. I was taken to see her in Paris with a man who was a judge at Nuremberg. She didn't pick it up at all.

INTERVIEWER: You were in Paris again recently, I believe?

WEST: To film *The Birds Fall Down,* yes, for the BBC. It was quite fun. It was uncomfortable in many ways and I was so horrified by the cheap food in Paris. It was so bad. Terribly bad. The film turned out to be visually very beautiful. Sometimes it seemed to me a little slow. Some of the dresses are lovely.

INTERVIEWER: Have you had other books adapted?

WEST: No, people always buy them and then find they can't do them, so that I've gained financially but otherwise hardly ever. A man called Van Druten, who's forgotten now, did *The Return of the Soldier* as a play and it wasn't really good, though some of his plays were. I can't remember who acted it, or indeed anything about it.

INTERVIEWER: You've never written for the stage yourself?

WEST: I've had so little time to write. Also, theatrical people can't be bothered with me. I wrote a play in the twenties which I think had lovely stuff in it, *Goodbye Nicholas*, and fourteen copies were lost by managers, fourteen, that's really true, and I just gave up. One of them, who lost three, was a man called Barry Jackson, who was at the Birmingham Repertory Theatre; after we'd had a terrific apologies and that kind of thing, about a year later he met me in the bar of some theater and said, "Rebecca, why have you never written a play?" They are like that.

INTERVIEWER: What was the play about?

WEST: Oh, it was about Kruger, the financier, who committed suicide. It just showed you how they did the fraud and what they thought about it. It was sound enough, but nobody was interested in it at all. Then I lent it to an old friend of mine. I'm sorry to say he used a lot of it, without acknowledgment, in a play of his, an American man.

INTERVIEWER: Who was that?

WEST: I won't tell you, but it was very naughty. But never mind. His play died a death too. I would like to write old-fashioned plays like de Musset's. I think they're lovely. I think de Musset's essay on Rachel and Malibran is one of the loveliest things in the world. It's lovely about acting and romanticism. It's beautifully written and it's quite wonderful.

INTERVIEWER: Rachel is quite important to you, because you wrote a beautiful thing in your lecture on McLuhan about her.

WEST: Oh, not *my* beauty, not *my* beauty, it's Valéry's, who wrote the beautiful thing and who loved Rachel. Isn't it a beautiful thing? The ear of the lover took down what his beloved Rachel was saying and commemorated the secret of it. It's really wonderful. It's about as nice a form of immortality as anyone could have, isn't it? I fell on the essay, when I was quite young, and then I read it again because Malibran [Maria-Felicia García, d. 1836] was the sister of Madame Viardot [Pauline García, d. 1910] who is, you know, the lady who is supposed to have been the mistress—but I think the duties were light—of Turgenev. Turgenev lived in the house of Madame Viardot nearly all his life, and she brought up his illegitimate daughter. She was an opera singer but she had a dreadful time getting jobs at the opera because she and her husband were anti-Bonapartist and the Bonapartists had command of the opera. She was a great girl, and it's a very terrible thing: all her life she wrote compositions but nobody has ever played them. She was terribly busy. There's a description of her as "*too busy*" in the letters of Brahms and Clara Schumann. The Garcías were people who had two odd genetic streaks: one was for longevity, the other was for music. The first García bumped his family all over the Americas and all over Europe as a musical troupe. There were several in the family; the brother taught at the Royal Academy of Music in London, where my uncle was principal, and he used to give children's parties. I remember going to a children's party and being kissed by the old gentleman who was the brother of Malibran. He lived to be a hundred and one. I think his descendants transplanted themselves to somewhere in the north of England. The life of the family has all sorts of odd things embedded in it. You know how in du Maurier's books, how in *Trilby*, she vocalized to the music of Chopin's Nocturnes and people say that's so absurd. But Viardot did it and it apparently came off and Chopin himself liked it.

INTERVIEWER: Did you used to go to concerts a lot?

WEST: Yes, I used to and I used to listen on the radio. I can't do even the radio any longer. It doesn't seem to *respond*, as the Americans say.

INTERVIEWER: You said once that all your intelligence is in your hands.

WEST: Yes, a lot, I think. Isn't yours? My memory is certainly in my hands. I can remember things only if I have a pencil and I can write with it and I can play with it.

INTERVIEWER: You use a pencil, do you, when you write?

WEST: When anything important has to be written, yes. I think your hand concentrates for you. I don't know why it should be so.

INTERVIEWER: You never typed?

WEST: I did, but not now. I can't see in front and behind a typewriter now with cataract-operated eyes. If you have the spectacles for the front thing, you can't see the back, and I can't do with bifocals. I just get like a distracted hen. I can't do it. Hens must wear bifocals, if one looks closely. It explains it all. It's so difficult dealing with ribbons too. I can only write by hand now. I used to do a rough draft longhand and then another on the typewriter. I'm a very quick typist. When I had mumps I was shut up in a bedroom, because both my sisters had to sit examinations. When I came out, I could type.

INTERVIEWER: Do you do many drafts?

WEST: I fiddle away a lot at them. Particularly if it's a fairly elaborate thing. I've never been able to do just one draft. That seems a wonderful thing. Do you know anyone who can?

INTERVIEWER: I think D. H. Lawrence did.

WEST: You could often tell.

INTERVIEWER: How many hours a day do you write?

WEST: I don't manage much. When I write uninterrupted, I *can* write all day, straight through.

INTERVIEWER: Did you find any of your books especially easy to write?

WEST: No. It's a nauseating process. They're none of them easy.

INTERVIEWER: Have you ever abandoned a book before it was finished?

WEST: I've abandoned work because I've not had time. I've had a worrisome family thinking up monkey tricks to prevent me finishing books, and I had a terrible time when I was young and in the country, because I had no money, and no reference books, and I couldn't get up to London and to the London Library, where I had a subscription.

INTERVIEWER: There is a great diversity in your work. Did you find it difficult to combine criticism and journalism and history and fiction?

WEST: I did, really. My life has been dictated to and broken up by forces beyond my control. I couldn't control the two wars! The second war had a lot of personal consequences for me, both before and after. But I had enough money at that time, because I had a large herd of cows and a milk contract. I had to take some part in looking after the cows, but the dear things worked for me industriously. At one time I had to write articles because I had to put up a lot of money for family reasons. Everyone has to pay for their families every now and then.

INTERVIEWER: Who are the writers you admire? You commented recently that Tolstoy was most overrated.

WEST: I'm a heretic about Tolstoy. I really don't see *War and Peace* as a great novel because it seems constantly to be trying to prove that nobody who was in the war knew what was going on. Well, I don't know whoever thought they would . . . that if you put somebody down in the wildest sort of mess they understand what's happening. The point's very much better done, I think, by Joseph de Maistre. He wrote a very interesting essay in the late eighteenth century, saying how more and more people would not be able to know what was happening to them in wartime because it was all too complicated. He was in a very complicated state himself because he came from Aspramonte, which is a village on a hill near Nice. The people of Aspramonte were of the original Mediterranean population. They wore long hair all through the centuries, the conservative hippies. He was descended from a family who went round getting mulberry leaves for the silkworms. He got into the service of the king of Sardinia. He was sent as an ambassador to St. Petersburg. He wrote *Les Soirées de St.-Pétersbourg*, which is marvelous descriptive writing. He did a very good thing about hanging. He was for it, but his essay demonstrates the painfulness of ever considering whether you do hang people or not. I don't know how he became a diplomat for the king of Sardinia. I'm very often curious about people in history; they turn up in the oddest places. They strayed like goats in a road, but from class to class.

INTERVIEWER: Do you admire E. M. Forster?

WEST: No. I think the Indian one [*A Passage to India*] is very funny because it's all about people making a fuss about nothing, which isn't really enough. I can never understand how people read Proust at the same time. But they did. You can read Proust all the time. There is a book of that period that I do like very much, and that is *They Went* by Norman Douglas. It's about the king of a legendary country. I've read it several times and I've always found it beautiful.

INTERVIEWER: Are you interested in T. S. Eliot's writing?

WEST: Goodness! T. S. Eliot, whom I didn't like a bit? He was a poseur. He was married to this woman who was very pretty. My husband and I were asked to see them, and my husband roamed around the flat and there were endless photographs of T. S. Eliot and bits of his poetry done in embroidery by pious American ladies, and only one picture of his wife, and that was when she was getting married. Henry pointed it out to me and said, "I don't think I like that man."

INTERVIEWER: What about the work of Somerset Maugham, whom you also knew?

WEST: He couldn't write for toffee, bless his heart. He wrote conventional short stories, much inferior to the work of other people. But they were much better than his plays, which were too frightful. He was an extremely interesting man, though, not a bit clever or cold or cynical. I know of many affectionate things he did. He had a great capacity for falling in love with the wrong people. His taste seemed to give way under him so extraordinarily sometimes. He fascinated me by his appearance; he was so neatly made, like a swordstick that fits just so. Occasionally his conversation was beautifully funny and quite unmalicious. I object strongly to pictures of Maugham as if he were a second-rate Hollywood producer in the lavish age. His house was very pleasant and quiet and agreeable.

INTERVIEWER: Some critics think that sex is still written about with great awkwardness. Why is this?

WEST: I would have thought that was completely true of Kafka, who couldn't write about sex or value its place in life. I think there's an awful lot of nonsense in Lawrence when he writes about Mexican sacrifices and sexual violence. Their only relevance was to the Mexicans' lack of protein, as in the South Sea Islands. Funny, that's a wonderful thing. I don't know why more people don't write about it: how the whole of life must have been different when four-footed animals came in. They had just a few deer before, but not enough to go round, and so they prevented the deer from becoming extinct by making them sacred to the kings. It's much more interesting to write about that than about sex, which most of your audience knows about.

INTERVIEWER: Have you ever worked closely with a publisher who has suggested ideas to you?

WEST: No. I write books to find out about things. I wrote *Saint Augustine* because, believe it or not, there was no complete life in English at the time.

INTERVIEWER: Have you never had a close relationship with an editor, who has helped you after the books were written?

WEST: No. I never met anybody with whom I could have discussed books before or after. One doesn't have people on one's wavelength as completely as that. And I very rarely found the *New Yorker* editors any good.

INTERVIEWER: They have a tremendous reputation.

WEST: I don't know why.

INTERVIEWER: When you read, do you just follow your imagination completely?

WEST: Well, I've had eighty-five years to read in.

INTERVIEWER: I wondered whether you made book lists?

WEST: Yes, I do, but I'm often disappointed. I do think modern novels are boring on the whole. Somebody told me I ought to read a wonderful thing about how a family of children buried Mum in a cellar under concrete and she began to smell. But that's the sole point of the story. Mum just smells. That's all that happens. It is not enough.

INTERVIEWER: This is a new Ian McEwan, isn't it? I thought you, in your book on Augustine, made a marvelous comment which applies to him and to some of the other fashionable novelists now. You say that Augustinianism is "the ring-fence, in which the modern mind is still prisoner." I think that Ian McEwan is very Augustinian in his sense of unmovable evil in human life.

WEST: Yes, but he doesn't really do very much with it, does he? This thing just presents you with the hairs along people's groins and the smell, and very little else.

INTERVIEWER: Do you feel this relates to your feeling about the will to die in people, that this kind of very black outlook on the human body and human emotions is part of the suicidal streak that you've written about in both individuals and in society?

WEST: Oh, I suppose it is. It's very far-fetched, isn't it? One rarely recognizes the smell of Mum under the concrete, does one? I don't know. I cannot see the abysmal silliness of a lot of novels. Did you read a book called *The Honey Tree*? By Janice Elliott. If you didn't read it, it's no use talking about it. It's all about people who take a house and fornicate all over it, and they all have children, and their swollen bodies are a great source of satisfaction to Mrs. Elliott, and paternity does all sorts of things to men which I doubt, don't you?

INTERVIEWER: Perhaps. I believe you admire A. L. Barker.

WEST: Enormously, but I'm the only person who does, so far as I can make out. I think she's the best novelist now writing, not always, but I think *The Middling* is a magnificent novel. And *A Source of Embarrassment*, about the woman who knew she was going to die. This last book, *The Heavy Feather*, is so good I can't believe it, and nobody likes it. And they are wrong. I am exaggerating, of course. Lots of people do admire her, but not enough.

INTERVIEWER: What are the particular qualities that you think she has that others at the moment haven't?

WEST: She really tells you what people do, the extraordinary things that people think, how extraordinary circumstances are, and how unexpected the effect of various incidents. There's a terribly good thing in *The Heavy Feather*, where a woman goes home and there's a railway accident. The train is just jarred and the poor woman is sitting with a suitcase over her head. The suitcase falls on top of the woman sitting opposite her and kills her. This woman has been saying how happy she is and how all her children love her and how ideal her life is. Then the other, when she gets home, finds she's taken the woman's suitcase instead of her own, and it's got the address and she goes to take back the suitcase and try and get her own from the husband, who turns out to be Hindustani. The woman was white, and he's living there with a Hindustani girl and they're both terrified because they have been waiting for this white woman, who had no children and wasn't adored and was utterly miserable. The people come off the page to tell you what this would be like. You feel: Now I understand this better. And she also has in the book very good heterosexuals and very good homosexuals . . . with the different quality quite marked.

INTERVIEWER: Yes. Would you place her as high as the women writers that you have said overcome the problem of being female in their writing? I am thinking of Madame de Sévigné, Madame de La Fayette, Jane Austen, Willa Cather, Virginia Woolf, Colette.

WEST: Oh, she's almost better than anybody, I think. She's much better than Iris Murdoch, I think. But then Iris Murdoch I like enormously except when she begins to clown and be funny, because I don't think she ever is very funny. She writes curious books on goodness. Have you read her philosophic works? I can't make head or tail of them. They're better written than anything else she writes. They are so strange. She says that one has to study what goodness is by looking at good people. She says that the trouble with good people is that, if they're men, usually very little is known about them because they're so obscure, and, as for women, goodness is rarely found in women except in the inarticulate mothers of large families, which is just such an idiotic remark, you can't believe it. Is she pulling one's leg? One hopes so. But even so, why?

INTERVIEWER: Do you have a high opinion of Ivy Compton-Burnett?

WEST: She had her own stereotype, and wrote too many books exactly like each other in form. But it was a damn good form. At the time of a rising in South Africa, when it seemed that the colored races were going to burst forth and one was afraid that the white suburbs were being set on fire, I managed to get in happy nights reading the novels of Ivy Compton-Burnett. But it was very funny that people believed in her story of herself. She was a nanny, and you had only to meet her to see it; all her stories are nanny stories, about how awful the family is. She was very, very clever. You'd have to be very tasteless not to see she had something unique to give her age . . .

INTERVIEWER: How do you feel about Doris Lessing?

WEST: I wish I knew her. I think she's a marvelous writer. There's a peculiar book about European refugees in Africa, but it fascinates. It's beautifully done, the play side of philosophy. They were talking about all their ideas and it was as if the children were trying to go into a shop and buy things not with coins but with butterscotch or toffee apples. It's very curious. Yes, she's the only person who absolutely gets the mood of today right, I think. An absolutely wonderful writer. She wrote a picaresque novel, *The Children of Violence*, I thought was very fine. Who got the Booker Prize? Does anybody know? [Iris Murdoch won it for *The Sea, The Sea*, after this meeting.]

INTERVIEWER: Do you follow prizes?

WEST: Not very much. I was on the Booker Prize Committee twice. It almost drove me mad. I think they give people prizes too late. This is a sad thought. They've been heard of as failures and they have become conditioned to failure, so it is rather wide of the point. It's nice for them, though.

INTERVIEWER: Do you feel that public taste has declined as expressed in things like prizes?

WEST: People in England read books. I have read Mr. McEwan, and I read new books all the time, whether I review them or not, but you see, most people in America are reading the same books over and over again. They read Scott Fitzgerald and Hemingway and James Joyce and Nabokov, and they haven't moved on anywhere for years.

INTERVIEWER: John Gross says in his book on the English man of letters that we are now as far from Joyce as Joyce was from George Eliot, but in terms of the progress of literature, we haven't moved at all.

WEST: Yes. It's curious. People have no desire to read anything new. It is bad that English is taught in universities. It's bad over here, where it's sometimes not badly taught, but over there, where it's horribly badly taught, it simply stops the thing in its tracks.

INTERVIEWER: Because people always look back on the past?

WEST: They don't even look onto the past. They look onto the certified past. There really were beautiful writers in America like G. W. Cable, who wrote about the South in the middle of the last century. It's very rich, rather Balzacian sort of stuff about the South, New Orleans and so on. But nobody reads him now.

INTERVIEWER: Why do you think English is so badly taught in America?

WEST: It's an absurd error to put modern English literature in the curriculum. You should read contemporary literature for pleasure or not read it at all. You shouldn't be taught to monkey with it. It's ghastly to think of all the little girls who are taught to read *To the Lighthouse*. It's not really substantial food for the young because there's such a strong feeling that Virginia Woolf was doing a set piece and it didn't really matter very much. She was putting on an act. Shakespeare didn't put on an act. But *Orlando* is a lovely original splash, a beautiful piece of fancy. Leonard Woolf had a tiresome mind. When you read his books about Malaya, and then the books of the cadets who went out there, he's so petty, and they have such an enthusiasm and such tolerance for the murderous habits of the natives. But he was certainly good to Virginia. I couldn't forgive Vanessa Bell for her awful muddy decorations and those awful pictures of Charlotte Brontë. And I hated Duncan Grant's pictures too. The best thing that was ever said about Bloomsbury was said by a lovely butler of mine. At dinner one evening, they began to talk of Faulkner's book in which someone uses a corncob for the purposes of rape. They were being terribly subtle, and doing this and that gesture over the table. The butler came in to my son Anthony's room and asked, "Do you know where they keep the Faulkners? It seems they're very saucy." . . . Virginia Woolf's criticism was much better than criticism others were writing then.

INTERVIEWER: Amongst critics, do you admire Cyril Connolly? Or Malcolm Muggeridge?

WEST: Connolly? What an extraordinary thing to ask! He was a very good editor of *Horizon*, but he wasn't an interesting person. As for writing, he was fond of it, as you might say. But he didn't know much about it, did he? I've got no opinion of Muggeridge. He's very nice and friendly. Whatever have I read of his in the past? I can never think Christ is grateful for being alluded to as if He were a lost cause.

INTERVIEWER: Did you want to write about trials?

WEST: Not at all. I had done it once or twice, when I was very hard up, when I was young, just to get some money, and so I learned how to do them, and then I used to sit and listen to William Joyce [Lord Haw-Haw, hanged 1945] when he was broadcasting. Then I arranged to go to his trial because I was interested in him. A man called Theo Matthew, who was director of public prosecutions, though not a prosecuting sort of person, said, "I wish you'd report a lot of these trials because otherwise they will go unnoticed because there is so little newsprint." He said, "Really, if you will consider it as war work, it would be extremely valuable." So I did that for one book [*The New Meaning of Treason*, 1947] and then I did it for another [*A Train of Powder*, 1955]. Most of the people in intelligence didn't agree with my views. I don't know whether it had any effect on them at all. Someone asked me recently how did I think intelligence had found out John Vassal? [British spy, jailed in 1963]. It seemed to me such a silly question. He had it tattooed on his forehead. I never know how people don't find out spies.

INTERVIEWER: Are you interested in espionage still?

WEST: I won't say I'm interested in spies, but they do turn up in my life in quite funny ways. There was a man called Sidney Reilly, who was a famous spy, a double agent. My mother-in-law was very upset because my husband married me instead of the daughter of a civil servant. My husband's mother thought she was a nice Catholic girl, who'd be so nice for my husband, and it always tickled me because it gradually emerged that this girl was the mistress of this *very* famous and very disreputable spy. It was a wonderful thing to have in your pocket against your mother-in-law. My mother-in-law was an enormous, huge woman, and extremely pathetic. She had had her life broken up so often. By the First World War, and then the Second. Between the wars she was perfectly happy going to tea at those old-fashioned tea places they had—Rumpelmayer's. But her other son was very ill and he went out to Australia and he had a weak lung, and she went to see him and she got caught by the war there. If you like Rumpelmayer's, you wouldn't want to be in Australia for six years.

INTERVIEWER: Do you enjoy reviewing for the *Sunday Telegraph*?

WEST: Yes, I do. I do. I would feel awfully cut off if I didn't review; I think it's such a good discipline. It makes you really open your mind to the book. Probably you wouldn't, if you just read it.

INTERVIEWER: Oh, yes. It concentrates one, yes. I thought your review of Christopher Isherwood's *Christopher and His Kind* was dazzling. You demolished him.

WEST: I was so horrified by the way he treated the little German pansy. Also I thought it must have been so disgusting for the people in the village on the Greek island. I know Greeks love money, but I think a lot of money would have to pass before you'd be reconciled to Isherwood making such a noise.

INTERVIEWER: When I read your review, I was completely

convinced by your argument, that it was an extraordinary sort of obliviousness that comes from class privilege.

WEST: Well, I didn't want to make a butt of him. Do you know, a bookseller's assistant said to him, "What do you think of Rebecca West's review of your book?" and he is alleged to have said such a lovely thing: "I shall think of some way of turning it to my advantage." You can't think how bad reviewing was when I first started to review, so dull and so dreadful. Nobody good but Lady Robert Cecil, one of the Salisbury family.

INTERVIEWER: But your reviews were absolutely sparkling. I love the essay you wrote about *The Uncles*.

WEST: Oh, Bennett was horrible about it. He was a horrible, mean-spirited, hateful man. I hated Arnold Bennett.

INTERVIEWER: But you were very nice about him.

WEST: Well, I thought so, and I think he was sometimes a very good writer. I do think *The Old Wives' Tale* is very good, don't you? He was a horrible man.

INTERVIEWER: Was he in a position to make things difficult for you then?

WEST: Yes. He was not nice. He lived with these two women, the Frenchwoman to whom he was married and also the woman who was with him when he died. He was always telling other people how tiresome these women were. It was all very, as people say, unchivalrous.

INTERVIEWER: English writing hasn't really produced the kind of giants it produced in the twenties. The stagnation of English writing since then is extraordinary. Joyce, Virginia Woolf, Wells, Shaw: all these people were writing, and who have we got to compare now?

WEST: I find Tom Stoppard just as amusing as I ever found Shaw. Very amusing, both as a playwright and as himself. But I'm not now an admirer of Shaw. It was a poor mind, I think. I liked his wife so much better. He *was* conceited, but in an odd way. Usually, you know, it's people shouting to keep their spirits up, but he really did think he was better than most people. I thought that book on Yeats's postbag was so good, letters that people wrote to Yeats. Did you read that? It's absolutely delightful. It's got delightful things like a very nicely phrased letter from a farmer, saying that he understands Yeats writes about supernatural matters and can he recommend a reliable witch? You know, charming things like that.

INTERVIEWER: Did you meet Yeats?

WEST: Yes. He wasn't a bit impressive and he wasn't my sort of person at all. He boomed at you like a foghorn. He was there one time when Philip Guedalla and two or three of us were all very young, and were talking nonsense about murderers in Shakespeare and whether a third murderer ever became a first murderer by working hard or were they, sort of, hereditary slots? Were they like Japanese specialists and one did one kind of murder, another did another? It was really awfully funny. Philip was very funny to be with. Then we started talking about something on the Western Isles but Yeats wouldn't join in, until we fussed round and were nice to him. But we were all wrong; what he liked was solemnity and, if you were big enough, heavy enough, and strong enough, he loved you. He loved great big women. He would have been mad about Vanessa Redgrave.

INTERVIEWER: Is your Irish birth important to you?

WEST: Frightfully, yes. I loved my family. I have a great affiliation to relations of mine called Denny. The present man is an architect, Sir Anthony Denny. He's exactly like Holbein's drawing of his ancestor, Anthony Denny, which I think is a great testimonial. Anthony Denny lives up in the Cotswolds and he and his wife are most glamorous people in a very quiet way. They have two charming sons, one of them paints very well, and they adopted a child, a Vietnamese child. Tony went out to see his brother, who had fever there, and he was walking along a quay and one of the refugee babies, who was sitting about, suddenly ran up to him and clasped him round the knees and looked up in his face. So he just said, "I'll have this one"—and took him home. It was a most lovely reason. The Dennys did nice things like that. And then my father used to speak about this cousin in Ireland, in the west of Ireland, called Dickie Shoot. Dickie Shoot beggared himself by helping people.

INTERVIEWER: I always think it's astonishing how much literature Protestant Ireland has produced.

WEST: I don't think they're very poetical people or sensitive people really, but what a lot of literature they've produced compared with the Scotch, who I think have really deeper emotions. It's most peculiar.

INTERVIEWER: Shaw. Wilde. Whatever one thinks of their quality, there they are. Samuel Beckett. All from Protestant Irish stock.

WEST: You know, an Irish priest said a most beautiful thing to me the other day, and I absolutely loved it. He looked at those books and said—a very old man he is, he's older than I am, he must be over ninety—and he said to me, "What are you doing with all your books, when you're dead? You must have planned for them." I said, "I'm giving those Oxford dictionaries to the grandson of Oscar Wilde, Merlin Holland." And he said, "Oh, how beautiful that makes it all. It's rather as if it hadn't happened." I said, "What do you mean?" He said, "Well, your family lives in Fitzwilliam Square and Wilde's people lived in Merrion Square and it's such a natural thing to do for a family in Fitzwilliam Square to give their Oxford dictionary to the son of a family living in Merrion Square." Almost as if it hadn't happened. He couldn't have added a word to it. I love Merlin. I went to see him out in Beirut with his mother, which was rather a trial. She's Australian in a big way but you know, it was so extraordinary, the glimpse I had of her. He was very fond of a ballet dancer, and we went out to lunch. We went up to her house, and after dinner Mrs. Holland, who is plump and sixty-something, got up and she turned on one of the records, *Swan*

Lake, and danced to it, as she'd learned to, and she was quite beautiful. Obviously she should have been a dancer.

INTERVIEWER: Do you think it has become easier for women to follow their vocations?

WEST: I don't know. It's very hard. I've always found I've had too many family duties to enable me to write enough. I would have written much better and I would have written much more. Oh, men, whatever they may say, don't really have any barrier between them and their craft, and certainly I had.

INTERVIEWER: What inspired you later to write your great book on Yugoslavia? Was it the contact with the people?

WEST: What I was interested in really was wandering about with Henry. I wanted to write a book on Finland, which is a wonderful case of a small nation with empires here and there, so I learned Finnish and I read a Finnish novel. It was all about people riding bicycles. But then, when I went to Yugoslavia, I saw it was much more exciting with Austria and Russia and Turkey, and so I wrote that. I really did enjoy it terribly, loved it. I loved writing about Saint Augustine, too. I like writing about heretics, anyway.

INTERVIEWER: You consider Augustine a heretic, do you?

WEST: Oh, no, he wasn't a heretic. Most of his life he wasn't at all a nice man, but that's quite a different thing. I like to think about people like the Donatists, who were really suffering agonies of one kind and another because the Roman Empire was splitting up and it was especially uncomfortable to be in Roman Africa. But they didn't know anything about economics, and did know about theology. Theology had taught them that if you suffered, it was usually because you'd offended God: so they invented an offense against God, which was that unworthy priests were celebrating the Sacraments. So that satisfied them and then they went round the country, looting and getting the food and the property they wanted because they said that they were punishing heretics. I think it's wonderful that in the past people overlooked things that now seem to us quite obvious, and thought they were doing things for the reasons they weren't, and tried to remedy them by actions. Perhaps there's some quite simple thing we'll think of someday, which will make us much happier.

—MARINA WARNER

1981

DOROTHY PARKER

———◆◆▷◆✳◆◁◆———

Dorothy Parker was born Dorothy Rothschild in West End, New Jersey, in 1893. Her mother died shortly before her fourth birthday: she was sent to a convent school and then to boarding school by her father and stepmother but left school permanently at age fourteen. In 1914 she sold her first poem to *Vanity Fair.* In 1916 she went to work for *Vogue* at ten dollars a week. The following year Parker replaced P. G. Wodehouse as the drama critic for *Vanity Fair,* where she met the group of writers that would become known as the Algonquin Round Table. Parker's stories began appearing in *The New Yorker* soon after its founding in 1925, and in 1927 she became a regular book reviewer there, using the byline Constant Reader. That same year saw the publication of her first collection of verse, *Enough Rope.* In 1929 Parker won the O. Henry Prize for "Big Blonde," which she included in her first collection of stories, *Laments for the Living* (1930). Her subsequent books include the story collections *After Such Pleasures* (1933), *Here Lies* (1939) and *Collected Stories* (1942); the poetry collections *Sunset Gun* (1928), *Death and Taxes* (1931) and *Not So Deep as a Well* (1936); *The Viking Portable Library: Dorothy Parker* (1944), her own selection of stories and poems; and the plays *Close Harmony* (with Elmer Rice, 1924), *The Coast of Illyria* (1949) and *The Ladies of the Corridor* (with Arnaud D'Usseau, 1953). She also wrote or cowrote many Hollywood screenplays, including *A Star Is Born* (1937), for which she received an Oscar nomination. Almost all of Parker's poetry collections were best-sellers and her stories were immensely successful, but she, ironically, preferred her plays, which never achieved the same degree of critical success. Whatever the genre, Parker's work is defined by her pithy, acerbic, sometimes malicious wit; her writing, in the words of Alexander Woollcott, was a potent "distillation of nectar and wormwood, of ambrosia and deadly nightshade." Dorothy Parker died of a heart attack at the Hotel Volney in New York in 1967.

DOROTHY PARKER

A t the time of this interview, Dorothy Parker was living in a midtown New York hotel. She shared her small apartment with a youthful poodle that had the run of the place and had caused it to look, as Mrs. Parker said apologetically, somewhat "Hogarthian": newspapers spread about the floor, picked lamb chops here and there, and a rubber doll—its throat torn from ear to ear—which Mrs. Parker lobbed left-handed from her chair into corners of the room for the poodle to retrieve—as it did, never tiring of the opportunity. The room was sparsely decorated, its one overpowering fixture being a large dog portrait, not of the poodle, but of a sheepdog owned by the author Philip Wylie and painted by his wife. The portrait indicated a dog of such size that if it were real, would have dwarfed Mrs. Parker, who was a small woman, her voice gentle, her tone often apologetic, but occasionally, given the opportunity to comment on matters she felt strongly about, she spoke almost harshly, and her sentences were punctuated with observations phrased with lethal force. Hers was still the wit that made her a legend as a member of the Round Table of the Algonquin—a humor whose particular quality seemed a coupling of brilliant social commentary with a mind of devastating inventiveness. She seemed able to produce the well-turned phrase for any occasion. A friend remembered sitting next to her at the theater when the news was announced of the death of

I Live on Your Visits
Dorothy Parker
(2)

and, on consoles and desk and table, photographs of himself at two
and a half and five and seven and nine, framed in broad mirror
bands. Whenever his mother settled in a new domicile, and she
removed often, those photographs were the first things out of the
luggage. The boy hated them. He had had to pass his fifteenth
birthday before his body had caught up with his head; in those
presentments of his former selves, that pale, enormous blob.
Once he had asked his mother to put the pictures somewhere else -
preferably some small, dark place that could be locked. But he
had had the bad fortune to make his request on one of the occasions
when she was given to weeping suddenly and long. So the photographs stood out on parade, with their frames twinkling away.

There were twinkings, too, to the silver top of the
fat crystal cocktail shaker, but the liquid low within the crystal
was pale and dull. There was no shine, either, to the glass his
mother held. It was cloudy from the clutch of her
hand, and on the inside there were oily dribbles/what what it had
contained.

His mother shut the door by which she had admitted him
and followed him into the room. She looked at him with her head
tilted to the side.

"Well, aren't you going to kiss me?" she said in a
charming, wheedling voice, the voice of a little, little girl.
"Aren't you, you beautiful big ox, you?"

"Sure," he said. He bent down toward her, but she
stepped suddenly away. A sharp change came over her. She drew
herself tall, with her shoulders back and her head flung high.
Her upper lip lifted over her teeth, and her gaze came cold beneath

A manuscript page from a short story by Dorothy Parker.

*the stolid Calvin Coolidge. "How do they know?" whispered Mrs. Parker.
Readers of this interview, however, will find that Mrs. Parker had only
contempt for the eager reception accorded her wit. "Why, it got so bad," she had
said bitterly, "that they began to laugh before I opened my mouth." And she had
a similar attitude toward her value as a serious writer.*

*But Mrs. Parker was her own worst critic. Her three books of poetry may
have established her reputation as a master of light verse, but her short stories
were essentially serious in tone—serious in that they reflected her own life,
which was in many ways an unhappy one—and also serious in their intention. Franklin P. Adams described them in an introduction to her work:
"Nobody can write such ironic things unless he has a deep sense of injustice—
injustice to those members of the race who are the victims of the stupid, the pre-
tentious and the hypocritical."*

INTERVIEWER: Your first job was on *Vogue*, wasn't it? How did
you go about getting hired, and why *Vogue*?

PARKER: After my father died there wasn't any money. I had
to work, you see, and Mr. Crowninshield, God rest his soul,
paid twelve dollars for a small verse of mine and gave me a job
at ten dollars a week. Well, I thought I was Edith Sitwell. I lived
in a boarding house at 103rd and Broadway, paying eight dollars a week for my room and two meals, breakfast and dinner.
Thorne Smith was there, and another man. We used to sit
around in the evening and talk. There was no money, but, Jesus,
we had fun.

INTERVIEWER: What kind of work did you do at *Vogue*?

PARKER: I wrote captions. "This little pink dress will win
you a beau," that sort of thing. Funny, they were plain women
working at *Vogue*, not chic. They were decent, nice women—the
nicest women I ever met—but they had no business on such a
magazine. They wore funny little bonnets and in the pages of
their magazine they virginized the models from tough babes
into exquisite little loves. Now the editors are what they should

be: all chic and worldly; most of the models are out of the mind of a Bram Stoker, and as for the caption writers—*my* old job—they're recommending mink covers at seventy-five dollars apiece for the wooden ends of golf clubs "—for the friend who has everything." Civilization is coming to an end, you understand.

INTERVIEWER: Why did you change to *Vanity Fair?*

PARKER: Mr. Crowninshield wanted me to. Mr. Sherwood and Mr. Benchley—we always called each other by our last names—were there. Our office was across from the Hippodrome. The midgets would come out and frighten Mr. Sherwood. He was about seven feet tall and they were always sneaking up behind him and asking him how the weather was up there. "Walk down the street with me," he'd ask, and Mr. Benchley and I would leave our jobs and guide him down the street. I can't tell you, we had more fun. Both Mr. Benchley and I subscribed to two undertaking magazines: *The Casket* and *Sunnyside.* Steel yourself: *Sunnyside* had a joke column called "From Grave to Gay." I cut a picture out of one of them, in color, of how and where to inject embalming fluid, and had it hung over my desk until Mr. Crowninshield asked me if I could possibly take it down. Mr. Crowninshield was a lovely man, but puzzled. I must say we behaved extremely badly. Albert Lee, one of the editors, had a map over *his* desk with little flags on it to show where our troops were fighting during the First World War. Every day he would get the news and move the flags around. I was married, my husband was overseas, and since I didn't have anything better to do I'd get up half an hour early and go down and change his flags. Later on, Lee would come in, look at his map, and he'd get very serious about spies—shout, and spend his morning moving his little pins back into position.

INTERVIEWER: How long did you stay at *Vanity Fair?*

PARKER: Four years. I'd taken over the drama criticism from P. G. Wodehouse. Then I fixed three plays—one of them *Caesar's Wife*, with Billie Burke in it—and as a result I was fired.

INTERVIEWER: You *fixed* three plays?

PARKER: Well, *panned*. The plays closed and the producers, who were the big boys—Dillingham, Ziegfeld and Belasco—didn't like it, you know. *Vanity Fair* was a magazine of no opinion, but *I* had opinions. So I was fired. And Mr. Sherwood and Mr. Benchley resigned their jobs. It was all right for Mr. Sherwood, but Mr. Benchley had a family—two children. It was the greatest act of friendship I'd known. Mr. Benchley did a sign, "Contributions for Miss Billie Burke," and on our way out we left it in the hall of *Vanity Fair*. We behaved very badly. We made ourselves discharge chevrons and wore them.

INTERVIEWER: Where did you all go after *Vanity Fair*?

PARKER: Mr. Sherwood became the motion-picture critic for the old *Life*. Mr. Benchley did the drama reviews. He and I had an office so tiny that an inch smaller and it would have been adultery. We had *Parkbench* for a cable address, but no one ever sent us one. It was so long ago—before you were a gleam in someone's eyes—that I doubt there *was* a cable.

INTERVIEWER: It's a popular supposition that there was much more communication between writers in the twenties. The Round Table discussions in the Algonquin, for example.

PARKER: I wasn't there very often—it cost too much. Others went. Kaufman was there. I guess he was sort of funny. Mr. Benchley and Mr. Sherwood went when they had a nickel. Franklin P. Adams, whose column was widely read by people who wanted to write, would sit in occasionally. And Harold Ross, the *New Yorker* editor. He was a professional lunatic, but I don't know if he was a great man. He had a profound ignorance. On one of Mr. Benchley's manuscripts he wrote in the margin opposite "Andromache," "Who he?" Mr. Benchley wrote back, "You keep out of this." The only one with stature who came to the Round Table was Heywood Broun.

INTERVIEWER: What was it about the twenties that inspired people like yourself and Broun?

PARKER: Gertrude Stein did us the most harm when she said,

"You're all a lost generation." That got around to certain people and we all said, "Whee! We're lost." Perhaps it suddenly brought to us the sense of change. Or irresponsibility. But don't forget that, though the people in the twenties seemed like flops, they weren't. Fitzgerald, the rest of them, reckless as they were, drinkers as they were, they worked damn hard and all the time.

INTERVIEWER: Did the "lost generation" attitude you speak of have a detrimental effect on your own work?

PARKER: Silly of me to blame it on dates, but so it happened to be. Dammit, it *was* the twenties and we had to be smarty. I *wanted* to be cute. That's the terrible thing. I should have had more sense.

INTERVIEWER: And during this time you were writing poems?

PARKER: My verses. I cannot say poems. Like everybody was then, I was following in the exquisite footsteps of Miss Millay, unhappily in my own horrible sneakers. My verses are no damn good. Let's face it, honey, my verse is terribly dated—as anything once fashionable is dreadful now. I gave it up, knowing it wasn't getting any better, but nobody seemed to notice my magnificent gesture.

INTERVIEWER: Do you think your verse writing has been of any benefit to your prose?

PARKER: Franklin P. Adams once gave me a book of French verse forms and told me to copy their design, that by copying them I would get precision in prose. The men you imitate in verse influence your prose, and what I got out of it was precision, all I realize I've ever had in prose writing.

INTERVIEWER: How did you get started in writing?

PARKER: I fell into writing, I suppose, being one of those awful children who wrote verses. I went to a convent in New York—The Blessed Sacrament. Convents do the same things progressive schools do, only they don't know it. They don't teach you how to read; you have to find out for yourself. At my convent we *did* have a textbook, one that devoted a page and a half to Adelaide Ann Proctor; but we couldn't read Dickens; he was vulgar, you know. But *I* read him and Thackeray, and I'm the one woman you'll ever know who's read every word of Charles Reade, the author of *The Cloister and the Hearth*. But as for helping me in the outside world, the convent taught me only that if you spit on a pencil eraser it will erase ink. And I remember the smell of oilcloth, the smell of nuns' garb. I was fired from there, finally, for a lot of things, among them my insistence that the Immaculate Conception was spontaneous combustion.

INTERVIEWER: Have you ever drawn from those years for story material?

PARKER: All those writers who write about their childhood! Gentle God, if I wrote about mine you wouldn't sit in the same room with me.

INTERVIEWER: What, then, would you say is the source of most of your work?

PARKER: Need of money, dear.

INTERVIEWER: And besides that?

PARKER: It's easier to write about those you hate—just as it's easier to criticize a bad play or a bad book.

INTERVIEWER: What about "Big Blonde"? Where did the idea for that come from?

PARKER: I knew a lady—a friend of mine who went through holy hell. Just say I knew a woman once. The purpose of the writer is to say what he feels and sees. To those who write fantasies—the Misses Baldwin, Ferber, Norris—I am not at home.

INTERVIEWER: That's not showing much respect for your fellow women, at least not the writers.

PARKER: As artists they're not, but as providers they're oil wells; they gush. Norris said she never wrote a story unless it was fun to do. I understand Ferber whistles at her typewriter.

And there was that poor sucker Flaubert rolling around on his floor for three days looking for the right word. I'm a feminist, and God knows I'm loyal to my sex, and you must remember that from my very early days, when this city was scarcely safe from buffaloes, I was in the struggle for equal rights for women. But when we paraded through the catcalls of men and when we chained ourselves to lamp posts to try to get our equality— dear child, we didn't foresee *those* female writers. Or Clare Boothe Luce, or Perle Mesta, or Oveta Culp Hobby.

INTERVIEWER: You have an extensive reputation as a wit. Has this interfered, do you think, with your acceptance as a serious writer?

PARKER: I don't want to be classed as a humorist. It makes me feel guilty. I've never read a good tough quotable female humorist, and I never was one myself. I couldn't do it. A "smart-cracker" they called me, and that makes me sick and unhappy. There's a hell of a distance between wisecracking and wit. Wit has truth in it; wisecracking is simply calisthenics with words. I didn't mind so much when they were good, but for a long time anything that was called a crack was attributed to me—and then they got the shaggy dogs.

INTERVIEWER: How about satire?

PARKER: Ah, satire. That's another matter. They're the big boys. If I'd been called a satirist there'd be no living with me. But by satirist I mean those boys in the other centuries. The people we call satirists now are those who make cracks at topical topics and consider themselves satirists—creatures like George S. Kaufman and such who don't even know what satire is. Lord knows, a writer should show his times, but not show them in wisecracks. Their stuff is not satire; it's as dull as yesterday's newspaper. Successful satire has got to be pretty good the day after tomorrow.

INTERVIEWER: And how about contemporary humorists? Do you feel about them as you do about satirists?

PARKER: You get to a certain age and only the tired writers are funny. I read my verses now and I ain't funny. I haven't been funny for twenty years. But anyway there aren't any humorists anymore, except for Perelman. There's no need for them. Perelman must be very lonely.

INTERVIEWER: Why is there no need for the humorist?

PARKER: It's a question of supply and demand. If we needed them, we'd have them. The new crop of would-be humorists doesn't count. They're like the would-be satirists. They write about topical topics. Not like Thurber and Mr. Benchley. Those two were damn well read and, though I hate the word, they were cultured. What sets them apart is that they both had a point of view to express. That is important to all good writing. It's the difference between Paddy Chayefsky, who just puts down lines, and Clifford Odets, who in his early plays not only sees but has a point of view. The writer must be aware of life around him. Carson McCullers is good, or she used to be, but now she's withdrawn from life and writes about freaks. Her characters are grotesques.

INTERVIEWER: Speaking of Chayefsky and McCullers, do you read much of your own or the present generation of writers?

PARKER: I will say of the writers of today that some of them, thank God, have the sense to adapt to their times. Mailer's *The Naked and the Dead* is a great book. And I thought William Styron's *Lie Down in Darkness* an extraordinary thing. The start of it took your heart and flung it over there. He writes like a god. But for most of my reading I go back to the old ones—for comfort. As you get older you go much farther back. I read *Vanity Fair* about a dozen times a year. I was a woman of eleven when I first read it—the thrill of that line "George Osborne lay dead with a bullet through his head." Sometimes I read, as an elegant friend of mine calls them, "who-did-its." I love Sherlock Holmes. My life is so untidy and he's so neat. But as for living novelists, I suppose E. M. Forster is the best, not knowing what that is, but at least he's a semifinalist, wouldn't you think? Somerset Maugham once said to me, "We have a novelist over here, E. M. Forster, though I don't suppose he's familiar to you." Well, I could have kicked him. Did he think I carried a papoose on my back? Why, I'd go on my hands and knees to get to Forster. He once wrote something I've always remembered: "It has never happened to me that I've had to choose between betraying a friend and betraying my country, but if it ever does so happen I hope I have the guts to betray my country." Now doesn't that make the Fifth Amendment look like a bum?

INTERVIEWER: Could I ask you some technical questions? How do you actually write out a story? Do you write out a draft and then go over it or what?

PARKER: It takes me six months to do a story. I think it out and then write it sentence by sentence—no first draft. I can't write five words but that I change seven.

INTERVIEWER: How do you name your characters?

PARKER: The telephone book and from the obituary columns.

INTERVIEWER: Do you keep a notebook?

PARKER: I tried to keep one, but I never could remember where I put the damn thing. I always say I'm going to keep one tomorrow.

INTERVIEWER: How do you get the story down on paper?

PARKER: I wrote in longhand at first, but I've lost it. I use two fingers on the typewriter. I think it's unkind of you to ask. I know so little about the typewriter that once I bought a new one because I couldn't change the ribbon on the one I had.

INTERVIEWER: You're working on a play now, aren't you?

PARKER: Yes, collaborating with Arnaud d'Usseau. I'd like to do a play more than anything. First night is the most exciting thing in the world. It's wonderful to hear your words spoken.

Unhappily, our first play, *The Ladies of the Corridor*, was not a success, but writing that play was the best time I ever had, both for the privilege and the stimulation of working with Mr. d'Usseau and because that play was the only thing I have ever done in which I had great pride.

INTERVIEWER: How about the novel? Have you ever tried that form?

PARKER: I wish to God I could do one, but I haven't got the nerve.

INTERVIEWER: And short stories? Are you still doing them?

PARKER: I'm trying now to do a story that's purely narrative. I think narrative stories are the best, though my past stories make themselves stories by telling themselves through what people say. I haven't got a visual mind. I hear things. But I'm not going to do those *he-said she-said* things anymore, they're over, honey, they're over. I want to do the story that can only be told in the narrative form, and though they're going to scream about the rent, I'm going to do it.

INTERVIEWER: Do you think economic security an advantage to the writer?

PARKER: Yes. Being in a garret doesn't do you any good unless you're some sort of a Keats. The people who lived and wrote well in the twenties were comfortable and easy-living. They were able to find stories and novels, and good ones, in conflicts that came out of two million dollars a year, not a garret. As for me, I'd like to have money. And I'd like to be a good writer. These two can come together, and I hope they will, but if that's too adorable, I'd rather have money. I hate almost all rich people, but I think I'd be darling at it. At the moment, however, I like to think of Maurice Baring's remark: "If you would know what the Lord God thinks of money, you have only to look at those to whom he gives it." I realize that's not much help when the wolf comes scratching at the door, but it's a comfort.

INTERVIEWER: What do you think about the artist being supported by the state?

PARKER: Naturally, when penniless, I think it's superb. I think that the art of the country so immeasurably adds to its prestige that if you want the country to have writers and artists—persons who live precariously in our country—the state must help. I do not think that any kind of artist thrives under charity, by which I mean one person or organization giving him money. Here and there, this and that—that's no good. The difference between the state giving and the individual patron is that one is charity and the other isn't. Charity is murder and you know it. But I do think that if the government supports its artists, they need have no feeling of gratitude—the meanest and most sniveling attribute in the world—or baskets being brought to them, or apple-polishing. Working for the state—for Christ's sake, are you grateful to your employers? Let the state see what its artists are trying to do—like France with the Académie Française. The artists are a part of their country and their country should recognize this, so both it and the artists can take pride in their efforts. Now I mean that, my dear.

INTERVIEWER: How about Hollywood as provider for the artist?

PARKER: Hollywood money isn't money. It's congealed snow, melts in your hand, and there you are. I can't talk about Hollywood. It was a horror to me when I was there and it's a horror to look back on. I can't imagine how I did it. When I got away from it I couldn't even refer to the place by name. "Out there," I called it. You want to know what "out there" means to me? Once I was coming down a street in Beverly Hills and I saw a Cadillac about a block long, and out of the side window was a wonderfully slinky mink, and an arm, and at the end of the arm a hand in a white suede glove wrinkled around the wrist, and in the hand was a bagel with a bite out of it.

INTERVIEWER: Do you think Hollywood destroys the artist's talent?

PARKER: No, no, no. I think nobody on earth writes down. Garbage though they turn out, Hollywood writers aren't writing down. That is their best. If you're going to write, don't pretend to write down. It's going to be the best you can do, and it's the fact that it's the best you can do that kills you. I want so much to write well, though I know I don't, and that I didn't make it. But during and at the end of my life, I will adore those who have.

INTERVIEWER: Then what is it that's the evil in Hollywood?

PARKER: It's the people. Like the director who put his finger in Scott Fitzgerald's face and complained, "Pay *you*. Why, you ought to pay us." It was terrible about Scott; if you'd seen him you'd have been sick. When he died no one went to the funeral, not a single soul came, or even sent a flower. I said, "Poor son of a bitch," a quote right out of *The Great Gatsby*, and everyone thought it was another wisecrack. But it was said in dead seriousness. Sickening about Scott. And it wasn't only the people, but also the indignity to which your ability was put. There was a picture in which Mr. Benchley had a part. In it Monty Woolley had a scene in which he had to enter a room through a door on which was balanced a bucket of water. He came into the room covered with water and muttered to Mr. Benchley, who had a part in the scene, "Benchley? Benchley of *Harvard*?" "Yes," mumbled Mr. Benchley and he asked, "Woolley? Woolley of *Yale*?"

INTERVIEWER: How about your political views? Have they made any difference to you professionally?

PARKER: Oh, certainly. Though I don't think this "blacklist" business extends to the theater or certain of the magazines, in Hollywood it exists because several gentlemen felt it best to drop names like marbles which bounced back like rubber balls about people they'd seen in the company of what they charmingly called "commies." You can't go back thirty years to Sacco and Vanzetti. I won't do it. Well, well, well, that's the way it is. If all this means something to the good of the movies, I don't know what it is. Sam Goldwyn said, "How'm I gonna do decent pictures when all my good writers are in jail?" Then he added, the infallible Goldwyn, "Don't misunderstand me, they all ought to be hung." Mr. Goldwyn didn't know about "hanged." That's all there is to say. It's not the tragedies that kill us, it's the messes. I can't stand messes. I'm not being a smartcracker. You know I'm not when you meet me—don't you, honey?

—MARION CAPRON

1956

P. L. TRAVERS

W e have no idea where childhood ends and maturity begins," says Pamela Lyndon Travers. "It is one unending thread, not a life chopped up into sections out of touch with one another." In touch with a childlike wisdom, joy and simplicity, this Australian-born woman, while convalescing in a Sussex cottage, wrote *Mary Poppins* in order to amuse herself. Submitted on the advice of a friend, it was published in 1934 and later turned into a film by Walt Disney. Travers followed the instant success of the book with *Mary Poppins Comes Back* (1935), *Mary Poppins Opens the Door* (1944), *Mary Poppins in the Park* (1952), *Mary Poppins in Cherry Tree Lane* (1982), and, in 1989, *Mary Poppins and the House Next Door.* Her other works include *I Go by Sea, I Go by Land* (1944), *The Fox at the Manger* (1962), *Friend Monkey* (1971), *About the Sleeping Beauty* (1975), and three books based on preceding Mary Poppins stories, *Mary Poppins from A to Z* (1962), *A Mary Poppins Story for Colouring* (1969), and *Mary Poppins in the Kitchen* (1975). She published several articles on mythology, children's literature and her own work, the most important of the latter being "Only Connect" (1967), which was an address to the Library of Congress. She collected her essays and lectures on these topics into *What the Bee Knows: Reflections on Myth, Symbol and Story,* published in 1989. Travers was writer-in-residence at various American universities and received honorary degrees from universities in the United States and Britain. She died at her home in London at the age of ninety-six in April 1996.

P. L. TRAVERS

P. *L. Travers's terraced house in Chelsea has a pink door, the color of the cover of* Mary Poppins in Cherry Tree Lane. *In the hall is an antique rocking horse. Her study is at the top of the house: a white-walled room, crowded with books and papers, its austerity relieved by a modern rocking chair. Pamela Travers, tall and handsome, with short whitish hair, is a strong woman of great humor and charm. Once a dancer, she moves smoothly and gracefully; once an actress, she speaks with the deep clear tones of another era. Before answering a question she sometimes closes her eyes as if in meditation. There is something both mythic and modern about her. She was wearing a blue-and-white flowing dress and white pumps and silver ethnic jewelry. As she spoke, her tongue sometimes darted from the corner of her mouth, reminding one perhaps of the hamadryad in* Mary Poppins—*the wise snake that lectures to the transfixed Banks children. She is a master of pith and anecdote, as shown in the story she tells about paying a visit to Yeats. A young woman then, traveling by train in Ireland, it occurred to her to stop and bring a gift to the poet. She persuaded a boatman to take her to the Isle of Innisfree, where she collected great branches of rowan for her gift. A storm came up as she struggled with her branches into the train car. Finally, at Yeats's door in Dublin, a startled maid took her in and dried her clothes by the fire. By this*

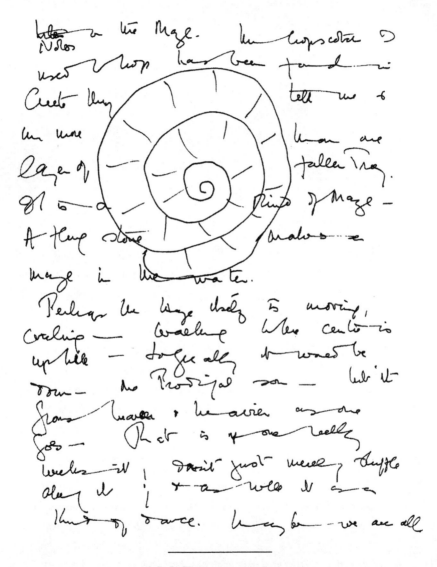

A P. L. Travers manuscript page.

time, Travers, quite embarrassed, was planning an opportune escape, but as she made for the door the servant told her that Yeats was ready to see her. She ascended the stairs to meet a grandfatherly Yeats who proudly showed her an egg his canary had just laid. As they talked, Travers noticed on his desk a vase with a small slip from the colossus of branches she had brought. "That's when I learned," Travers concludes, "that you can say more with less."

INTERVIEWERS: That recalls your meeting with AE [George Russell]. You must have had great courage as a young woman to call on these venerable Irishmen.

TRAVERS: I read AE's poems when I was a child in Australia. Later I came to England to see my relatives. But before I did that, I sent a poem to AE, who was then editing *The Irish Statesman*, and with all the arrogance of youth I didn't put any letter with it explaining myself or saying that I was Irish or anything. I just sent it with a stamped addressed envelope.

And sure enough, the stamped envelope came back. But in it was a check for two guineas and a letter that said: "I'm accepting your poem, which is a very good one, and I think it could not have been written by anyone who wasn't Irish. If you're ever coming to Ireland, be sure to come and see me." Since I was going to Ireland, I did go to see him and was greatly welcomed and more poems were taken. I felt immediate mutuality with him, this great elderly man bothering about me. But he bothered about all young poets. They were always welcome.

After our visit he said to me, "On your way back through Dublin you come and see me again." I said, "Of course, I will." But when the time arrived and I was back in Dublin, an awful timidity came upon me. I thought he was a great man and I shouldn't take up his time; he was doing this for *politesse*. And so I refrained from going to see him and went back to England. Sometime later when I opened the door, there was AE. He said to me, "You're a faithless girl. You promised to see me on your way back through Dublin and you didn't." And he added, "I meant to give you my books then and, as you weren't there, I brought them." And there were all his books.

INTERVIEWERS: He sought you out, then?

TRAVERS: Oh, he didn't come to London specially to see me. He had come to see his old friend George Moore. But he took me in during that time, and had time for me. I often went out to Dublin after that and saw a good deal of AE and Yeats and James Stephens. Among the young people like myself was Frank O'Connor, who used to be called Michael O'Donovan. He was one of AE's protégés. There were many of them.

INTERVIEWERS: AE's reaction to *Mary Poppins* is very interesting. You report his saying, "Had [Mary Poppins] lived in another age, in the old times to which she certainly belongs, she would undoubtedly have had long golden tresses, a wreath of flowers in one hand, and perhaps a spear in the other. Her eyes would have been like the sea, her nose comely, and on her feet winged sandals. But, this age being the Kali Yuga, as the Hindus call it, she comes in habiliments suited to it." It seems that AE was suggesting that your English nanny was some twentieth-century version of the Mother Goddess Kali.

TRAVERS: Indeed, he was throwing me a clue, but I didn't seize upon that for a long time. I've always been interested in the Mother Goddess. Not long ago, a young person, whom I don't know very well, sent a message to a mutual friend that said: "I'm an addict of *Mary Poppins,* and I want you to ask P. L. Travers if Mary Poppins is not really the Mother Goddess." So, I sent back a message: "Well, I've only recently come to see that. She is either Mother Goddess or one of her creatures—that is, if we're going to look for mythological or fairy tale origins of *Mary Poppins."*

I've spent years thinking about it because the questions I've been asked, very perceptive questions by readers, have led me to examine what I wrote. The book was entirely spontaneous and not invented, not thought out. I never said, "Well, I'll write a story about Mother Goddess and call it *Mary Poppins.*" It didn't happen like that. I cannot summon up inspiration; I myself am summoned.

Once when I was in the United States I went to see a psychologist. It was during the war when I was feeling very cut off. I thought, Well, these people in psychology always want to see the kinds of things you've done, so I took as many of my books as were then written. I went and met the man, and he gave me another appointment. And at the next appointment the books were handed back to me with the words: "You know, you don't really need me. All you need to do is read your own books."

That was so interesting to me. I began to see, thinking about it, that people who write spontaneously as I do, not with invention, never really read their own books to learn from them. And I set myself to reading them. Every now and then I found myself saying, "But this is true. How did she know?" And then I realized that she is me. Now I can say much more about *Mary Poppins* because what was known to me in my blood and instincts has now come up to the surface in my head.

INTERVIEWERS: Has Mary Poppins changed for you over the years?

TRAVERS: Not at all, not at all.

INTERVIEWERS: Has she changed for other people, do you think? Has their attitude to her altered at all?

TRAVERS: I don't think that she *must* change for other people very much; I think that they would be bitterly disappointed. The other day two little boys accosted me in the street and said to me, "You are the lady who wrote *Mary Poppins,* aren't you?" And I admitted it, and said, "How do you know?" And they said, "Because we sing in the choir, and the vicar told us." So, clearly, they had thrown off their surplices and rushed after me to catch me. So I said, "Well, do you like her?" And they both nodded vigorously. I then said, "What is it you like about her?"

And one of them said, "Well, she's so *ordinary* and then . . ." and having said "and then" he looked around for the proper word, and couldn't find it. And I said, "You don't have to say any more. That 'and then' says everything." And the other little boy said, "Yes, and I'm going to marry her when I grow up." And I saw the first one clench his fists and look very belligerent. I felt there might be trouble and so I said, "Well, we'll just have to see what *she* thinks about it, won't we? And in the meantime, my house is just there—come in and have a lemonade." So they did. With regard to your question about her altering, I do not think that people who read her would want her to be altered. And what I liked so much about that—I felt it was the highest praise—was that the boy should say, "Well, she's so *ordinary.*" But that's what she is. And it is only through the ordinary that the extraordinary can make itself perceived.

INTERVIEWERS: Speaking about children's reactions, when a little girl was asked why she liked Mary Poppins, she said, "Because she is so *mad.*"

TRAVERS: She *is* mad. Only the mad can be so sane. A young man in my house—he's now grown up and has his own children—but when he was sixteen he said to me, "Make me a promise." And I thought, Well, an open-ended promise is very difficult and dangerous . . . but he said, "Don't worry, you can easily afford it." (Of course he might have been about to ask me for a Rolls-Royce, and what would I have done then?) But I said, "Yes, very well." So he said, "Promise me never to be clever." "Oh," I said, "I can easily do that, because you know I'm a perfect fool and I'm not in the least bit clever. But why do you ask that?" He said, "I've just been reading *Mary Poppins* again, and it could only have been written by a lunatic." That goes with your girl, you see. And I knew perfectly well, because we understand each other's language very well, that he meant "lunatic" as high praise.

INTERVIEWERS: Virginia Woolf when going through a

"mad" period thought she heard the birds singing in Greek. This reminds one of the babies in *Mary Poppins* and *Mary Poppins Comes Back* who understand what the Starling says. Maybe it's the same kind of "madness"?

TRAVERS: Possibly. My Starlings in *Mary Poppins* talk Cockney, as far as I remember.

INTERVIEWERS: Mary Poppins is always teaching, isn't she?

TRAVERS: Well, yes, but I think she teaches by the way; I don't think she sets herself up as a governess. You remember there was a governess called Miss Andrew. She's very different from that.

INTERVIEWERS: Miss Andrew's a horror. But is Mary Poppins perhaps instructing the children in the "difficult truths" you mention in "Only Connect" as being contained in fairy tale, myth and nursery rhyme?

TRAVERS: Exactly. Well, you see, I think if she comes from anywhere that has a name, it is out of myth. And myth has been my study and joy ever since—oh, the age, I would think . . . of three. I've studied it all my life. No culture can satisfactorily move along its forward course without its myths, which are its teachings, its fundamental dealing with the truth of things, and the one reality that underlies everything. Yes, in that way you could say that it was teaching, but in no way deliberately doing so.

INTERVIEWERS: Jane and Michael, then, learn about tears and suffering from Mary Poppins when she leaves them?

TRAVERS: She doesn't hold back anything from them. When they beg her not to depart, she reminds them that nothing lasts forever. She's as truthful as the nursery rhymes. Remember that all the King's horses and all the King's men couldn't put Humpty-Dumpty together again. There's such a tremendous truth in that. It goes into children in some part of them that they don't know, and indeed perhaps *we* don't know. But eventually they realize—and that's the great truth.

INTERVIEWERS: Does Mary Poppins's teaching—if one can call it that—resemble that of Christ in his parables?

TRAVERS: My Zen master, because I've studied Zen for a long time, told me that every one (and all the stories weren't written then) of the Mary Poppins stories is in essence a Zen story. And someone else, who is a bit of a Don Juan, told me that every one of the stories is a moment of tremendous sexual passion, because it begins with such tension and then it is reconciled and resolved in a way that is gloriously sensual.

INTERVIEWERS: So people can read anything and everything into the stories?

TRAVERS: Indeed. A great friend of mine at the beginning of our friendship (he was himself a poet) said to me very defiantly, "I have to tell you that I *loathe* children's books." And I said to him, "Well, won't you just read this just for my sake?" And he said grumpily, "Oh, very well, send it to me." I did, and I got a letter back saying: "Why didn't you *tell* me? Mary Poppins with her cool green core of sex has me enthralled forever."

INTERVIEWERS: And what about love? Are you implying in the Mary Poppins books that a child needs more than the love of family and friends?

TRAVERS: I have always thought that if the child doesn't need it, it benefits by having that extra, that plus. Every child needs to have for itself not only its loving parents and siblings and friends of its own age, but a grown-up friend. It is the fashion now to make a gap between child and grown-up, but this, I believe, has been made by the media. I was older than Jane and Michael, but I had a grown-up friend when I was about eleven. How wonderful it was to be able to have somebody other than your parents that you could talk to, who treated you as though you were a human being, with your proper place in the world. Your parents did so too (my parents were most loving, I had a most loving childhood), but the extra friend was a tremendous plus.

INTERVIEWERS: That is the kind of love that both Mary Poppins and Friend Monkey give?

TRAVERS: Yes, there is a great deal in common between Mary Poppins and Friend Monkey. *Friend Monkey* is really my favorite of all my books because the Hindu myth on which it is based is my favorite—the myth of the Monkey Lord who loved so much that he created chaos wherever he went.

INTERVIEWERS: Almost a Christ figure?

TRAVERS: Indeed, I hadn't dared to think of that, but yes, indeed, when you read the *Ramayana* you'll come across the story of Hanuman on which I built my version of that very old myth.

I love *Friend Monkey.* I love the story of Hanuman. For many years, it remained in my very blood because he's someone who loves too much and can't help it. I don't know where I first heard of him, but the story remained with me and I knew it would come out of me somehow or other. But I didn't know what shape it would take.

The book hasn't been very well received. It wasn't given very good notices. Everybody said, "Oh, *Friend Monkey.* She's writing about a monkey now. Why not more of Mary Poppins?" I wanted to do something new and, strangely enough, it wasn't something so very new after all.

INTERVIEWERS: Let's talk about another reaction to *Mary Poppins.* As you know, the book was recently removed from the children's shelves of the San Francisco libraries. The charge has been made that the book is racist and presents an unflattering view of minorities.

TRAVERS: The Irish have an expression: "Ah, my grief!" It means "the pity of things." The objections had been made to the chapter "Bad Tuesday," where Mary Poppins goes to the four points of the compass. She meets a mandarin in the East, an Indian in the West, an Eskimo in the North, and blacks in the South who speak in a pickaninny language. What I find strange is that, while my critics claim to have children's best interests in mind, children themselves have never objected to the book. In fact, they love it. That was certainly the case when I was asked to speak to an affectionate crowd of children at a library in Port-of-Spain in Trinidad. On another occasion, when a white teacher friend of mine explained how she felt uncomfortable reading the pickaninny dialect to her young students, I asked her, "And are the black children affronted?" "Not at all," she replied, "it appeared they loved it." "Minorities" is not a word in my vocabulary. And I wonder, sometimes, how much disservice is done children by some individuals who occasionally offer, with good intentions, to serve as their spokesmen. Nonetheless, I have rewritten the offending chapter, and in the revised edition I have substituted a Panda, Dolphin, Polar Bear, and Macaw. I have done so not as an apology for anything I have written. The reason is much more simple: I do not wish to see Mary Poppins tucked away in the closet. Aside from this issue, there is something else you should remember. I never wrote my books especially for children.

INTERVIEWERS: You have said that before. What do you mean?

TRAVERS: When I sat down to write *Mary Poppins* or any of the other books, I did not know children would read them. I'm sure there must be a field of "children's literature"—I hear about it so often—but sometimes I wonder if it isn't a label created by publishers and booksellers who also have the impossible presumption to put on books such notes as "from five to seven" or "from nine to twelve." How can they know when a book will appeal to such and such an age?

If you look at other so-called children's authors, you'll see they never wrote directly for children. Though Lewis Carroll dedicated his book to Alice, I feel it was an afterthought once the whole was already committed to paper. Beatrix Potter declared, "I write to please myself!" And I think the same can be said of Milne or Tolkien or Laura Ingalls Wilder.

I certainly had no specific child in mind when I wrote *Mary Poppins*. How could I? If I were writing for the Japanese child who reads it in a land without staircases, how could I have written of a nanny who slides up the banister? If I were writing for the African child who reads the book in Swahili, how could I have written of umbrellas for a child who has never seen or used one?

But I suppose if there is something in my books that appeals to children, it is the result of my not having to go *back* to my childhood; I can, as it were, turn *aside* and consult it (James Joyce once wrote, "My childhood bends beside me"). If we're completely honest, not sentimental or nostalgic, we have no idea where childhood ends and maturity begins. It is one unending thread, not a life chopped up into sections out of touch with one another.

Once, when Maurice Sendak was being interviewed on television a little after the success of *Where the Wild Things Are*, he was asked the usual questions: Do you have children? Do you like children? After a pause, he said with simple dignity: "I was a child." That says it all.

But don't let me leave you with the impression that I am ungrateful to children. They have stolen much of the world's treasure and magic in the literature they have appropriated for themselves. Think, for example, of the myths or Grimm's fairy tales—none of which were written especially for them—this ancestral literature handed down by the folk. And so despite publishers' labels and my own protestations about not writing especially for them, I am grateful that children have included my books in their treasure trove.

INTERVIEWERS: Don't you have a new Mary Poppins book coming out?

TRAVERS: You know, for the longest time I thought I was done with Mary Poppins. Then I found out she was not done with me. My English publisher, William Collins, will release

Mary Poppins in Cherry Tree Lane. It will be out in the U.S. in the fall of 1982 with Delacorte/Dell. After all those years, Mary Poppins showed me new dimensions of herself and other characters. I will be interested to learn how you and other readers find it. Then in the fall my English publisher will reissue *Friend Monkey.*

INTERVIEWERS: Could you write a *Mary Poppins* book to order?

TRAVERS: No, never. As I have said, I am summoned. I do not wait around, though; I write on other things. For example, I am a regular contributor to the periodical *Parabola: Myth and the Quest for Meaning,* my latest piece being "Leda's Lament." Anyway, everything comes out of living with an idea. If I knew how to summon up inspiration, would I give my secret away?

INTERVIEWERS: Even if you might be termed an "inspired" or mystical writer, do you have to set yourself a daily schedule of writing?

TRAVERS: In a way I'm never not doing it. When I'm going to buy, let us say, a tube of toothpaste, I have it in me. The story or lecture or article is moving. And I make a point of writing, if only a little, every day, as a kind of discipline so that it is not a whim but a piece of work.

INTERVIEWERS: Do you read much before or during writing?

TRAVERS: No. I read myth and fairy tale and books about them a great deal now, but I very seldom read novels. I find modern novels bore me. I can read Tolstoy and the Russians, but mostly I read comparative mythology and comparative religion. I need matter to carry with me.

INTERVIEWERS: Do you compose in longhand or at the typewriter?

TRAVERS: I do a little bit of both. It's very strange. My handwriting, when I'm writing on paper before I put it onto the typewriter, is quite different—it's somebody else's handwriting. I'm always surprised to see it. Perhaps I'm not writing at all;

perhaps there is somebody else doing it. I so often wonder: do these ideas come into the mind or are they just instinctive or are they . . . ?

INTERVIEWERS: "Throngs of living souls," as AE suggests.

TRAVERS: I just don't know. I don't think I'm a very mental person. When I write it's more a process of listening. I don't pretend that there is some spirit standing beside me that tells me things. More and more I've become convinced that the great treasure to possess is the Unknown. I'm going to write, I hope, a lot about that. It's with my unknowing that I come to the myths. If I came to them knowing, I would have nothing to learn. But I bring my unknowing, which is a tangible thing, a clear space, something that's been made room for out of the muddle of ordinary psychic stuff, an empty space.

INTERVIEWERS: In one of your essays you recall the Zen statement "Summoned not created" when speaking about this.

TRAVERS: Yes, that really describes it. You know C. S. Lewis, whom I greatly admire, said: "There's no such thing as creative writing." I've always agreed with that and always refuse to teach it when given the opportunity. He said: "There is, in fact, only one Creator and we mix." That's our function, to mix the elements He has given us. See how wonderfully anonymous that leaves us? You can't say, "I did this; this gross matrix of flesh and blood and sinews and nerves did this." What nonsense! I'm given these things to make a pattern out of. Something gave it to me.

I've always loved the idea of the craftsman, the anonymous man. For instance, I've always wanted my books to be called the work of Anon, because Anon is my favorite literary character. If you look through an anthology of poems that go from the far past into the present time, you'll see that all the poems signed "Anon" have a very specific flavor that is one flavor all the way through the centuries. I think, perhaps arrogantly, of myself as "Anon." I would like to think that *Mary Poppins* and the other books could be called back to make that change. But I suppose it's too late for that.

INTERVIEWERS: What do you think of the books of Carlos Castaneda?

TRAVERS: I like them very much. They take me into a world where I fear I will not belong. It's a bit more occult than my world, but I like Don Juan's idea about what a warrior is and how a warrior should live. In a way, we all have to live like warriors; that's the same as being the hero of one's own story. I feel that Castaneda has been taken into other dimensions of thinking and experiencing. I don't pretend to understand them, and I think I understand why Castaneda is so slow to give interviews and tries to separate himself from all of that. He doesn't want to explain. These things can't be explained in ordinary terms.

You know, in America, everybody thinks there's an answer to every question. They're always saying, "But why and how?" They always think there is a solution. There is a great fortitude in that and a great sense of optimism. In Europe, we are so old that we know there are certain things to which there is not an answer. And you will remember, in this regard, that Mary Poppins's chief characteristic, apart from her tremendous vanity, is that she never explains. I often wonder why people write and ask me to explain this and that. I'll write back and say that Mary Poppins didn't explain, so neither can I or neither will I. So many people ask me, "Where does she go?" Well, I say, if the book hasn't said that, then it's up to you to find out. I'm not going to write footnotes to *Mary Poppins.* That would be absolutely presumptuous, and at the same time it would be assuming that I know. It's the fact that she's unknown that's so intriguing to readers.

INTERVIEWERS: There's that same quality about Castaneda.

TRAVERS: There is. His is a more deliberate unknown. It's as though he were hiding, I often think. And I don't know why, psychologically, he is doing that but I respect that hiding nonetheless. He has some idea in it.

You see, you've got a great wealth of myth in America and he has tapped it. And some of the writers on American Indian affairs have tapped it. But in a way it's foreign to us. You see how often Castaneda, as a modern man and non-Indian, becomes sick, physically sick, with the experiences. It almost seems to be that they're not for us. The Mexican Indians are, after all, a very old race.

I lived with the Indians, or I lived on the reservations, for two summers during the war. John Collier, who was then the administrator for Indian Affairs, was a great friend of mine and he saw that I was very homesick for England but couldn't go back over those mined waters. And he said, "I'll tell you what I'll do for you. I'll send you to live with the Indians." "That's mockery," I replied. "What good will that do me?" He said, "You'll see."

I'd never been out West and I went to stay on the Navajo reservation at Administration House, which is at Window Rock beyond Gallup. Collier had sent a letter to the members of the committee at Administration House and asked them to take me about so that I could see the land and meet the Indians. They very kindly did. Fortunately, I was able to ride and I was equipped with jeans and boots and a western saddle. Then I saw that the Indian women wore big, wide, flounced Spanish skirts with little velvet jackets. And I, who don't like trousers very much, said I must have one of those. So they made me a flounced skirt and a velvet jacket, and I rode with the Indians. It was wonderful the way they turned towards me when, instead of being an Eastern dude, I put on their skirt.

One day the head of Administration House asked me if I would give a talk to the Indians. And I said, "How could I talk to them, these ancient people? It is they who could tell me things." He said, "Try." So they came into what I suppose was a clubhouse, a big place with a stage, and I stood on the stage and the place was full of Indians. I told them about England, because she was at war then, and all that was happening. I said that for me England was the place "Where the Sun Rises" because, you see, England is east of where I was. I said, "Over large water." And I told them about the children who were being evacuated from the cities and some of the experiences of the children. I put it as mythologically as I could, just very simple sayings.

At the end there was dead silence. I turned to the man who had introduced me and said, "I'm sorry. I failed, I haven't got across." And he said, "You wait. You don't know them as well as I do." And every Indian in that big hall came up and took me silently by the hand, one after another. That was their way of expressing feeling with me.

I never knew such depths of silence, internally and externally, as I experienced in the Navajo desert. One night I was taken at full moon away into the desert where they were having a meeting before they had their dancing. There were crowds of Indians there, about two thousand under the moon. And before the proceedings began there was no sound in the desert amongst those people except the occasional cry of a baby or the rattle of a horse's harness or the crackling of fire under a pot— those natural sounds that really don't take anything from the silence.

They waited it seemed to me hours before the first man got up to speak. Naturally, I didn't understand what they were saying. But I listened to the speeches and I enjoyed the silences all night long. And when the night was far spent, they began to dance. Not in the usual dances of the corn dance; they had their ordinary clothes on and were dancing two-and-two, going around and around a fire, a man and a woman. And I was told that if you're asked to dance by a man and you don't want to dance, you give him a silver coin. So one Indian did come up but I went with him. I couldn't do the dance, even though it wasn't a very intricate dance; it was more a little short step round and round, just these two people together. So we two strangers danced around the fire. It was very moving to me. And we came back to the House in the early morning.

And, of course, I saw lots of the regular dances with Navajos and the Hopis, and later with the Pueblos. The Indians in the Pueblo tribe gave me an Indian name and they said I must never reveal it. Every Indian has a secret name as well as his public name. This moved me very much because I have a strong feeling about names, that names are a part of a person, a very private thing to each one. I'm always amazed at the way Christian names are seized upon in America as if by right instead of as something to be given. One of the fairy tales, "Rumplestiltskin," deals with the extraordinary privacy and inward nature of the name. It's always been a big taboo in the fairy tales and in myth that you do not name a person. Many primitive people do not like you to speak and praise a child to its face, for instance, and they will make a cross or sign against evil when you do that, even in Ireland sometimes.

INTERVIEWERS: What do you think of the contemporary interest in religion and myth, particularly among young people? Do you sense that in the last few years a large number of people have grown interested in spiritual disciplines—yoga, Zen, meditation, and the like?

TRAVERS: Yes, definitely. It shows the deep, disturbed undercurrents that there are in man, that he is really looking for something that is more than a thing. This is a civilization devoted to things. What they're looking for is something that they cannot possess but serve, something higher than themselves.

I'm all with them in their search because it is my search, too. But I've searched for it all my life. And when I'm asked to speak about myth, I nearly always find it's not known. There's no preparation. There's nothing for the words to fall on. People haven't read the fairy tales.

INTERVIEWERS: What reading would you recommend for children and adults?

TRAVERS: I should send people right back to the fairy tales. The Bible, of course. Even the nursery rhymes. You can find things there. As I was saying, when you think of "Humpty-Dumpty"—". . . All the King's horses and all the King's men couldn't put Humpty together again"—that's a wonderful story, a fable that some things are impossible. And when children learn that, they accept that there are certain things that can't be, and it's a most delicate and indirect way to have it go into them.

I feel that the indirect teaching is what is needed. All school teaching is a direct giving of information. But everything I do is by hint and suggestion. That's what I think gets into the inner ear.

INTERVIEWERS: Nowadays, then, you see behind the headlines a renewed interest in the Divine Mother.

TRAVERS: I've said several times that I think women's liberation is, in a way, an aspect of realizing the Divine Mother. Not that I think women's libbers are Divine Mothers. Far from it. But I think the feminine principle, which we could say the Divine Mother embodies, is rising. All I want is that they don't use the feminine principle in order to turn themselves into men. We have all that we need as women. We just don't recognize it, some of us.

I am happily a woman. Nothing in me resents it. All of me accepts it and always has. Mind you, I haven't suffered. I haven't been in a profession where women are paid less than men. Nothing has been hard for me as a woman. But I sympathize with women who want to live themselves to the full. But I don't think you can do that by being a Madison Avenue executive or president of a women's bank. All those things I've never wanted.

Women belong in myth. We have to think of the ideas of yin and yang. So I feel we're really sitting, if we only knew, exactly where we ought to be, where the Divine Mother sits. If we don't know this is so, then it isn't so.

INTERVIEWERS: If Mary Poppins invented you, not vice versa, as you say, can you imagine what would have happened to you if she hadn't come along?

TRAVERS: Oh, I've never thought about it. It has never occurred to me to think that way, because, you see, we aren't given the opportunity of leading parallel lives. What would I have done if I hadn't done this? I have no means of knowing, because one life is all we get. It would have had something to do with the stage, dancing. But then, actresses grow old, dancers grow wobbly, whereas a writer still has a typewriter. And I think I've been learning and growing in writing all these years. If there's a life after death, I want to work.

INTERVIEWERS: Is there going to be another Mary Poppins book?

TRAVERS: Well, I have a sense of another lurking—"lurking" is the word, like a burglar, round and round the house. That's all I can say at the moment.

—EDWINA BURNESS
—JERRY GRISWOLD
1976, 1981

SIMONE DE BEAUVOIR

French novelist, memoirist and philosopher Simone de Beauvoir is most widely read today for her classic feminist work, *The Second Sex* (*Le Deuxième Sexe*, 1949), a radical critique of patriarchal Western culture that caused considerable scandal among French readers at the time and established her reputation as an intellectual. But the bulk of de Beauvoir's works are fiction or memoir. In 1954 she became the third woman ever to receive the prestigious Prix Goncourt for her novel *The Mandarins* (*Les Mandarins*).

De Beauvoir was born in Montparnasse on January 9, 1908, to a conservative middle-class family and received the limited education then considered appropriate for a gentlewoman. After her father's bankruptcy, however, her parents permitted de Beauvoir to undertake further study in preparation for a teaching career. At the Sorbonne, where she prepared for the *agrégation* in philosophy, she met Jean-Paul Sartre, who became the most important figure in her life and with whom she maintained an intimate, unorthodox relationship—they rejected the ideas of marriage, children and monogamy—until his death in 1980.

From her Sorbonne years until the Second World War, de Beauvoir supported herself teaching philosophy at *lycées* in Marseilles, Rouen and Paris. Her fiction was repeatedly rejected by journals and publishing houses until, in 1943, her first novel, *She Came to Stay (L'Invitée)*, appeared. From that time she devoted herself full-time to writing. A second novel, *The Blood of Others (Le Sang des autres, 1945)*, about the French resistance during the occupation, swiftly followed the first, and in the next five years de Beauvoir published a third novel and numerous nonfiction works, including a play, a travel diary and philosophical works, culminating in the 1949 publication of *The Second Sex*. In 1945, de Beauvoir and Sartre founded *Les Temps Modernes*, a monthly journal that became the mouthpiece of French existentialism.

In the fifties de Beauvoir first expressed her long-standing Communist sympathies through activism, traveling to Russia and China with Sartre, and publishing an enthusiastic endorsement of Chinese Communism, *The Long March (La Longue March, 1957)*. In 1958 she published the first of her numerous volumes of intellectual autobiography, *Memoirs of a Dutiful Daughter (Mémoirs d'une jeune fille rangée)*, followed by *The Force of Age (La Force de l'âge, 1960)*, *The Force of Circumstance (La Force des choses, 1963)*, *A Very Easy Death (Une Morte très douce, 1966)*, *All Said and Done (Tout compte fait, 1972)* and *Adieux: A Farewell to Sartre (La Cérémonie des adieux suivie d'entretiens avec Jean-Paul Sartre, 1981)* among others. De Beauvoir died in 1986 and was buried alongside Sartre in the Montparnasse cemetery near her home.

A manuscript page from Simone de Beauvoir's La Force de Choses.

SIMONE DE BEAUVOIR

Simone de Beauvoir had introduced me to Jean Genet and Jean-Paul Sartre, whom I had interviewed. But she hesitated about being interviewed herself: "Why should we talk about me? Don't you think I've done enough in my three books of memoirs?" It took several letters and conversations to convince her otherwise, and then only on the condition "that it wouldn't be too long."

The interview took place in Miss de Beauvoir's studio on the rue Schoëlcher in Montparnasse, a five-minute walk from Sartre's apartment. We worked in a large, sunny room which serves as her study and sitting room. Shelves are crammed with surprisingly uninteresting books. "The best ones," she told me, "are in the hands of my friends and never come back." The tables are covered with colorful objects brought back from her travels, but the only valuable work in the room is a sculpture given to her by Giacometti. Scattered throughout the room are dozens of phonograph records, one of the few luxuries that Miss de Beauvoir permits herself.

Apart from her classically featured face, what strikes one about Simone de Beauvoir is her fresh, rosy complexion and her clear blue eyes, extremely young and lively. One gets the impression that she knows and sees everything; this inspires a certain timidity. Her speech is rapid, her manner direct without being brusque, and she is rather smiling and friendly.

INTERVIEWER: For the last seven years you've been writing your *Memoires*, in which you frequently wonder about your vocation and your profession. I have the impression that it was the loss of religious faith that turned you toward writing.

DE BEAUVOIR: It's very hard to review one's past without cheating a little. My desire to write goes far back. I wrote stories at the age of eight, but lots of children do the same. That doesn't really mean they have a vocation for writing. It may be that in my case the vocation was accentuated because I had lost religious faith; it's also true that when I read books that moved me deeply, such as George Eliot's *The Mill on the Floss*, I wanted terribly much to be, like her, someone whose books would be read, whose books would move readers.

INTERVIEWER: Have you been influenced by English literature?

DE BEAUVOIR: The study of English has been one of my passions ever since childhood. There's a body of children's literature in English far more charming than what exists in French. I loved to read *Alice in Wonderland*, *Peter Pan*, George Eliot, and even Rosamond Lehmann.

INTERVIEWER: *Dusty Answer?*

DE BEAUVOIR: I had a real passion for that book. And yet it was rather mediocre. The girls of my generation adored it. The author was very young, and every girl recognized herself in Judy. The book was rather clever, even rather subtle. As for me, I envied English university life. I lived at home. I didn't have a room of my own. In fact, I had nothing at all. And though that life wasn't free, it did allow for privacy and seemed to me magnificent. The author had known all the myths of adolescent girls—handsome boys with an air of mystery about them and so on. Later, of course, I read the Brontës and the books of Virginia Woolf: *Orlando*, *Mrs. Dalloway*. I don't care much for *The Waves*, but I'm very, very fond of her book on Elizabeth Barrett Browning.

INTERVIEWER: What about her journal?

DE BEAUVOIR: It interests me less. It's too literary. It's fascinating, but it's foreign to me. She's too concerned with whether she'll be published, with what people will say about her. I liked very much "A Room of One's Own" in which she talks about the situation of women. It's a short essay, but it hits the nail on the head. She explains very well why women can't write. Virginia Woolf is one of the woman writers who have interested me most. Have you seen any photos of her? An extraordinarily lonely face . . . in a way, she interests me more than Colette. Colette is, after all, very involved in her little love affairs, in household matters, laundry, pets. Virginia Woolf is much broader.

INTERVIEWER: Did you read her books in translation?

DE BEAUVOIR: No, in English. I read English better than I speak it.

INTERVIEWER: What do you think about college and university education for a writer? You yourself were a brilliant student at the Sorbonne and people expected you to have a brilliant career as a teacher.

DE BEAUVOIR: My studies gave me only a very superficial knowledge of philosophy but sharpened my interest in it. I benefited greatly from being a teacher—that is, from being able to spend a great deal of time reading, writing and educating myself. In those days, teachers didn't have a very heavy program. My studies gave me a solid foundation because in order to pass the state exams you have to explore areas that you wouldn't bother about if you were concerned only with general culture. They provided me with a certain academic method that was useful when I wrote *The Second Sex* and that has been useful, in general, for all my studies. I mean a way of going through books very quickly, of seeing which works are important, of classifying them, of being able to reject those which are unimportant, of being able to summarize, to browse.

INTERVIEWER: Were you a good teacher?

DE BEAUVOIR: I don't think so, because I was interested only in the bright students and not at all in the others, whereas a good teacher should be interested in everyone. But if you teach philosophy you can't help it. There were always four or five students who did all the talking, and the others didn't care to do anything. I didn't bother about them very much.

INTERVIEWER: You had been writing for ten years before you were published, at the age of thirty-six. Weren't you discouraged?

DE BEAUVOIR: No, because in my time it was unusual to be published when you were very young. Of course, there were one or two examples, such as Radiguet, who was a prodigy. Sartre himself wasn't published until he was about thirty-five, when *Nausea* and *The Wall* were brought out. When my first more or less publishable book was rejected, I was a bit discouraged. And when the first version of *She Came to Stay* was rejected, it was very unpleasant. Then I thought that I ought to take my time. I knew many examples of writers who were slow in getting started. And people always spoke of the case of Stendhal, who didn't begin to write until he was forty.

INTERVIEWER: Were you influenced by any American writers when you wrote your early novels?

DE BEAUVOIR: In writing *She Came to Stay*, I was certainly influenced by Hemingway insofar as it was he who taught us a certain simplicity of dialogue and the importance of the little things in life.

INTERVIEWER: Do you draw up a very precise plan when you write a novel?

DE BEAUVOIR: I haven't, you know, written a novel in ten years, during which time I've been working on my memoirs.

When I wrote *The Mandarins*, for example, I created characters and an atmosphere around a given theme, and little by little the plot took shape. But in general I start writing a novel long before working out the plot.

INTERVIEWER: People say that you have great self-discipline and that you never let a day go by without working. At what time do you start?

DE BEAUVOIR: I'm always in a hurry to get going, though in general I dislike starting the day. I first have tea and then, at about ten o'clock, I get under way and work until one. Then I see my friends and after that, at five o'clock, I go back to work and continue until nine. I have no difficulty in picking up the thread in the afternoon. When you leave, I'll read the paper or perhaps go shopping. Most often it's a pleasure to work.

INTERVIEWER: When do you see Sartre?

DE BEAUVOIR: Every evening and often at lunchtime. I generally work at his place in the afternoon.

INTERVIEWER: Doesn't it bother you to go from one apartment to another?

DE BEAUVOIR: No. Since I don't write scholarly books, I take all my papers with me and it works out very well.

INTERVIEWER: Do you plunge in immediately?

DE BEAUVOIR: It depends to some extent on what I'm writing. If the work is going well, I spend a quarter or half an hour reading what I wrote the day before, and I make a few corrections. Then I continue from there. In order to pick up the thread I have to read what I've done.

INTERVIEWER: Do your writer friends have the same habits as you?

DE BEAUVOIR: No, it's quite a personal matter. Genet, for example, works quite differently. He puts in about twelve hours a day for six months when he's working on something and when he has finished he can let six months go by without doing anything. As I said, I work every day except for two or three months of vacation when I travel and generally don't work at all. I read very little during the year, and when I go away I take a big valise full of books, books that I didn't have time to read. But if the trip lasts a month or six weeks, I do feel uncomfortable, particularly if I'm between two books. I get bored if I don't work.

INTERVIEWER: Are your original manuscripts always in longhand? Who deciphers them? Nelson Algren says that he's one of the few people who can read your handwriting.

DE BEAUVOIR: I don't know how to type, but I do have two typists who manage to decipher what I write. When I work on the last version of a book, I copy the manuscript. I'm very careful. I make a great effort. My writing is fairly legible.

INTERVIEWER: In *The Blood of Others* and *All Men Are Mortal* you deal with the problem of time. Were you influenced, in this respect, by Joyce or Faulkner?

DE BEAUVOIR: No, it was a personal preoccupation. I've always been keenly aware of the passing of time. I've always thought that I was old. Even when I was twelve, I thought it was awful to be thirty. I felt that something was lost. At the same time, I was aware of what I could gain, and certain periods of my life have taught me a great deal. But, in spite of everything, I've always been haunted by the passing of time and by the fact that death keeps closing in on us. For me, the problem of time is linked up with that of death, with the thought that we inevitably draw closer and closer to it, with the horror of decay. It's that, rather than the fact that things disintegrate, that love peters out. That's horrible too, though I personally have never been troubled by it. There's always been great continuity in my life. I've always lived in Paris, more or less in the same neighborhoods. My relationship with Sartre has lasted a very long time. I have very old friends whom I continue to see. So it's not that I've felt that time breaks things up, but rather the fact that I always take my bearings. I mean the fact that I have so many years behind me, so many ahead of me. I count them.

INTERVIEWER: In the second part of your memoirs, you draw a portrait of Sartre at the time he was writing *Nausea*. You picture him as being obsessed by what he calls his "crabs," by anguish. You seem to have been, at the time, the joyous member of the couple. Yet, in your novels you reveal a preoccupation with death that we never find in Sartre.

DE BEAUVOIR: But remember what he says in *The Words*. That he never felt the imminence of death, whereas his fellow students—for example, Nizan, the author of *Aden Arabia*—were fascinated by it. In a way, Sartre felt he was immortal. He had staked everything on his literary work and on the hope that his work would survive, whereas for me, owing to the fact that my personal life will disappear, I'm not the least bit concerned about whether my work is likely to last. I've always been deeply aware that the ordinary things of life disappear, one's day-to-day activities, one's impressions, one's past experiences. Sartre thought that life could be caught in a trap of words, and I've always felt that words weren't life itself but a reproduction of life, of something dead, so to speak.

INTERVIEWER: That's precisely the point. Some people claim that you haven't the power to transpose life in your novels. They insinuate that your characters are copied from the people around you.

DE BEAUVOIR: I don't know. What is the imagination? In the long run, it's a matter of attaining a certain degree of generality, of truth about what is, about what one actually lives. Works which aren't based on reality don't interest me unless they're out and out extravagant, for example the novels of Alexandre Dumas or of Victor Hugo, which are epics of a kind. But I don't call "made-up" stories works of the imagination but rather works of artifice. If I wanted to defend myself, I could refer to Tolstoy's *War and Peace*, all the characters of which were taken from real life.

INTERVIEWER: Let's go back to your characters. How do you choose their names?

DE BEAUVOIR: I don't consider that very important. I chose the name Xavière in *She Came to Stay* because I had met only one person who had that name. When I look for names, I use the telephone directory or try to remember the names of former pupils.

INTERVIEWER: To which of your characters are you most attached?

DE BEAUVOIR: I don't know. I think that I'm interested less in the characters themselves than in their relationships, whether it be a matter of love or friendship. It was the critic Claude Roy who pointed that out.

INTERVIEWER: In every one of your novels we find a female character who is misled by false notions and who is threatened by madness.

DE BEAUVOIR: Lots of modern women are like that. Women are obliged to play at being what they aren't, to play, for example, at being great courtesans, to fake their personalities. They're on the brink of neurosis. I feel very sympathetic toward women of that type. They interest me more than the well-balanced housewife and mother. There are, of course, women who interest me even more, those who are both true and independent, who work and create.

INTERVIEWER: None of your female characters are immune from love. You like the romantic element.

DE BEAUVOIR: Love is a great privilege. Real love, which is very rare, enriches the lives of the men and women who experience it.

INTERVIEWER: In your novels, it seems to be the women— I'm thinking of Françoise in *She Came to Stay* and Anne in *The Mandarins*—who experience it most.

DE BEAUVOIR: The reason is that, despite everything, women give more of themselves in love because most of them don't have much else to absorb them. Perhaps they're also more capable of deep sympathy, which is the basis of love. Perhaps it's also because I can project myself more easily into women than into men. My female characters are much richer than my male characters.

INTERVIEWER: You've never created an independent and really free female character who illustrates in one way or other the thesis of *The Second Sex.* Why?

DE BEAUVOIR: I've shown women as they are, as divided human beings, and not as they ought to be.

INTERVIEWER: After your long novel, *The Mandarins,* you stopped writing fiction and began to work on your memoirs. Which of these two literary forms do you prefer?

DE BEAUVOIR: I like both of them. They offer different kinds of satisfaction and disappointment. In writing my memoirs, it's very agreeable to be backed up by reality. On the other hand, when one follows reality from day to day, as I have, there are certain depths, certain kinds of myth and meaning that one disregards. In the novel, however, one can express these horizons, these overtones of daily life, but there's an element of fabrication that is nevertheless disturbing. One should aim at inventing without fabricating. I had been wanting to talk about my childhood and youth for a long time. I had maintained very deep relationships with them, but there was no sign of them in any of my books. Even before writing my first novel, I had a desire to have, as it were, a heart-to-heart talk. It was a very emotional, a very personal need. After *The Memoirs of a Dutiful Daughter* I was unsatisfied, and then I thought of doing something else. But I was unable to. I said to myself, "I've fought to be free. What have I done with my freedom, what's become of it?" I wrote the sequel that carried me from the age of twenty-one to the present time, from *The Prime of Life* to *Force of Circumstance*—

INTERVIEWER: At the meeting of writers in Formentor a few

years ago, Carlo Levi described *The Prime of Life* as "the great love story of the century." Sartre appeared for the first time as a human being. You revealed a Sartre who had not been rightly understood, a man very different from the legendary Sartre.

DE BEAUVOIR: I did it intentionally. He didn't want me to write about him. Finally, when he saw that I spoke about him the way I did, he gave me a free hand.

INTERVIEWER: In your opinion, why is it that, despite the reputation he's had for twenty years, Sartre the writer remains misunderstood and is still violently attacked by critics?

DE BEAUVOIR: For political reasons. Sartre is a man who has violently opposed the class into which he was born and which therefore regards him as a traitor. But that's the class which has money, which buys books. Sartre's situation is paradoxical. He's an antibourgeois writer who is read by the bourgeoisie and admired by it as one of its products. The bourgeoisie has a monopoly on culture and thinks that it gave birth to Sartre. At the same time, it hates him because he attacks it.

INTERVIEWER: In an interview with Hemingway in *The Paris Review*, he said, "All you can be sure about, in a political-minded writer, is that if his work should last, you will have to skip the politics when you read it." Of course, you don't agree. Do you still believe in "commitment"?

DE BEAUVOIR: Hemingway was precisely the type of writer who never wanted to commit himself. I know that he was involved in the Spanish Civil War, but as a journalist. Hemingway was never deeply committed, so he thinks that what is eternal in literature is what isn't dated, isn't committed. I don't agree. In the case of many writers, it's also their political stand which makes me like or dislike them. There aren't many writers of former times whose work was really committed. And although one reads Rousseau's *Social Contract* as eagerly as one reads his *Confessions*, one no longer reads *The New Héloïse*.

INTERVIEWER: The heyday of existentialism seems to have

been the period from the end of the war to 1952. At the present time, the "new novel" is in fashion; and such writers as Drieu La Rochelle and Roger Nimier.

DE BEAUVOIR: There's certainly a return to the right in France. The new novel itself isn't reactionary, nor are its authors. A sympathizer can say that they want to do away with certain bourgeois conventions. These writers aren't disturbing. In the long run, Gaullism brings us back to Pétainism, and it's only to be expected that a collaborator like Drieu La Rochelle and an extreme reactionary like Nimier be held in high esteem again. The bourgeoisie is showing itself again in its true colors—that is, as a reactionary class. Look at the success of Sartre's *The Words.* There are several things to note. It's perhaps—I won't say his best book, but one of his best. At any rate, it's an excellent book, an exciting display of virtuosity, an amazingly written work. At the same time, the reason it has had such success is that it's a book that is not "committed." When the critics say that it's his best book, along with *Nausea,* one should bear in mind that *Nausea* is an early work, a work that is not committed, and that it is more readily accepted by the left and right alike than are his plays. The same thing happened to me with *The Memoirs of a Dutiful Daughter.* Bourgeois women were delighted to recognize their own youth in it. The protests began with *The Prime of Life* and continued with *Force of Circumstance.* The break is very clear, very sharp.

INTERVIEWER: The last part of *Force of Circumstance* is devoted to the Algerian war, to which you seem to have reacted in a very personal way.

DE BEAUVOIR: I felt and thought about things in a political way, but I never engaged in political action. The entire last part of *Force of Circumstance* deals with the war. And it seems anachronistic in a France that is no longer concerned with that war.

INTERVIEWER: Didn't you realize that people were bound to forget about it?

DE BEAUVOIR: I deleted lots of pages from that section. I therefore realized that it would be anachronistic. On the other hand, I absolutely wanted to talk about it, and I'm amazed that people have forgotten it to such a degree. Have you seen the film *La Belle Vie*, by the young director Robert Enrico? People are stupefied because the film shows the Algerian war. Claude Mauriac wrote in *Le Figaro Litteraire*: "Why is it that we're shown parachute troopers on public squares. It's not true to life." But it is true to life. I used to see them every day from Sartre's window at Saint Germain des Prés. People have forgotten. They wanted to forget. They wanted to forget their memories. That's the reason why, contrary to what I expected, I wasn't attacked for what I said about the Algerian war but for what I said about old age and death. As regards the Algerian war, all Frenchman are now convinced that it never took place, that nobody was tortured, that insofar as there was torture they were always against torture.

INTERVIEWER: At the end of *Force of Circumstance* you say: "As I look back with incredulity at that credulous adolescent, I am astounded to see how I was swindled." This remark seems to have given rise to all kinds of misunderstandings.

DE BEAUVOIR: People—particularly enemies—have tried to interpret it to mean that my life has been a failure, either because I recognize the fact that I was mistaken on a political level or because I recognize that after all a woman should have had children, etc. Anyone who reads my book carefully can see that I say the very opposite, that I don't envy anyone, that I'm perfectly satisfied with what my life has been, that I've kept all my promises and that consequently if I had my life to live over again I wouldn't live it any differently. I've never regretted not having children insofar as what I wanted to do was to write.

Then why "swindled"? When one has an existentialist view of the world, like mine, the paradox of human life is precisely that one tries to *be* and, in the long run, merely exists. It's because of this discrepancy that when you've laid your stake on being—and, in a way you always do when you make plans, even if you actually know that you can't succeed in being—when you turn around and look back on your life, you see that you've simply existed. In other words, life isn't behind you like a solid thing, like the life of a god (as it is conceived, that is, as something impossible). Your life is simply a human life.

So one might say, as Alain did, and I'm very fond of that remark, "Nothing is promised us." In one sense, it's true. In another, it's not. Because a bourgeois boy or girl who is given a certain culture is actually promised things. I think that anyone who had a hard life when he was young won't say in later years that he's been "swindled." But when I say that I've been swindled I'm referring to the seventeen-year-old girl who daydreamed in the country near the hazel bush about what she was going to do later on. I've done everything I wanted to do, writing books, learning about things, but I've been swindled all the same because it's never anything more. There are also Mallarmé's lines about "the perfume of sadness that remains in the heart," I forget exactly how they go. I've had what I wanted, and, when all is said and done, what one wanted was always something else. A woman psychoanalyst wrote me a very intelligent letter in which she said that "in the last analysis, desires always go far beyond the object of desire." The fact is that I've had everything I desired, but the "far beyond" which is included in the desire itself is not attained when the desire has been fulfilled. When I was young, I had hopes and a view of life which all cultured people and bourgeois optimists encourage one to have and which my readers accuse me of not encouraging in them. That's what I meant, and I wasn't regretting anything I've done or thought.

INTERVIEWER: Some people think that a longing for God underlies your works.

DE BEAUVOIR: No. Sartre and I have always said that it's not because there's a desire to *be* that this desire corresponds to any reality. It's exactly what Kant said on the intellectual level. The fact that one believes in causalities is no reason to believe that there is a supreme cause. The fact that man has a desire to be does not mean that he can ever attain being or even that being is a possible notion, at any rate the being that is a reflection and at the same time an existence. There is a synthesis of existence and being that is impossible. Sartre and I have always rejected it, and this rejection underlies our thinking. There is an emptiness in man, and even his achievements have this emptiness. That's all. I don't mean that I haven't achieved what I wanted to achieve but rather that the achievement is never what people think it is. Furthermore, there is a naïve or snobbish aspect, because people imagine that if you have succeeded on a social level you must be perfectly satisfied with the human condition in general. But that's not the case.

"I'm swindled" also implies something else—namely, that life has made me discover the world as it is, that is, a world of suffering and oppression, of undernourishment for the majority of people, things that I didn't know when I was young and when I imagined that to discover the world was to discover something beautiful. In that respect, too, I was swindled by bourgeois culture, and that's why I don't want to contribute to the swindling of others and why I say that I was swindled, in short, so that others aren't swindled. It's really also a problem of a social kind. In short, I discovered the unhappiness of the world little by little, then more and more, and finally, above all, I felt it in connection with the Algerian war and when I traveled.

INTERVIEWER: Some critics and readers have felt that you spoke about old age in an unpleasant way.

DE BEAUVOIR: A lot of people didn't like what I said because they want to believe that all periods of life are delightful, that children are innocent, that all newlyweds are happy, that all old people are serene. I've rebelled against such notions all my life, and there's no doubt about the fact that the moment, which for me is not old age but the beginning of old age, represents— even if one has all the resources one wants, affection, work to be done—represents a change in one's existence, a change that is manifested by the loss of a great number of things. If one isn't sorry to lose them it's because one didn't love them. I think that people who glorify old age or death too readily are people who really don't love life. Of course, in present-day France you have to say that everything's fine, that everything's lovely, including death.

INTERVIEWER: Beckett has keenly felt the swindle of the human condition. Does he interest you more than the other "new novelists"?

DE BEAUVOIR: Certainly. All the playing around with time that one finds in the "new novel" can be found in Faulkner. It was he who taught them how to do it, and in my opinion he's the one who does it best. As for Beckett, his way of emphasizing the dark side of life is very beautiful. However, he's convinced that life is dark and only that. I too am convinced that life is dark, and at the same time I love life. But that conviction seems to have spoiled everything for him. When that's all you can say, there aren't fifty ways of saying it, and I've found that many of his works are merely repetitions of what he said earlier. *Endgame* repeats *Waiting for Godot,* but in a weaker way.

INTERVIEWER: Are there many contemporary French writers who interest you?

DE BEAUVOIR: Not many. I receive lots of manuscripts, and the annoying thing is that they're almost always bad. At the present time, I'm very excited about Violette Leduc. She was first published in 1946 in *Collection Espoir,* which was edited by Camus. The critics praised her to the skies. Sartre, Genet and Jouhandeau liked her very much. She never sold. She recently published a great autobiography called *The Bastard,* the beginning of which was published in *Les Temps Modernes*, of which Sartre is editor-in-chief. I wrote a preface to the book because I thought that she was one of the unappreciated postwar French writers. She's having great success in France at the present time.

INTERVIEWER: And how do you rank yourself among contemporary writers?

DE BEAUVOIR: I don't know. What is it that one evaluates? The noise, the silence, posterity, the number of readers, the absence of readers, the importance at a given time? I think that people will read me for some time. At least, that's what my readers tell me. I've contributed something to the discussion of women's problems. I know I have from the letters I receive. As for the literary *quality* of my work, in the strict sense of the word, I haven't the slightest idea.

—MADELEINE GOBEIL

Translated by Bernard Frechtman

EUDORA WELTY

Eudora Welty has lived almost all of her life in Jackson, Mississippi, where she was born in 1909. She attended Mississippi State College for Women for two years and received her B.A. from the University of Wisconsin in 1929. After a year at the Columbia School of Advertising, she returned to Jackson in 1932 to pursue her writing. Since then she has departed only for a rare visit to Europe, an annual trip to New York, and an occasional reading at a college. The South has always been the setting of Welty's work, and the short story her forte, although she has written a number of novels: *The Robber Bridegroom* (1942), *Delta Wedding* (1946), *The Ponder Heart* (1954), *Losing Battles* (1970), and *The Optimist's Daughter* (1972), which won the Pulitzer Prize.

Her first published story, "Death of a Traveling Salesman," appeared in 1936 in *Manuscript*, an obscure quarterly. During the next five years she was published in many distinguished periodicals, most frequently *The Southern Review*. Welty's first collection of stories, *A Curtain of Green*, did not appear until 1941. It was followed by three more collections: *The Wide Net* (1943), *The Golden Apples* (1949), and *The Bride of Innisfallen* (1955). She has also written a children's book, *The Shoe Bird* (1964), and published a collection of photographs, *One Time, One Place* (1971). Her first work of nonfiction, *The Eye of the Story: Selected Essays and Reviews,* appeared in 1978, and *One Writer's Beginnings,* her autobiography, was published in 1984.

Welty was recipient of the Creative Arts Medal for Fiction at Brandeis University in 1966. She is a member of the National Institute of Arts and Letters and since 1958 has been an honorary consultant in American letters of the Library of Congress. She has been awarded the National Medal for Literature, the National Institute of Arts and Letters' Gold Medal, and the Modern Language Association's Commonwealth Award.

EUDORA WELTY

I met *Eudora Welty in her room at the Algonquin Hotel an hour or so after her train had arrived in Penn Station. She had given me the wrong room number, so I first saw her peering out of her door as the elevator opened. A tall, large-boned, gray-haired woman greeted me apologetically. She was admittedly nervous about being interviewed, particularly on a tape recorder. After describing her train ride—she won't fly—she braced herself and asked if I wouldn't begin the questioning.*

Once the interview got under way, she grew more at ease. As she herself might say, she was "not unforthcoming." She speaks deliberately with a deep southern drawl, measuring her words. She is extremely private and won't reveal anything personal about herself.

INTERVIEWER: You wrote somewhere that we should still tolerate Jane Austen's kind of family novel. Is Austen a kindred spirit?

WELTY: *Tolerate?* I should just think so! I love and admire all she does, and profoundly, but I don't read her or anyone else for "kindredness." The piece you're referring to was written on as-

"Bywy River, my father killed his last bear. Blessed old
Dragged her Home,
sow/ Laid her across ~~the~~ doorstep."

"Granny! Did you ever have a <u>father</u>? And <u>mother</u>?" cried

Elvie.

"Mama said, 'Take that back where you found it, Mr. Blaikie.
You're nothing but bragging now,'" said Granny.

~~"When & then, Granny ~~~~ ~~~~ Elvie pleaded~~

~~"When ~~~~ ~~~~ to know.~~

"Was you <u>born</u>?" Elvie pleaded to know: "Granny!
Like Lady May?"

"Granny'd like <u>her</u> picture taken!" Aunt Beck divined. "Ninety
today!"

"With all of us!" cried Aunt Birdie. "A picture with Granny
in the middle. Haul her out here in the broil, see what you can
get, Sister Cleo!"

Miss Beulah was summoned, and stood at center back, the ~~Reuben~~
~~Beecham~~   The men squatted or reclined on the ground.
~~Renos~~ wives lined up at her sides. Granny sat composed in the center, and for the only time that day drew the pipe from her pocket,
in order to pose with it cocked in her mouth. ~~Then~~ The aunts as
one dropped their hands before them, as if called to the door in
their aprons. ~~But as Aunt Nannie, her great bosom like~~
~~pleased arms only folded across it front.~~

How Cleo a
~~stranger~~ to all
"Try my ~~history~~"

———————————

A Eudora Welty manuscript page.

signment for *Brief Lives*, an anthology Louis Kronenberger was editing. He did offer me either Jane Austen or Chekhov, and Chekhov I do dare to think is more "kindred." I feel closer to him in spirit, but I couldn't read Russian, which I felt whoever wrote about him should be able to do. Chekhov is one of us—so close to today's world, to my mind, and very close to the South—which Stark Young pointed out a long time ago.

INTERVIEWER: Why is Chekhov close to today's South?

WELTY: He loved the singularity in people, the individuality. He took for granted the sense of family. He had the sense of fate overtaking a way of life, and his Russian humor seems to me kin to the humor of a southerner. It's the kind that lies mostly in character. You know, in *Uncle Vanya* and *The Cherry Orchard*, how people are always gathered together and talking and talking, no one's really listening. Yet there's a great love and understanding that prevails through it, and a knowledge and acceptance of each other's idiosyncrasies, a tolerance of them, and also an acute enjoyment of the dramatic. Like in *The Three Sisters*, when the fire is going on, how they talk right on through their exhaustion, and Vershinin says, "I feel a strange excitement in the air," and laughs and sings and talks about the future. That kind of responsiveness to the world, to whatever happens, out of their own deeps of character seems very southern to me. Anyway, I took a temperamental delight in Chekhov, and gradually the connection was borne in upon me.

INTERVIEWER: Do you ever return to Virginia Woolf?

WELTY: Yes. She was the one who opened the door. When I read *To the Lighthouse*, I felt, Heavens, *what is this?* I was so excited by the experience I couldn't sleep or eat. I've read it many times since, though more often these days I go back to her diary. Any day you open it to will be tragic, and yet all the marvelous things she says about her work, about working, leave you filled with joy that's stronger than your misery for her. Remember—

"I'm not very far along, but I think I have my statues against the sky"? Isn't that beautiful?

INTERVIEWER: About your own work, are you surprised that *Losing Battles* was on the best-seller list—a first for you, I believe?

WELTY: It occurred to me right at first it must be a fluke—that whoever had that place on the best-seller list had just got up and given me his seat—let the lady sit down, she's tottering. Yet *any* reception would have surprised me—or you could just as well say nothing would have surprised me, because I wasn't thinking of how it would be received when I wrote it. I thought about the opinion of a handful of friends I would love to have love that book, but not about the public.

INTERVIEWER: Do you write for your friends?

WELTY: At the time of writing, I don't write for my friends or myself, either; I write for *it*, for the pleasure of *it*. I believe if I stopped to wonder what So-and-so would think, or what I'd feel like if this were read by a stranger, I would be paralyzed. I care what my friends think, very deeply—and it's only after they've read the finished thing that I really can rest, deep down. But in the writing, I have to just keep going straight through with only the *thing* in mind and what it dictates.

It's so much an inward thing that reading the proofs later can be a real shock. When I received them for my first book—no, I guess it was for *Delta Wedding*—I thought, *I* didn't write this. It was a page of dialogue—I might as well have never seen it before. I wrote to my editor, John Woodburn, and told him something had happened to that page in the typesetting. He was kind, not even surprised—maybe this happens to all writers. He called me up and read me from the manuscript—word for word what the proofs said. Proofs don't shock me any longer, yet there's still a strange moment with every book when I move from the position of writer to the position of reader, and I suddenly see my words with the eyes of the cold public. It gives me a terrible sense of exposure, as if I'd gotten sunburned.

INTERVIEWER: Do you make changes in galleys?

WELTY: I correct or change words, but I can't rewrite a scene or make a major change because there's a sense then of someone looking over my shoulder. It's necessary, anyway, to trust that moment when you were sure at last you had done all you could, done your best for that time. When it's finally in print, you're delivered—you don't ever have to look at it again. It's too late to worry about its failings. I'll have to apply any lessons this book has taught me toward writing the next one.

INTERVIEWER: Is *Losing Battles* a departure from your previous fiction?

WELTY: I wanted to see if I could do something that was new for me: translating every thought and feeling into action and speech, speech being another form of action—to bring the whole life of it off through the completed gesture, so to speak. I felt that I'd been writing too much by way of description, of introspection on the part of my characters. I tried to see if I could make everything shown, brought forth, without benefit of the author's telling any more about what was going on inside the characters' minds and hearts. For me, this makes almost certainly for comedy—which I love to write best of all. Now I see it might be a transition toward writing a play.

INTERVIEWER: Did you know what you were going to write before you put it on paper?

WELTY: Yes, it was there in my head, but events proliferated as I went along. For instance, I thought all the action in the novel would be contained in one day and night, but a folder started to fill up with things marked "Next A.M." I didn't foresee the stories that grew out of the stories—that was one of the joys of working the novel out. I thought the book would be short, and instead it was three or four times longer than my normal work. There's no way of estimating its original length because I had great chunks of things in paper clips which weren't numbered until they went to the printer. And I must have thrown away at least as much as I kept in the book.

INTERVIEWER: Did you learn anything new about writing dialogue?

WELTY: I believe so. In its beginning, dialogue's the easiest thing in the world to write when you have a good ear, which I think I have. But as it goes on, it's the most difficult, because it has so many ways to function. Sometimes I needed to make a speech do three or four or five things at once—reveal what the character said but also what he thought he said, what he hid, what others were going to think he meant, and what they misunderstood, and so forth—all in his single speech. And the speech would have to keep the essence of this one character, his whole particular outlook in concentrated form. This isn't to say I succeeded. But I guess it explains why dialogue gives me my greatest pleasure in writing. I used to laugh out loud sometimes when I wrote it—the way P. G. Wodehouse is said to do. I'd think of some things my characters would say, and even if I couldn't use it, I would write the scene out just to let them loose on something—my private show.

INTERVIEWER: Where does the dialogue come from?

WELTY: Familiarity. Memory of the way things get said. Once you have heard certain expressions, sentences, you almost never forget them. It's like sending a bucket down the well and it always comes up full. You don't know you've remembered, but you have. And you listen for the right word, in the present, and you hear it. Once you're into a story everything seems to apply—what you overhear on a city bus is exactly what your character would say on the page you're writing. Wherever you go, you meet part of your story. I guess you're tuned in for it, and the right things are sort of magnetized—if you can think of your ears as magnets. I could hear someone saying—and I had to cut this out—"What, you never ate goat?" And someone answering, "Goat! Please don't say you serve *goat* at this reunion. I wasn't told it was *goat* I was served. I thought—" and so on, and then the recipe, and then it ended up with—I can't remember exactly now—it ended with, "You can do a whole lot of things with vinegar." Well, all these things I would just laugh about and think about for so long and put them in. And then I'd think, that's just plain indulgence. Take it out! And I'd take it out.

INTERVIEWER: Are you an eavesdropper?

WELTY: I'm not as much as I used to be, or would like to be, because I don't hear as well as I used to, or there's too much other noise everywhere. But I've heard some wonderful remarks. Well, in the South, everybody stays busy talking all the time— they're not sorry for you to overhear their tales. I don't feel in helping myself I ever did anything underhanded. I was *helping out.*

INTERVIEWER: Do you think this oral tradition, so to speak, accounts for your vigorous use of dialogue?

WELTY: I think it accounts for the pleasure people take in a story told. It's a treasure I helped myself to. I took it for my ways and means, and that's proper and justified: Our people talk that way. They learn and teach and think and enjoy that way. Southerners do have, they've inherited, a narrative sense of human destiny. This may or may not come out in *Losing Battles.* A reunion is everybody remembering together—remembering and relating when their people were born and what happened in their lives, what that made happen to their children, and how it was that they died. There's someone to remember a man's whole life, every bit of the way along. I think that's a marvelous thing, and I'm glad I got to know something of it. In New York you may have the greatest and most congenial friends, but it's extraordinary if you ever know anything about them except that little wedge of their life that you meet with the little wedge of your life. You don't get that sense of a continuous narrative line. You never see the full circle. But in the South, where people don't move about as much, even now, and where they once hardly ever moved away at all, the pattern of life was always right there.

INTERVIEWER: Would you say that southerners—deep southerners—are more open than northerners?

WELTY: I think we have a sort of language we all understand and speak—a shorthand of some kind, based on familiarity—but I'm not sure we're more open. We may not tell as much as we think we do, and we may not hide as much as we think we do. We're just more used to talking—as you can see—and the subject doesn't especially cut us down.

INTERVIEWER: And that profoundly affects your fiction?

WELTY: I think that's what gives a pattern to it, and a sense of its shape to me. I do want to say that I'm only speaking for myself when I speak of southern qualities, because I don't know how other people work. It may be entirely different, especially with a genius like William Faulkner, who had such a comprehensive sense of the whole deep, deep past and more far-reaching, bred-in country knowledge than I have, which is so valuable, besides all the rest of his equipment that I don't need to tell you about.

INTERVIEWER: Did you know Faulkner?

WELTY: Slightly and over a long period of time, but not well. I liked him ever so much. We met at a dinner party in Oxford, just old friends of his and old friends of mine, which was the right way for it to happen, and it was just grand. We sang hymns, and we sang some old ballads—and the next day he invited me to go sailing. If we ever met in New York, we just talked about being in Oxford. *He* didn't bring up writing, and if he didn't, you know *I* wasn't going to bring it up! But when he was working in Hollywood, he once wrote me a two-line letter—this was long before we met—and told me he liked a little book of mine called *The Robber Bridegroom* and said would I let him know if he could ever do anything for me. It was on a little piece of notebook paper, written in that fine, neat, sort of unreadable hand, in pencil—and I've lost it.

INTERVIEWER: Did you feel at all influenced by his presence?

WELTY: I don't honestly think so. It is hard to be sure about such things. I was naturally in the deepest awe and reverence of him. But that's no help in your own writing. Nobody can help you but yourself. So often I'm asked how I could have written a word with William Faulkner living in Mississippi, and this question amazes me. It was like living near a big mountain, something majestic—it made me happy to know it was there, all that work of his life. But it wasn't a helping or hindering presence. Its magnitude, all by itself, made it something remote in my own working life. When I thought of Faulkner it was when I *read*.

On the other hand, he didn't seem remote to everybody in being our great writer. I know a story about him, though he never knew anybody knew of it, I'd bet. Mississippi is full of writers, and I heard this from the person it was told to. A lady had decided she'd write a novel and got along fine till she came to the love scene. "So," she told my friend, "I thought, there's William Faulkner, sitting right up there in Oxford. Why not send it to William Faulkner and ask him?" So she sent it to him, and time went by, and she didn't ever hear from him, and so she called him up. Because there he was. She said, "Mr. Faulkner, did you ever get that love scene I sent you?" He said yes, he had got it. And she said, "Well, what did you think of it?" And he said, "Well, honey, it's not the way I'd do it—but you go *right ahead.*" Now, wasn't that gentle of him?

INTERVIEWER: Do people give you unpublished manuscripts to read? I mean, women especially tend to write voluminous historical novels, and I wonder if any of them are in Jackson.

WELTY: I wouldn't be surprised. I don't think there's any neck of the woods they're not in. Yes, I get sent manuscripts, but those historical and Gothic novels are really a subject on which I know nothing, and I say so. There is, in point of fact, a good deal of writing talent in general around our state now—a lot of good young ones, serious ones.

INTERVIEWER: Did you ever feel part of a literary community, along with people like Flannery O'Connor, Carson McCullers, Katherine Anne Porter, or Caroline Gordon?

WELTY: I'm not sure there's any dotted line connecting us up, though all of us knew about each other, and all of us, I think, respected and read each other's work and understood it. And some of us are friends of long standing. I don't think there was any passing about of influences, but there's a lot of pleasure in thinking in whose lifetimes your own lifetime has happened to come along. Of course, Katherine Anne Porter was wonderfully generous to me from the beginning. At the time I began sending my first stories to *The Southern Review*, she read them and wrote to me from Baton Rouge inviting me to come down to see her. It took me, I suppose, six months or a year to fully get up my nerve. Twice I got as far as Natchez and turned around and came back. But I finally did get there, and Katherine Anne couldn't have been more welcoming. Later on, she wrote the introduction to my first book of stories, and I owe her very much for that. We've been friends all these years.

INTERVIEWER: How would you feel about a biography about yourself?

WELTY: Shy, and discouraged at the very thought, because to me a writer's work should be everything. A writer's whole feeling, the force of his whole life, can go into a story—but what he's worked for is to get an objective piece down on paper. That should be read instead of some account of his life, with that understanding—here is something which now exists and was made by the hands of this person. Read it for what it is. It doesn't even matter too much whose hands they were. Well, of course, it does—I was just exaggerating to prove my point. But your private life should be kept private. My own I don't think would particularly interest anybody, for that matter. But I'd guard it; I feel strongly about that. They'd have a hard time trying to find something about me. I think I'd better burn everything up. It's best to burn letters, but at least I've never kept diaries or journals. All my manuscripts I've given to the Department of Archives and History in Jackson as they came out because that's my hometown and the director is a lifelong friend. But I don't give them everything. I must have a trunk full of stuff that I didn't give because I didn't think it was anybody else's concern, or that anybody would even care to see my mistakes and false turns. Like about eating goat and all the million things that I left out.

INTERVIEWER: Why do *Losing Battles* and *Delta Wedding* take place back in the 1920s and 1930s?

WELTY: It was a matter of setting the stage and confining the story. These are both family stories, and I didn't want them inhibited by outward events I couldn't control. In the case of *Delta Wedding,* I remember I made a careful investigation to find the year in which nothing very terrible had happened in the Delta by way of floods or fires or wars which would have taken the men away. I settled it by the almanac. It was a little inconvenient for me because I myself was only a little girl during the era I was writing about—that's why I let a little girl be the observer of part of it. In the case of *Losing Battles,* I wanted to write about a family who had *nothing.* A bare stage. I chose the time that was the very hardest, when people had the least and the stage could be the barest—and that was the Depression, of course.

INTERVIEWER: Do you prefer working with a bare stage?

WELTY: In this case, it was in order to overcrowd it with people. I start with ideas about character and situation, and the technique grows out of these as I grow into the work. It's different, of course, for every story. In *Losing Battles* I wanted to write about people who had nothing at all and yet had all the resources of their own character and situation to do what they could about their lives.

INTERVIEWER: Were you familiar with plantation life when you wrote *Delta Wedding?*

WELTY: No, but I had some friends who came from there,

and I used to hear their stories, and I'd be taken on picnics and visits there. Family visits. The Delta is very rich and visually striking, but completely flat. I would find it maddening after days with nothing but the horizon. Just before you reach it, there are high bluffs, and to get in you plunge down a deep hill, and from then on there's nothing but flatness. Some of the things I saw and heard began to stick. Some family tales and sayings are right in the book, though by now I can't remember which are true and which are made up.

INTERVIEWER: John Crowe Ransom wrote in a review that *Delta Wedding* might well be "one of the last novels in the tradition of the Old South."

WELTY: I revere Mr. Ransom, but his meaning here is not quite clear to me. I wasn't trying to write a novel of the Old South. I don't think of myself as writing out of any special tradition, and I'd hesitate to accept that sanction for *Delta Wedding.* I'd hesitate still more today because the term itself, "Old South," has a connotation of something unreal and not quite straightforward.

INTERVIEWER: Your parents weren't from the Deep South originally. Do you think that contributed to your ironic perspective?

WELTY: It may have given me balance. But other factors mattered more. My father's father owned a farm in southern Ohio, and my mother's father was a country lawyer and farmer in West Virginia, and both my mother's parents came from Virginia families made up mostly of teachers and preachers. Some of these wrote for newspapers or kept journals, though none wrote fiction. But the family influence I felt came from the important fact that they all loved to read and that I was brought up with books. Yet my parents would have been the people they were, people of character, no matter where they were from, and I would have been their child wherever I was born. I'm a native southerner, but as a writer I think background matters most in how well it teaches you to look around and see clearly what's there and in how deeply it nourishes your imagination.

INTERVIEWER: "Where is the Voice Coming From?" is about the Medgar Evers assassination and must be your only topical story.

WELTY: I'm certain it is. It pushed up through something else I was working on. I had been having a feeling of uneasiness over the things being written about the South at that time because most of them were done in other parts of the country, and I thought most were synthetic. They were perfectly well-intentioned stories but generalities written from a distance to illustrate generalities. When that murder was committed, it suddenly crossed my consciousness that I knew what was in that man's mind because I'd lived all my life where it happened. It was the strangest feeling of horror and compulsion all in one. I tried to write from the interior of my own South, and that's why I dared to put it in the first person. The title isn't very good; I'd like to get a better one. At the time I wrote it—it was overnight—no one knew who the murderer was, and I just meant by the title that whoever was speaking, I—the writer—knew, was in a position to know, what the murderer must be saying and why.

INTERVIEWER: Do real events hinder you in writing?

WELTY: Well, if you write about an actual event, you can't shape it the way you can an imaginary one. In "The Voice" I was writing about the real thing, and at the point of its happening. I was like a real-life detective trying to discover who did it. I don't mean the name of the murderer but his *nature.* That's not really a short-story writer's prerogative, or is it? Anyway, as events went to prove, I think I came close to pinpointing the mind, but I went a bit wide of the mark in placing the social background of the person arrested for it. As a friend of mine said, "You thought it was a Snopes, and it was a Compson." However, in some ways, that isn't a very lasting distinction anymore.

INTERVIEWER: Do you see a difference between your early stories in *A Curtain of Green* and *The Wide Net* where you deal more with the grotesque and grim than you do in *The Bride of the Innisfallen?*

WELTY: It's a difference not really in subject matter so much as in the ways I approached it. In those early stories I'm sure I needed the device of what you call the "grotesque." That is, I hoped to differentiate characters by their physical qualities as a way of showing what they were like inside—it seemed to me then the most direct way to do it. This is an afterthought, though. I don't suppose I did it as consciously as all that, and I didn't know it was the easiest way. But it is easier to show somebody as lonely if you make him deaf and dumb than if you go feeling your way into his mind. And there was another reason for making the boy in "First Love" a deaf character: one of the other characters—Aaron Burr—was a real person. I couldn't invent conversation for him as I could for an imaginary character, so I had him speak in front of a deaf boy who could report and interpret him in his own way—that is, to suit the story. It's instinctive for a writer to show acute feeling or intense states of emotion by translating it into something visible—red hair, if nothing else. But it's not necessary. I believe I'm writing about the same inward things now without resorting to such obvious devices. But all devices—and the use of symbols is another—must come about organically, out of the story. I feel emphatic about that.

INTERVIEWER: Are you also talking here about other early stories like "Lily Daw and the Three Ladies" and "Petrified Man"?

WELTY: Well, when I wrote my first stories, I wrote much faster, and it failed to occur to me that I could write them any other way, and perhaps better the second time. They show all the weaknesses of the headlong. I never rewrote, I just wrote. The plots in these stories are weak because I didn't know enough to worry about plots. In the dialogue stories, they came into being exactly as the dialogue led them along. I didn't realize their real weakness until I began reading stories in public—and my ear told me. They could have been made stronger so easily. Sometimes I fixed them up a little for my readings—cut, transposed—small things, just to see the difference.

INTERVIEWER: What inspired "Powerhouse"?

WELTY: I wrote it in one night after I'd been to a concert and dance in Jackson where Fats Waller played. I tried to write my idea of the life of the traveling artist and performer—not Fats Waller himself, but any artist—in the alien world and tried to put it in the words and plot suggested by the music I'd been listening to. It was a daring attempt for a writer like me—as daring as it was to write about the murderer of Medgar Evers on *that* night—and I'm not qualified to write about music or performers. But trying it pleased me then, and it still does please me.

INTERVIEWER: Are there problems with ending a story?

WELTY: Not so far, but I could have made mistakes without knowing it yet. It's really part of plotting to know the exact moment you're through. I go by my ear, and this may trick me. When I read, I hear what's on the page. I don't know whose voice it is, but some voice is reading to me, and when I write my own stories, I hear it, too. I have a visual mind, and I *see* everything I write, but I have to hear the words when they're put down. Oh, that sounds absurd. This is not the same as working with dialogue, which of course is another, specialized, kind of hearing.

INTERVIEWER: Your first stories were about Paris.

WELTY: It's not worth remembering. That was when I was a college freshman, sixteen years old. Oh, you know, I was writing about the great world, of which I only knew Jackson, Mississippi. But part of it stemmed from my sense of mystery in people and places, and that's legitimate and lifelong. As for

Paris, I remember a sentence I opened one story with, to show you how bad I was: "Monsieur Boule inserted a delicate dagger in Mademoiselle's left side and departed with a poised immediacy." I like to think I didn't take myself seriously then, but I did.

INTERVIEWER: When you sent out "Death of a Traveling Salesman," how did you know you had ended your apprenticeship?

WELTY: I was just beginning it! I was thrilled to find that out. I hadn't conceived of a story's actually being taken. A boy up the street, an old friend, Hubert Creekmore, who's dead now, knew all about sending stories out. He was a writer who started before I did and published many good novels and poems. I wouldn't let him read anything I wrote but just asked him, "Hubert, do you know where I can send this?"—and he said to John Rood of *Manuscript*. So I sent it off, and John Rood took it, and of course I was flabbergasted. So was Hubert! I believe I've always been lucky—my work has always landed safely and among friends.

INTERVIEWER: You were lucky to escape the novel-first requirement that publishers seem to impose upon young writers. They're wary of short-story collections.

WELTY: I owe that to John Woodburn, my first editor, who was then at Doubleday, and to Diarmuid Russell, my agent and friend of many years now. I owe it to my nature, too, because I never wrote anything that didn't spring naturally to mind and engage my imagination.

INTERVIEWER: Compared to your stories, I see your novels as looser, freer, happier works that enjoy reconciliations and a final sense of communion.

WELTY: My natural temperament is one of positive feelings, and I really do work for resolution in a story. I don't think we often see life resolving itself, not in any sort of perfect way, but I like the fiction writer's feeling of being able to confront an experience and resolve it as art, however imperfectly and briefly—to give it a form and try to embody it—to hold it and express it in a story's terms. You have more chance to try it in a novel. A short story is confined to one mood, to which everything in the story pertains. Characters, setting, time, events, are all subject to the mood. And you can try more ephemeral, more fleeting things in a story—you can work more by suggestion—than in a novel. Less is resolved, more is suggested, perhaps.

INTERVIEWER: You reserve the short story for the ephemeral and the novel for the resolution?

WELTY: I can only say such things after the fact. If I'd known I was going to finish *Losing Battles* as a long novel, I don't know that I'd have begun it. I'm a short-story writer who writes novels the hard way, and by accident. You see, all my work grows out of the work itself. It seems to set its form from the idea, which is complete from the start, and a sense of the form is like a vase into which you pour something and fill it up. I have that completely in mind from the beginning, and I don't realize how far I can wander and yet come back. The flexibility and freedom are exciting to me, not being used to them, and they are hard to come by. But no one could have enjoyed more learning those lessons than I did. There's no end to what can be tried, is there? So better luck next time.

INTERVIEWER: Do you think critics have made too much of you as a regional writer, taking off from your own essays on the subject?

WELTY: I don't mind being called a regional writer. It's the critic's job to place and judge. But the critic can't really have a say in what a writer chooses to write about—that's the writer's lone responsibility. I just think of myself as writing about human beings, and I happen to live in a region, as do we all, so I write about what I know—it's the same case for any writer living anywhere. I also happen to love my particular region. If this shows, I don't mind.

INTERVIEWER: Is place your source of inspiration?

WELTY: Not only that, it's my source of knowledge. It tells me the important things. It steers me and keeps me going straight, because place is a definer and a confiner of what I'm doing. It helps me to identify, to recognize and explain. It does so much for you of itself. It saves me. Why, you couldn't write a story that happened nowhere. *I* couldn't, anyway. I couldn't write anything that abstract. I wouldn't be interested in anything that abstract.

INTERVIEWER: How about the function of place in "No Place for You, My Love"?

WELTY: That story is the one that place did the most for. It really wrote the story. I saw that setting only one time—the Delta of the Mississippi River itself, down below New Orleans where it winds toward the Gulf—one time only. Which smote me. It started the story and made it for me—and *was* the story, really. At its very least, place is essential, though. Time and place make the framework that any story's built on. To my mind, a fiction writer's honesty begins right there, in being true to those two facts of time and place. From there, imagination can take him anywhere at all.

You can equally well be true, I feel, to an *impression* of place. A new place seen in a flash may have an impact almost as strong as the place you've grown up in, one you're familiar with down to the bone and know what it's like without having to think. I've written about place from either one extreme or the other but not from partial familiarity or guessing—there's no solidity there.

INTERVIEWER: "Music from Spain" takes place in San Francisco.

WELTY: That's using impression of place. I was in San Francisco for only three or four months—that's seeing it in a flash. That story was all a response to a place, an act of love at first sight. It's written from the point of view of the stranger, of course—the only way to write about a strange place. On the other hand, I couldn't write a story laid in New York, where I've come so many times—because it's both familiar and unfamiliar, a no-man's-land.

INTERVIEWER: Where is Morgana, in *The Golden Apples*?

WELTY: It's a made-up Delta town. I was drawn to the name because I always loved the conception of fata morgana—the illusory shape, the mirage that comes over the sea. All Delta places have names after people, so it was suitable to call it Morgana after some Morgans. My population might not have known there was such a thing as fata morgana, but illusions weren't unknown to them, all the same—coming in over the cottonfields.

INTERVIEWER: Do you see a similarity between Miss Eckhart in *The Golden Apples* and Julia Mortimer in *Losing Battles*, both being schoolteachers who were civilizing agents and therefore outsiders?

WELTY: It doesn't have to be "therefore"—though mine were indeed outsiders. I suppose they are kin, but teachers like those are all over the South and maybe everywhere else, too—dedicated, and losing their battles, but not losing them every time. I went all through grammar school in Jackson under a principal all of us who went there still remember and talk about—Miss Lorena Duling. This isn't to say I based my character on her, but she gave me insight into what it meant to be a great teacher. And so was my mother one. All her teaching was done by the time I came along, but she told me stories about it. She taught in the little mountain schools in West Virginia, riding to her school on horseback and crossing the river in a boat, teaching children older than she was—she started at fifteen. I think it was my mother who made seventeen silver dollars the first month she taught, and after that they never could quite come up to that high a standard—which also happened to Miss Julia Mortimer. The shaping influence of teachers like that stays real for a lifetime.

INTERVIEWER: I see another group of characters forming a pattern in your work. Virgie Rainey, in *The Golden Apples*, is an individualist and outsider and similar in that respect to Robbie Reid of *Delta Wedding* and Gloria Short of *Losing Battles.*

WELTY: In looking back I can see the pattern. It's funny—when I'm writing, I never see a repeat I make in large or small degree. I learn about it later. In Jackson they were recently doing a play of *The Ponder Heart* when I had just finished writing *Losing Battles.* The new novel was so fresh in my mind, whereas I hadn't thought of *The Ponder Heart* for years. But when I sat in at rehearsals, I kept seeing bits and pieces come up that I thought I had invented for *Losing Battles,* and there they were in another version in *Ponder Heart.* So I thought, it's sort of dismaying, but there it is. Your mind works that way. Yet they occur to me as new every time.

INTERVIEWER: Do you write when you're away from home?

WELTY: I've found it possible to write almost anywhere I've happened to try. I like it at home better because it's much more convenient for an early riser, which I am. And it's the only place where you can really promise yourself time and keep out interruptions. My ideal way to write a short story is to write the whole first draft through in one sitting, then work as long as it takes on revisions, and then write the final version all in one, so that in the end the whole thing amounts to one long sustained effort. That's not possible anywhere, but it comes nearest to being possible in your own home.

INTERVIEWER: Do you typewrite?

WELTY: Yes, and that's useful—it helps give me the feeling of making my work objective. I can correct better if I see it in typescript. After that, I revise with scissors and pins. Pasting is too slow, and you can't undo it, but with pins you can move things from anywhere to anywhere, and that's what I really love doing—putting things in their best and proper place, revealing things at the time when they matter most. Often I shift things from the very beginning to the very end. Small things—one fact, one word—but things important to me. It's possible I have a reverse mind and do things backwards, being a broken left-hander. Just so I've caught on to my weakness.

INTERVIEWER: You rewrite considerably?

WELTY: Yes, I do. Some things I let alone from first to last— the kernel of the story. You know enough not to touch something if it's right. The hardest thing for me is getting people in and out of rooms—the mechanics of a story. A simple act of putting on clothes is almost impossible for me to describe without many false starts. You have to be quick and specific in conveying that sort of action or fact, and also as neat and quiet about it as possible so that it doesn't obtrude. And I find that very challenging, especially to describe an action that I don't do very well myself, like sewing. I made Aunt Lexie in *Losing Battles* a poor sewer so that I wouldn't have to describe it too well. The easiest things to write about are emotions.

INTERVIEWER: And yet the most difficult thing would seem to be the hidden reaches of the human heart, the mystery, those impalpable emotions.

WELTY: For a writer those things are what you start with. You wouldn't have started a story without that awareness— that's what made you begin. That's what makes a character, projects the plot. Because you write from the inside. You can't start with how people look and speak and behave and come to know how they feel. You must know exactly what's in their hearts and minds before they ever set visible foot on the stage. You must know all, then not tell it all, or not tell too much at once: simply the right thing at the right moment. And the same character would be written about entirely differently in a novel as opposed to a short story. In a story you don't go into a character in order to develop him. He was born full grown, and he's present there to perform his part in the story. He's subservient to his function, and he doesn't exist outside it. But in a novel, he may. So you may have to allow for his growth and maybe hold him down and not tell everything you know, or else let him have his full sway—make room for a hero, even, in more spacious premises.

INTERVIEWER: Can you talk objectively about your language, perhaps about your use of metaphor?

WELTY: I don't know how to because I think of the actual writing as having existence only in the story. When I think of something, I put it into a narrative form, not in analytical form, and so anything I say would be artificial. Which reminds me of an Armenian friend of mine, an artist, who told me that his dreams all happened in the same place. When he went to bed, he'd imagine himself on a sled going down a steep hill; at the foot of the hill was a little town, and by the time he reached it, he was asleep, and his dreams happened right there. He didn't know why or how. And to go to the ridiculous and yet the sublime, there's W. C. Fields, who read an analysis of how he juggled. He couldn't juggle for six years afterwards. He'd never known that was how it was done. He'd just thrown up the balls and juggled.

—LINDA KUEHL

1972

ELIZABETH BISHOP

Elizabeth Bishop's father died eight months after her birth in April 1911. Her mother subsequently suffered a mental breakdown, and although she lived until 1934, her daughter, only five, saw her for the last time in 1916. The young girl was juggled from relative to relative until her boarding-school years, a circumstance that may explain the importance of travel to both her life and her poetry. While she was at Vassar College she published work in *Hound & Horn* and the college literary magazines. She graduated in 1934 with a degree in music and aspired to become a composer, but that same year she met Marianne Moore, who encouraged her to continue writing poetry and was to remain an important influence on Bishop's work. *Partisan Review* published her story "In Prison" in 1938, and *The New Yorker* published her poem "Cirque d'Hiver" in 1939. Her first collection, *North & South*, published in 1946, won the Houghton Mifflin Poetry Award. In 1956 she won the Pulitzer Prize for her second collection, *Poems*, and in 1969 she won the National Book Award for *The Complete Poems*, a volume titled with her characteristic irony. Bishop became the first woman and the first American to win the prestigious Neustadt International Prize for Literature in April 1976. Her last volume of poetry, *Geography III*, published the following December, won the Book Critics' Circle Award.

Bishop lived at various times in New York, Boston, Key West and Brazil, which she visited in 1951, intending to stay two weeks; in fact she remained for over fifteen years—the first truly happy period of her life, she said—living with Lota de Macedo Soares until her friend's suicide in 1967. After Lota's death Bishop held poet-in-residence posts at numerous universities; she had been on the verge of beginning a new semester at MIT when she died suddenly on October 6, 1979.

ELIZABETH BISHOP

The interview took place at Lewis Wharf, Boston, on the afternoon of June 28, 1978, three days before Miss Bishop and two friends were to leave for North Haven, a Maine island in Penobscot Bay where she summered. Her living room, on the fourth floor of Lewis Wharf, had a spectacular view of Boston Harbor; when I arrived, she immediately took me out on the balcony to point out such Boston landmarks as Old North Church in the distance, mentioning that Old Ironsides was moored nearby.

Her living room was spacious and attractive, with wide-planked polished floors, a beamed ceiling, two old brick walls, and one wall of books. Besides some comfortable modern furniture, the room included a jacaranda rocker and other old pieces from Brazil, two paintings by Loren MacIver, a giant horse conch from Key West and a Franklin stove with firewood in a donkey pannier, also from Brazil. The most conspicuous piece was a large carved figurehead of an unknown beast, openmouthed, with horns and blue eyes, which hung on one wall below the ceiling.

Her study, a smaller room down the hall, was in a state of disorder. Literary magazines, books and papers were piled everywhere. Photographs of Marianne Moore, Robert Lowell and other friends hung on the walls; one of Dom Pedro, the last emperor of Brazil, she especially liked to show to her

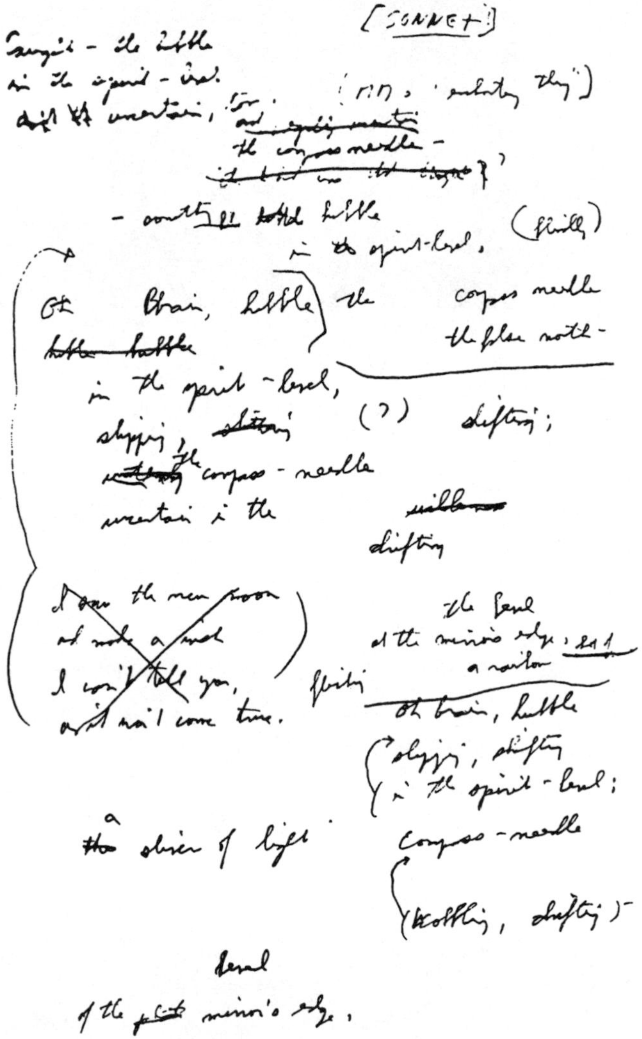
[SONNET]
in the spirit-level
the compass-needle
in the spirit-level.
Oh Brain, bubble
compass needle
in the spirit-level,
(?)
drifting;
compass-needle
uncertain in the
drifting
the bevel
of the mirror's edge
Oh brain, bubble
slipping, shifting
in the spirit-level;
compass-needle
drifting
a slice of light
bevel
of the mirror's edge.

A manuscript page from Elizabeth Bishop's "Sonnet," 1979.

Brazilian visitors. "Most have no idea who he is," she said. "This is after he abdicated and shortly before he died—he looked very sad." Her desk was tucked in a far corner by the only window, also with a north view of the harbor.

At sixty-seven, Miss Bishop was striking, her short, swept-back white hair setting off an unforgettably noble face. She was wearing a black tunic shirt, gold watch and earrings, gray slacks, and flat brown Japanese sandals that made her appear shorter than her actual height: five feet, four inches. Although she looked well and was in high spirits, she complained of having had a recent hay fever attack and declined to have her photograph taken with the wry comment "Photographers, insurance salesmen, and funeral directors are the worst forms of life."

Seven or eight months later, after reading a profile I had written for The Vassar Quarterly *(which had been based on this interview) and worrying that she sounded like "the soul of frivolity," she wrote me: "I once admired an interview with Fred Astaire in which he refused to discuss 'the dance,' his partners, or his 'career' and stuck determinedly to golf—so I hope that some readers will realize I do think about art once in a while even if babbling along like a very shallow brook . . ."*

Though Miss Bishop did have the opportunity of correcting those portions of this interview incorporated in the Vassar Quarterly *article, she never saw it in this form.*

◆◆

INTERVIEWER: Your living room seems to be a wonderful combination of the old and new. Is there a story behind any of the pieces, especially that figurehead? It's quite imposing.

BISHOP: I lived in an extremely modern house in Brazil. It was very beautiful, and when I finally moved I brought back things I liked best. So it's just a kind of mixture. I really like modern things, but while I was there I acquired so many other things I couldn't bear to give them up. This figurehead is from the São Francisco River. Some are more beautiful; this is a very ugly one.

INTERVIEWER: Is it supposed to ward off evil spirits?

BISHOP: Yes, I think so. They were used for about fifty years on one section, two or three hundred miles, of the river. It's nothing compared to the Amazon but it's the next biggest river in Brazil. This figurehead is primitive folk art. I think I even know who made it. There was a black man who carved twenty or thirty, and it's exactly his style. Some of them are made of much more beautiful wood. There's a famous one called the Red Horse made of jacaranda. It's beautiful, a great thing like this one, a horse with its mouth open, but for some reason they all just disappeared. I made a weeklong trip on that river in 1967 and didn't see one. The riverboat, a sternwheeler, had been built in 1880—something for the Mississippi, and you can't believe how tiny it was. We splashed along slowly for days and days . . . a very funny trip.

INTERVIEWER: Did you spend so much of your life traveling because you were looking for a perfect place?

BISHOP: No, I don't think so. I really haven't traveled that much. It just happened that although I wasn't rich I had a very small income from my father, who died when I was eight months old, and it was enough when I got out of college to go places on. And I traveled extremely cheaply. I could get along in Brazil for some years but now I couldn't possibly live on it. But the biographical sketch in the first anthology I was in said, "Oh, she's been to Morocco, Spain, etc.," and this has been repeated for years even though I haven't been back to any of these places. But I never traveled the way students travel now. Compared to my students, who seem to go to Nepal every Easter vacation, I haven't been anywhere at all.

INTERVIEWER: Well, it always sounds as if you're very adventurous.

BISHOP: I want to do the Upper Amazon. Maybe I will. You start from Peru and go down—

INTERVIEWER: Do you write when you're actually traveling?

BISHOP: Yes, sometimes. It depends. I usually take notes but not always. And I keep a kind of diary. The two trips I've made that I liked best were the Amazon trip and one to the Galapagos Islands three or four years ago . . . I'd like very much to go back to Italy again because I haven't seen nearly enough of it. And Sicily. Venice is wonderful. Florence is rather strenuous, I think. I was last there in '64 with my Brazilian friend. We rented a car and did northern Italy for five or six weeks. We didn't go to Rome. I *must* go back. There are so many things I haven't seen yet. I like painting probably better than I like poetry. And I haven't been back to Paris for years. I don't like the prices!

INTERVIEWER: You mentioned earlier that you're leaving for North Haven in several days. Will this be a "working vacation"?

BISHOP: This summer I want to do a lot of work because I really haven't done anything for ages and there are a couple of things I'd like to finish before I die. Two or three poems and two long stories. Maybe three. I sometimes feel that I shouldn't keep going back to this place that I found just by chance through an ad in the Harvard *Crimson.* I should probably go to see some more art, cathedrals, and so on. But I'm so crazy about it that I keep going back. You can see the water, a great expanse of water and fields from the house. Islands are beautiful. Some of them come right up, granite, and then dark firs. North Haven isn't like that exactly, but it's very beautiful. The island is sparsely inhabited and a lot of the people who have homes there are fearfully rich. Probably if it weren't for these people the island would be deserted the way a great many Maine islands are, because the village is very tiny. But the inhabitants almost all work—they're lobstermen but they work as caretakers. . . . The electricity there is rather sketchy. Two summers ago it was one hour on, one hour off. There I was with *two* electric typewriters and I couldn't keep working. There was a cartoon in the grocery store—it's eighteen miles from the mainland—a man in a hardware store saying, "I want an extension cord eighteen miles long!" Last year they did plug into the mainland—they put in cables. But once in a while the power still goes off.

INTERVIEWER: So you compose on the typewriter?

BISHOP: I can write prose on a typewriter. Not poetry. Nobody can read my writing so I write letters on it. And I've finally trained myself so I can write prose on it and then correct a great deal. But for poetry I use a pen. About halfway through sometimes I'll type out a few lines to see how they look.

William Carlos Williams wrote entirely on the typewriter. Robert Lowell printed—he never learned to write. He printed everything.

INTERVIEWER: You've never been as prolific as many of your contemporaries. Do you start a lot of poems and finish very few?

BISHOP: Yes. Alas, yes. I begin lots of things and then I give up on them. The last few years I haven't written as much because of teaching. I'm hoping that now that I'm free and have a Guggenheim I'll do a lot more.

INTERVIEWER: How long did it take you to finish "The Moose"?

BISHOP: That was funny. I started that *years* ago—twenty years ago, at least—I had a stack of notes, the first two or three stanzas, and the last.

INTERVIEWER: It's such a dreamy poem. It seems to move the way a bus moves.

BISHOP: It was all true. The bus trip took place before I went to Brazil. I went up to visit my aunt. Actually, I was on the wrong bus. I went to the right place but it wasn't the express I was supposed to get. It went roundabout and it was all exactly the way I described it, except that I say "seven relatives." Well, they weren't really relatives, they were various stepsons and so on, but that's the only thing that isn't quite true. I wanted to finish it because I liked it, but I could never seem to get the middle part, to get from one place to the other. And then when I was still living in Cambridge I was asked to give the Phi Beta Kappa poem at Harvard. I was rather pleased and I remembered that I had another unfinished poem. It's about whales and it was written a long time ago, too. I'm afraid I'll never publish it because it looks as if I were just trying to be up-to-date now that whales are a "cause."

INTERVIEWER: But it's finished now?

BISHOP: I think I could finish it very easily. I'm going to take it to Maine with me. I think I'll date it or nobody will believe I started it so long ago. At the time, though, I couldn't find the one about whales—this was in '73 or '74, I think—so I dug out "The Moose" and thought, "Maybe I can finish it," and I did. The day of the ceremony for Phi Beta Kappa (which I'd never made in college) we were all sitting on the platform at Sanders Theater. And the man who had asked me to give the poem leaned across the president and said to me whispering, "What is the name of your poem?" I said, "'The Moose,' M-o-o-s-e," and he got up and introduced me and said, "Miss Bishop will now read a poem called 'The *Moos*.'" Well, I choked and my hat was too big. And later the newspaper account read, "Miss Bishop read a poem called 'The Moose' and the tassle of her mortarboard swung back and forth over her face like a windshield wiper"!

The Glee Club was behind us and they sang rather badly, I thought, everybody thought. A friend of mine who couldn't come to this occasion but worked in one of the Harvard houses and knew some of the boys in the Glee Club asked one of them when they came back in their red jackets, "Well, how was it?" He said, "Oh, it was all right but we didn't sing well"—which was true—and then he said, "A woman read a poem." My friend said, "How was it?" And he said, "Well, as poems go, it wasn't bad"!

INTERVIEWER: Have you ever had any poems that were gifts? Poems that seemed to write themselves?

BISHOP: Oh yes. Once in a while it happens. I wanted to write a villanelle all my life but I never could. I'd start them but for some reason I never could finish them. And one day I couldn't believe it—it was like writing a letter.* There was one rhyme I couldn't get that ended in e-n-t and a friend of mine, the poet Frank Bidart, came to see me and I said, "Frank, give me a rhyme." He gave me a word offhand and I put it in. But neither he nor I can remember which word it was. But that kind of thing doesn't happen very often. Maybe some poets always write that way. I don't know.

INTERVIEWER: Didn't you used to give Marianne Moore rhymes?

BISHOP: Yes, when she was doing the La Fontaine translations. She'd call me up and read me something when I was in New York—I was in Brazil most of that time—and say she needed a rhyme. She said that she admired rhymes and meters very much. It was hard to tell whether she was pulling your leg or not sometimes. She was Celtic enough to be somewhat mysterious about these things.

INTERVIEWER: Critics often talk about your more recent poems being less formal, more "open," so to speak. They point out that *Geography III* has more of "you" in it, a wide emotional range. Do you agree with these perceptions?

BISHOP: This is what critics say. I've never written the things I'd like to write that I've admired all my life. Maybe one never does. Critics say the most incredible things!

INTERVIEWER: I've been reading a critical book about you that Anne Stevenson wrote. She said that in your poems nature was neutral.

BISHOP: Yes, I remember the word "neutral." I wasn't quite sure what she meant by that.

---

*The poem is "One Art," in *Geography III*

INTERVIEWER: I thought she might have meant that if nature is neutral there isn't any guiding spirit or force.

BISHOP: Somebody famous—I can't think who it was—somebody extremely famous was asked if he had one question to ask the Sphinx and get an answer, what would it be? And he said, "Is nature for us or against us?" Well, I've never really thought about it one way or the other. I like the country, the seashore especially, and if I could drive, I'd probably be living in the country. Unfortunately, I've never learned to drive. I bought two cars. At least. I had an MG I adored for some years in Brazil. We lived on top of a mountain peak, and it took an hour to get somewhere where I could practice. And nobody really had time to take an afternoon off and give me driving lessons. So I never got my license. And I *never* would have driven in Rio, anyway. But if you can't drive, you can't live in the country.

INTERVIEWER: Do you have the painting here that your uncle did? The one "about the size of an old-style dollar bill" that you wrote about in "Poem"?

BISHOP: Oh, sure. Do you want to see it? It's not good enough to hang. Actually, he was my great-uncle. I never met him.

INTERVIEWER: The cows in this really are just one or two brushstrokes!

BISHOP: I exaggerated a little bit. There's a detail in the poem that isn't in the painting. I can't remember what it is now. My uncle did another painting when he was fourteen or fifteen years old that I wrote about in an early poem ["Large Bad Picture"]. An aunt who lived in Montreal had both of these and they used to hang in her front hall. I was dying to get them and I went there once and tried to buy them, but she wouldn't sell them to me. She was rather stingy. She died some years ago. I don't know who has the large one now.

INTERVIEWER: When you were showing me your study, I noticed a shadow box hanging in the hall. Is it by Joseph Cornell?

BISHOP: No, I did that one. That's one of my little works. It's about infant mortality in Brazil. It's called *anjinhos*, which means "little angels." That's what they call the babies and small children who die.

INTERVIEWER: What's the significance of the various objects?

BISHOP: I found the child's sandal on a beach wading east of Rio one Christmas and I finally decided to do something with it. The pacifier was bright red rubber. They sell them in big bottles and jars in drugstores in Brazil. I decided it couldn't be red, so I dyed it black with India ink. A nephew of my Brazilian friend, a very smart young man, came to call while I was doing this. He brought two American rock-and-roll musicians and we talked and talked and talked, and I never thought to explain in all the time they were there what I was doing. When they left, I thought, My God, they must think I'm a witch or something!

INTERVIEWER: What about the little bowls and skillets filled with rice?

BISHOP: Oh, they're just things children would be playing with. And of course rice and black beans are what Brazilians eat every day.

Cornell is superb. I first saw the *Medici Slot Machine* when I was in college. Oh, I loved it. To think one could have *bought* some of those things then. He was very strange. He got crushes on opera singers and ballet dancers. When I looked at his show in New York two years ago I nearly fainted, because one of my favorite books is a book he liked and used. It's a little book by an English scientist who wrote for children about soap bubbles [*Soap Bubbles; their colours and the forces which mold them*, by Sir C. V. Boys, 1889].

His sister began writing me after she read Octavio Paz's poem for Cornell that I translated. (She doesn't read Spanish.) She sent me a German-French grammar that apparently he meant to do something with and never did. A lot of the pages were folded over and they're all made into star patterns with red ink around them. . . . He lived in what was called Elysian Park. That's an awfully strange address to have.

INTERVIEWER: Until recently you were one of the few American poets who didn't make their living teaching or giving readings. What made you decide to start doing both?

BISHOP: I never wanted to teach in my life. I finally did because I wanted to leave Brazil and I needed the money. Since 1970 I've just been *swamped* with people sending me poems. They start to when they know you're in the country. I used to get them in Brazil, but not so much. They got lost in the mail quite often. I don't believe in teaching poetry at all, but that's what they want one to do. You see so many poems every week, you just lose all sense of judgment.

As for readings, I gave a reading in 1947 at Wellesley College two months after my first book appeared. And I was *sick* for days ahead of time. Oh, it was absurd. And then I did one in Washington in '49 and I was sick again and nobody could hear me. And then I didn't give any for twenty-six years. I don't mind reading now. I've gotten over my shyness a little bit. I think teaching helps. I've noticed that teachers aren't shy. They're rather aggressive. They get to be, finally.

INTERVIEWER: Did you ever take a writing course as a student?

BISHOP: When I went to Vassar I took sixteenth-century, seventeenth-century and eighteenth-century literature, and then a course in the novel. The kind of courses where you have to do a lot of reading. I don't think I believe in writing courses at all. There weren't any when I was there. There was a poetry-writing course in the evening, but not for credit. A couple of my friends went to it, but I never did.

The word "creative" drives me crazy. I don't like to regard it as therapy. I was in the hospital several years ago and somebody gave me Kenneth Koch's book, *Rose, Where Did You Get That Red?*

And it's true, children sometimes write wonderful things, paint wonderful pictures, but I think they should be *dis*couraged. From everything I've read and heard, the number of students in English departments taking literature courses has been falling off enormously. But at the same time the number of people who want to get in the writing classes seems to get bigger and bigger. There are usually two or three being given at Harvard every year. I'd get forty applicants for ten or twelve places. Fifty. It got bigger and bigger. I don't know if they do this to offset practical concerns, or what.

INTERVIEWER: I think people want to be able to say they do something creative like throw pots or write poems.

BISHOP: I just came back in March from reading in North Carolina and Arkansas, and I swear if I see any more handcrafts I'll go mad! I think we should go right straight back to the machine. You can only use so many leather belts, after all. I'm sorry. Maybe you do some of these things.

INTERVIEWER: Do many strangers send you poems?

BISHOP: Yes. It's very hard to know what to do. Sometimes I answer. I had a fan letter the other day, and it was adorable. It was in this childish handwriting. His name was Jimmy Sparks and he was in the sixth grade. He said his class was putting together a booklet of poems and he liked my poems very much—he mentioned three—because they rhymed and because they were about nature. His letter was so cute I did send him a postcard. I think he was supposed to ask me to send a handwritten poem or photograph—schools do this all the time—but he didn't say anything like that, and I'm sure he forgot his mission.

INTERVIEWER: What three poems did he like? "The Sandpiper"?

BISHOP: Yes, and the one about the mirror and the moon, "Insomnia," which Marianne Moore said was a cheap love poem.

INTERVIEWER: The one that ends, ". . . and you love me"?

BISHOP: Yes. I never liked that. I almost left it out. But last year it was put to music by Elliott Carter along with five other poems of mine* and it sounded much better as a song. Yes, Marianne was very opposed to that one.

INTERVIEWER: Maybe she didn't like the last line.

BISHOP: I don't think she ever believed in talking about the emotions much.

INTERVIEWER: Getting back to teaching, did you devise formal assignments when you taught at Harvard? For example, to write a villanelle?

BISHOP: Yes, I made out a whole list of weekly assignments that I gave the class; but every two or three weeks was a free assignment and they could hand in what they wanted. Some classes were so prolific that I'd declare a moratorium. I'd say, "Please, nobody write a poem for two weeks!"

INTERVIEWER: Do you think you can generalize that beginning writers write better in forms than not?

BISHOP: I don't know. We did a sestina—we started one in class by drawing words out of a hat—and I wish I'd never suggested it because it seemed to have *swept* Harvard. Later, in the applications for my class, I'd get dozens of sestinas. The students seemed to think it was my favorite form—which it isn't.

INTERVIEWER: I once tried a sestina about a woman who watches soap operas all day.

BISHOP: Did you watch them in college?

INTERVIEWER: No.

BISHOP: Well, it seemed to be a fad at Harvard. Two or three years ago I taught a course in prose and discovered my students were watching the soap operas every morning and afternoon. I don't know when they studied. So I watched two or three just to see what was going on. They were *boring*. And the advertising!

---

*"Anaphora," "The Sandpiper," "Argument," "O Breath," and "View of the Capitol from The Library of Congress."

One student wrote a story about an old man who was getting ready to have an old lady to dinner (except she was really a ghost), and he polished a plate till he could see his face in it. It was quite well done, so I read some of it aloud, and said, "But look, this is impossible. You can never see your face in a plate." The whole class, in unison, said, "Joy!" I said, "What? What are you talking about?" Well, it seems there's an ad for Joy soap liquid in which a woman holds up a plate and sees—you know the one? Even so, you can't! I found this very disturbing. TV was *real* and no one had observed that it wasn't. Like when Aristotle was right and no one pointed out, for centuries, that women *don't* have fewer teeth than men.

I had a friend bring me a small TV, black-and-white, when I was living in Brazil. We gave it to the maid almost immediately because we watched it only when there were things like political speeches, or a revolution coming on. But she loved it. She slept with it in her bed! I think it meant so much to her because she couldn't read. There was a soap opera that year called *The Right to Life*. It changed the whole schedule of Rio society's hours because it was on from eight to nine. The usual dinner hour's eight, so either you had to eat dinner before so that the maid could watch *The Right to Life* or eat much later, when it was over. We ate dinner about ten o'clock finally so that Joanna could watch this thing. I finally decided I had to see it, too. It became a chic thing to do and everybody was talking about it. It was absolutely ghastly! They got the programs from Mexico and dubbed them in Portuguese. They were very corny and always very lurid. Corpses lying in coffins, miracles, nuns, even incest.

I had friends in Belo Horizonte, and the mother and their cook and a grandchild would watch the soap operas, the *novellas*, they're called, every night. The cook would get so excited she'd talk to the screen: "No! No! Don't do that! You know he's a bad man, Doña So-and-so!" They'd get so excited, they'd cry. And I knew of two old ladies, sisters, who got a TV. They'd knit and knit and watch it and cry and one of them would get up and say "Excuse me, I have to go to the bathroom" to the television!

INTERVIEWER: You were living in Brazil, weren't you, when you won the Pulitzer Prize in 1956?

BISHOP: Yes, it was pretty funny. We lived on top of a mountain peak—really way up in the air. I was alone in the house with Maria, the cook. A friend had gone to market. The telephone rang. It was a newsman from the American embassy and he asked me who it was in English, and of course it was very rare to hear someone speak in English. He said, "Do you know you've won the Pulitzer Prize?" Well, I thought it was a joke. I said, "Oh, come on." And he said, "Don't you hear me?" The telephone connection was very bad and he was shrieking. And I said, "Oh, it can't be." But he said it wasn't a joke. I couldn't make an impression on Maria with this news, but I felt I had to share it, so I hurried down the mountain a half mile or so to the next house, but no one was at home. I thought I should do something to celebrate, have a glass of wine or something. But all I could find in that house, a friend's, were some cookies from America, some awful chocolate cookies—Oreos, I think—so I ended up eating two of those. And that's how I celebrated winning the Pulitzer Prize.

The next day there was a picture in the afternoon paper— they take such things very seriously in Brazil—and the day after that my Brazilian friend went to market again. There was a big covered market with stalls for every kind of comestible, and there was one vegetable man we always went to. He said, "Wasn't that Doña Elizabetchy's picture in the paper yesterday?" She said, "Yes, it was. She won a prize." And he said, "You know, it's amazing! Last week Señora (Somebody) took a chance on a bicycle and *she* won! My customers are so lucky!" Isn't that marvelous?!

INTERVIEWER: I'd like to talk a little bit about your stories, especially "In the Village," which I've always admired. Do you see any connection, other than the obvious one of shared subject matter, between your stories and poems? In "method of attack," for example?

BISHOP: They're very closely related. I suspect that some of the stories I've written are actually prose poems and not very good stories. I have four about Nova Scotia. One came out last year in the *Southern Review.* I'm working on a long one now that I hope to finish this summer. . . . "In the Village" was funny. I had made notes for various bits of it and was given too much cortisone—I have very bad asthma from time to time—and you don't need any sleep. You feel wonderful while it's going on, but to get off it is awful. So I couldn't sleep much and I sat up all night in the tropical heat. The story came from a combination of cortisone, I think, and the gin and tonic I drank in the middle of the night. I wrote it in two nights.

INTERVIEWER: That's incredible! It's a long, long story.

BISHOP: Extraordinary. I wish I could do it again but I'll never take cortisone again, if I can possibly avoid it.

INTERVIEWER: I'm always interested in how different poets go about writing about their childhood.

BISHOP: Everybody does. You can't help it, I suppose. You are fearfully observant then. You notice all kinds of things, but there's no way of putting them all together. My memories of some of those days are so much clearer than things that happened in 1950, say. I don't think one should make a cult of writing about childhood, however. I've always tried to avoid it. I find I have written some, I must say. I went to an analyst for a couple of years off and on in the forties, a very nice woman who was especially interested in writers, writers and blacks. She said it was amazing that I would remember things that happened to me when I was two. It's very rare, but apparently writers often do.

INTERVIEWER: Do you know what your earliest memory is?

BISHOP: I think I remember learning to walk. My mother was away and my grandmother was trying to encourage me to walk. It was in Canada and she had lots of plants in the window the way all ladies do there. I can remember this blur of plants and my grandmother holding out her arms. I must have toddled. It seems to me it's a memory. It's very hazy. I told my grandmother years and years later and she said, "Yes, you did learn to walk while your mother was visiting someone." But you walk when you're one, don't you?

I remember my mother taking me for a ride on the swan boats here in Boston. I think I was three then. It was before we went back to Canada. Mother was dressed all in black— widows were in those days. She had a box of mixed peanuts and raisins. There were real swans floating around. I don't think they have them anymore. A swan came up and she fed it and it bit her finger. Maybe she just told me this, but I believed it because she showed me her black kid glove and said, "See." The finger was split. Well, I was thrilled to death! Robert Lowell put those swan boats in two or three of the *Lord Weary's Castle* poems.

INTERVIEWER: Your childhood was difficult, and yet in many of your stories and poems about that time there's a tremendously lyrical quality as well as a great sense of loss and tragedy.

BISHOP: My father died, my mother went crazy when I was four or five years old. My relatives, I think they all felt so sorry for this child that they tried to do their very best. And I think they did. I lived with my grandparents in Nova Scotia. Then I lived with the ones in Worcester, Massachusetts, very briefly, and got terribly sick. This was when I was six and seven. Then I lived with my mother's older sister in Boston. I used to go to Nova Scotia for the summer. When I was twelve or thirteen I was improved enough to go to summer camp at Wellfleet until I went away to school when I was fifteen or sixteen. My aunt was devoted to me and she was awfully nice. She was married and had no children. But my relationship with my relatives—I was always a sort of a guest, and I think I've always felt like that.

INTERVIEWER: Was your adolescence a calmer time?

BISHOP: I was very romantic. I once walked from Nauset Light—I don't think it exists anymore—which is the beginning of the elbow [of Cape Cod], to the tip, Provincetown, all alone. It took me a night and a day. I went swimming from time to time but at that time the beach was absolutely deserted. There wasn't anything on the back shore, no buildings.

INTERVIEWER: How old would you have been?

BISHOP: Seventeen or eighteen. That's why I'd never go back—because I can't bear to think of the way it is now. . . . I haven't been to Nantucket since—well, I hate to say. My senior year at college I went there for Christmas with my then boyfriend. Nobody knew we were there. It was this wonderful, romantic trip. We went the day after Christmas and stayed for about a week. It was terribly cold but beautiful. We took long walks on the moors. We stayed at a very nice inn and we thought that probably the landlady would throw us out (we were very young and this kind of thing wasn't so common then). We had a bottle of sherry or something innocent like that. On New Year's Eve about ten o'clock there was a knock on the door. It was our landlady with a tray of hot grogs! She came in and we had the loveliest time. She knew the people who ran the museum and they opened it for us. There are a couple of wonderful museums there.

INTERVIEWER: I heard a story that you once spent a night in a tree at Vassar outside Cushing dormitory. Is it true?

BISHOP: Yes, it was me, me and a friend whose name I can't remember. We really were crazy and those trees were wonderful to climb. I used to be a great tree climber. Oh, we probably gave up about three in the morning. How did that ever get around? I can't imagine! We stopped being friends afterwards. Well, actually she had invited two boys from West Point for the weekend and I found myself *stuck* with this youth all in—[her hands draw an imagined cape and uniform in the air]—the dullest boy! I didn't know what to say! I nearly went mad. I think I sort of dropped the friend at that point. . . . I lived in a great big corner room on the top floor of Cushing and I apparently had registered a little late because I had a roommate whom I had never wanted to have. A strange girl named Constance. I remember her entire side of the room was furnished in Scottie dogs—pillows, pictures, engravings and photographs. And mine was rather bare. Except that I probably wasn't a good roommate either, because I had a theory at that time that one should write down all one's dreams. That that was the way to write poetry. So I kept a notebook of my dreams and thought if you ate a lot of awful cheese at bedtime you'd have interesting dreams. I went to Vassar with a pot about this big—it did have a cover!—of Roquefort cheese that I kept in the bottom of my bookcase. . . . I think everyone's given to eccentricities at that age. I've heard that at Oxford Auden slept with a revolver under his pillow.

INTERVIEWER: As a young woman, did you have a sense of yourself as a writer?

BISHOP: No, it all just happens without your thinking about it. I never meant to go to Brazil. I never meant doing any of these things. I'm afraid in my life everything has just *happened.*

INTERVIEWER: You like to think there are reasons—

BISHOP: Yes, that people plan ahead, but I'm afraid I really didn't.

INTERVIEWER: But you'd always been interested in writing?

BISHOP: I'd written since I was a child, but when I went to Vassar I was going to be a composer. I'd studied music at Walnut Hill and had a rather good teacher. I'd had a year of counterpoint and I also played the piano. At Vassar you had to perform in public once a month. Well, this terrified me. I really was sick. So I played once and then I gave up the piano because I couldn't bear it. I don't think I'd mind now, but I can't play the piano anymore. Then the next year I switched to English.

It was a very literary class. Mary McCarthy was a year ahead of me. Eleanor Clark was in my class. And Muriel Rukeyser, for freshman year. We started a magazine you may have heard of, *Con Spirito.* I think I was a junior then. There were six or seven of us—Mary, Eleanor Clark and her older sister, my friends Margaret Miller and Frani Blough, and a couple of others. It was during Prohibition and we used to go downtown to a speakeasy and drink wine out of teacups. That was our big vice. Ghastly stuff! Most of us had submitted things to the *Vassar Review* and they'd been turned down. It was very old-fashioned then. We were all rather put out because *we* thought we were good. So we thought, Well, we'll start our own magazine. We thought it would be nice to have it anonymous, which it was. After its third issue the *Vassar Review* came around and a couple of our editors became editors on it and then they published things by us. But we had a wonderful time doing it while it lasted.

INTERVIEWER: I read in another interview you gave that you had enrolled or were ready to enroll after college in Cornell Medical School.

BISHOP: I think I had all the forms. This was the year after I had graduated from Vassar. But then I discovered I would have to take German and I'd already given up on German once, I thought it was so difficult. And I would have had to take another year of chemistry. I'd already published a few things and I think Marianne [Moore] discouraged me, and I didn't go. I just went off to Europe instead.

INTERVIEWER: Did the Depression have much reality for college students in the thirties?

BISHOP: Everybody was frantic trying to get jobs. All the intellectuals were Communist except me. I'm always very perverse so I went in for T. S. Eliot and Anglo-Catholicism. But the spirit was pretty radical. It's funny. The girl who was the biggest radical—she was a year ahead of me—has been married for years and years to one of the heads of Time-Life. I've forgotten his name. He's very famous and couldn't be more conservative. He writes shocking editorials. I can still see her standing outside the library with a tambourine collecting money for this cause and that cause.

INTERVIEWER: Wanting to be a composer, a doctor or a writer—how do you account for it?

BISHOP: Oh, I was interested in all those things. I'd like to be a painter most, I think. I never really sat down and said to myself, "I'm going to be a poet." Never in my life. I'm still surprised that people think I am. . . . I started publishing things in my senior year, I think, and I remember my first check for thirty-five dollars and that was rather an exciting moment. It was from something called *The Magazine*, published in California. They took a poem, they took a story—oh, I wish those poems had never been published! They're terrible! I did show the check to my roommate. I was on the newspaper, *The Miscellany*—and I really was, I don't know, mysterious. On the newspaper board they used to sit around and talk about how they could get published and so on and so on. I'd just hold my tongue. I was embarrassed by it. And still am. There's nothing more embarrassing than being a poet, really.

INTERVIEWER: It's especially difficult to tell people you're meeting for the first time that that's what you do.

BISHOP: Just last week a friend and I went to visit a wonderful lady I know in Quebec. She's seventy-four or seventy-five. And she didn't say this to me but she said to my friend, Alice, "I'd like to ask my neighbor who has the big house next door to dinner, and she's so nice, but she'd be bound to ask Elizabeth what she does and if Elizabeth said she wrote poetry, the poor woman wouldn't say another word all evening!" This is awful, you know, and I think no matter how modest you think you feel or how minor you think you are, there must be an awful core of ego somewhere for you to set yourself up to write poetry. I've never *felt* it, but it must be there.

INTERVIEWER: In your letter to me, you sounded rather wary of interviewers. Do you feel you've been misrepresented in interviews? For example, that your refusal to appear in all-women poetry anthologies has been misunderstood as a kind of disapproval of the feminist movement.

BISHOP: I've always considered myself a strong feminist. Recently I was interviewed by a reporter from the *Chicago Tribune.* After I talked to the girl for a few minutes, I realized that she wanted to play me off as an "old-fashioned" against Erica Jong, and Adrienne [Rich], whom I like, and other violently feminist people. Which isn't true at all. I finally asked her if she'd ever read any of my poems. Well, it seemed she'd read *one* poem. I didn't see how she could interview me if she didn't know anything about me at all, and I told her so. She was nice enough to print a separate piece in the *Chicago Tribune* apart from the longer article on the others. I had said that I didn't believe in propaganda in poetry. That it rarely worked. What she had me saying was "Miss Bishop does not believe that poetry should convey the poet's personal philosophy." Which made me sound like a complete dumbbell! Where she got that, I don't know. This is why one gets nervous about interviews.

INTERVIEWER: Do you generally agree with anthologists' choices? Do you have any poems that are personal favorites? Ones you'd like to see anthologized that aren't?

BISHOP: I'd rather have—well, anything except "The Fish"! I've declared a moratorium on that. Anthologists repeat each other so finally a few years ago I said nobody could reprint "The Fish" unless they reprinted three others because I got so sick of it.

INTERVIEWER: One or two more questions. You went to Yaddo several times early in your career. Did you find the atmosphere at an artist's colony helpful to your writing?

BISHOP: I went to Yaddo twice, once in the summer for two weeks, and for several months the winter before I went to Brazil. Mrs. Ames was very much in evidence then. I didn't like it in the summer because of the incessant coming and going, but the winter was rather different. There were only six of us, and just by luck we all liked each other and had a very good time. I wrote one poem, I think, in that whole stretch. The first time I liked the horse races, I'm afraid. In the summer—I think this still goes on—you can walk through the Whitney estate to the tracks. A friend and I used to walk there early in the morning and sit at the track and have coffee and blueberry muffins while they exercised the horses. I loved that. We went to a sale of yearlings in August and that was beautiful. The sale was in a big tent. The grooms had brass dustpans and brooms with brass handles and they'd go around after the little colts and sweep up the manure. That's what I remember best about Yaddo.

INTERVIEWER: It was around the time that you went to Yaddo, wasn't it, that you were consultant in poetry to the Library of Congress? Was that year in Washington more productive than your Yaddo experience?

BISHOP: I've suffered because I've been so shy all my life. A few years later I might have enjoyed it more but at the time I didn't like it much. I hated Washington. There were so many government buildings that looked like Moscow. There was a very nice secretary, Phyllis Armstrong, who got me through. I think she did most of the work. I'd write something and she'd say, "Oh, no, that isn't official," so then she'd take it and rewrite it in gobbledegook. We used to bet on the horses—Phyllis always bet the daily double. She and I would sit there reading the *Racing Form* and poets would come to call and Phyllis and I would be talking about our bets!

All the "survivors" of that job—a lot of them are dead—were invited to read there recently. There were thirteen of us, unfortunately.

INTERVIEWER: A friend of mine tried to get into that reading and she said it was jammed.

BISHOP: It was *mobbed!* And I don't know why. It couldn't have been a duller, more awful occasion. I think we were supposedly limited to ten minutes. I *stuck* to it. But there's no stopping somebody like James Dickey. Stafford was good. I'd never heard him and never met him. He read one very short poem that really brought tears to my eyes, he read it so beautifully.

I'm not very fond of poetry readings. I'd much rather read the book. I know I'm wrong. I've only been to a few poetry readings I could *bear.* Of course, you're too young to have gone through the Dylan Thomas craze. . . .

When it was somebody like Cal Lowell or Marianne Moore, it's as if they were my children. I'd get terribly upset. I went to hear Marianne several times and finally I just couldn't go because I'd sit there with tears running down my face. I don't know, it's sort of embarrassing. You're so afraid they'll do something wrong.

Cal thought that the most important thing about readings was the remarks poets made in between the poems. The first time I heard him read was years ago at the New School for Social Research in a small, gray auditorium. It was with Allen Tate and Louise Bogan. Cal was very much younger than anybody else and had published just two books. He read a long, endless poem—I've forgotten its title*—about a Canadian nun in New Brunswick. I've forgotten what the point of the poem is, but it's very, very long and it's quite beautiful, particularly in the beginning. Well, he started, and he read very badly. He kind of droned and everybody was trying to get it. He had gotten about two thirds of the way through when somebody yelled, "Fire!" There was a small fire in the lobby, nothing much, that was put out in about five minutes and everybody went back to their

*"Mother Marie Therese" in *The Mills of the Kavanaughs*

seats. Poor Cal said, "I think I'd better begin over again," so he read the whole thing all over again! But his reading got much, much better in later years.

INTERVIEWER: He couldn't have done any better than the record the Poetry Center recently put out. It's wonderful. And very funny.

BISHOP: I haven't the courage to hear it.

—ELIZABETH SPIRES

1978

MARY MCCARTHY

Mary McCarthy was born in Seattle, Washington, on June 21, 1912, and raised by grandparents, uncles, and aunts after her parents died of influenza in 1918. At the age of eight she won a state prize for an essay entitled "The Irish in American History." She was educated at the Forest Ridge Convent in Seattle, Annie Wright Seminary in Tacoma, and Vassar College, where she was elected to Phi Beta Kappa and graduated in 1933.

After her graduation from college she began to write book reviews for *The Nation* and *The New Republic.* In 1936 and 1937 she was an editor for Covici Friede, and from 1937 to 1948 she was an editor and theater critic for *Partisan Review.* During this period she wrote articles, stories and, finally, novels.

Her son was born in 1938. After her divorce from Edmund Wilson, she taught for a short time at Bard College and at Sarah Lawrence. She was a Guggenheim Fellow during 1949 and 1950, and again in 1959 and 1960. In 1949 she received the *Horizon* prize, and in 1957 a National Institute grant.

McCarthy's numerous works of fiction and criticism include *The Company She Keeps* (1942), *The Groves of Academe* (1952), *A*

Charmed Life (1955), *Memories of a Catholic Girlhood* (1957), *The Stones of Florence* (1959), *The Group* (1963), *The Writing on the Wall and Other Literary Essays* (1970) and *Ideas and the Novel* (1980). In 1984 McCarthy won both the Edward McDowell Award and the National Award for Literature. She is a member of the National Institute of Arts and Letters. Her autobiography, *How I Grew*, was published in 1987. She was at work on a second volume when she died in 1989.

who would advise me about budgeting and not letting friends make long-distance calls on my wire. But all that was normal; it was happening to everybody and nobody could feel it as a profound or permanent change, for it was like the life of a college student prolonged; middle-class college students always overspent their allowances and ran up bills that scared them because they couldn't pay. ####### The thirties proper, which I was inducted into in about 1936, were something harsher. They were Armageddon. This panel itself is rather thirtyish. The idea behind it is that we (or you) are sitting in judgment on a period of history. The thirties ## being presented as a choice. Are you for them or against them, and as you answer, so will you be defined. The rhetorical form that best expresses the thirties is the debate. Today, perhaps, it is the panel, which recognizes the possibility of shades of opinion; in the thirties, the meetings of this sort that I remember ######## featured only a pair of antagonists. People used to tell about a debate, so called, at the University of Chicago, when President Hutchins represented Aristotle, Mortimer Adler represented Aquinas, and a student wearing a dunce-cap (yes, literally) represented Hume. Thus the debate shaded into the trial, and in the thirties the weaker member of a pair of debaters found himself, always, on trial. This state of war, of incessant belligerency, was not confined to politics. It infected literature, education, psychiatry, art. The word, re- conciliation, which was often used at that time, testifies to the state of belli- gerency. Certain mediators were always trying to "reconcile" Freud with Marx, or, a little later, Freud with religion. A common form of speech was "How do you re- concile what you say with----?" In practice, there were some very strange reconciliations. The tiara at the Waldorf strike; the gold evening dress to go to Madrid in the Spanish Civil War. Those women were trying to reconcile the twenties (fun) with the thirties. There was a strong affinity in the thirties for the absurd. Looking back, people remember grotesque and unbelievable events#, events that flew, as they say, in the face of Nature. But I will come back to that in a minute.

    The thirties are presented now, nostalgically, as a time of freedom. Not so.

A manuscript page from an essay by Mary McCarthy.

MARY MCCARTHY

T he interview took place in the living room of the apartment in Paris where Miss McCarthy was staying during the winter of 1961. It was a sunny, pleasant room, not too large, with long windows facing south toward the new buildings going up along the avenue Montaigne. A dining-cum-writing table stood in an alcove at one end; on it were a lamp, some books and papers, and a rather well-worn portable typewriter. At the other end of the room were several armchairs and a low sofa where Miss McCarthy sat while the interview was recorded. On this early-spring afternoon, the windows were open wide, letting in a warm breeze and the noise of construction work nearby. An enormous pink azalea plant bloomed on the balcony, and roses graced a small desk in one corner.

McCarthy settled down on the sofa and served coffee. She was wearing a simple beige dress with little jewelry—a large and rather ornate ring was her one elaborate ornament. She is a woman of medium height, dark, with straight hair combed back from a center part into a knot at the nape of her neck; this simple coiffure sets off a profile of beautiful, almost classic regularity. Her smile is a generous one, flashing suddenly across her face, crinkling up her wide-set eyes. She speaks not quickly, but with great animation and energy, gesturing seldom; it is typical of her that she matches the tremendously elegant *carriage of her arms and neck and handsomely poised head with a deliberate, almost jerky motion in taking a step.*

While McCarthy's conversation was remarkably fluent and articulate, she nevertheless often interrupted herself in order to reword or qualify a phrase, sometimes even impatiently destroying it and starting again in the effort to express herself as exactly as possible. Several times during the interview she seized upon a question in such a way that one felt she had decided upon certain things she wanted to say about herself and would willy-nilly create the opportunity to do so. At other moments, some of them hilarious—her pitiless wit is justifiably celebrated—she would indulge in unpremeditated extravagances of description or speculation that she would then laughingly censor as soon as the words were out of her mouth. She was extremely generous in the matter of silly or badly worded questions, turning them into manageable ones by the nature of her response. In all, her conversation was marked by a scrupulous effort to be absolutely fair and honest, and by a kind of natural and exuberant enjoyment of her own intellectual powers.

<hr>

INTERVIEWER: Do you like writing in Europe?

MCCARTHY: I don't really find much difference. I think if you stayed here very long, you'd begin to notice a little difficulty about language.

INTERVIEWER: Did you write about Europe when you first came here after the war?

MCCARTHY: Only in that short story, "The Cicerone." That was in the summer of 1946. We were just about the only tourists because you weren't allowed to travel unless you had an official reason for it. I got a magazine to give me some sort of *carnet.*

INTERVIEWER: Did the old problem, the American in Europe, interest you as a novelist?

MCCARTHY: I suppose at that time, at least in that story somewhat, it did. But no, not further. For one thing, I don't know whether I cease to feel so much like an American or what; New York is, after all, so Europeanized, and so many of one's friends are European, that the distinction between you as an American and the European blurs. Also Europe has become so much more Americanized. No, I no longer see that Jamesian distinction. I mean, I see it in James, and I could see it even in 1946, but I don't see it anymore. I don't feel anymore this antithesis of Young America, Old Europe. I think that's really gone. For better or worse, I'm not sure. Maybe for worse.

INTERVIEWER: What about the novel you're writing while you're here—have you been working on it a long time?

MCCARTHY: Oh, years! Let me think, I began it around the time of the first Stevenson campaign. Then I abandoned it and wrote the books on Italy, and *A Charmed Life*, and *Memories of a Catholic Girlhood*. When did I begin this thing again? A year ago last spring, I guess. Part of it came out in *Partisan Review*. The one called "Dotty Makes an Honest Woman of Herself."

INTERVIEWER: Is it unfair to ask you what it will be about?

MCCARTHY: No, it's very easy. It's called *The Group*, and it's about eight Vassar girls. It starts with the inauguration of Roosevelt, and—well, at first it was going to carry them up to the present time, but then I decided to stop at the inauguration of Eisenhower. It was conceived as a kind of mock-chronicle novel. It's a novel about the idea of progress, really. The idea of progress seen in the female sphere, the feminine sphere. You know, home economics, architecture, domestic technology, contraception, childbearing; the study of technology in the home, in the playpen, in the bed. It's supposed to be the history of the loss of faith in progress, in the idea of progress, during that twenty-year period.

INTERVIEWER: Are these eight Vassar girls patterned more or less after ones you knew when you were there in college?

MCCARTHY: Some of them are drawn pretty much from life, and some of them are rather composite. I've tried to keep myself out of this book. Oh, and all their mothers are in it. That's the part I almost like the best.

INTERVIEWER: Just the mothers, not the fathers?

MCCARTHY: Not the fathers. The fathers vaguely figure, offstage and so on, but the mothers are really monumentally present!

INTERVIEWER: Does it matter to you at all where you write?

MCCARTHY: Oh, a nice peaceful place with some good light.

INTERVIEWER: Do you work regularly, every morning, say?

MCCARTHY: Normally; right now I haven't been. Normally I work from about nine to two, and sometimes much longer—if it's going well, sometimes from nine to seven.

INTERVIEWER: Typewriter?

MCCARTHY: Typewriter, yes. This always has to get into a *Paris Review* interview! I very rarely go out to lunch. That's a rule. I've been accepting lunch dates recently—*why* didn't I remember that? My excuse—the excuse I've been forgetting—is simply that I don't go out to lunch! And in general, I don't. That was the best rule I ever made.

INTERVIEWER: Once you've published part of a novel separately, in a magazine or short-story collection, do you do much work on it afterwards, before it is published in the novel itself?

MCCARTHY: It depends. With this novel, I have.

INTERVIEWER: Speaking not of a novel, but of your autobiography, I remember that you published parts of *Memories of a Catholic Girlhood* as one section in *Cast a Cold Eye.* You changed the story about your nickname a great deal, reducing it to just a small incident in *Catholic Girlhood.*

MCCARTHY: I couldn't *bear* that one! It had appeared years ago in *Mademoiselle*, and when I put it in *Cast a Cold Eye*, I didn't realize how much I disliked it. When I came to put *Catholic Girlhood* together, I simply couldn't stand it, and when I was reading the book in proof, I decided to tear it out, to reduce it to a tiny,

tiny incident. As it stood, it was just impossible, much too rhetorical.

INTERVIEWER: When you publish chapters of a book separately on their own, do you think of them as chapters, or as independent short stories?

MCCARTHY: As chapters, but if somebody, a magazine editor, thought they were what *Partisan Review* calls a "self-contained chapter," all right, but I've never tried to make them into separate units. If one happens to be, all right—if they want to publish it as such. *The New Yorker* has given me surprises: they've printed things that I would never have thought could stand by themselves. But *they* thought so.

INTERVIEWER: Did you, when you saw them in print?

MCCARTHY: Surprisingly, yes.

INTERVIEWER: What about in your first novel, *The Company She Keeps*?

MCCARTHY: Those chapters were written originally as short stories. About halfway through, I began to think of them as a kind of unified story. The same character kept reappearing, and so on. I decided finally to call it a novel, in that it does in a sense tell *a* story, one story. But the first chapters were written without any idea of there being a novel. It was when I was doing the one about the Yale man that I decided to put the heroine of the earlier stories in that story too. The story of the Yale man is not a bit autobiographical, but the heroine appears anyway, in order to make a unity for the book.

INTERVIEWER: Were you also interested simply in the problem of writing one story from various different points of view, in experimenting with the different voices?

MCCARTHY: There were no voices in that. I don't think I was really very much interested in the technical side of it. It was the first piece of fiction I had ever written, I mean I'd never made any experiments before. I was too inexperienced to worry about technical problems.

INTERVIEWER: You hadn't written any fiction before then?

MCCARTHY: No. Well, in college I had written the tiniest amount of fiction: very bad short stories, very unrealized short stories, for courses, and that was all. I once started a detective story to make money—but I couldn't get the murder to take place! At the end of three chapters I was still describing the characters and the milieu, so I thought, this is not going to work. No corpse! And that was all. Then I simply did *The Company She Keeps*, and was only interested in the technical side from the point of view of establishing the truth, of trying to recreate what happened. For instance, the art-gallery story was written in the first person because that's the way you write that kind of story—a study of a curious individual.

INTERVIEWER: You imply that most of the stories were distinctly autobiographical.

MCCARTHY: They all are, more or less, except the one about the Yale man.

INTERVIEWER: Is this distinction between autobiography and fiction clear in your mind before you begin writing a story, or does it become so as you write? Or is there no such distinction?

MCCARTHY: Well, I think it depends on what you're doing. Let's be frank. Take "The Man in the Brooks Brothers Shirt"; in that case it was an attempt to describe something that really happened—though naturally you have to do a bit of name-changing and city-changing. And the first story, the one about the divorce: that was a stylization—there were no proper names in it or anything—but still, it was an attempt to be as exact as possible about something that had happened. The Yale man was based on a real person. John Chamberlain, actually, whom I didn't know very well. But there it was an attempt to make this real man a broad type. You know, to use John Chamberlain's boyish looks and a few of the features of his career, and then draw all sorts of other Yale men into it. Then the heroine was put in, in an imaginary love affair, which *had* to be because she had to be in the story. I always thought that was all very hard on John Chamberlain, who was married. But of course he knew it wasn't true, and he knew that I didn't know him very well, and that therefore in the story he was just a kind of good-looking clothes hanger. Anything else that I've written later—I may make a mistake—has been, on the whole, a fiction. Though it may have autobiographical elements in it that I'm conscious of, it has been conceived as a fiction, even a thing like *The Oasis*, that's supposed to have all these real people in it. The whole story is a complete fiction. Nothing of the kind ever happened; after all, it happens in the future. But in general, with characters, I do try at least to be as exact as possible about the essence of a person, to find the key that works the person both in real life and in the fiction.

INTERVIEWER: Do you object to people playing the *roman à clef* game with your novels?

MCCARTHY: I suppose I really ask for it, in a way. I *do* rather object to it at the same time, insofar as it deflects attention from what I'm trying to do in the novel. What I really do is take real plums and put them in an imaginary cake. If you're interested in the cake, you get rather annoyed with people saying what species the real plum was. In *The Groves of Academe*, for instance. I had taught at Bard College and at Sarah Lawrence, but I didn't want to make a composite of those two places: I really wanted to make a weird imaginary college of my own. I even took a trip to the Mennonite country in Pennsylvania to try to find a perfect location for it, which I found—now, where was it? Somewhere near Ephrata—yes, it was Lititz, Pennsylvania, the home of the pretzel. There's a very charming old-fashioned sort of academy, a girls' college there—I'd never heard of it before and can't remember the name. It had the perfect setting, I thought, for this imaginary college of mine. Anyway, I would get terribly annoyed if people said it had to do with Sarah

Lawrence, which it had almost no resemblance to. It was quite a bit like Bard. Sarah Lawrence is a much more *borné* and dull place than Bard, or than my college. And of course I was even more annoyed if they said it was Bennington. There was not supposed to be anything there of Bennington at all!

INTERVIEWER: When were you at Bard?

MCCARTHY: '45 to '46.

INTERVIEWER: And at Sarah Lawrence?

MCCARTHY: I was there just for one term, the winter of '48.

INTERVIEWER: Did you enjoy teaching?

MCCARTHY: I adored teaching at Bard, yes. But the students were so poor at Sarah Lawrence that I didn't much enjoy it there. I don't think anyone I knew who was teaching there then did. But at Bard it was very exciting. It was all quite mad, crazy. I had never taught before, and I was staying up till two in the morning every night trying to keep a little bit behind my class. Joke.

INTERVIEWER: Did they ask you to teach "creative writing"?

MCCARTHY: I've always refused to teach creative writing. Oh, I had in addition to two courses, about seven or eight tutorials, and some of those tutees wanted to study creative writing. I think I finally weakened and let one boy who was utterly ungifted for it study creative writing because he was so incapable of studying anything else.

INTERVIEWER: But mostly it was these two courses.

MCCARTHY: Yes, and then you had to keep up with all these students. I had one boy doing all the works of James T. Farrell and a girl who was studying Marcus Aurelius and Dante. That was fun. That one I did the work for. And one girl was doing a thesis on Richardson; that was just hopeless. I mean, I couldn't even try to keep up with teaching Russian novels, and, say, Jane Austen—who in my course came under the head of Modern Novel—*and* all the works of Richardson. So I could never tell, you know, whether she had read what she was supposed to have read, because I couldn't remember it! Everything was reversed! The student was in a position to see whether the professor was cheating, or had done her homework. Anyway, everybody ended up ill after this year—you know, various physical ailments. But it was exciting, it was fun. The students were fun. The bright ones were bright, and there wasn't much of a middle layer. They were either bright or they were just cretins. I must say, there are times when you welcome a B student.

I liked teaching because I loved this business of studying. I found it quite impossible to give a course unless I'd read the material the night before. I absolutely couldn't handle the material unless it was fresh in my mind. Unless you give canned lectures, it really has to be—though that leads, I think, to all sorts of very whimsical, perhaps, and capricious interpretations; that is, you see the whole book, say *Anna Karenina*, in terms that are perhaps dictated by the moment. One wonders afterwards whether one's interpretation of *Anna Karenina* that one had rammed down the throats of those poor students was really as true as it seemed to one at the time.

INTERVIEWER: Which books did you teach in the Modern Novel?

MCCARTHY: Well, you had to call everything at Bard either modern or contemporary, or the students wouldn't register for it. Everyone thinks this a joke, but it was true. I originally was going to teach a whole course on critical theory, from Aristotle to T. S. Eliot or something, and only three students registered for it, but if it had been called Contemporary Criticism, then I think we would have had a regular class. So we called this course the Modern Novel, and it began with Jane Austen, I think, and went up, well, certainly to Henry James. That was when I taught novels in pairs. I taught *Emma* and *Madame Bovary* together. Then *The Princess Casamassima*, with the anarchist plot in it and everything, with *The Possessed*. *The Red and the Black* with

Great Expectations. And *Fontamara* with something. I only taught novels I liked.

INTERVIEWER: Would it be roughly the same list, were you teaching the course now? Or do you have new favorites?

MCCARTHY: Oh I don't know, I might even add something like *Dr. Zhivago* at the end. I would probably do some different Dickens. I've read an awful lot of Dickens over again since then. Now I think I'd teach *Our Mutual Friend* or *Little Dorritt.*

INTERVIEWER: Why did you start reading Dickens over again?

MCCARTHY: I don't know, I got interested in Dickens at Bard, and then at Sarah Lawrence. Another stimulus was a book done by a man called Edgar Johnson, a biographer of Dickens. Anthony West had attacked it in *The New Yorker,* and this made me so angry that I reviewed the book, and that set off another kind of chain reaction. I really *passionately* admire Dickens.

INTERVIEWER: Could I go back for a moment to what you said about your early writing at college? I think you said that *The Company She Keeps* was the first fiction you ever wrote, but that was some years after you left Vassar, wasn't it?

MCCARTHY: Oh, yes. You know, I had been terribly discouraged when I was at Vassar, and later, by being told that I was really a critical mind, and that I had no creative talent. Who knows? they may have been right. This was done in a generous spirit, I don't mean that it was harsh. Anyway, I hadn't found any way at all, when I was in college, of expressing anything in the form of short stories. We had a rebel literary magazine that Elizabeth Bishop and Eleanor Clark were on, and Muriel Rukeyser and I. I wrote, not fiction, but sort of strange things for this publication.

INTERVIEWER: A rebel magazine?

MCCARTHY: There was an official literary magazine, which we were all against. Our magazine was anonymous. It was called *Con Spirito.* It caused a great sort of scandal. I don't know why—

it was one of these perfectly innocent undertakings. But people said, "How awful, it's anonymous." The idea of anonymity was of course to keep the judgment clear, especially the editorial board's judgment—to make people read these things absolutely on their merits. Well, anyway, *Con Spirito* lasted for only a few numbers. Elizabeth Bishop wrote a wonderful story for it which I still remember, called "Then Came the Poor." It was about a revolution, a fantasy that took place in modern bourgeois society, when the poor invade, and take over a house.

INTERVIEWER: When you left Vassar, what then?

MCCARTHY: Well, I went to New York, and I began reviewing for *The New Republic* and *The Nation*—right away. I wrote these little book reviews. Then there was a series about the critics. *The Nation* wanted a large-scale attack on critics and book reviewers, chiefly those in the *Herald Tribune*, the *Times*, and the *Saturday Review* and so on. I had been doing some rather harsh reviews, so they chose me as the person to do this. But I was so young—I think I was twenty-two—that they didn't *trust* me. So they got Margaret Marshall, who was the assistant literary editor then, to do it with me: actually we divided the work up and did separate pieces. But she was older and was supposed to be—I don't know—a restraining influence on me; anyway, someone more responsible. That series was a great sensation at the time, and it made people very mad. I continued just to do book reviews, maybe one other piece about the theater, something like the one on the literary critics. And then nothing more until *Partisan Review* started. That was when I tried to write the detective story—before *Partisan Review*. To be exact, *Partisan Review* had existed as a Stalinist magazine, and then it had died, gone to limbo. But after the Moscow trials, the PR boys, Rahv and Phillips, revived it, got a backer, merged with some other people—Dwight Macdonald and others—and started it again. As an anti-Stalinist magazine. I had been married to an actor, and was supposed to know something about the theater, so I began writing a theater column for them. I didn't have any other ambitions at all. Then I married Edmund Wilson, and after we'd been married about a week, he said, "I think you have a talent for writing fiction." And he put me in a little room. He didn't literally lock the door, but he said, "Stay in there!" And I did. I just sat down, and it just came. It was the first story I had ever written, really: the first story in *The Company She Keeps*. Robert Penn Warren published it in the *Southern Review*. And I found myself writing fiction, to my great surprise.

INTERVIEWER: This was when you became involved in politics, wasn't it?

MCCARTHY: No. Earlier. In 1936, at the time of the Moscow trials. That changed absolutely everything. I got swept into the whole Trotskyite movement. But by accident. I was at a party. I knew Jim Farrell—I'd reviewed one of his books, I think it was *Studs Lonigan*—in any case, I knew Jim Farrell, and I was asked to a party given by his publisher for Art Young, the old *Masses* cartoonist. There were a lot of Communists at this party. Anyway, Farrell went around asking people whether they thought Trotsky was entitled to a hearing and to the right of asylum. I said yes, and that was all. The next thing I discovered I was on the letterhead of something calling itself the American Committee for the Defense of Leon Trotsky. I was furious, of course, at this use of my name. Not that my name had any consequence, but still, it was mine. Just as I was about to make some sort of protest, I began to get all sorts of calls from Stalinists, telling me to get off the committee. I began to see that other people were falling off the committee, like Freda Kirchwey—she was the first to go, I think—and this cowardice impressed me so unfavorably that naturally I didn't say anything about my name having got on there by accident, or at least without my realizing. So I stayed.

I began to know all the people on the committee. We'd attend meetings. It was a completely different world. Serious, you know. Anyway, that's how I got to know the PR boys. They hadn't yet revived the *Partisan Review*, but they were both on the Trotsky committee, at least Philip was. We—the committee, that is—used to meet in Farrell's apartment. I remember once when we met on St. Valentine's Day and I thought, Oh, this is so strange, because I'm the only person in this room who realizes that it's Valentine's Day. It was true! I had a lot of rather rich Stalinist friends, and I was always on the defensive with them, about the Moscow trial question, Trotsky and so on. So I had to inform myself, really, in order to conduct the argument. I found that I was reading more and more, getting more and more involved in this business. At the same time I got a job at Covici Friede, a rather left-wing publishing house now out of business, also full of Stalinists. I began to see Philip Rahv again because Covici Friede needed some readers' opinions on Russian books, and I remembered that he read Russian, so he came around to the office, and we began to see each other. When *Partisan Review* was revived I appeared as a sort of fifth wheel—there may have been more than that—but in any case as a kind of appendage of *Partisan Review*.

INTERVIEWER: Then you hadn't really been interested in politics before the Moscow trials?

MCCARTHY: No, not really. My first husband had worked at the Theater Union, which was a radical group downtown that put on proletarian plays, and there were lots of Communists in that. Very few Socialists. And so I knew all these people; I knew that kind of person. But I wasn't very sympathetic to them. We used to see each other, and there were a lot of jokes. I even marched in May Day parades. Things like that. But it was all . . . fun. It was all done in that spirit. And I remained, as the *Partisan Review* boys said, absolutely bourgeois throughout. They always said to me very sternly, "You're really a throwback. You're really a twenties figure."

INTERVIEWER: How did you react to that?

MCCARTHY: Well, I suppose I was wounded. I was a sort of gay, good-time girl, from their point of view. And they were men of the thirties. Very serious. That's why my position was so insecure on *Partisan Review;* it wasn't exactly insecure, but . . . lowly. I mean, in *fact.* And that was why they let me write about the theater, because they thought the theater was of absolutely no consequence.

INTERVIEWER: How did the outbreak of the war affect your political opinion? The *Partisan Review* group split apart, didn't it?

MCCARTHY: At the beginning of the war we were all isolationists, the whole group. Then I think the summer after the fall of France—certainly before Pearl Harbor—Philip Rahv wrote an article in which he said in a measured sentence, "In a certain sense, this is our war." The rest of us were deeply shocked by this, because we regarded it as a useless imperialist war. You couldn't beat Fascism that way: "Fight the enemy at home," and so on. In other words, we reacted to the war rather in the manner as if it had been World War I. This was after Munich, after the so-called "phony war." There was some reason for having certain doubts about the war, at least about the efficacy of the war. So when Philip wrote this article, a long controversy began on *Partisan Review.* It split between those who supported the war, and those who didn't. I was among those who didn't—Edmund Wilson also, though for slightly different reasons. Dwight Macdonald and Clement Greenberg split off, and Dwight founded his own magazine, *Politics,* which started out as a Trotskyite magazine, and then became a libertarian, semi-anarchist one. Meyer Shapiro was in this group, and I forget who else. Edmund was really an unreconstructed isolationist. The others were either Marxist or libertarian. Of course there was a split in the Trotskyite movement at that period.

Toward the end of the war I began to realize that there was something hypocritical about my position—that I was really supporting the war. I'd go to a movie—there was a marvelous documentary called *Desert Victory* about the British victory over Rommel's Africka Korps—and I'd find myself weeping madly when Montgomery's bagpipers went through to El Alamein. In other words, cheering the war, and on the other hand, being absolutely against Bundles for Britain, against Lend Lease—this was after Lend Lease, of course—against every practical thing. And suddenly, I remember—it must have been the summer of '45 that I first said this aloud—I remember it was on the Cape, at Truro. There were a lot of friends, Chiaromonte, Lionel Abel, Dwight, et cetera, at my house—by this time I was divorced from Edmund, or separated, anyway. And I said, "You know, I think I, and all of us, are really *for* the war." This was the first time this had been said aloud by me. Dwight indignantly denied it. "I'm *not* for the war!" he said. But he was. Then I decided I wanted to give a blood transfusion. And I practically had to get cleared! Now no one was making me do this, but I felt I had to go and get cleared by my friends first. Was it wrong of me to support the war effort by giving blood? It was agreed that it was all right. All this *fuss!* So I gave blood, just once. Some other people were doing it too, I believe, independently, at the same time, people of more or less this tendency. That is the end of that story.

Years later, I realized I really thought that Philip had been right, and that the rest of us had been wrong. Of course we didn't know about the concentration camps: the death camps hadn't started at the beginning. All that news came in fairly late. But once this news was in, it became clear—at least to me, and I still believe it—that the only way to have stopped it was in a military way. That only the military defeat of Hitler could stop this, and it had to be stopped. But it took a long, long time to come to this view. You're always afraid of making the same mistake over again. But the trouble is you can always correct an earlier mistake like our taking the attitude to World War II as if it were World War I, but if you ever try to project the correction of a mistake into the future, you may make a different one. That is, many people now are talking about World War III as if it were World War II.

INTERVIEWER: What I don't see, though, is how all this left you once the war was over.

MCCARTHY: Actually, as I remember, after the war was the very best period, politically, that I've been through. At that time, it seemed to me there was a lot of hope around. The war was over! Certain—perhaps—mistakes had been recognized. The bomb had been dropped on Hiroshima, and there was a kind of general repentance of this fact. This was before the hydrogen bomb; and we never even dreamed that the Russians were going to get the atomic bomb. The political scene looked free. This was not only true for us—it seemed a good moment. At least there was still the hope of small libertarian movements. People like Dwight and Chiaromonte and I used to talk about it a great deal, and even Koestler was writing at that period about the possibility of founding oases—that's where I took the title of that book from. It seemed possible still, utopian but possible, to change the world on a small scale. Everyone was trying to live in a very principled way, but with quite a lot of energy, the energy that peace had brought, really. This was the period of the Marshall Plan, too. It was a good period. Then of course the Russians got the atom bomb, and the hydrogen bomb came. That was the end of *any* hope, or at least any hope that I can see of anything being done except in a massive way.

INTERVIEWER: How do you characterize your political opinion now?

MCCARTHY: Dissident!

INTERVIEWER: All the way round?

MCCARTHY: Yes! No, I still believe in what I believed in then—I still believe in a kind of libertarian socialism, a decentralized socialism. But I don't see any possibility of achieving it.

That is, within the span that I can see, which would be, say, to the end of my son's generation, your generation. It really seems to me sometimes that the only hope is space. That is to say, perhaps the most energetic—in a bad sense—elements will move on to a new world in space. The problems of mass society will be transported into space, leaving behind this world as a kind of Europe, which then eventually tourists will visit. The Old World. I'm only half joking. I don't think that the problem of social equality has ever been solved. As soon as it looks as if it were going to be solved, or even as if it were going to be confronted—say, as at the end of the eighteenth century—there's a mass move to a new continent which defers this solution. After '48, after the failure of the '48 revolutions in Europe, hope for an egalitarian Europe really died, and the forty-eighters, many of them, went to California in the Gold Rush as forty-niners. My great-grandfather, from central Europe, was one of them. The Gold Rush, the Frontier was a substitute sort of equality. Think of Chaplin's film. And yet once the concept of equality had entered the world, life becomes intolerable without it; yet life continues without its being realized. So it may be that there will be another displacement, another migration. The problem, the solution, or the confrontation, will again be postponed.

INTERVIEWER: Do you find that your critical work, whether it's political or literary, creates any problems in relation to your work as a novelist?

MCCARTHY: No, except that you have the perpetual problem, if somebody asks you to do a review, whether to interrupt what you're writing—if you're writing a novel—to do the review. You have to weigh whether the subject interests you enough, or whether you're tired at that moment, emotionally played out by the fiction you're writing. Whether it would be a good thing to stop and concentrate on something else. I just agreed to and did a review of Camus's collected fiction and journalism. That *was* in some way connected with my own work, with the question of the novel in general. I thought, yes, I will do this because I want to read all of Camus and decide what I think about him finally. (Actually, I ended up almost as baffled as when I started.) But in general, I don't take a review unless it's something like that. Or unless Anthony West attacks Dickens. You know. Either it has to be some sort of thing that I want very much to take sides on, or something I'd like to study a bit, that I want to find out about anyway. Or where there may, in the case of study, be some reference—very indirect—back to my own work.

INTERVIEWER: This is quite a change from the time when you wrote criticism and never even thought of writing fiction. But now you consider yourself a novelist? Or don't you bother with these distinctions?

MCCARTHY: Well, I suppose I consider myself a novelist. Yes. Still, whatever way I write was really, I suppose, formed critically. That is, I learned to write reviews and criticism and then write novels, so that however I wrote, it was formed that way. George Eliot, you know, began by translating Strauss, began by writing about German philosophy—though her philosophic passages are not at all good in *Middlemarch.* Nevertheless, I *think* that this kind of training really makes one more interested in the subject than in the style. Her work certainly doesn't suffer from any kind of stylistic frippery. There's certainly no voluminous drapery around. There is a kind of concision in it, at her best—that passage where she's describing the character of Lydgate—which shows, I think, the critical and philosophic training. I've never liked the conventional conception of "style." What's confusing is that style usually means some form of fancy writing—when people say, oh yes, so and so's such a "wonderful stylist." But if one means by style the voice, the irreducible and always recognizable and alive thing, then of course style is really everything. It's what you find in Stendhal, it's what you find in Pasternak. The same thing you find in a poet—the sound of, say, Donne's voice. In a sense, you can't go further in an analysis of Donne than to be able to place this voice, in the sense that you recognize Don Giovanni by the voice of Don Giovanni.

INTERVIEWER: In speaking of your own writing, anyway, you attribute its "style" to your earlier critical work—then you don't feel the influence of other writers of fiction?

MCCARTHY: I don't think I have any influences. I think my first story, the first one in *The Company She Keeps*, definitely shows the Jamesian influence—James is so terribly catching. But beyond that, I can't find any influence. That is, I can't as a detached person—as detached as I can be—look at my work and see where it came from the point of view of literary sources.

INTERVIEWER: There must be certain writers, though, that you are *drawn* to more than others.

MCCARTHY: Oh, yes! But I don't think I write like them. The writer I really like best is Tolstoy, and I *know* I don't write like Tolstoy. I wish I did! Perhaps the best English prose is Thomas Nash. I don't write at all like Thomas Nash.

INTERVIEWER: It would seem also, from hints you give us in your books, that you like Roman writers as well.

MCCARTHY: I did when I was young, very much. At least, I adored Catullus, and Juvenal; those were the two I really passionately loved. And Caesar, when I was a girl. But you couldn't say that I had been influenced by *Catullus!* No! And Stendhal I like very, very much. Again, I would be happy to write like Stendhal, but I don't. There are certain sentences in Stendhal that come to mind as how to do it if one could. I can't. A certain kind of clarity and brevity—the author's attitude summed up in a sentence, and done so simply, done without patronizing. Some sort of joy.

INTERVIEWER: It's a dangerous game to play, the influence one.

MCCARTHY: Well, in some cases it's easy to see, and people themselves acknowledge it, and are interested in it, as people are interested in their genealogy. I simply can't find my ancestors. I was talking to somebody about John Updike, and he's another one I would say I can't find any sources for.

INTERVIEWER: Do you like his writing?

MCCARTHY: Yes. I've not quite finished *Rabbit, Run*—I must get it back from the person I lent it to and finish it. I thought it was very good, and so stupidly reviewed. I'd read *Poorhouse Fair*, which I thought was really remarkable. Perhaps it suffered from the point-of-view problem, the whole virtuosity of doing it through the eyes of this old man sitting on the veranda of the poorhouse, through his eyes with their refraction, very old eyes, and so on. I think, in a way, this trick prevents him saying a good deal in the book. Nevertheless, it's quite a remarkable book. But anyway, I nearly didn't read *Rabbit, Run* because I thought, Oh my God! from reading those reviews. The reviewers seemed to be under the impression that the hero was a terrible character. It's incredible! No, I think it's the most interesting American novel I've read in quite a long time.

INTERVIEWER: What about others? Did you like *Henderson the Rain King*?

MCCARTHY: Well, yes, the first part of *Henderson* I think is marvelous. The vitality! I still think it's an amusing novel right through the lions, almost like a French eighteenth-century novel, or *conte*, very charming. But it doesn't have this tremendous blast of vitality that the first part has, and it doesn't have the density.

INTERVIEWER: What other recent American novels have you been interested by?

MCCARTHY: Well, name one. There really aren't any! I mean, are there? I can't think of any. I don't like Salinger, not at all. That last thing isn't a novel anyway, whatever it is. I don't like it. Not at all. It suffers from this terrible sort of metropolitan sentimentality and it's *so* narcissistic. And to me, also, it seemed so false, so calculated. Combining the plain man with an absolutely megalomaniac egoism. I simply can't stand it.

INTERVIEWER: What do you think of women writers, or do you think the category "woman writer" should not be made?

MCCARTHY: Some women writers make it. I mean, there's a certain kind of woman writer who's a capital W, capital W. Virginia Woolf certainly was one, and Katherine Mansfield was one, and Elizabeth Bowen is one. Katherine Anne Porter? Don't think she really is—I mean, her writing is certainly very feminine, but I would say that there wasn't this "WW" business in Katherine Anne Porter. Who else? There's Eudora Welty, who's certainly not a "Woman Writer." Though she's become one lately.

INTERVIEWER: What is it that happens to make this change?

MCCARTHY: I think they become interested in décor. You notice the change in Elizabeth Bowen. Her early work is much more masculine. Her later work has much more drapery in it. Who else? Jane Austen was never a "woman writer," I don't think. The cult of Jane Austen pretends that she was, but I don't think she was. George Eliot *certainly* wasn't, and George Eliot is the kind of woman writer I admire. I was going to write a piece at some point about this called "Sense and Sensibility," dividing women writers into these two. I *am* for the ones who represent sense, and so was Jane Austen.

INTERVIEWER: Getting away from novels for a moment, I'd like to ask you about *Memories of a Catholic Girlhood* if I might. Will you write any more autobiography?

MCCARTHY: I was just reading—oh God, actually I *was* just starting to read Simone de Beauvoir's second volume, *La Force de l'âge*, and she announces in the preface that she can't write about her later self with the same candor that she wrote about her girlhood.

INTERVIEWER: You feel that too?

MCCARTHY: On this one point I agree with her. One has to be really old, I think, really quite an old person—and by that time I don't know what sort of shape one's memory would be in.

INTERVIEWER: You don't agree with her on other points?

MCCARTHY: I had an interview with *L'Express* the other day, and I gave Simone de Beauvoir the works. Let's not do it twice. I think she's pathetic, that's all. This book is supposed to be better, more interesting anyway, than the first one because it's about the thirties, and everyone wants to read about the thirties. And her love affair with Sartre, which is just about the whole substance of this book, is supposed to be very touching. The book *is* more interesting than the first one. But I think she's odious. A mind totally bourgeois turned inside out.

INTERVIEWER: I have something else to ask, apropos of *Memories of a Catholic Girlhood.* There are certain points, important points and moments in your novels, where you deepen or enlarge the description of the predicament in which a character may be by reference to a liturgical or ecclesiastical or theological parallel or equivalence. What I want to know is, is this simply a strict use of analogy, a technical literary device, or does it indicate any conviction that these are valid and important ways of judging a human being?

MCCARTHY: I suppose it's a reference to a way of thinking about a human being. But I think at their worst they're rather just literary references. That is, slightly show-off literary references. I have a terrible compulsion to make them—really a dreadful compulsion. The first sentence of *The Stones of Florence* begins, "How can you stand it? This is the first thing, and the last thing, the eschatological question that the visitor leaves echoing in the air behind him." Something of that sort. Well, everybody was after me to take out that word. I left it out when I published that chapter in *The New Yorker,* but I put it back in the book. No, I do have this great compulsion to make those references. I think I do it as a sort of secret signal, a sort of looking over the heads of the readers who don't recognize them to the readers who do understand them.

INTERVIEWER: If these references *are* only literary ones, secret signals, then they are blasphemous.

MCCARTHY: Yes, I see what you mean. I suppose they are. Yes, they are secret jokes, they are blasphemies. But—I think I said something of this in the introduction of *Catholic Girlhood*—I think that religion offers to Americans (I mean the Roman Catholic religion) very often the only history and philosophy they ever get. A reference to it somehow opens up that historical vista. In that sense it is a device for deepening the passage.

INTERVIEWER: Could we go back to your novels for a moment? I'd like to ask you about how you begin on them. Do you start with the characters, the situation, the plot? What comes first? Perhaps that's too hard a question, too general.

MCCARTHY: Very hard, and I'm awfully specific. I can really only think in specific terms, at least about myself. *The Groves of Academe* started with the plot. The plot and this figure: there can't be the plot without this figure of the impossible individual, the unemployable professor and his campaign for justice. Justice, both in quotes, you know, and serious in a way. What *is* justice for the unemployable person? That was conceived from the beginning as a plot: the whole idea of the reversal at the end, when Mulcahy is triumphant and the president is about to lose his job or quit, when the worm turns and is triumphant. I didn't see exactly what would happen in between; the more minute details weren't worked out. But I did see that there would be his campaign for reinstatement and then his secret would be discovered. In this case that he had *not* been a Communist. *A Charmed Life* began with a short story; the first chapter was written as a short story. When I conceived the idea of its being a novel, I think about all I knew was that the heroine would have to die in the end. Everybody objected to that ending, and said that it was terrible to have her killed in an automobile accident in the last paragraph—utterly unprepared for, and so on. But the one thing I knew absolutely certainly was that the heroine had to die in the end. At first I was going to have her have an abortion, and have her die in the abortion. But that seemed to me so trite. Then I conceived the idea of having her drive on the correct side of the road and get killed, because in this weird place everyone is always on the wrong side of the road. But all that is really implicit in the first chapter.

INTERVIEWER: So the charge that readers are unprepared for the last paragraph you feel is unfair?

MCCARTHY: There may be something wrong with the novel, I don't know. But it was always supposed to have a fairy tale element in it. New Leeds is *haunted!* Therefore nobody should be surprised if something unexpected happens, or something catastrophic, for the place is also pregnant with catastrophe. But it may be that the treatment in between was too realistic, so that the reader was led to expect a realistic continuation of everything going on in a rather moderate way. It was, to some extent, a symbolic story. The novel is supposed to be about doubt. All the characters in different ways represent doubt, whether it is philosophical or ontological doubt as in the case of the strange painter who questions everything—"Why don't I murder my grandmother?" and so on. Or the girl's rather nineteenth-century self-doubt, doubt of the truth, of what she perceives. In any case, everyone is supposed to represent one or another form of doubt. When the girl finally admits to herself that she's pregnant, and also recognizes that she must do something about it, in other words, that she has to put up a real stake— and she does put up a real stake—at that moment she becomes mortal. All the other characters are immortal. They have dozens of terrible accidents, and they're all crippled in one way or another, and yet they have this marvelous power of survival. All those drunks and human odds and ends. Anyway, the girl

makes the decision—which from the point of view of conventional morality is a wicked decision—to have an abortion, to
kill life. Once she makes this decision, she becomes mortal, and
doesn't belong to the charmed circle anymore. As soon as she
makes it, she gets killed—to get killed is simply a symbol of
the fact that she's mortal.

INTERVIEWER: You say that her decision makes her mortal.
But her decision has also included someone else, the painter.

MCCARTHY: Yes, yes. I see what you mean. I hadn't thought
of that, that when she asks somebody to help her it implies
some sort of social bond, some sort of mutual bond between
people in society, while the rest of these people are still a community of isolates.

INTERVIEWER: His joining her in this mortal, social bond,
that doesn't make him mortal as well? He is still a part of the
charmed circle?

MCCARTHY: He's too sweet to be mortal! Well, he's a comic
figure, and I have this belief that all comic characters are immortal. They're eternal. I believe this is Bergson's theory too.
He has something, I'm told, about comic characters being *figé*.
Like Mr. and Mrs. Micawber: they all have to go on forever and
be invulnerable. Almost all Dickens's characters have this peculiar existence of eternity, except the heroes, except Pip, or
Nicholas Nickleby, or David Copperfield.

INTERVIEWER: What other characters in your novels do you
consider—

MCCARTHY: The comic ones? Who knows whether they're
immortal! As far as I'm concerned, they're immortal!

INTERVIEWER: Then you haven't thought of this distinction
between "mortal" and "immortal" in relation to characters in
other of your novels besides *A Charmed Life*?

MCCARTHY: I didn't think of this distinction until just recently, and not in connection with myself. It's just at this very
moment—*now* talking with you—that I'm thinking of it in

connection with myself. I would say that it is a law that applies to *all* novels: that the comic characters are *figé*, are immortal, and that the hero or heroine exists in time, because the hero or heroine is always in some sense equipped with purpose.

The man in *The Groves of Academe.* Well, he's immortal, yes. He is a comic villain, and villains too always—I think—partake in this comic immortality. I *think* so. I'm not sure that you couldn't find an example, though, of a villain it wasn't true of. In Dickens again. In the late novels, somebody like Bradley Headstone, the schoolmaster, he's a mixed case. He's certainly not a villain in the sense of, say, the villain in *Little Dorritt,* who belongs to the old-fashioned melodramatic immortal type of villain. Headstone is really half a hero, Steerforth is half a hero, and therefore they don't conform to this.

This all came to me last year, this distinction, when I was thinking about the novel. Not my novel: The Novel.

But maybe that's really part of the trouble I'm having with *my* novel! These girls are all essentially comic figures, and it's awfully hard to make anything happen to them. Maybe this is really the trouble! Maybe I'm going to find out something in this interview! That the whole problem is *time!* I mean for me, in this novel. The passage of time, to show development. I think maybe my trouble is that these girls are comic figures, and that therefore they really can't develop! You see what I mean? They're not all so terribly comic, but most of them are.

How're they ever going to progress through the twenty years between the inauguration of Roosevelt and the inauguration of Eisenhower? This has been the great problem, and here I haven't had a form for it. I mean, all I know is that they're supposed to be middle-aged at the end.

Yes, I think maybe that *is* the trouble. One possibility would be . . . I've been introducing them one by one, chapter by chapter. They all appear at the beginning, you know, like the beginning of an opera, or a musical comedy. And then I take them one by one, chapter by chapter. I have been bringing each one on a little later on in time. But perhaps I can make bigger and bigger jumps so that you could meet, say, the last one when she is already middle-aged. You see what I mean. Maybe this would solve the problem. One five years later, another eight years later, and so on. I could manage the time problem that way. This has been very fruitful! Thank you!

INTERVIEWER: I want to ask you about the problem of time in the novel. You have written that a novel's action cannot take place in the future. But you have said that the action described in *The Oasis* all takes place in the future.

MCCARTHY: *The Oasis* is not a novel. I don't classify it as such. It was terribly criticized, you know, on that ground; people objected, said it wasn't a novel. But I never meant it to be. It's a *conte*, a *conte philosophique*.

INTERVIEWER: And *A Charmed Life* you say has fairy-tale elements.

MCCARTHY: I'm not sure any of my books are novels. Maybe none of them are. Something happens in my writing—I don't mean it to—a sort of distortion, a sort of writing on the bias, seeing things with a sort of swerve and swoop. *A Charmed Life*, for instance. You know, at the beginning I make a sort of inventory of all the town characters, just telling who they are. Now I did this with the intention of describing, well, this nice, ordinary, old-fashioned New England town. But it ended up differently. Something is distorted, the description takes on a sort of extravagance—I don't know exactly how it happens. I know I don't mean it to happen.

INTERVIEWER: You say in one of your articles that perhaps the fault lies simply in the material which the modern world affords, that it itself lacks—

MCCARTHY: Credibility? Yes. It's a difficulty I think all modern writers have.

INTERVIEWER: Other than the problem of arrangement of

time, are there other specific technical difficulties about the novel you find yourself particularly concerned with?

MCCARTHY: Well, the whole question of the point of view, which tortures everybody. It's the problem that everybody's been up against since Joyce, if not before. Of course James really began it, and Flaubert even. You find it as early as *Madame Bovary.* The problem of the point of view, and the voice: *style indirect libre*—the author's voice, by a kind of ventriloquism, disappearing in and completely limited by the voices of his characters. What it has meant is the complete banishment of the author. I would like to restore the author! I haven't tried yet, but I'd like to try after this book, which is as far as I can go in ventriloquism. I would like to try to restore the author. Because you find that if you obey this Jamesian injunction of "Dramatize, dramatize," and especially if you deal with comic characters, as in my case, there is so much you can't say because you're limited by these mentalities. It's just that a certain kind of intelligence—I'm not only speaking of myself, but of anybody, Saul Bellow, for example—is more or less absent from the novel, and has to be, in accordance with these laws which the novel has made for itself. I think one reason that everyone—at least I—welcomed *Dr. Zhivago* was that you had the author in the form of the hero. And this beautiful tenor voice, the hero's voice and the author's—this marvelous voice, and this clear sound of intelligence. The Russians have never gone through the whole development of the novel you find in Joyce, Faulkner, et cetera, so that Pasternak was slightly unaware of the problem! But I think this technical development has become absolutely killing to the novel.

INTERVIEWER: You say that after this novel about the Vassar girls, you—

MCCARTHY: I don't know what I'm going to do, but I want to try something that will introduce, at least back into my work, my own voice. And not in the disguise of a heroine. I'm awfully sick of my heroine. I don't mean in this novel: my heroine of the past. Because the sensibility in each novel got more and more localized with this heroine, who became an agent of perception, et cetera.

Let me make a jump now. The reason that I enjoyed doing those books on Italy, the Venice and Florence books, was that I was writing *in my own voice*. One book was in the first person, and one was completely objective, but it doesn't make any difference. I felt, you know, now I can talk freely! The books were written very fast, the Venice one faster. Even the Florence book, with masses of research in it, was written very fast, with a great deal of energy, with a kind of liberated energy. And without the peculiar kind of painstakingness that's involved in the dramatization that one does in a novel—that is, when nothing can come in that hasn't been perceived through a character. The technical difficulties are so great, in projecting yourself, in feigning an alien consciousness, that too much energy gets lost, I think, in the masquerade. And I think this is not only true of me.

INTERVIEWER: How did you come to write those books about Florence and Venice?

MCCARTHY: By chance. I was in Paris, just about to go home to America, and somebody called up and asked if I would come and have a drink at the Ritz before lunch, that he wanted to ask me something. It was an intermediary from the Berniers, who edit *L'Oeil.* They were in Lausanne, and this man wanted to know whether I would write a book on Venice for them. I had been in Venice once for ten days, years ago, but it seemed somehow adventurous. And there were other reasons too. So I said yes. I went out to meet the Berniers in Lausanne. I had absolutely no money left, about twenty dollars, and I thought, what if all this is a terrible practical joke? You know. I'll get to Lausanne and there won't be any of these people! There'll be nobody! I ran into Jay Laughlin that night, and he said that his aunt was in Lausanne at the moment, so that if anything happened to me, I could call on her! But in any case, I went to Lausanne, and they were real, they were there. And we drove to Venice together.

I knew nothing about the subject—maybe I exaggerate my ignorance now—but I was *appalled*. I was afraid to ask any questions—whenever I'd ask a question Georges Bernier would shudder because it revealed such absolutely terrifying depths of ignorance. So I tried to be silent. I'd never heard before that there was more than one Tiepolo, or more than one Tintoretto, that there was a son. I vaguely knew Bellini, but didn't have any idea there were three Bellinis. Things like that. I couldn't have been expected to know Venetian history, but actually Venetian history is very easy to bone up on, and there isn't much. But the art history! And I considered myself a reasonably cultivated person! My art history was of the most fragmentary nature!

But it was fun, and then that led me into doing the Florence book. I didn't want to, at first. But everything in Venice—in Italy, for that matter—really points to Florence, everything in the Renaissance anyway, like signposts on a road. Whenever you're near discovery, you're near Florence. So I felt that this was all incomplete; I thought I had to go to Florence. It was far from my mind to write a book. Then various events happened, and slowly I decided, All right, I would do the book on Florence. After that I went back to Venice and studied the Florentines in Venice, just for a few days. It was *so* strange to come back to Venice after being immersed in Florence. It looked so terrible! From an architectural point of view, *so* scrappy and nondescript, if you'd been living with the Florentine substance and monumentality, and intellectuality of architecture. At first coming back was a real shock. Oh, and I discovered I liked history! And I thought, my God, maybe I've made a mistake. Maybe I should have been an historian.

INTERVIEWER: It would also appear that you discovered you loved Brunelleschi.

MCCARTHY: Oh, yes! Yes! Also, I felt a great, great congeniality—I don't mean with Brunelleschi personally, I would flatter myself if I said that—but with the history of Florence, the Florentine temperament. I felt that through the medium of writing about this city I could set forth what I believed in, what I was for; that through this city, its history, its architects and painters—more its sculptors than its painters—it was possible for me to say what I believed in. And say it very affirmatively, even though this all ended in 1529, you know, long before the birth of Shakespeare.

INTERVIEWER: In reading the Florence book, I remember being very moved by the passage where you talk of Brunelleschi, about his "absolute integrity and essence," that solidity of his, both real and ideal. When you write about Brunelleschi, you write about this sureness, this "being-itself," and yet as a novelist—in *The Company She Keeps* for instance— you speak of something so very different, and you take almost as a theme this fragmented unplaceability of the human personality.

MCCARTHY: But I was very young then. I think I'm really not interested in the quest for the self anymore. Oh, I suppose everyone continues to be interested in the quest for the self, but what you feel when you're older, I think, is that—how to express this—that you really must *make* the self. It's absolutely useless to look for it, you won't find it, but it's possible in some sense to make it. I don't mean in the sense of making a mask, a Yeatsian mask. But you finally begin in some sense to make and to choose the self you want.

INTERVIEWER: Can you write novels about that?

MCCARTHY: I never have. I never have, I've never even thought of it. That is, I've never thought of writing a developmental novel in which a self of some kind is discovered or is made, is forged, as they say. No. I suppose in a sense I don't know any more today than I did in 1941 about what my identity is. But I've stopped looking for it. I must say, I believe much more in truth now than I did. I do believe in the solidity of truth much more. Yes. I believe there is a truth, and that it's knowable.

—ELISABETH SIFTON

1961

NADINE GORDIMER

Nadine Gordimer was born in 1923, in Springs, the Transvaal, a small town near Johannesburg, South Africa. Her father was a Jewish watchmaker who had immigrated from Lithuania at the age of thirteen; her mother was an Englishwoman. Raised "on the soft side" of South Africa's color bar, her concern with South African apartheid plays a large role in her novels.

Gordimer began writing at the age of nine; six years later she published her first story in *Forum*, a Johannesburg weekly. Though her formal education was interrupted by illness and she was taught primarily by a private tutor, Gordimer did study for one year at the University of Witwatersrand in 1945. Her first collection of short stories, *Face to Face*, was published in 1949. Gordimer's novels include *The Conservationist* (1976), which was awarded the Booker Prize, *Burger's Daughter* (1979), *July's People* (1981), *A Sport of Nature* (1987) and *My Son's Story* (1990). Her eight short-story collections include *A Soldier's Embrace* (1980) and *Something Out There* (1984), and a collection of her essays, *The Essential Gesture: Writing, Politics and Places*, was published in 1988. Her first novel, *The Lying Days*, appeared in 1953.

In 1991 Gordimer received the Nobel Prize for literature, the culmination of the many awards bestowed on her in her career, including the W. H. Smith Literary Award, the James Tait Black Memorial Prize, and France's Grand Aigle d'Or in 1975. She is an honorary member of the American Academy of Arts & Letters and the African National Congress and has served as vice president of PEN International.

NADINE GORDIMER

This interview with Nadine Gordimer was conducted in two parts—in the fall of 1979, when she was in America on a publicity tour for her most recent novel, Burger's Daughter, and in the spring of 1980, when she was here to see her son graduate from college.

Our first meeting was in a room set aside for us by her publisher, the Viking Press—one of those conference rooms made cozy by lots of books and claustrophobic by its lack of windows. The hotel room where our second meeting took place was slightly more conducive to amiable conversation. But Gordimer does not waste words in conversation any more than she does in her prose. On both occasions she was ready to begin our interview the moment I walked in the door and ready to end it the moment the hour she had suggested for our meeting was up. Her clarity and mental focus allow her to express a great deal in a short amount of time.

A petite, birdlike, soft-spoken woman, Gordimer manages to combine a fluidity and gentleness with the seemingly restrained and highly structured workings of her mind. It was as if the forty-odd years that she had devoted to writing had trained her to distill passion—and as a South African writer she is necessarily aware of being surrounded by passion on all sides—into form, whether of the written or spoken word. At the same time, she conveyed a sense

. 2.

youôve escaped altogether. Because without the Kafka will-

power you can|t reach out or be caught (the same thing, here)

in nothing and nowhere. I was going to call it a desert,

from old habit, but where's the sand, where's the camels,

where's the air?— I'm still mensch enough to crack a joke—

you see? Oh but I forgot—you didn't like my jokes, my
                                        unfortunately you had no life in you,
fooling around with kids.   My poor boy, in all those books

and diaries and letters (the ones you posted, to strangers,
                        it   before you put the words
to women) you said a hundred times xaxxaxxxxxxxfxxxfxxxxxxx

xxxxxxxxxxxxxxxxxxxxxxx in my mouth, in your literary way,

in xxxxxxxxxxx (imaginary) letter: you were 'unfit for life',

and so death was always, how would you say, naturally to you.
                                            of vigour
It doesn't come so easily to a man like me I was, I can tell

you, and so here I am writing, talking— I don't know if there

is a word for this/s Anyway, it's Hermann Kafka; I outlived

you, there, the same as

here.

   That is what you really accuse me of, you know,

sixty or so pages the length of that letter varies a bit bit

little from language to language, of course it's been translated

into everything — I don't know what, Hottentot and Iceland-

ic Chinese, though you wrote it 'for me' in German.)

I outlived you, not for seven years, as an old sick man, after

you died, but while you were young and alive. It's clear

as daylight, from the examples you give of being afraid of

me, from the time you were a little boy. You were not

afraid, you were envious. At first, when I took you swimming

and you say you felt yourself a nothing, puny and weak,

beside my big, strong naked body in the change-house, all

right, you say you were proud of such a father, a father

with a fine physique... And may I remind you that father

A manuscript page from a short story by Nadine Gordimer.

of profound caring about the subject matter of her writing; those subjects natural to any writer concerned with the human condition, but set, in her case, in the heightened context of South African life. Her manner seemed to say, "Yes, these are important subjects we're discussing. Now let's get through talking about them so I can get back to the business of writing about them."

INTERVIEWER: Do you have seasons in South Africa, or is it hot all year round?

GORDIMER: Oh no, we have seasons. Near the equator, there's very little difference in the seasons. But right down where we are, at the end of the continent, and also high up where I live in Johannesburg—six thousand feet up—you have very different seasons. We have a sharp, cold winter. No snow—it's rather like your late fall or early spring—sunny, fresh, cold at night. We have a very definite rainy season. But you don't see rain for about half the year. You forget that rain exists. So it's a wonderful feeling when you wake up one day and you smell the rain in the air. Many of the old houses, like ours, have galvanized iron or tin roofs. It's very noisy when there's a heavy rain—it just gallops down on the roof. The house that I was brought up in had a tin roof, so it's one of my earliest memories, lying in bed and listening to the rain . . . and hail, which, of course, on a tin roof is deafening.

INTERVIEWER: When was your first trip out of South Africa?

GORDIMER: My first trip out was to what was then called Rhodesia—Zimbabwe. That might seem very much the same thing as South Africa to you, but it isn't. Zimbabwe is Central Africa, subtropical, shading into tropical. But my first real trip out was much later. I had already published two books—I was thirty years old. I went to Egypt, on my way to England, and America. Perhaps it was a good transition. In London I felt at home, but in an unreal way—I realized when I got there that my picture of London came entirely from books. Particularly

Dickens and Virginia Woolf. The writers who, I'd thought, had impressed me with the features of English life, like Orwell, did not have this evocation when I was actually in the place; they were not writers with a strong sense of place. Woolf and Dickens obviously were. So that when I walked around in Chelsea I felt that this was definitively Mrs. Dalloway's country. I remember I stayed in a hotel near Victoria Station. And at night, these dark, sooty buildings, the dampness when one leant against a wall—absolutely decayed buildings . . .

INTERVIEWER: Were you as unprepared for this first trip off the African continent, and as awed by it, as Rebecca in your novel, *Guest of Honour?*

GORDIMER: No, my mother, who hadn't been back to England for about twenty years, prepared me. She provided me with woolly underwear and whatnot, which I threw away after I arrived. But Rebecca's trip to Switzerland . . . I think descriptions of impressions from the air are something that writers nowadays have to be careful of. Like train journeys in mid-nineteenth-century literature . . . they made such a change in people's lives. They produced a . . . leap in consciousness, especially so far as time was concerned. I can imagine what it must have been, the thought of taking a train that was to go rushing through the countryside. There were so many descriptions of trains in the literature of the day. But I think writers must be careful now not to overdo the use of travel as a metaphor for tremendous internal changes. "The journey" now is by air, and think of how many writers use this—in my own books it appears in *The Conservationist* and in *Guest of Honour.* And indeed, in *Burger's Daughter,* Rosa Burger takes her first trip out of South Africa; I had to resist the temptation to talk about the journey—I describe only the landing, because that particular piece of the landscape could be useful later on.

INTERVIEWER: Was this trip to England a sort of "back to the roots" expedition?

GORDIMER: No. But it brought an understanding of what I was, and helped me to shed the last vestiges of colonialism. I didn't know I was a colonial, but then I had to realize that I was. Even though my mother was only six when she came to South Africa from England, she still would talk about people "going home." But after my first trip out, I realized that "home" was certainly and exclusively—Africa. It could never be anywhere else.

INTERVIEWER: What brought your parents to South Africa?

GORDIMER: The same thing brought them both. They were part of the whole colonial expansion. My maternal grandfather came out in the 1890s with a couple of brothers. South Africa was regarded as a land of opportunity for Europeans. And indeed, he went prospecting for diamonds in Kimberley. I don't think he found very much—maybe some small stones. After that, his entire life was the stock exchange. He was what we call a "tickey-snatcher." A tickey was a tiny coin like a dime—alas, we don't have it anymore. It was equal to three English pence. "Tickey" is a lovely word, don't you think? Well, my grandfather was a tickey-snatcher on the stock exchange, which meant that he sat there all day, and that he bought and sold stocks— making a quick buck.

My father's story is really not such a happy one. He was born in Lithuania, and he went through the whole Jewish pogrom syndrome, you know. He had hardly any schooling. There wasn't any high school for Jewish kids in his village. His father was a shipping clerk and there were twelve children. I'm sure they must have been very poor. Their mother was a seamstress. As soon as my father was twelve or thirteen the idea was that he would just go—*somewhere*, either to America or wherever—it was the time of the great expansion, you know, the early 1900s. So his was the classic Ellis Island story—thirteen years old, not speaking a word of English, traveling in the hold of a ship, but all the way to Africa instead of America—it must have been extraordinary. He was a very unadventurous man; he didn't have a strong personality—he was timid. He still is a mystery to me. I wonder if he didn't burn himself out in this tremendous initial adventure, whether it wasn't really too much for him, and once having found a niche for himself somewhere, he just didn't have the guts to become much of a personality. There was something *arrested* about my father.

INTERVIEWER: What did he do once he got to Africa?

GORDIMER: Like many poor Jews—one either became a shoemaker, a tailor or a watchmaker. He had learned watchmaking. All he had was a little bag with his watchmaking tools. He went to the Transvaal, to the goldfields. He took his little suitcase and went around the mines and asked the miners if anybody wanted a watch fixed. And he would take the watches away to a little room he had somewhere: he would just sit there and mend watches. Then he bought a bicycle and he'd go back round the mines. But by the time I came on the scene he had a little jeweler's shop and he was no longer a watchmaker—he employed one. Indeed, he imported his brother-in-law from Russia to do it. By now my father was the tycoon of the family. He brought *nine* sisters out of Lithuania—the poor man— saving up to bring one after the other. I found out later that he hated them all—we didn't ever have family gatherings. I don't know why he hated them so much.

INTERVIEWER: Where exactly was this jeweler's shop?

GORDIMER: In a little town called Springs, which was thirty miles from Johannesburg. I grew up in a small, gold-mining town of about twenty thousand people.

INTERVIEWER: What were the schools like there?

GORDIMER: Well, I've had little formal education, really. I had a very curious childhood. There were two of us—I have an elder sister—and I was the baby, the spoiled one, the darling. I was awful—brash, a show-off, a dreadful child. But maybe that had something to do with having a lot of energy that didn't find any outlet. I wanted to be a dancer—this was my passion, from the age of about four to ten. I absolutely adored dancing. And I can still remember the pleasure, the release, of using the body in this way. There was no question but that I was to be a dancer, and I suppose maybe I would have been. But at the age of ten, I suddenly went into a dead faint one day, having been a very skinny but very healthy child. Nobody took much notice. But then it happened again. So I was taken to the family doctor, and it was discovered that I had an incredibly rapid heartbeat. Nobody had noticed this; it was, I suppose, part of my excitability and liveliness. It was discovered that I had an enlarged thyroid gland, which causes a fast heartbeat and makes one hyperactive. Well, I've since discovered that this isn't a serious malady at all. It happens to hundreds of people—usually at puberty. But my mother got very alarmed. This rapid pulse should have been ignored. But my mother was quite sure that it meant that I had a "bad heart." So she went immediately to the convent where I attended school and told the nuns, "This child mustn't have any physical training, she mustn't play tennis, she mustn't even swim." At ten, you know, you don't argue with your mother—she tells you you're sick, you believe her. When I would be about to climb stairs, she would say, "Now, take it slowly, *remember your heart.*" And then of course the tragedy was that I was told I mustn't dance anymore. So the dancing stopped like that, which was a terrible deprivation for me.

It's really only in the last decade of my life that I've been able to face all this. When I realized what my mother had done to me, I went through, at the age of twenty, such resentment—this happens to many of us, but I *really* had reason. When I was thirty, I began to understand why she did it, and thus to pity her. By the time she died in '76 we were reconciled. But it was an extraordinary story.

In brief, my mother was unhappily married. It was a dreadful marriage. I suspect she was sometimes in love with other men; but my mother would never have dreamt of having an affair. Because her marriage was unhappy, she concentrated on her children. The chief person she was attracted to was our family doctor. There's no question. I'm sure it was *quite* unconscious, but the fact that she had this "delicate" daughter, about whom she could be constantly calling the doctor—in those days doctors made house calls, and there would be tea and cookies and long chats—made her keep my "illness" going in this way. Probably I was being wrongly treated anyway, so that what medication should have cleared up, it didn't, and symptoms persisted. Of course, I began to feel terribly important. By that time I was reading all sorts of books that led me to believe my affliction made me very interesting. I was growing up with this legend that I was very delicate, that I had something wrong with my heart.

When I was eleven—I don't know how my mother did this—she took me out of school completely. For a year I had no education at all. But I read tremendously. And I retreated into myself, I became very introspective. She changed my whole character. Then she arranged for me to go to a tutor for three hours a day. She took me there at ten in the morning and picked me up at one. It was such incredible loneliness—it's a terrible thing to do to a child. There I was, all on my own, doing my work; a glass of milk was brought to me by this woman—she was very nice, but I had no contact with other children. I spent my whole life, from eleven to sixteen, with older people, with people of my mother's generation. She carted me around to tea parties—I simply lived her life. When she and my father went out at night to dinner she took me along . . . I got to the stage where I could really hardly talk to other children. I was a little old woman.

INTERVIEWER: What about your sister's relationship to you during this time?

GORDIMER: My sister is four years older than I am. She went

away to university; she wasn't really a companion to me. I stopped going to the tutor when I was fifteen or sixteen. So that was the extent of my formal education.

When I was twenty-one or twenty-two, already a published writer, I wanted to go to university to get a little more formal education. But since I hadn't matriculated, I could only do occasional courses at the University of the Witwatersrand—that's Afrikaans for "ridge of white waters." There was something called "general studies"—this was just after the war, and there were lots of veterans who had interrupted their education, and so it was very nice for me—there were people my own age mixed up with the others. A few years ago I gave a graduation address at that same university.

INTERVIEWER: Are you one of these writers to whom they're always trying to give honorary degrees?

GORDIMER: I don't accept them in South Africa. I've taken one—in Belgium in 1981, from the University of Leuven. It turned out to be quite extraordinary, because the man who got an honorary degree with me, Monsignor Oscar Romero, was assassinated two weeks later in El Salvador. In Belgium he had given the most marvelous address. He was such a striking man. He received a standing ovation for about eight minutes from the students. And two weeks later he was lying on the floor of a church, dead.

INTERVIEWER: How long did you go to university?

GORDIMER: One year. This was the first time in my life I'd mixed with blacks, and was more or less the beginning of my political consciousness. Perhaps the good thing about being carted around with my parents was that they would sit playing gin rummy or something while I wandered around the host's house seeing what I could find to read. I discovered everybody from Henry Miller to Upton Sinclair. It was Sinclair's *The Jungle* that really started me thinking about politics: I thought, good God, these people who are exploited in a meatpacking factory—they're just like blacks here. And the whole idea that people came to America, not knowing the language, having to struggle in sweatshops . . . I didn't relate this to my own father, because my father was bourgeois by then . . . but I related it to the blacks. Again, what a paradox that South Africa was the blacks' *own country*, but they were recruited just as if they had been migrant workers for the mines. So I saw the analogy. And that was the beginning of my thinking about my position vis-à-vis blacks. But though I didn't know anything—I was twelve or thirteen, and leading the odd kind of life I did, living in books—I began to think about these things before, perhaps, I was ready for them. When I got to university, it was through mixing with other people who were writing or painting that I got to know black people as equals. In a general and inclusive, nonracial way, I met people who lived in the world of ideas, in the world that interested me passionately.

In the town where I lived, there was no mental food of this kind at all. I'm often amazed to think how they live, those people, and what an oppressed life it must be, because human beings *must* live in the world of ideas. This dimension in the human psyche is very important. It was there, but they didn't know how to express it. Conversation consisted of trivialities. For women, household matters, problems with children. The men would talk about golf or business or horse racing or whatever their practical interests were. Nobody ever talked about, or even around, the big things—life and death. The whole existential aspect of life was never discussed. I, of course, approached it through books. Thought about it on my own. It was as secret as it would have been to discuss my parents' sex life. It was something so private, because I felt that there was nobody with whom I could talk about these things, just *nobody*. But then, of course, when I was moving around at university, my life changed. From Europe—it was just after the war—came Existentialism, and at home in South Africa there was great interest in movements of the Left, and black national movements. At that time, the Communist party and various other leftist movements were not banned. So there were all sorts of Marxist discussion groups. This was an area of thought and conviction I simply never had heard mentioned before. I'd only read about it. And there, of course, were people who were mixing with blacks. So it was through people who were writing, painting or acting that I started mixing with blacks.

INTERVIEWER: What did you do after that year at university? Did you begin any political activity?

GORDIMER: No, you see I was writing then—a lot. I was concentrating tremendously on writing. I wasn't really interested in politics. My approach to living as a white supremacist, perforce, among blacks, was, I see now, the humanist approach, the individualistic approach. I felt that all I needed, in my own behavior, was to ignore and defy the color bar. In other words, my own attitude toward blacks seemed to be sufficient action. I didn't see that it was pretty meaningless until much later.

INTERVIEWER: Were you living on your own then?

GORDIMER: No, I wasn't. In that way I was extremely backward. But you have to look at the kind of dependency that had been induced in me at the crucial age of ten. When other kids were going off to the equivalent of what's known as "summer camp"—"Nadine can't go camping, she's got a *bad heart!* If people go on a hike, she can't go. She's got to stay with mama." A child like that becomes very corrupt, a kind of jester, an entertainer for grown-ups. Especially at the age of fifteen and sixteen. Adults find you charming. You flirt with other people's husbands instead of with boys your own age. It's a very corrupting thing. I was rather a good mimic. Perhaps it was the beginning of having an ear for dialogue? So I would take off people. Grown-ups would sit around at drink parties, getting a little tight, and there was Nadine prancing around, rather cruelly imitating people whom they knew. It didn't occur to them that the moment their backs were turned I was doing it to them as well.

At any rate, I was still living at home when I went to university, and I used to commute by train into Johannesburg. Then my sister got married and lived in Johannesburg, so that when I didn't want to go home I would go to her, which was very nice for me, to have a base there. But I still didn't have the guts, I don't know why, to move out of home, the mining town of Springs. And you see, I wasn't earning enough by my writing, heaven knows, to live on. I was doing something that no kid does nowadays—I was living off my father. On the other hand, my needs were so modest. It never occurred to me that one would want a car—now every kid has a jalopy—this was just not the kind of thing that I would have dreamt of. All I wanted was to buy books. I earned enough with my writing here and there to do this, and of course I also used the library tremendously, which, again, people don't seem to do so much anymore. When I talk to young writers, and I say, "Have you read this or that?"—"Well, no, but books are so expensive . . ."—I say, "Well, for God's sake! The central library is a wonderful library. For heaven's sake, use it! You're never going to be able to write if you don't read!"

INTERVIEWER: Perhaps the isolation of your childhood helped you to become a writer—because of all the time it left you for reading—lonely though it must have been.

GORDIMER: Yes . . . perhaps I would have become a writer anyway. I was doing a bit of writing before I got "ill." I wanted to be a journalist as well as a dancer. You know what made me want to become a journalist? Reading Evelyn Waugh's *Scoop* when I was about eleven. Enough to make anybody want to be a journalist! I absolutely adored it. I was already reading a lot, obviously, but of course I was reading without any discrimination. I would go to the library and wander around, and one book led to another. But I think that's the best way. An Oxford student who is doing a thesis on my writing came to visit me in Johannesburg the other day. I did something I've not done before. I told him, "Right, here are boxes of my papers, just do what you like." I liked him so much—he was so very intelligent and lively. I would meet him at lunch. He would emerge, and so would I, from our separate labors. Suddenly he brought out a kid's exercise book—a list, that I'd kept for about six months when I was twelve, of books that I'd read, and I'd written little book reviews. There was a review of Gone With the Wind. Do you know what was underneath it? My "review" of Pepys's Diary. And I was still reading kids' books at the time, devouring those, and I didn't see that there was any difference between these and Gone With the Wind or Pepys's Diary.

INTERVIEWER: Were you publishing stories in The New Yorker before you published your first book?

GORDIMER: No. I published a book of stories in South Africa, in 1949. I must have started publishing stories in The New Yorker when I was twenty-six. I had one story in The New Yorker, and several in journals like Virginia Quarterly Review, the Yale Review—the traditional places where young writers in the fifties submitted their work. Then my first book was published abroad—a book of short stories.

INTERVIEWER: You sent your manuscripts around to these magazines?

GORDIMER: No, no, by that time I had an agent. It came about that I had an agent in New York. I never sent anything on impulse to those magazines, because I wasn't familiar at all with American publications. The publications I was familiar with were the English ones. Of course, publishers in those days usually watched magazines. And my first publisher, Simon and Schuster, became interested in me through reading that first story of mine in The New Yorker. Katharine White became my editor and friend at The New Yorker. She told me, years after, that all those other stories which were in my first book had already been submitted to *The New Yorker* via my agent. But they had been read by the slush-pile people. She had never seen them, and she regretted very much that she hadn't. But of course these things happen. And I don't quite know how that *one* story surfaced.

INTERVIEWER: Who was your agent?

GORDIMER: My agent was an extraordinary man called Sidney Satenstein. He was an extremely rich man who loved writers. He had no children, and I think writers were his children. He had very few writers really, because he wasn't principally an agent. I came to him through somebody who knew him and knew my work and said, "It's ridiculous—you should have an agent abroad." He was such an incredible man—a sort of John O'Hara character, or even coarser, really. He spent half his time flying to Las Vegas to gamble, or to Florida to play golf. He was a kind of caricature rich American. He always had a cigar in his mouth. He was big, and wore the most ghastly clothes— checked trousers and things like that. He was an absolute darling. Of course he gave me a completely false idea of what an agent was. When I met him I was exactly thirty—though he had taken me on in my mid-twenties—and he was in his mid-sixties. He established a sort of fatherly relationship with me, very fond. Strangely enough, he really liked my writing, which surprised me. One wouldn't have thought that my writing— especially my stories—would have interested *him*. But they did. He was incredible. He knew the circumstances of my life. I was newly divorced, I had a small child—a baby, indeed, eighteen months old—and I had no money. And he really fought for me. If somebody bought something of mine—and after all, I was totally unknown—he insisted that I was a hot property. He got sufficient money for me to live on. When Simon and Schuster bought my first book of stories, they wanted to know if I was writing a novel, and indeed I was. And again he pushed them to give me what would now be considered a *teeny* advance, the amount someone would get to write a line today, but then publishers were not so generous, nor writers so demanding. But at least they gave me a modest sum that I could live on. And once the book was well along, and they saw part of it, Satenstein said to them, you've just *got* to give her more, she's got nothing. So they gave me another advance—all due to him. He used to send me enormous bottles of French perfume. The times I came here—twice—while he was alive, he threw parties for me at the "21" Club, with caviar and sturgeon . . . he had a big heart, and style.

Unfortunately, he died—of a heart attack—just when I began to get known and make a success. He deserved better, because it would have been terribly exciting for him. At least he was able to be thrilled with the response to my first novel. Though not a best-seller—I've never been that—it was a big critical success here . . . a completely unknown writer with a front-page review in *The New York Times.*

INTERVIEWER: What role do you feel politics and the constant conflict it evokes in South Africa have played in your development as a writer?

GORDIMER: Well, it has turned out to have played a very important role. I would have been a writer anyway; I was writing before politics impinged itself upon my consciousness. In my writing, politics comes through in a didactic fashion very rarely. The kind of conversations and polemical arguments you get in *Burger's Daughter,* and in some of my other books—these really play a very minor part. For various reasons to do with the story, they had to be there. But the real influence of politics on my writing is the influence of politics on people. Their lives, and I believe their very personalities, are changed by the extreme political circumstances one lives under in South Africa. I am dealing with people; here are people who are shaped and changed by politics. In that way my material is profoundly influenced by politics.

INTERVIEWER: Do you see that as an advantage for a writer?

GORDIMER: Not really. Life is so apparently amorphous. But as soon as you burrow down this way or that . . . you know Goethe's maxim? "Thrust your hand deep into life, and whatever you bring up in it, that is you, that is your subject." I think that's what writers do.

INTERVIEWER: If you had grown up in a country that was not politically oppressed, might you have become a more abstract writer?

GORDIMER: Maybe. Take a writer whom I admire tremendously, the greatest American short-story writer ever, Eudora Welty. In a strange way, if she had lived where I've lived, she might have turned these incredible gifts of hers more outward—she might have written more, she might have tackled wider subjects. I hesitate to say this, because what she's done she's done wonderfully. But the fact is that she hasn't written very much; I don't think she ever developed fully her gifts as a novelist. She was not forced by circumstance to come to grips with something different. And I don't believe it's just a matter of temperament, because my early writing had qualities similar to hers. I got to hate that word about my work—"sensitive." I was constantly being compared to Katherine Mansfield. I am *not* by nature a political creature, and even now there is so much I don't like in politics, and in political people—though I admire tremendously people who are politically active—there's so much lying to oneself, self-deception, there has to be—you don't make a good political fighter unless you can pretend the warts aren't there.

INTERVIEWER: Do you have the same complaint about Virginia Woolf's novels as you do with Eudora Welty's?

GORDIMER: No, because Virginia Woolf extended herself the other way. I mean she really concentrated totally on that transparent envelope that she'd find for herself. There are two ways to knit experience, which is what writing is about. Writing is making sense of life. You work your whole life and perhaps you've made sense of one small area. Virginia Woolf did this incomparably. And the complexity of her human relationships, the economy with which she managed to portray them . . . staggering. But you can't write a novel like *Burger's Daughter* with the sensibility of a Virginia Woolf. You have to find some other way. You're always trying to find some other way. I'm interested in both ways of writing. I started off by being interested in that transparent envelope.

INTERVIEWER: Was Woolf a big influence when you began writing?

GORDIMER: Midway, I think—after I'd been writing for about five years. She can be a very dangerous influence on a young writer. It's easy to fall into the cadence. But the content isn't there. The same could be said for a completely different kind of writer like Dos Passos, or Hemingway. You've got to be very careful, or you do if you are a writer like me, starting out with an acute sensibility and a poor narrative gift. My narrative gift was weak in my early novels—they tend to fall into beautiful set pieces. It was only with *The Late Bourgeois World*, which was published in 1966, that I began to develop narrative muscle. From then on, my struggle has been not to lose the acute sensitivity—I mean the acuteness of catching nuance in behavior (not in description, because as you get more mature that falls into place) and to marry it successfully to a narrative gift. Because the kind of subjects that are around me, that draw me, that I see motivating me, require a strong narrative ability.

INTERVIEWER: Do you feel that your political situation—the political situation in South Africa—gave you a particular incentive as a writer?

GORDIMER: No. For instance, in *Burger's Daughter*, you could say on the face of it that it's a book about white Communists in South Africa. But to me, it's something else. It's a book about commitment. Commitment is not merely a political thing. It's part of the whole ontological problem in life. It's part of my feeling that what a writer does is to try to make sense of life. I think that's what writing is, I think that's what painting is. It's seeking that thread of order and logic in the disorder, and the incredible waste and marvelous profligate character of life. What all artists are trying to do is to make sense of life. So you see, I would have found my themes had I been an American or an English writer. They are there if one knows where to look . . . if one is pushed from within.

INTERVIEWER: How do you feel that fiction from relatively nonoppressed countries compares with that produced in countries where the political situation necessitates a certain amount of political consciousness?

GORDIMER: To me, it's all a matter of the quality of the writing. To me, that is everything. I can appreciate a tremendously subjective and apolitical piece of writing. If you're a writer, you can make the death of a canary stand for the whole mystery of death. That's the challenge. But, of course, in a sense you are "lucky" if you have great themes. One could say that about the Russians in the nineteenth century. Would they have been the wonderful writers they are if they hadn't had that challenge? They also had the restrictions that we chafe against in South Africa—censorship, and so on. And yet it seems on the face of it to have had only a good effect on writing. Then I think it depends. It can have a deleterious effect. In South Africa, among young blacks who are writing—it's difficult for them to admit it, but they know this—they have to submit to an absolute orthodoxy within black consciousness. The poem or the story or the novel must follow a certain line—it's a kind of party line even though what is in question is not a political party, but it *is*, in the true sense of the word, a party line. For example, nobleness of character in blacks must be shown. It's pretty much frowned upon if there's a white character who is human. It's easy enough to understand this and it's important as a form of consciousness-raising for young blacks to *feel* their own identity, to recite poems which simply exalt blackness and decry everything else, and often to exalt it in crude terms, in crude images, clichés. That's fine as a weapon of propaganda in the struggle, which is what such writing is, primarily. But the *real* writers are victims of this, because as soon as they stray from one or two clearly defined story lines, they're regarded as—

INTERVIEWER: Traitors. Are there many blacks writing and publishing in South Africa?

GORDIMER: There are a lot, and there's a fairly good relationship between black and white writers. Literature is one of the few areas left where black and white feel some identity of purpose; we all struggle under censorship, and most white writers feel a strong sense of responsibility to promote, defend, and help black writers where possible.

INTERVIEWER: *Burger's Daughter* was banned three weeks after it was published, wasn't it?

GORDIMER: Yes, and it remained banned for several months. Then it was unbanned. I was pleased, as you can imagine. Not only for myself, but because it established something of a precedent for other writers, since there are in that book blatant contraventions of certain Acts. In that book I published a document that was a real document, distributed by the students in the 1976 riots in Soweto, and banned by the government. It's in the book with all the misspellings and grammatical mistakes . . . everything exactly as it was; and indeed that's important because, as Rosa points out, these kids rioted because they felt their education wasn't good enough. And when you read the text of that pathetic little pamphlet you can see what the young blacks meant, because that's as well as they could write at the age of sixteen or seventeen, when they were ready to matriculate. So here is one example where, indeed, I flagrantly crossed the line to illegality. Now that the book has been unbanned, it's going to be a difficult thing for the censors to ban other books on evidence of such transgressions.

INTERVIEWER: Why was the book unbanned?

GORDIMER: If I hadn't been a writer who's known abroad and if this hadn't been a book that happened to receive serious attention at a high level abroad—it obviously made the censors feel rather foolish—the book would not have been released. So there we are.

INTERVIEWER: Is it common for a book to be unbanned?

GORDIMER: Well, not so quickly. Of my two previous books, one, *A World of Strangers*, was banned for twelve years, and the other, entitled *The Late Bourgeois World*, for ten; after that length of time most books are pretty well dead.

INTERVIEWER: How does a book get banned?

GORDIMER: First of all, if the book is imported, the authorities embargo it. In other words, it's just like any other cargo arriving at the docks. It is embargoed at customs and the customs officer sends the book off to the Censorship Board. He's got a list of suspects. For instance, a South African writer like myself would be on it, you see, because they know the kind of subjects I've chosen, and, in any case, I've had three books banned previously. So would somebody like James Baldwin; several of his books were banned. Then there's another way that books get embargoed with the possible outcome of a ban. After normal distribution, somebody, some Mother Grundy, old busybody, reads a book that's already in the bookshops, objects to it, and sends it off to the Censorship Board with a complaint. On the recommendation of just one person, a committee will read the book to see if it's "objectionable." But while it's being read by the censors, it's under embargo, which means that although there are copies in the bookshops the bookseller can't sell them; he's got to put them away, take them off the shelves. Sometimes the book is then released. It happened to my novel *A Guest of Honour;* it happened to *The Conservationist. The Conservationist*, I think, was held by the censors for ten weeks, which is iniquitous because the first ten weeks in a book's life are crucial from the point of view of sales. Then it was released by the director of the board. The members of the censor's committee—there are a number of those, usually with three people constituting a committee—read the book, each writes an independent report, and if these concur that the book should be banned or released, right, it's done. If they don't concur, then a fourth person has to be brought in. If they concur that the book is undesirable, then it is banned. The author isn't told. The decision is published in the government gazette, which is published once a week. And that's the end of the book.

INTERVIEWER: What happens then? Is it like what happened with *Ulysses*? Do people scrounge around frantically trying to get hold of it and hide it when policemen walk by?

GORDIMER: People do, people do. Books are usually banned only for sale and distribution but not for *possession*, so that if you've already bought the book you may keep it; but you may not lend it to me or the person across the road, and you may not sell it.

INTERVIEWER: You can't lend it?

GORDIMER: No. This, of course, is perfectly ridiculous. Everybody lends banned books all the time. But people are very nervous, for instance, about buying them abroad or having them sent. They're rather too timid about that. They don't like to have to smuggle them in.

INTERVIEWER: So there isn't much smuggling going on?

GORDIMER: Some people don't, some do. But with some of us, it's a point of honor always to do this.

INTERVIEWER: To smuggle?

GORDIMER: Yes, of course. It's a legitimate form of protest. But unfortunately, when a book is banned, very few copies get around.

INTERVIEWER: Getting back to the idea that oppressed societies produce better writers . . .

GORDIMER: Well, I don't know. I think in the case of Latin American countries, they seem to have experienced so many forms of oppression and for so long that it's become a normal state. But notice that they all write about the same thing . . . the themes are as obsessive as the African ones. *The* theme among the remarkable Latin American writers is the corrupt dictator. Nevertheless, despite the sameness of theme, I regard this as the most exciting fiction in the world being written today.

INTERVIEWER: Which Latin American novelists?

GORDIMER: García Márquez, of course. Hardly necessary even to name Borges. Borges is the only living successor to Franz Kafka. Alejo Carpentier was absolutely wonderful. *The Kingdom of the Earth* is an exquisite little novel—it's brilliant. Then there's Carlos Fuentes, a magnificent writer. Mario Vargas Llosa. And Manuel Puig. These just roll off my tongue quickly; there are others. But always there's this obsessive theme—the corrupt dictator. They all write about it; they're obsessed by it.

INTERVIEWER: I suppose that an oppressed culture such as South Africa's creates the possibility for heroes to exist, and that this is why some of your novels, such as *A Guest of Honour* and *Burger's Daughter,* have heroes as their motivating force.

GORDIMER: Well, you know, it amazes me . . . I come to America, I go to England, I go to France . . . nobody's at risk. They're afraid of getting cancer, losing a lover, losing their jobs, being insecure. It's either something that you have no control over, like death—the atom bomb—or it's something with which you'd be able to cope anyway, and that is not the end of the world; you'll get another job or you'll go on state relief or something of this nature. It's only in my own country that I find people who voluntarily choose to put everything at risk— in their personal life. I mean to most of us, the whole business of falling in love is so totally absorbing, nothing else matters. It's happened to me. There have been times in my life when I have put the person I was in love with far ahead of my work. I would lose interest, I wouldn't even care if the book was coming out. I'd forget when it was being published and I wouldn't worry about the reception it got because I was in such a state of anguish over some man. And yet the people I know who are committed to a *political* cause never allow themselves to be deflected by this sort of personal consideration or ambition.

INTERVIEWER: How do you think romantic love manifests itself in families such as Rosa's, where people's passions lie in politics?

GORDIMER: This is what interested me so much, and this is what I partly tried to explore in the relationship between that girl and her family, who loved her, exploited her, but at the same time felt that they were doing this not for each other or to each other, but because the *cause* demanded it.

INTERVIEWER: We get only very brief glimpses of the love affair between Burger and his wife. In fact, the reader hardly gets any picture either of their relationship or of Rosa's mother at all.

GORDIMER: That was one of the points that's fascinated me about such people: you could know them very well, and yet even in their intimate relations with one another they remained intensely secretive; it's part of the discipline that you have to have. I have a very, very close friend—no character in the book is modeled on her, I might add—but much that I know or have discovered intuitively about such people started with my fascination with her. She has been my closest friend for many years—she's a political exile now—and we've talked nights and days. She's one of the few people for whom I suppose I'd put myself physically at risk if there were to be cause. There are so many things I don't know about her that normally would come out in confidences between people who are as close as we are, and it's because of her political commitment that I can't ask her and she won't tell me. I think that this could extend even to family relationships. It's part of the discipline that the more you know, the more dangerous you are to the people around you. If you and I are working together in an underground movement, the less I know about you the better.

INTERVIEWER: We've talked about the South American writers you admire. What about other writers?

GORDIMER: Lots of novelists say they don't read other novelists, contemporary ones. If this is true, it's a great pity. Imagine, if you had lived in the nineteenth century and not read the writers that we now turn back to so lovingly, or even if you had lived in the twentieth century and hadn't read Lawrence or Hemingway, Virginia Woolf and so on. At different times in my life I've—liked is not the word—I've been psychologically *dependent* upon different writers. Some have remained influential in my life and some haven't, and some I suppose I've forgotten and do them an injustice by not mentioning. When I first began to write, I wrote short stories, and of course I still do; I've written a great many. It's a form that I love to write and to read. I was very influenced by American, southern, short-story writers. Eudora Welty was a great influence on me. Years later, when I met Eudora, visited her in Jackson, there were such parallels between the way she was living, even then, and my life: a black man was mowing the lawn! There was a kind of understanding. Of course, this really had nothing to do with the fact that I thought she was a superb short-story writer. Katherine Anne Porter was an influence on me. Faulkner. Yes. But, again, you see, one lies, because I'm sure that when we were doing the five-finger exercises of short-story writing, Hemingway must have influenced *everybody* who began to write in the late forties, as I did. Proust has been an influence on me, all my life—an influence so deep it frightens me . . . not only in my writing, but in my attitudes to life. Then later came Camus, who was quite a strong influence, and Thomas Mann, whom I've come to admire more and more. E. M. Forster, when I was a young girl; when I was in my twenties—he was very important to me. And I still think *Passage to India* is an absolutely wonderful book that cannot be killed by being taught in the universities.

INTERVIEWER: In what way did Hemingway influence you?

GORDIMER: Oh, through his short stories. The reduction, you know, and also the use of dialogue. Now I think a great failure in Hemingway's short stories is the omnipresence of Hemingway's voice. People do not speak for themselves, in their own thought patterns; they speak as Hemingway does. The "he said," "she said" of Hemingway's work. I've cut these attributions out of my novels, long ago. Some people complain that this makes my novels difficult to read. But I don't care. I simply cannot stand he-said/she-said anymore. And if I can't make readers *know* who's speaking from the tone of voice, the turns of phrase, well, then I've failed. And there's nothing anyone can do about it.

INTERVIEWER: It certainly enforces concentration when one is reading your novels.

GORDIMER: Yes.

INTERVIEWER: The dashes are very effective.

GORDIMER: Oh, that's very old. It started with Sterne's *Tristram Shandy.*

INTERVIEWER: What technique did you use that was the same?

GORDIMER: A kind of interior monologue that jumps about from different points of view. In *The Conservationist,* sometimes it's Mehring speaking from inside himself, observing, and sometimes it's a totally dispassionate view from outside.

INTERVIEWER: It's a much more standard narrative technique than that of *Burger's Daughter.*

GORDIMER: Well, no, it isn't, you know. In *The Conservationist* you've got interior monologue and you have a real narrator. It's not always Mehring speaking. But the line between when he is and when he isn't is very vague, my theory being that the central personality is there, whether it's being observed from outside or whether from inside—it's the same entity.

INTERVIEWER: You mentioned that the way in which you came up with the structure of *Burger's Daughter,* in which Rosa is always speaking to somebody, was from the idea that when one is writing one always has a listener in mind.

GORDIMER: Oh, no, not in your writing, in your *life.* I believe that in your life, in your thoughts when you are alone, you are always addressing yourself to somebody.

INTERVIEWER: And you are not doing this when you write?

GORDIMER: No, because you're no longer yourself when you're writing; you're projecting into other people. But I think in your life, and sometimes even in the conduct of your life, you're imagining that some particular person is seeing your actions. And you're turning away, sometimes, from others.

INTERVIEWER: How has Faulkner influenced you? Do you see any similarities in the structure of *Burger's Daughter* and, say, *As I Lay Dying?*

GORDIMER: No, none at all, and I don't think there could be any influence there. I think the big time when people influence you is when you're very young and you start to write; after that you slough off what you don't need and you painfully hammer out your own style.

INTERVIEWER: There's a similarity between the way your method of narration in *Burger's Daughter* and some of Faulkner's books address themselves to the relative nature of "truth."

GORDIMER: Yes. Well, of course it is a method that points out the relativity of truth. The point I'm trying to make is about the relationship between style and point of view; in a sense, style is the point of view, or the point of view is the style.

INTERVIEWER: Right, and that's why you choose to structure your narratives in the way that you do.

GORDIMER: And then it was Proust who said that style is the moment of identification between the writer and his situation. Ideally that is what it should be—one allows the situation to dictate the style.

INTERVIEWER: So that you are expressing a point of view, with the style that you choose, about the way life is in South Africa.

GORDIMER: Yes. I'm expressing a point of view of the way life is for that particular person and the people around her (in the case of *Burger's Daughter*), and, by extension, a view of life itself.

INTERVIEWER: In Conor Cruise O'Brien's review of *Burger's Daughter*, which appeared in *The New York Review of Books*, he says that your novel is constructed with a "properly deceptive art." He talks about how the construction makes the book seem as if it were a book in which nothing happens, and then several cataclysmic things do, in fact, happen. I was wondering if you have any response.

GORDIMER: For me again, so little of the construction is objectively conceived. It's organic and instinctive and subconscious. I can't tell you how I arrive at it. Though, with each book, I go through a long time when I know what I want to do and I'm held back and puzzled and appalled because I don't know before I begin to write how I'm going to do it, and I always fear that I can't do it. You see, in *Guest of Honour,* I wrote a political book, a book that needed certain objective entities relating to and acting upon the character's life in particular. And I wrote that book as a conventional narrative so that at the point where there was indeed a big Party congress there was no difficulty then in presenting it almost like a play. Then I wrote *The Conservationist,* where I chose to ignore that one had to explain anything at all. I decided that if the reader didn't make the leap in his mind, if the allusions were puzzling to him—too bad. But the narrative would have to carry the book in the sense of what is going on in the characters' minds and going on in their bodies; the way they believed things that they did *really were.* Either the reader would make the leap or not, and if the reader was puzzled now and then—too bad. In other words, the novel was full of private references between the characters. Of course, you take a tremendous risk with such a narrative style, and when you do succeed, I think it's the ideal. When you don't, of course, you irritate the reader or you leave him puzzled. Personally, as a reader, I don't mind being puzzled. Perhaps the writer doesn't know the consequences implied in his/her books, because there's a choice of explanations; and, as a reader, I enjoy that. To me, it's an important part of the exciting business of reading a book, of being stirred, and of having a mind of your own. And so, as a writer, I take the liberty of doing this.

INTERVIEWER: You don't consciously create a complete structure before you begin writing a novel?

GORDIMER: No. For *Burger's Daughter,* perhaps four or five pages of very scrappy notes for the whole book. But, for me, those half sentences or little snatches of dialogue are tremendously important; they are the core of something. And I've only got to look at them, and know that that's the next stage in the book that I'm coming to.

INTERVIEWER: Is this the way you usually write your novels?

GORDIMER: Yes. With me it's really a very natural process once I get started. An organic process.

INTERVIEWER: How long do you prepare before you get started?

GORDIMER: It's so difficult for me to say because, looking back at *Burger's Daughter,* for example, I know that I've been fascinated by the kind of person Rosa is for many years. It's as if the secret of a life is there, and slowly I'm circling, coming closer and closer to it. Perhaps there are other themes that present themselves but finally spin off instead of drawing me to them. I suppose one's ready for different things at different times in one's life. And also, in a country where so much is changing, the quality of life around one is changing; so that perhaps I wouldn't be attracted now to write the book that I wrote ten years ago, and vice versa.

INTERVIEWER: So you feel that the way your books are written is more an inevitable phenomenon than a conscious choice.

GORDIMER: I don't think any writer can say why he chooses this or that or how a theme impinges itself. It may have been around for a long time and then a stage comes in your life when your imagination is ready for it and you can deal with it.

INTERVIEWER: I wanted to ask you about *The Conservationist*, in which death is almost an obsessive theme. There are certain sections where it is continually brought up in ritualized ways: the man hopping up from his grave in different people's minds throughout the book, and the ritual of killing the goat to get back at Solomon's injury . . .

GORDIMER: In *The Conservationist* there's a resurrection theme, and that is also a political theme. At the end of the book there's a disguised message. The slogan of the biggest banned liberation movement, a kind of battle cry widely adopted, is the African word, "mayibuye." This means, "Africa, come back." You can see the whole idea of resurrection is there. And if you look at the end of *The Conservationist* you'll see that this thought is reworded, but it is actually what is said when the unknown man is reburied: that although he is nameless and childless, he has all the children of other people around him; in other words, the future. He has people around him who are not his blood brothers and sisters but who stand for them. And that he has now been put with proper ceremony into his own earth. He has taken possession of it. There's a suggestion of something that has been planted, that is going to grow again.

INTERVIEWER: This theme is repeated in one of your short stories—"Six Feet of the Country."

GORDIMER: Yes. But the repetition is in reverse: "Six Feet" was written years before *The Conservationist*. Oddly enough, that early story is based on a true incident.

INTERVIEWER: Do you have a fascination with death?

GORDIMER: Not consciously, but then . . . how can any thinking person not have? Death is really the mystery of life, isn't it? If you ask, "What happens when we die? Why do we die?" you are asking, "Why do we live?" Unless one has a religion . . . Without a religious explanation, one has only the Mount Everest argument: "I climb it because it's there. I live because there is the gift of life." It's not an answer, really, it's an evasion. Or, "I think my purpose on this earth is to make life better." Progress is the business of making life more safe and more enjoyable . . . fuller, generally. But that justification, it stops short of death, doesn't it? The only transcendent principle is that you are then seeking to improve the human lot for future generations. But we still don't get past the fact that it's a turnabout business; it's your turn and then it's mine, and life is taken up by somebody else. Human beings are never reconciled to this. In my own life I am made puzzled and uneasy by my attitude and that of others to death. If somebody dies young it's so terrible, it's such a tragedy, and the sense of waste is so strong; you think of all the promise that was there. And then if people live into old age, there's the horror of decay, especially—it's awful to say—but especially with exceptional people; when you see their minds going and their bodies falling to pieces, and they want to die and you want them to die, then that's equally terrible. So it's the mere fact of death that we can't accept? We say it's terrible if people die young, and we say it's terrible if they go on living too long.

INTERVIEWER: Are you a religious or mystical person?

GORDIMER: I'm an atheist. I wouldn't even call myself an agnostic. I am an atheist. But I think I have a basically religious temperament, perhaps even a profoundly religious one. I went through a stage in my life when I was about thirty-two or thirty-three years old—when I was very fascinated by the writings of Simone Weil. In the end, her religious philosophy left me where I was. But I felt that there was something there that answered to a need that I felt, my "need for roots" that she wrote about so marvelously. I couldn't find the same solution.

INTERVIEWER: How do you feel about Conor Cruise O'Brien's idea about there being Christian overtones in *Burger's Daughter?*

GORDIMER: Well, I'm thinking of that. I'm sure that many of my friends, people who know me well, laughed because they know that, as I say, I'm an atheist. But he hit on something that is there in me, a certain inclination—more than that—a pull. Perhaps, brought up differently in a different milieu, in a different way, I might have been a religious person.

INTERVIEWER: Then there is the resurrection of the black man in *The Conservationist.*

GORDIMER: But of course the idea of resurrection comes from the Greeks, from the Egyptians. You can begin to believe in a collective unconscious without having religious beliefs.

INTERVIEWER: I've noticed that sensual elements play a key role in your writing: smells, textures, sexuality, bodily functions. You don't write about the so-called "beautiful people," the leisured class of South Africa, and the beautiful environment in which they must live. In fact, I noticed that almost all of the white women in your *Selected Stories* are physically and mentally both highly unattractive and middle-class. Does this reflect the way in which you view white colonialists in your country?

GORDIMER: I don't make such judgments about people. After all, I'm a white colonial woman myself, of colonial descent. Perhaps I know us too well through myself. But if somebody is partly frivolous or superficial, has moments of cruelty or self-doubt, I don't write them off, because I think that absolutely everybody has what are known as human failings. My black characters are not angels either. All this role-playing that is done in a society like ours—it's done in many societies, but it's more noticeable in ours—sometimes the role is forced upon you. You fall into it. It's a kind of song-and-dance routine, and you find yourself, and my characters find themselves, acting out these preconceived, ready-made roles. But, of course, there are a large number of white women of a certain kind in the kind of society that I come from who . . . well, the best one can say of them is that one can excuse them because of their ignorance of what they have allowed themselves to become. I see the same kind of women here in the U.S. You go into one of the big stores here and you can see these extremely well-dressed, often rather dissatisfied-looking, even sad-looking middle-aged women, rich, sitting trying on a dozen pairs of shoes; and you can see they're sitting there for the morning. And it's a terribly agonizing decision, but maybe the heel should be a little higher or maybe . . . should I get two pairs? And a few blocks away it's appalling to see in what poverty and misery other people are living in this city, New York. Why is it that one doesn't criticize that American woman the same way one does her counterpart in South Africa? For me, the difference is that the rich American represents class difference and injustice, while in South Africa the injustice is based on both class *and* race prejudice.

INTERVIEWER: What about the "beautiful people" of South Africa?

GORDIMER: They're featured very prominently in an early book of mine called *A World of Strangers* but very rarely since then, until the character of Mehring in *The Conservationist.* They are not the most interesting people in South Africa, believe me . . . although they may regard themselves as such.

INTERVIEWER: Is it intentional that so often the physical details of characters are not brought home strongly in your work? One gets a very strong sense of the mind's workings in major characters, but often a very limited sense of what they actually look like.

GORDIMER: I think that physical descriptions of people should be minimal. There are exceptions—take Isaac Bashevis Singer. He very often starts off a story by giving you a full physical description. If you look very closely at the description, of course it's extremely good. He stamps character on a twist of the nose or a tuft of red beard. My own preference is for physical description to come piecemeal at times when it furthers other elements in the text. For instance, you might describe a character's eyes when another character is looking straight into them so it would be natural . . . a feature of that particular moment in the narrative. There might be another scene later, where the character whose eyes you've described is under tension, and is showing it by tapping her foot or picking at a hangnail—so if there was something particular about her hands, that would be the time to talk about them. I'm telling you this as if it were something to be planned. It isn't. It comes at the appropriate moment.

INTERVIEWER: In the introduction to your *Selected Stories*, you say: "My femininity has never constituted any special kind of solitude, for me. In fact, my only genuine connection with the social life of the town (when I was growing up) was through my femaleness. As an adolescent, at least, I felt and followed sexual attraction in common with others; that was a form of communion I could share. Rapunzel's hair is the right metaphor for this femininity: by means of it I was able to let myself out and live in the body, with others, as well as—alone—in the mind." You go on to say you "question the existence of the specific solitude of woman-as-intellectual when that woman is a writer, because when it comes to their essential faculty as writers, all writers are androgynous beings."

What about the process of becoming a writer, of becoming an androgynous being? Isn't that a struggle for women?

GORDIMER: I hesitate to generalize from my own experience. I would consider it an arrogance to state my own experience as true for all women. I really haven't suffered at all from being a woman. It's inconceivable, for example, that I could ever have become interested in a man who regarded women as nonbeings. It's never happened. There would be a kind of war between us. I just take it for granted, and it has always happened, that the men in my life have been people who treated me as an equal. There was never any question of fighting for this. I'm somebody who has lived a life as a woman. In other words, I've been twice married, I've brought up children, I've done all the things that women do. I haven't avoided or escaped this, supposing that I should have wished to, and I don't wish to and never wished to. But, as I say, I don't generalize, because I see all around me women who are gifted and intelligent who *do* have these struggles and who indeed *infuriate* me easier. But I did manage to maintain it when my children were young, I suppose, by being rather ruthless. I think writers, artists, are very ruthless, and they have to be. It's unpleasant for other people, but I don't know how else we can manage. Because the world will never make a place for you. My own family came to understand and respect this. Really, when my children were quite small they knew that in my working hours they must leave me alone; if they came home from school and my door was closed, they left and they didn't turn on the radio full blast. I was criticized for this by other people. But my own children don't hold it against me. I still had time that I spent with them. What I have also sacrificed, and it hasn't been a sacrifice for me, is a social life; and as I've got older, I'm less and less interested in that. When I was young I did go through some years when I enjoyed partygoing very much and stayed out all night. But in the end, the loss next day, the fact that I had a hangover and that I couldn't work, quickly outweighed the pleasure; and, as time has gone by, I've kept more and more to myself. Because a writer doesn't only need the time when he's actually writing—he or she has got to have time to think and time just to let things work out. Nothing is worse for this than society. Nothing is worse for this than the abrasive, if enjoyable, effect of other people.

INTERVIEWER: What conditions do you find to be most conducive to writing?

GORDIMER: Well, nowhere very special, no great, splendid

desk and cork-lined room. There have been times in my life, my God, when I was a young divorced woman with a small child living in a small apartment with thin walls when other people's radios would drive me absolutely mad. And that's still the thing that bothers me tremendously—*that* kind of noise. I don't mind people's voices. But Muzak or the constant clack-clack of a radio or television coming through the door . . . well, I live in a suburban house where I have a small room where I work. I have a door with direct access to the garden—a great luxury for me—so that I can get in and out without anybody bothering me or knowing where I am. Before I begin to work I pull out the phone and it stays out until I'm ready to plug it in again. If people really want you, they'll find you some other time. And it's as simple as that, really.

INTERVIEWER: How long do you usually work every day? Or do you work every day?

GORDIMER: When I'm working on a book I work every day. I work about four hours nonstop, and then I'll be very tired and nothing comes anymore, and then I will do other things. I can't understand writers who feel they shouldn't have to do any of the ordinary things of life, because I think that this is necessary; one has got to keep in touch with that. The solitude of writing is also quite frightening. It's quite close sometimes to madness, one just disappears for a day and loses touch. The ordinary action of taking a dress down to the dry cleaner's or spraying some plants infected with aphids is a very sane and good thing to do. It brings one back, so to speak. It also brings the world back. I have formed the habit, over the last two books I've written, of spending half an hour or so reading over what I'd written during the day just before I go to bed at night. Then, of course, you get tempted to fix it up, fuss with it, at night. But I find that's good. But if I've been with friends or gone out somewhere, then I won't do that. The fact is that I lead a rather solitary life when I'm writing.

INTERVIEWER: Is there a time of day that's best?

GORDIMER: I work in the morning. That's best for me.

INTERVIEWER: How long does it usually take you to write a book?

GORDIMER: It depends. The shortest has been about eighteen months. *Burger's Daughter* took me four years.

INTERVIEWER: Four years of steady writing?

GORDIMER: I wrote one or two other things, small things. Sometimes when I'm writing I get a block, and so I stop and write a short story, and that seems to set me going. Sometimes when I'm writing a book I get ideas for stories, and they're just tucked away. But alas, as I get older, I get fewer ideas for short stories. I used to be teeming with them. And I'm sorry about that because I like short stories.

INTERVIEWER: What about writer's block? Is that a problem for you?

GORDIMER: No. And I say so, as you see, with hesitation and fear and trembling because you always feel that that demon is waiting behind the back of your brain.

INTERVIEWER: You have the short story to loosen you up?

GORDIMER: Yes, and occasionally I do some nonfiction piece, usually something involving travel. For me, this is a kind of relaxation. During the time I was writing *Burger's Daughter* I did two such pieces.

INTERVIEWER: You don't even have minor fits of procrastination, endless cups of tea or things like that?

GORDIMER: No, no. Though I do have, not blocks but . . . problems moving on from one stage to the next; particularly when I've got something done with and it's worked well. For instance, I finished that chapter with Brandt Vermeulen, you know, the nationalist in *Burger's Daughter,* which went unexpectedly well. I simply wrote it just like that and it all came right. I had been dreading it. I had been dreading getting the tone of voice and everything right. And then, knowing where I was going on from there, there was suddenly an inability to get out of that mood and into another; and so there were perhaps a few awful days; because when that happens, I don't stop and do something else. I sit in front of that paper for the normal time that I would be writing. And then, well, I break through.

INTERVIEWER: There's no specific routine that gets you from the bedroom or the living room into the writing room, bridging that terrifying gap between not writing and writing?

GORDIMER: No—that's the advantage if you're free to choose the time you're going to write. That's the advantage of writing in the morning. Because then one gets up and in one's subconscious mind one knows: I am going to write. Whatever small thing you have to do, such as talking to other people at breakfast, it's only done with one part of you, so to speak; just done on the surface. The person with whom I live, my husband, understands this and has for a very long time. And he knows that to say to me at breakfast, "What shall we do about so-and-so?" or, "Would you read this letter?"—he knows that isn't the time to ask. I get irritable, and irritated, I don't want to be asked to do things then. And I don't want to phone an order to the grocer at that time. I just want to be left alone to eat my breakfast. Ideally, I like to walk around a bit outside, which you can do, of course, with a garden. But I often think that even that becomes a kind of procrastination because it's so easy then to see a weed that one has to stop and pull up and then one sees some ants and wonders, Where are they going? So the best thing to do is to go into the room and close the door and sit down.

INTERVIEWER: Do you go through much revision of your work?

GORDIMER: As time goes by, less and less. I used to. When I was young, I used to write three times as much as the work one finally reads. If I wrote a story, it would be three times the final length of that story. But that was in the very early times of my writing. Short stories are a wonderful discipline against over-writing. You get so used to cutting out what is extraneous.

INTERVIEWER: Do you ever find critics useful?

GORDIMER: Yes, but you must remember they're always after the event, aren't they? Because then the work's already done. And the time you find you agree with them is when they come to the same conclusions you do. In other words, if a critic objects to something that I know by my lights is right, that I did the best I could and that it's well done, I'm not affected by the fact that somebody didn't like it. But if I have doubts about a character or something that I've done, and these doubts are confirmed by a critic, then I feel my doubts confirmed and I'm glad to respect that critic's objections.

INTERVIEWER: Frequently writers say they don't read reviews because even one bad review among ten shining ones can be devastating.

GORDIMER: Of course, it depends very much on the reviewer. There are people who are not reviewers, one or two, to whom I give my books to read, perhaps even in manuscript. I am sick with apprehension while they are reading them. And certainly there are certain reviewers I would be very wounded by if they were to say, "Well, this one's rotten."

INTERVIEWER: But this hasn't happened yet.

GORDIMER: Not yet. With *Burger's Daughter* I've had, out of perhaps fifty or sixty reviews, two bad ones.

INTERVIEWER: You say that writers are androgynous. Do you recognize any difference between masculine and feminine writing, such as say, Woolf's versus Hemingway's writing?

GORDIMER: Hemingway is such an extreme example, and his writing is really an instance of machismo, isn't it? Henry James could have been a woman. E. M. Forster could have been. George Eliot could have been a man. I used to be too insistent on this point that there's no sex in the brain; I'm less insistent now—perhaps I'm being influenced by the changing attitude of women toward themselves in general? I don't think there's anything that women writers don't know. But it may be that there are certain aspects of life that they can deal with a shade better, just as I wonder whether any woman writer, however great, could have written the marvelous war scenes in *War and Peace*. By and large, I don't think it matters a damn what sex a writer is, so long as the work is that of a real *writer*. I think there *is* such a thing as "ladies' writing," for instance, feminine writing; there are "authoresses" and "poetesses." And there are men, like Hemingway, whose excessive "manliness" is a concomitant part of their writing. But with so many of the male writers whom I admire, it doesn't matter too much. There doesn't seem to be anything *they* don't know, either. After all, look at Molly Bloom's soliloquy. To me, that's the ultimate proof of the ability of either sex to understand and convey the inner workings of the other. No woman was ever "written" better by a woman writer. How did Joyce know? God knows how, and it doesn't matter. When I was a young woman, a young girl, I wrote a story about a man who had lost his leg. He couldn't accept this, the reality of it, until he was sitting recuperating in the garden and saw a locust that had its leg off; he saw the locust struggling because it felt its leg was still there. I don't know how I wrote that story, somehow I just imagined myself into it. A psychiatrist once told me it was a perfect example of penis envy.

INTERVIEWER: Is there anything, new or otherwise, that you hope to do with your writing in the future?

GORDIMER: I would always hope to find the one right way to tackle whatever subject I'm dealing with. To me, that's the real problem, and the challenge of writing. There's no such feeling as a general achievement. You cannot say that because I have managed to say what I wanted to say in one book, that it is now inside me for the next, because the next one is going to have a different demand. And until I find out how to write it, I can't tackle it.

INTERVIEWER: In other words, you don't know the question until you have the answer?

GORDIMER: Yes. I would like to say something about how I feel in general about what a novel, or any story, ought to be. It's a quotation from Kafka. He said, "A book ought to be an ax to break up the frozen sea within us."

—JANNIKA HURWITT

1980

MAYA ANGELOU

Maya Angelou is perhaps best known for the autobiographical series she began with *I Know Why the Caged Bird Sings* (1970), which was an immediate success and received a National Book Award nomination. In it, Angelou depicts her growing up in the segregated town of Stamps, Arkansas, where she had been sent by her divorced parents. In *Gather Together in My Name* (1974), Angelou recounts the first four years of her life as a single mother. *Singin' and Swingin' and Gettin' Merry Like Christmas* (1976) chronicles her life into the 1950s. *The Heart of a Woman* (1981) and *All God's Children Need Traveling Shoes* (1986) describe her travels in Africa, as well as her involvement in the civil rights movement in the United States.

Angelou's first volume of poetry, *Just Give Me a Cold Drink of Water 'fore I Die* (1971), was nominated for the Pulitzer Prize. Other collections include *Oh Pray My Wings Are Gonna Fit Me Well* (1975) and *And Still I Rise* (1978). *I Shall Not Be Moved* was published in 1990.

Throughout her life, Angelou's involvement in the performing arts has been varied and outstanding. She has danced under the tuition of Martha Graham, Pearl Primus and Ann Halprin;

she was the first black woman to have an original screenplay produced (*Georgia, Georgia,* 1971) and was the first black American woman to direct films.

Angelou has held academic posts at several universities in the United States, including the University of California and Wichita State. She has been honored by Smith College (1975), Mills College (1975), and Lawrence University (1976). In 1981 Wake University in Winston-Salem, North Carolina, appointed her to a lifetime position as the first Reynolds Professor of American Studies. In 1991 Angelou was named Distinguished Visiting Professor at Exeter University, England. She read her poem "On the Pulse of Morning" at the presidential inauguration in 1993.

MAYA ANGELOU

This interview was conducted on the stage of the YMHA on Manhattan's Upper East Side. An audience predominantly of women filled every seat, with standees in the back . . . a testament to Maya Angelou's drawing power. Close to the stage was a small contingent of black women dressed in the white robes of the Black Muslim order. Many of Angelou's remarks drew fervid applause, especially those that reflected her views on racial problems, the need to persevere, and "courage." She is an extraordinary performer and has a powerful stage presence. Many of the answers seemed as much directed to the audience as to the interviewer, so that when Maya Angelou concluded the evening by reading aloud from her work—again to a rapt audience—it seemed a logical extension of a planned entertainment.

INTERVIEWER: You once told me that you write lying on a made-up bed with a bottle of sherry, a dictionary, Roget's Thesaurus, yellow pads, an ashtray and a Bible. What's the function of the Bible?

ANGELOU: The language of all the interpretations, the translations, of the Judaic Bible and the Christian Bible, is musical,

Before a long journey begins which includes crossing

boundaries and time zones, the prudent traveler checks her *maps*

checks, addresses and

travel documents, passport, Visa, medical innoculations,

, makes certain that her ~~that she has~~

clothes ~~is~~ fit the weather, and apt currencies for the

will

destination. *If the journey include crossing regional*

national boundaries and time zones, the traveller

checks the validity of her

The less careful traveler is not so superb in her *disappointments*

and as a result frequently encounters delays, and

planning, *she* Once the journey commences she unfailingly *disappointment*

and despair

some

reaches ~~a~~ destination, *although possibly not the*

one of her choice

It is *who experiences*

The desperate traveler ~~affords~~ the greatest surprises and

the hold of the road unquestly for her, since her

the most exquisite thrills, ~~for~~ her sole preparation for

→ ~~the road~~ is the fierce determination to leave where she is,

and her only certain destination is somewhere other than

where she has been.

"I got the key to the Highway,

Booked down and I'm bound to go

L38235-0188

A manuscript page from an essay by Maya Angelou.

just wonderful. I read the Bible to myself; I'll take any translation, any edition, and read it aloud, just to hear the language, hear the rhythm, and remind myself how beautiful English is. Though I do manage to mumble around in about seven or eight languages, English remains the most beautiful of languages. It will do anything.

INTERVIEWER: Do you read it to get inspired to pick up your own pen?

ANGELOU: For melody. For content also. I'm working at trying to be a Christian, and that's serious business. It's like trying to be a good Jew, a good Muslim, a good Buddhist, a good Shintoist, a good Zoroastrian, a good friend, a good lover, a good mother, a good buddy: it's serious business. It's not something where you think, Oh, I've got it done. I did it all day, hot-diggety. The truth is, all day long you try to do it, try to be it, and then in the evening, if you're honest and have a little courage, you look at yourself and say, Hmm. I only blew it eighty-six times. Not bad. I'm trying to be a Christian, and the Bible helps me to remind myself what I'm about.

INTERVIEWER: Do you transfer that melody to your own prose? Do you think your prose has that particular ring that one associates with the King James version?

ANGELOU: I want to hear how English sounds; how Edna St. Vincent Millay heard English. I want to hear it, so I read it aloud. It is not so that I can then imitate it. It is to remind me what a glorious language it is. Then, I try to be particular, and even original. It's a little like reading Gerard Manley Hopkins or Paul Laurence Dunbar, or James Weldon Johnson.

INTERVIEWER: And is the bottle of sherry for the end of the day, or to fuel the imagination?

ANGELOU: I might have it at 6:15 A.M. just as soon as I get in, but usually it's about eleven o'clock when I'll have a glass of sherry.

INTERVIEWER: When you are refreshed by the Bible and the sherry, how do you start a day's work?

ANGELOU: I have kept a hotel room in every town I've ever lived in. I rent a hotel room for a few months, leave my home at six and try to be at work by 6:30. To write, I lie across the bed, so that this elbow is absolutely encrusted at the end, just so rough with calluses. I never allow the hotel people to change the sheets, because I never sleep there. I stay until 12:30 or 1:30 in the afternoon, and then I go home and try to breathe; I look at the work around five; I have an orderly dinner: proper, quiet, lovely dinner; and then I go back to work the next morning. Sometimes in hotels I'll go into the room, and there'll be a note on the floor which says, "Dear Miss Angelou, let us change the sheets. We think they are moldy." But I only allow them to come in and empty wastebaskets. I insist that all things are taken off the walls. I don't want anything in there. I go into the room, and I feel as if all my beliefs are suspended. Nothing holds me to anything. No milkmaids, no flowers, nothing. I just want to *feel* and then when I start to work I'll remember. I'll read something, maybe the Psalms, maybe, again, something from Mr. Dunbar, James Weldon Johnson. And I'll remember how beautiful, how pliable the language is, how it will lend itself. If you pull it, it says, "Okay." I remember that, and I start to write. Nathaniel Hawthorne says, "Easy reading is damn hard writing." I try to pull the language in to such a sharpness that it jumps off the page. It must look easy, but it takes me forever to get it to look so easy. Of course, there are those critics—New York critics, as a rule—who say, "Well, Maya Angelou has a new book out and, of course, it's good but then she's a natural writer." Those are the ones I want to grab by the throat and wrestle to the floor because it takes me forever to get it to sing. I *work* at the language. On an evening like this, looking out at the auditorium, if I had to write this evening from my point of view, I'd see the rust-red used worn velvet seats, and the lightness where people's backs have rubbed against the back of the seat so that it's a light orange; then, the beautiful colors of the people's faces, the white, pink-white, beige-white, light beige and brown and tan—I would have to look at all that, at all those faces and the way they sit on top of their necks. When I would end up writing after four hours or five hours in my room, it might sound like: "It was a rat that sat on a mat. That's that. Not a cat." But I would continue to play with it and pull at it and say, "I love you. Come to me. I love you." It might take me two or three weeks just to describe what I'm seeing now.

INTERVIEWER: How do you know when it's what you want?

ANGELOU: I know when it's the best I can do. It may not be the best there is. Another writer may do it much better. But I know when it's the best I can do. I know that one of the great arts that the writer develops is the art of saying, "No. No, I'm finished. Bye." And leaving it alone. I will not write it into the ground. I will not write the life out of it. I won't do that.

INTERVIEWER: How much revising is involved?

ANGELOU: I write in the morning, and then go home about midday and take a shower, because writing, as you know, is very hard work, so you have to do a double ablution. Then I go out and shop—I'm a serious cook—and pretend to be normal. I play sane: "Good morning! Fine, thank you. And you?" And I go home. I prepare dinner for myself and if I have houseguests, I do the candles and the pretty music and all that. Then, after all the dishes are moved away, I read what I wrote that morning. And more often than not, if I've done nine pages I may be able to save two and a half, or three. That's the cruelest time you know, to really admit that it doesn't work. And to blue-pencil it. When I finish maybe fifty pages, and read them—fifty acceptable pages—it's not too bad. I've had the same editor since 1967. Many times he has said to me over the years, or asked me, "Why would you use a semicolon instead of a colon?" And many times over the years I have said to him things like: "I will never speak to you again. Forever. Good-bye. That is it. Thank you very much." And I leave. Then I read the piece and I think of his suggestions. I send him a telegram that says, "OK, so you're right. So what? Don't ever mention this to me again. If you do, I will never speak to you again." About two years ago I was visiting him and his wife in the Hamptons. I was at the end of a dining room table with a sit-down dinner of about fourteen people. Way at the end I said to someone, "I sent him telegrams over the years." From the other end of the table he said, "And I've kept every one!" Brute! But the editing, one's own editing, before the editor sees it, is the most important.

INTERVIEWER: The five autobiographical books follow each other in chronological order. When you started writing *I Know Why the Caged Bird Sings*, did you know that you would move on from that? It almost works line by line into the second volume.

ANGELOU: I know, but I didn't really mean to. I thought I was going to write *Caged Bird* and that would be it and I would go back to playwriting and writing scripts for television. Autobiography is awfully seductive; it's wonderful. Once I got into it I realized I was following a tradition established by Frederick Douglass—the slave narrative—speaking in the first-person singular talking about the first-person plural, always saying "I" meaning "we." And what a responsibility! Trying to work with that form, the autobiographical mode, to change it, to make it bigger, richer, finer, and more inclusive in the twentieth century has been a great challenge for me. I've written five now, and I really hope—the works are required reading in many universities and colleges in the United States—that people *read* my work. The greatest compliment I receive is when people walk up to me on the street or in airports and say, "Miss Angelou, I *wrote* your books last year and I really—I mean I *read* . . ." That is it: that the person has come into the books so seriously, so completely, that he or she, black or white, male or female, feels, "That's my story. I told it. I'm making it up on the spot." That's the great compliment. I didn't expect, originally, that I was going to continue with the form. I thought I was going to write a little book and it would be fine, and I would go on back to poetry, write a little music.

INTERVIEWER: What about the genesis of the first book? Who were the people who helped you shape those sentences that leap off the page?

ANGELOU: Oh well, they started years and years before I ever wrote, when I was very young. I loved the black American minister. I loved the melody of the voice, and the imagery, so rich, and almost impossible. The minister in my church in Arkansas, when I was very young, would use phrases such as "God stepped out, the sun over his right shoulder, the moon nestling in the palm of his hand." I mean, I just loved it, and I loved the black poets, and I loved Shakespeare, and Edgar Allan Poe, and I liked Matthew Arnold a lot, still do. Being mute for a number of years, I read, and memorized, and all those people have had tremendous influence . . . in the first book, and even in the most recent book.

INTERVIEWER: Mute?

ANGELOU: I was raped when I was very young. I told my brother the name of the person who had done it. Within a few days the man was killed. In my child's mind—seven and a half years old—I thought my voice had killed him. So I stopped talking for five years. Of course I've written about this in *Caged Bird*.

INTERVIEWER: When did you decide you were going to be a writer? Was there a moment when you suddenly said, "This is what I wish to do for the rest of my life?"

ANGELOU: Well, I had written a television series for PBS, and I was going out to California. I thought I was a poet and playwright. That was what I was going to do the rest of my life. Or become famous as a real estate broker. This sounds like namedropping, and it really is—but James Baldwin took me over to dinner with Jules and Judy Feiffer one evening. All three of them are great talkers. They went on with their stories and I had to fight for the right to play it good. I had to insert myself to tell some stories too. Well, the next day, Judy Feiffer called Bob Loomis, an editor at Random House, and suggested that if he could get me to write an autobiography, he'd have something. So he phoned me and I said, "No, under no circumstances; I certainly will not do such a thing." So I went out to California to produce this series on African and black American culture. Loomis called me out there about three times. Each time I said no. Then he talked to James Baldwin. Jimmy gave him a ploy which always works with me—though I'm not proud to say that. The next time he called, he said, "Well, Miss Angelou. I won't bother you again. It's just as well that you don't attempt to write this book, because to write autobiography as literature is almost impossible." I said, "What are you talking about? I'll do it." I'm not proud about this button which can be pushed and I will immediately jump.

INTERVIEWER: Do you select a dominant theme for each book?

ANGELOU: I try to remember times in my life, incidents in which there was the dominating theme of cruelty, or kindness, or generosity, or envy, or happiness, glee . . . perhaps four incidents in the period I'm going to write about. Then I select the one which lends itself best to my device and which I can write as drama without falling into melodrama.

INTERVIEWER: Did you write for a particular audience?

ANGELOU: I thought early on if I could write a book for black girls it would be good, because there were so few books for a black girl to read that said "This is how it is to grow up." Then, I thought, I'd better, you know, enlarge that group, the market group that I'm trying to reach. I decided to write for black boys, and then white girls, and then white boys.

But what I try to keep in mind mostly is my craft. That's what I really try for; I try to allow myself to be impelled by my art—if that doesn't sound too pompous and weird—accept the impulse, and then try my best to have a command of the craft. If I'm feeling depressed, and losing my control, then I think about the reader. But that is very rare—to think about the reader when the work is going on.

INTERVIEWER: So you don't keep a particular reader in mind when you sit down in that hotel room and begin to compose or write. It's yourself.

ANGELOU: It's myself . . . and my reader. I would be a liar, a hypocrite, or a fool—and I'm not any of those—to say that I don't write for the reader. I do. But for the reader who hears, who really will work at it, going behind what I seem to say. So I write for myself and that reader who will pay the dues. There's a phrase in West Africa, in Ghana; it's called "deep talk." For instance, there's a saying: "The trouble for the thief is not how to steal the chief's bugle, but where to blow it." Now, on the face of it, one understands that. But when you really think about it, it takes you deeper. In West Africa they call that "deep talk." I'd like to think I write "deep talk." When you read me, you should be able to say "Gosh, that's pretty. That's lovely. That's nice. Maybe there's something else? Better read it again." Years ago I read a man named Machado de Assis who wrote a book called *Dom Casmurro*. Machado de Assis is a South American writer—black mother, Portuguese father—writing in 1865, say. I thought the book was very nice. Then I went back and read the book and said, "Hmm. I didn't realize all that was in that book." Then I read it again, and again, and I came to the conclusion that what Machado de Assis had done for me was almost a trick: he had beckoned me onto the beach to watch a sunset. And I had watched the sunset with pleasure. When I turned around to come back in I found that the tide had come in over my head. That's when I decided to write. I would write so that the reader says, "That's so nice. Oh boy, that's pretty. Let me read that again." I think that's why *Caged Bird* is in its twenty-first printing in hardcover and its twenty-ninth in paper.

All my books are still in print, in hardback as well as paper, because people go back and say, "Let me read that. Did she *really* say that?"

INTERVIEWER: The books are episodic, aren't they? Almost as if you had put together a string of short stories. I wondered if, as an autobiographer, you ever fiddled with the truth to make the story better.

ANGELOU: Well, sometimes. I love the phrase "fiddle with." It's so English. Sometimes I make a character from a composite of three or four people, because the essence in any one person is not sufficiently strong to be written about. Essentially though, the work is true though sometimes I fiddle with the facts. Many of the people I've written about are alive today, and I have them to face. I wrote about an ex-husband—he's an African—in *The Heart of a Woman*. Before I did, I called him in Dar-es-Salaam and said, "I'm going to write about some of our years together." He said, "Now before you ask, I want you to know that I shall sign my release, because I know you will not lie. However, I am sure I shall argue with you about your interpretation of the truth."

INTERVIEWER: Did he enjoy his portrait finally, or did you argue about it?

ANGELOU: Well, he didn't argue, but I was kind, too.

INTERVIEWER: I would guess this would make it very easy for you to move from autobiography into novel, where you can do anything you want with your characters.

ANGELOU: Yes, but for me, fiction is not the sweetest form. I really am trying to do something with autobiography now. It has caught me. I'm using the first-person singular, and trying to make that the first-person plural, so that anybody can read the work and say, "Hmm, that's the truth, yes, *uh-huh,*" and live in the work. It's a large ambitious dream. But I love the form.

INTERVIEWER: Aren't the extraordinary events of your life very hard for the rest of us to identify with?

ANGELOU: Oh my God, I've lived a very simple life! You can say, "Oh yes, at thirteen this happened to me, and at fourteen . . ." But those are facts. But the facts can obscure the truth, what it really felt like. Every human being has paid the earth to grow up. Most people don't grow up. It's too damn difficult. What happens is most people get older. That's the truth of it. They honor their credit cards, they find parking spaces, they marry, they have the nerve to have children, but they don't grow up. Not really. They get older. But to grow up costs the earth, the *earth*. It means you take responsibility for the time you take up, for the space you occupy. It's serious business. And you find out what it costs us to love and to lose, to dare and to fail. And maybe even more, to succeed. What it costs, in truth. Not superficial costs—anybody can have that—I mean in truth. That's what I write. What it really is like. I'm just telling a very simple story.

INTERVIEWER: Aren't you tempted to lie? Novelists lie, don't they?

ANGELOU: I don't know about lying for novelists. I look at some of the great novelists, and I think the reason they are great is that they're telling the truth. The fact is they're using made-up names, made-up people, made-up places, and made-up times, but they're telling the truth about the human being— what we are capable of, what makes us lose, laugh, weep, fall down and gnash our teeth and wring our hands and kill each other and love each other.

INTERVIEWER: James Baldwin, along with a lot of writers in this series, said that "when you're writing you're trying to find out something you didn't know." When you write, do you search for something that you didn't know about yourself or about us?

ANGELOU: Yes. When I'm writing, I am trying to find out who I am, who we are, what we're capable of, how we feel, how we lose and stand up, and go on from darkness into darkness.

I'm trying for that. But I'm also trying for the language. I'm trying to see how it can really sound. I really love language. I love it for what it does for us, how it allows us to explain the pain and the glory, the nuances and the delicacies of our existence. And then it allows us to laugh, allows us to show wit. Real wit is shown in language. We need language.

INTERVIEWER: Baldwin also said that his family urged him not to become a writer. His father felt that there was a white monopoly in publishing. Did you ever have any of those feelings: that you were going up against something that was really immensely difficult for a black writer?

ANGELOU: Yes, but I didn't find it so just in writing. I've found it so in all the things I've attempted. In the shape of American society, the white male is on top, then the white female, and then the black male, and at the bottom is the black woman. So that's been always so. That is nothing new. It doesn't mean that it doesn't shock me, shake me up. . . .

INTERVIEWER: I can understand that in various social stratifications, but why in art?

ANGELOU: Well, unfortunately, racism is pervasive. It doesn't stop at the university gate, or at the ballet stage. I knew great black dancers, male and female, who were told early on that they were not shaped, physically, for ballet. Today, we see very few black ballet dancers. Unfortunately, in the theater and in film, racism and sexism stand at the door. I'm the first black female director in Hollywood; in order to direct, I went to Sweden and took a course in cinematography so I would understand what the camera would do. Though I had written a screenplay, and even composed the score, I wasn't allowed to direct it. They brought in a young Swedish director who hadn't even shaken a black person's hand before. The film was *Georgia, Georgia* with Diane Sands. People either loathed it or complimented me. Both were wrong, because it was not what I wanted, not what I would have done if I had been allowed to direct it.

So I thought, Well, what I guess I'd better do is be ten times as prepared. That is not new. I wish it was. In every case I know I have to be ten times more prepared than my white counterpart.

INTERVIEWER: Even as a writer where—

ANGELOU: Absolutely.

INTERVIEWER: Yet a manuscript is what arrives at the editor's desk, not a person, not a body.

ANGELOU: Yes. I must have such control of my tools, of words, that I can make this sentence leap off the page. I have to have my writing so polished that it doesn't look polished at all. I want a reader, especially an editor, to be a half hour into my book before he realizes it's reading he's doing.

INTERVIEWER: But isn't that the goal of every person who sits down at a typewriter?

ANGELOU: Absolutely. Yes. It's possible to be overly sensitive, to carry a bit of paranoia along with you. But I don't think that's a bad thing. It keeps you sharp, keeps you on your toes.

INTERVIEWER: Is there a thread one can see through the five autobiographies? It seems to me that one prevailing theme is the love of your child.

ANGELOU: Yes, well, that's true. I think that that's a particular. I suppose, if I'm lucky, the particular is seen in the general. There is, I hope, a thesis in my work: we may encounter many defeats, but we must not be defeated. That sounds Goody Two-shoes, I know, but I believe that a diamond is the result of extreme pressure and time. Less time is crystal. Less than that is coal. Less than that is fossilized leaves. Less than that it's just plain dirt. In all my work, in the movies I write, the lyrics, the poetry, the prose, the essays, I am saying that we may encounter many defeats—maybe it's imperative that we encounter the defeats—but we are much stronger than we appear to be, and maybe much better than we allow ourselves to be. Human beings are more alike than unalike. There's no real mystique. Every human being, every Jew, Christian, back-slider, Muslim, Shintoist, Zen Buddhist, atheist, agnostic, every human being wants a nice place to live, a good place for the children to go to school, healthy children, somebody to love, the courage, the unmitigated gall to accept love in return, someplace to party on Saturday or Sunday night, and someplace to perpetuate that God. There's no mystique. None. And if I'm right in my work, that's what my work says.

INTERVIEWER: Have you been back to Stamps, Arkansas?

ANGELOU: About 1970, Bill Moyers, Willie Morris, and I were at some affair. Judith Moyers as well—I think she was the instigator. We may have had two or three scotches, or seven or eight. Willie Morris was then with *Harper's* magazine. The suggestion came up: "Why don't we all go back south." Willie Morris was from Yazoo, Mississippi. Bill Moyers is from Marshall, Texas, which is just a hop, skip and a jump—about as far as you can throw a chitterling—from Stamps, my hometown. Sometime in the middle of the night there was this idea: "Why don't Bill Moyers and Maya Angelou go to Yazoo, Mississippi, to visit Willie Morris? Then why don't Willie Morris and Maya Angelou go to Marshall, Texas, to visit Bill Moyers?" I said, "Great." I was agreeing with both. Then they said Willie Morris and Bill Moyers would go to Stamps, Arkansas, to visit Maya Angelou, and I said, "No way, José. I'm not going back to that little town with two white men! I will not do it!" Well, after a while Bill Moyers called me—he was doing a series on "creativity"—and he said, "Maya, come on, let's go to Stamps." I said, "No way." He continued, "I want to talk about creativity." I said, "You know, I don't want to know where it resides." I really don't, and I still don't. One of the problems in the West is that people are too busy putting things under microscopes and so forth. Creativity is greater than the sum of its parts. All I want to know is that creativity is there. I want to know that I can put my hand behind my back like Tom Thumb and pull out a plum. Anyway, Moyers went on and on and so did Judith and before I knew it, I found myself in Stamps, Arkansas. Stamps, Arkansas! With Bill Moyers, in front of my grandmother's door. My God! We drove out of town: me with Bill and Judith. Back of us was the crew, a New York crew, you know, very "Right, dig where I'm comin' from, like, get it on," and so forth. We got about three miles outside of Stamps and I said, "Stop the car. Let the car behind us pull up. Get those people in with you and I'll take their car." I suddenly was taken back to being twelve years old in a southern, tiny town where my grandmother told me, "Sistah, never be on a country road with any white boys." I was two hundred years older than black pepper, but I said, "Stop the car." I did. I got out of the car. And I knew these guys—certainly Bill. Bill Moyers is a friend and brother-friend to me; we care for each other. But dragons, fears, the grotesques of childhood always must be confronted at childhood's door. Any other place is esoteric and has nothing to do with the great fear that is laid upon one as a child. So anyway, we did Bill Moyers's show. And it seems to be a very popular program, and it's the first of the "creativity" programs. . . .

INTERVIEWER: Did going back assuage those childhood fears?

ANGELOU: They are there like griffins hanging off the sides of old and tired European buildings.

INTERVIEWER: It hadn't changed?

ANGELOU: No, worse if anything.

INTERVIEWER: But it was forty years before you went back to the South, to North Carolina. Was that because of a fear of finding griffins everywhere, Stamps being a typical community of the South?

ANGELOU: Well, I've never felt the need to prove anything to an audience. I'm always concerned about who I am to me first, to myself and God. I really am. I didn't go south because I didn't want to pull up whatever clout I had, because that's boring, that's not real, not true; that doesn't tell me anything. If I had known I was afraid, I would have gone earlier. I just thought I'd find the South really unpleasant. I have moved south now. I *live* there.

INTERVIEWER: Perhaps writing the autobiographies, finding out about yourself, would have made it much easier to go back.

ANGELOU: I know many think that writing sort of "clears the air." It doesn't do that at all. If you are going to write autobiography, don't expect that it will clear anything up. It makes it more clear to you, but it doesn't alleviate anything. You simply know it better, you have names for people.

INTERVIEWER: There's a part in *Caged Bird* where you and your brother want to do a scene from *The Merchant of Venice*, and you don't dare do it because your grandmother would find out that Shakespeare was not only deceased but white.

ANGELOU: I don't think she'd have minded if she'd known he was deceased. I tried to pacify her—my mother knew Shakespeare, but my grandmother was raising us. When I told her I wanted to recite—it was actually Portia's speech—Mama said to me, "Now, sistah, what are you goin' to render?" The phrase was so fetching. The phrase was: "Now, little mistress Marguerite will render her rendition." Mama said, "Now, sistah, what are you goin' to render?" I said, "Mama, I'm going to render a piece written by William Shakespeare." My grandmother asked me, "Now, sistah, who is this very William Shakespeare?" I had to tell her that he was white, it was going to come out. Somebody would let it out. So I told Mama, "Mama, he's white, but he's dead." Then I said, "He's been dead for centuries," thinking she'd forgive him because of this little idiosyncrasy. She said, "No, ma'am, little mistress, you will not. No, ma'am, little mistress, you will not." So I rendered James Weldon Johnson, Paul Laurence Dunbar, Countee Cullen, Langston Hughes.

INTERVIEWER: Were books allowed in the house?

ANGELOU: None of those books were in the house; they were in the school. I'd bring them home from school, and my brother gave me Edgar Allan Poe because he knew I loved him. I loved him so much I called him "EAP." But as I said, I had a problem when I was young: from the time I was seven and a half to the time I was twelve and a half I was a mute. I could speak, but I didn't speak for five years, and I was what was called a "volunteer mute." But I read and I memorized just masses—I don't know if one is born with photographic memory, but I think you can develop it. I just have that.

INTERVIEWER: What is the significance of the title, *All God's Children Need Traveling Shoes?*

ANGELOU: I never agreed, even as a young person, with the Thomas Wolfe title *You Can't Go Home Again.* Instinctively I didn't. But the truth is, you can never *leave* home. You take it with you; it's under your fingernails; it's in the hair follicles; it's in the way you smile; it's in the ride of your hips, in the passage of your breasts; it's all there, no matter where you go. You can take on the affectations and the postures of other places, and even learn to speak their ways. But the truth is, home is between your teeth. Everybody's always looking for it. Jews go to Israel; black-Americans and Africans in the Diaspora go to Africa; Europeans, Anglo-Saxons go to England and Ireland; people of Germanic background go to Germany. It's a very queer quest. We can kid ourselves; we can tell ourselves, "Oh yes, honey, I live in Tel Aviv, actually. . . ." The truth is a stubborn fact. So this book is about trying to go home.

INTERVIEWER: If you had to endow a writer with the most necessary pieces of equipment, other than, of course, yellow legal pads, what would these be?

ANGELOU: Ears. Ears. To hear the language. But there's no one piece of equipment that is most necessary. Courage, first.

INTERVIEWER: Did you ever feel that you could not get your

work published? Would you have continued to write if Random House had returned your manuscript?

ANGELOU: I didn't think it was going to be very easy, but I knew I was going to do something. The real reason black people exist at all today is because there's a resistance to a larger society that says, "You can't do it. You can't survive. And if you survive, you certainly can't thrive. And if you thrive, you can't thrive with any passion or compassion or humor or style." There's a saying, a song which says, "Don't you let nobody turn you 'round, turn you 'round. Don't you let nobody turn you 'round." Well, I've always believed that. So knowing that, knowing that nobody could turn me 'round, if I didn't publish, well, I would design this theater we're sitting in. Yes. Why not? Some human being did it. I agree with Terence. Terence said, *"Homo sum: humani nil a me alienum puto."* I am a human being. Nothing human can be alien to me. When you look up Terence in the encyclopedia, you see beside his name, in italics: "Sold to a Roman senator, freed by that senator." He became the most popular playwright in Rome. Six of his plays and that statement have come down to us from 154 B.C. This man, not born white, not born free, without any chance of ever receiving citizenship, said, "I am a human being. Nothing human can be alien to me." Well, I believe that. I ingested that, internalized that at about thirteen or twelve. I believed if I set my mind to it, maybe I wouldn't be published, but I would write a great piece of music, or do something about becoming a real friend. Yes, I would do something wonderful. It might be with my next-door neighbor, my gentleman friend, with my lover, but it would be wonderful as far as I could do it. So I never have been very concerned about the world telling me how successful I am. I don't need that.

INTERVIEWER: You mentioned courage—

ANGELOU:—the most important of all the virtues. Without that virtue you can't practice any other virtue with consistency.

INTERVIEWER: What do you think of white writers who have written of the black experience: Faulkner's *The Sound and the Fury*, or William Styron's *Confessions of Nat Turner?*

ANGELOU: Well, sometimes I am disappointed—more often than not. That's unfair, because I'm not suggesting the writer is lying about what he or she sees. It's my disappointment, really, in that he or she doesn't see more deeply, more carefully. I enjoy seeing Peter O'Toole or Michael Caine enact the role of an upper-class person in England. There the working class has had to study the upper class, has been obliged to do so, to lift themselves out of their positions. Well, black Americans have had to study white Americans. For centuries under slavery, the smile or the grimace on a white man's face, or the flow of a hand on a white woman could inform a black person: "You're about to be sold, or flogged." So we have studied the white American, where the white American has not been obliged to study us. So often it is as if the writer is looking through a glass darkly. And I'm always a little—not a little—saddened by that poor vision.

INTERVIEWER: And you can pick it up in an instant if you—

ANGELOU: Yes, yes. There are some who delight and inform. It's so much better, you see, for me, when a writer like Edna St. Vincent Millay speaks so deeply about her concern for herself, and does not offer us any altruisms. Then when I look through her eyes at how she sees a black or an Asian my heart is lightened. But many of the other writers disappoint me.

INTERVIEWER: What is the best part of writing for you?

ANGELOU: Well, I could say the end. But when the language lends itself to me, when it comes and submits, when it surrenders and says "I am yours, darling"—that's the best part.

INTERVIEWER: You don't skip around when you write?

ANGELOU: No, I may skip around in revision, just to see what connections I can find.

INTERVIEWER: Is most of the effort made in putting the words down onto the paper, or is it in revision?

ANGELOU: Some work flows, and you know, you can catch three days. It's like . . . I think the word in sailing is "scudding"—you know, three days of just scudding. Other days it's just awful—plodding and backing up, trying to take out all the ands, if, tos, fors, buts, wherefores, therefores, howevers; you know, all those.

INTERVIEWER: And then, finally, you write "The End" and there it is; you have a little bit of sherry.

ANGELOU: A lot of sherry then.

—GEORGE PLIMPTON

1990

ANNE SEXTON

The third of three daughters, Anne Harvey Sexton was born in 1928 in Newton, Massachusetts. She grew up in the affluent suburbs of Boston, attended a public high school and began writing at an early age. In 1948 she married Alfred Sexton, a premedical student who dropped out of college shortly after their wedding. They raised a family near Boston, but parted in divorce in 1973, a year before Sexton committed suicide.

Though she never attended college, Sexton taught creative writing at Boston University between 1970 and 1974. Her only formal education consisted of adult education classes at a handful of Boston-area colleges. Yet the poetry she wrote as a young housewife won immediate attention through the medium of literary magazines and newspapers, and with the publication of each of her first three books, a stream of grants and awards followed.

Her first collection, *To Bedlam and Part Way Back* (1960), received a National Book Award nomination. Like many of her books, it contained poems that dealt in an explicit manner with Sexton's private life—particularly the bouts of suicidal depression that interrupted her career. *All My Pretty Ones* (1962) brought her the first traveling fellowship offered by the American Academy of Arts and Letters, a Ford Foundation grant in playwriting, and the first Literary Magazine Travel Grant from the Congress for Cultural Freedom. In 1965 her *Selected Poems* appeared in England, where Sexton was elected to the Royal Society of Literature. Her fourth book, *Live or Die* (1966), won the Pulitzer Prize and the Shelley Memorial Prize from the Poetry Society of America. Five more books followed: *Love Poems* (1969), *Transformations* (1971), *The Book of Folly* (1972), *The Death Notebooks* (1974) and *An Awful Rowing Towards God* (1975).

ANNE SEXTON

T *he interview took place over three days in the middle of August 1968. When asked about dates of publications or other events, Anne Sexton kept saying, "Let me think, I want this to be accurate," and she'd use the births of her children as reference dates to chronicle the event in question. Sometimes her distinctions between real and imagined life blurred, as in scenes from Pirandello. Often, her answers sounded like incantations, repetitious chants that, if pared down, would lose something of their implications, and so, for the most part, they are preserved in their entirety. Even when replying from written notes, she read with all the inflections and intonations of—as she described her readings—"an actress in her own autobiographical play."*

INTERVIEWER: You were almost thirty before you began writing poetry. Why?

SEXTON: Until I was twenty-eight I had a kind of buried self who didn't know she could do anything but make white sauce and diaper babies. I didn't know I had any creative depths. I was a victim of the American Dream, the bourgeois, middle-class dream. All I wanted was a little piece of life, to be married, to

Moon song

I am alive at night
I am dead in the morning—
an old vessel who used up her oil,
bleak and pale-boned
No miracle No dazzle
I'm out of repair,
but you are tall in your battle dress
and I must arrange for your journey

I was always a virgin,
old and pitted
Before the world was, I was,

I have been oranging and fat,
carrot-colored, gaped at,
allowing my cracked O's to drop on the sea
near Venice and Mombasa
Over Maine I have rested
I have fallen like a jet into the Pacific.
I have committed perjury over Japan
I have dangled my pendulum,
my fat bag, my gold, gold,
blinkedy light
over you all

So if you must inquire, do so
After all, I am not artificial.
I looked long upon you,
love-bellied and empty,
flipping my endless display
for you, my cold, cold
coverall man.
You need only request it
and I will grant it
It is virtually guaranteed
That you will walk into me like a barracks
So come cruising, come cruising,
You of the blast off,
you of the bastion,
you of the scheme,
I will shut my fat eye down,
headquarters of an area
house of a dream

The manuscript of "Moon Song" by Anne Sexton.

have children. I thought the nightmares, the visions, the demons would go away if there was enough love to put them down. I was trying my damnedest to lead a conventional life, for that was how I was brought up, and it was what my husband wanted of me. But one can't build little white picket fences to keep nightmares out. The surface cracked when I was about twenty-eight. I had a psychotic break and tried to kill myself.

INTERVIEWER: And you began to write after the nervous breakdown?

SEXTON: It isn't quite as simple as all that. I said to my doctor at the beginning, "I'm no good; I can't do anything; I'm dumb." He suggested I try educating myself by listening to Boston's educational TV station. He said I had a perfectly good mind. As a matter of fact, after he gave me a Rorschach test, he said I had creative talent that I wasn't using. I protested, but I followed his suggestion. One night I saw I. A. Richards on educational television reading a sonnet and explaining its form. I thought to myself, "I could do that, maybe; I could try." So I sat down and wrote a sonnet. The next day I wrote another one, and so forth. My doctor encouraged me to write more. "Don't kill yourself," he said. "Your poems might mean something to someone else someday." That gave me a feeling of purpose, a little cause, something to *do* with my life, no matter how rotten I was.

INTERVIEWER: Hadn't you written limericks before that?

SEXTON: I did write some light verse—for birthdays, for anniversaries, sometimes thank-you notes for weekends. Long before, I wrote some serious stuff in high school; however, I hadn't been exposed to any of the major poets, not even the minor ones. No one taught poetry at that school. I read nothing but Sara Teasdale. I might have read other poets, but my mother said as I graduated from high school that I had plagiarized Sara Teasdale. Something about that statement of hers ...

I had been writing a poem a day for three months, but when she said that, I stopped.

INTERVIEWER: Didn't anyone encourage you?

SEXTON: It wouldn't have mattered. My mother was top billing in our house.

INTERVIEWER: In the beginning, what was the relationship between your poetry and your therapy?

SEXTON: Sometimes, my doctors tell me that I understand something in a poem that I haven't integrated into my life. In fact, I may be concealing it from myself, while I was revealing it to the readers. The poetry is often more advanced, in terms of my unconscious, than I am. Poetry, after all, milks the unconscious. The unconscious is there to feed it little images, little symbols, the answers, the insights I know not of. In therapy, one seeks to hide sometimes. I'll give you a rather intimate example of this. About three or four years ago my analyst asked me what I thought of my parents having intercourse when I was young. I couldn't talk. I knew there was suddenly a poem there, and I selfishly guarded it from him. Two days later, I had a poem, entitled, "In the Beach House," which describes overhearing the primal scene. In it I say, "Inside my prison of pine and bedspring, / over my window sill, under my knob, / it is plain they are at / the royal strapping." The point of this little story is the image, "the royal strapping." My analyst was quite impressed with that image, and so was I, although I don't remember going any further with it then. About three weeks ago, he said to me, "Were you ever beaten as a child?" I told him that I had been when I was about nine. I had torn up a five-dollar bill that my father gave to my sister; my father took me into his bedroom, laid me down on his bed, pulled off my pants, and beat me with a riding crop. As I related this to my doctor, he said, "See, that was quite a royal strapping," thus revealing to me, by way of my own image, the intensity of that moment, the sexuality of that beating, the little masochistic seizure—it's so classic, it's almost corny. Perhaps it's too intimate an example, but then both poetry and therapy are intimate.

INTERVIEWER: Are your poems still closely connected to your therapy as in the past?

SEXTON: No. The subject of therapy was an early theme—the process itself as in "Said the Poet to the Analyst," the people of my past, admitting what my parents were really like, the whole Gothic New England story. I've had about eight doctors, but only two that count. I've written a poem for each of the two—"You, Doctor Martin" and "Cripples and Other Stories." And that will do. Those poems are about the two men as well as the strange process. One can say that my new poems, the love poems, come about as a result of new attitudes, an awareness of the possibly good as well as the possibly rotten. Inherent in the process is a rebirth of a sense of self, each time stripping away a dead self.

INTERVIEWER: Some critics admire your ability to write about the terror of childhood guilts, parental deaths, breakdowns, suicides. Do you feel that writing about the dark parts of the human psyche takes a special act of courage?

SEXTON: Of course, but I'm tired of explaining it. It seems to be self-evident. There are warnings all along the way. "Go—children—slow." "It's dangerous in there." The appalling horror that awaits you in the answer.

INTERVIEWER: People speak of you as a primitive. Was it so natural for you to dig so deeply into the painful experiences of your life?

SEXTON: There was a part of me that was horrified, but the gutsy part of me drove on. Still, part of me was appalled by what I was doing. On the one hand I was digging up shit; with the other hand I was covering it with sand. Nevertheless, I went on ahead. I didn't know any better. Sometimes, I felt like a reporter researching himself. Yes, it took a certain courage, but as a writer one has to take the chance on being a fool . . . yes, to be a fool, that perhaps requires the greatest courage.

INTERVIEWER: Once you began writing, did you attend any formal classes to bone up on technique?

SEXTON: After I'd been writing about three months, I dared to go into the poetry class at the Boston Center for Adult Education taught by John Holmes. I started in the middle of the term, very shy, writing very bad poems, solemnly handing them in for the eighteen others in the class to hear. The most important aspect of that class was that I felt I belonged somewhere. When I first got sick and became a displaced person, I thought I was quite alone, but when I went into the mental hospital, I found I wasn't, that there were other people like me. It made me feel better—more real, sane. I felt, These are my people. Well, at the John Holmes class that I attended for two years, I found I belonged to the poets, that I was *real* there, and I had another, "These are my people." I met Maxine Kumin, the poet and novelist, at that class. She is my closest friend. She is part superego, part sister, as well as pal of my desk. It's strange because we're quite different. She is reserved, while I tend to be flamboyant. She is an intellectual, and I seem to be a primitive. That is true about our poetry as well.

INTERVIEWER: You once told me, "I call Maxine Kumin every other line." Is that a slight exaggeration?

SEXTON: Yes. But often, I call her draft by draft. However, a lot of poems I did without her. The year I was writing my first book, I didn't know her well enough to call that often. Later, when she didn't approve of such poems as "Flee on Your Donkey"—that one took four years to complete—I was on my own. Yet once, she totally saved a poem, "Cripples and Other Stories."

INTERVIEWER: In the early days, how did your relatives react to the jangling of family skeletons?

SEXTON: I tried not to show my relatives any of the poems.

I do know that my mother snuck into my desk one time and read "The Double Image" before it was printed. She told me just before she died that she liked the poem, and that saved me from some added guilt. My husband liked that poem, too. Ordinarily, if I show him a poem, something I try not to do, he says, "I don't think that's too hotsy-totsy," which puts me off. I try not to do it too often. My in-laws don't approve of the poems at all. My children do—with a little pain, they do.

INTERVIEWER: In your poems, several family skeletons come out of the camphor balls—your father's alcoholic tendencies, your mother's inability to deal with your suicide attempt, your great-aunt in a straitjacket. Is there any rule you follow as to which skeletons you reveal and which you don't?

SEXTON: I don't reveal skeletons that would hurt anyone. They may hurt the dead, but the dead belong to me. Only once in a while do they talk back. For instance, I don't write about my husband or his family, although there are some amazing stories there.

INTERVIEWER: How about Holmes or the poets in your class, what did they say?

SEXTON: During the years of that class, John Holmes saw me as something evil and warned Maxine to stay away from me. He told me I shouldn't write such personal poems about the madhouse. He said, "That isn't a fit subject for poetry." I knew no one who thought it was; even my doctor clammed up at that time. I was on my own. I tried to mind them. I tried to write the way the others, especially Maxine, wrote, but it didn't work. I always ended up sounding like myself.

INTERVIEWER: You have said, "If anything influenced me, it was W. D. Snodgrass's 'Heart's Needle.'" Would you comment on that?

SEXTON: If he had the courage, then I had the courage. That poem about losing his daughter brought me to face some of the facts about my own life. I had lost a daughter, lost her because I was too sick to keep her. After I read the poem, "Heart's Needle," I ran up to my mother-in-law's house and brought my daughter home. That's what a poem should do—move people to action. True, I didn't keep my daughter at the time—I wasn't ready. But I was beginning to be ready. I wrote a disguised poem about it, "Unknown Girl in the Maternity Ward." The pain of the loss . . .

INTERVIEWER: Did you ever meet Snodgrass?

SEXTON: Yes. I'd read "Heart's Needle" in *The New Poets of England and America*. I'd written about three quarters of *To Bedlam and Part Way Back* at the time, and I made a pilgrimage to Antioch Writers' Conference to meet and to learn from Snodgrass. He was a surprising person, surprisingly humble. He encouraged me, he liked what I was doing. He was the first established poet to like my work, and so I was driven to write harder and to allow myself, to dare myself to tell the whole story. He also suggested that I study with Robert Lowell. So I sent Mr. Lowell some of my poems and asked if he would take me into the class. By then I'd had poems published in *The New Yorker* and around a bit. At any rate, the poems seemed good enough for Lowell, and I joined the class.

INTERVIEWER: Which poems did you submit to Lowell?

SEXTON: As far as I can remember, the poems about madness—"You, Doctor Martin," "Music Swims Back to Me" . . . about ten or fifteen poems from the book.

INTERVIEWER: Was this before or after Lowell published *Life Studies*?

SEXTON: Before. I sent him the poems in the summer; the following spring *Life Studies* came out. Everyone says I was influenced by Robert Lowell's revelation of madness in that book, but I was writing *To Bedlam and Part Way Back*, the story of my madness, before *Life Studies* was published. I showed my poems to Mr. Lowell as he was working on his book. Perhaps

I even influenced him. I have never asked him. But stranger things have happened.

INTERVIEWER: And when was your first book, *To Bedlam and Part Way Back*, published?

SEXTON: It was accepted that January; it wasn't published for a year and a half after that, I think.

INTERVIEWER: Where was Lowell teaching then?

SEXTON: The class met at Boston University on Tuesdays from two to four in a dismal room. It consisted of some twenty students. Seventeen graduates, two other housewives who were graduates or something, and a boy who had snuck over from MIT. I was the only one in that room who hadn't read *Lord Weary's Castle.*

INTERVIEWER: And Lowell, how did he strike you?

SEXTON: He was formal in a rather awkward New England sense. His voice was soft and slow as he read the students' poems. At first I felt the impatient desire to interrupt his slow line-by-line readings. He would read the first line, stop, and then discuss it at length. I wanted to go through the whole poem quickly and then go back. I couldn't see any merit in dragging through it until you almost hated the damned thing, even your own poems, especially your own. At that point, I wrote to Snodgrass about my impatience, and his reply went this way, "Frankly, I used to nod my head at his every statement, and he taught me more than a whole gang of scholars could." So I kept my mouth shut, and Snodgrass was right. Robert Lowell's method of teaching is intuitive and open. After he had read a student's poem, he would read another evoked by it. Comparison was often painful. He worked with a cold chisel, with no more mercy than a dentist. He got out the decay, but if he was never kind to the poem, he was kind to the poet.

INTERVIEWER: Did you consult Robert Lowell on your manuscript of *To Bedlam and Part Way Back* before you submitted it to a publisher?

SEXTON: Yes. I gave him a manuscript to see if he thought it was a book. He was enthusiastic on the whole, but suggested that I throw out about half of it and write another fifteen or so poems that were better. He pointed out the weak ones, and I nodded and took them out. It sounds simple to say that I merely, as he once said, "jumped the hurdles that he had put up," but it makes a difference who puts up the hurdles. He defined the course, and acted as though, good racehorse that I was, I would just naturally run it.

INTERVIEWER: Ultimately, what can a teacher give a writer in a creative-writing class?

SEXTON: Courage, of course. That's the most important ingredient. Then, in a rather plain way, Lowell helped me to distrust the easy musical phrase and to look for the frankness of ordinary speech. Lowell is never impressed with a display of images or sounds—those things that a poet is born with anyhow. If you have enough natural imagery, he can show you how to chain it in. He didn't teach me what to put into a poem, but what to leave out. What he taught me was taste—perhaps that's the only thing a poet can be taught.

INTERVIEWER: Sylvia Plath was a member of Lowell's class also, wasn't she?

SEXTON: Yes. She and George Starbuck heard that I was auditing Lowell's class. They kind of joined me there for the second term. After the class, we would pile in the front seat of my old Ford, and I would drive quickly through the traffic to the Ritz. I would always park illegally in a "Loading Only" zone, telling them gaily, "It's OK, we're only going to get loaded." Off we'd go, each on George's arm, into the Ritz to drink three or four martinis. George even has a line about this in his first book of poems, *Bone Thoughts*. After the Ritz, we would spend our last pennies at the Waldorf Cafeteria—a dinner for seventy cents— George was in no hurry. He was separated from his wife; Sylvia's Ted [Hughes] was busy with his own work, and I had to stay in the city for a seven P.M. appointment with my psychiatrist . . . a funny three.

INTERVIEWER: In Sylvia Plath's last book, written just before her suicide, she was submerged by the theme of death, as you are in your book, *Live or Die*. Did you ever get around to talking about death or your suicides at the Ritz?

SEXTON: Often, very often. Sylvia and I would talk at length about our first suicide, in detail and in depth—between the free potato chips. Suicide is, after all, the opposite of the poem. Sylvia and I often talked opposites. We talked death with burned-up intensity, both of us drawn to it like moths to an electric lightbulb, sucking on it. She told the story of her first suicide in sweet and loving detail, and her description in *The Bell Jar* is just that same story. It is a wonder we didn't depress George with our egocentricity; instead, I think, we three were stimulated by it—even George—as if death made each of us a little more real at the moment.

INTERVIEWER: In a BBC interview, Sylvia Plath said, "I've been very excited by what I feel is the new breakthrough that came with, say, Robert Lowell's *Life Studies* . . . this intense breakthrough into very serious, very personal emotional experience, which I feel has been partly taboo. . . . I think particularly of the poetess Anne Sexton, who writes also about her experiences as a mother; as a mother who's had a nervous breakdown, as an extremely emotional and feeling young woman. And her poems are wonderfully craftsmanlike poems, and yet they have a kind of emotional psychological depth, which I think is something perhaps quite new and exciting." Do you agree that you influenced her?

SEXTON: Maybe. I did give her a sort of daring, but that's all she should have said. I remember writing to Sylvia in England after her first book, *The Colossus*, came out and saying something like "If you're not careful, Sylvia, you will out-Roethke Roethke." She replied that I had guessed accurately. But maybe she buried her so-called influences deeper than that, deeper than any one of us would think to look, and if she did, I say, "Good luck to her!" Her poems do their own work. I don't need to sniff them for distant relatives: I'm against it.

INTERVIEWER: Did Sylvia Plath influence your writing?

SEXTON: Her first book didn't interest me at all. I was doing my own thing. But after her death, with the appearance of *Ariel*, I think I was influenced, and I don't mind saying it. In a special sort of way, it was daring again. She had dared to do something quite different. She had dared to write hate poems, the one thing I had never dared to write. I'd always been afraid, even in my life, to express anger. I think the poem, "Cripples and Other Stories," is evidence of a hate poem somehow, though no one could ever write a poem to compare to her "Daddy." There was a kind of insolence in them, saying, "Daddy, you bastard, I'm through." I think the poem, "The Addict," has some of her speech rhythms in it. She had very open speech rhythms, something that I didn't always have.

INTERVIEWER: You have said, "I think the second book lacks some of the impact and honesty of the first, which I wrote when I was so raw that I didn't know any better." Would you describe your development from the second book to the third and from your third to the fourth?

SEXTON: Well, in the first book, I was giving the experience of madness; in the second book, the causes of madness; and in the third book, finally, I find that I was deciding whether to live or to die. In the third I was daring to be a fool again—raw, "uncooked," as Lowell calls it, with a little camouflage. In the fourth book, I not only have lived, come on to the scene, but loved, that sometime miracle.

INTERVIEWER: What would you say about the technical development from book to book?

SEXTON: In *Bedlam*, I used very tight form in most cases, feeling that I could express myself better. I take a kind of pleasure, even now, but more especially in *Bedlam*, in forming a stanza, a verse, making it an entity, and then coming to a little conclusion at the end of it, of a little shock, a little double rhyme shock. In my second book, *All My Pretty Ones*, I loosened up and in the last section didn't use any form at all. I found myself to be surprisingly free without the form which had worked as a kind of superego for me. The third book I used less form. In *Love Poems*, I had one long poem, eighteen sections, that is in form, and I enjoyed doing it in that way. With the exception of that and a few other poems, all of the book is in free verse, and I feel at this point comfortable to use either, depending on what the poem requires.

INTERVIEWER: Is there any particular subject which you'd rather deal with in form than in free verse?

SEXTON: Probably madness. I've noticed that Robert Lowell felt freer to write about madness in free verse, whereas it was the opposite for me. Only after I had set up large structures that were almost impossible to deal with did I think I was free to allow myself to express what had really happened. However in *Live or Die*, I wrote "Flee on Your Donkey" without that form and found that I could do it just as easily in free verse. That's perhaps something to do with my development as a human being and understanding of myself, besides as a poet.

INTERVIEWER: In *Live or Die*, the whole book has a marvelous structured tension—simply by the sequence of the poems which pits the wish to live against the death instinct. Did you plan the book this way? Lois Ames speaks of you as wishing to write more "live" poems because the "die" poems outnumbered them.

SEXTON: I didn't plan the book any way. In January of 1962, I started collecting new poems the way you do when a book is over. I didn't know where they would go or that they would go anywhere, even into a book. Then at some point, as I was collecting these poems, I was rereading *Henderson the Rain King*, by

Saul Bellow. I had met Saul Bellow at a cocktail party about a year before, and I had been carrying *Henderson the Rain King* around in my suitcase everywhere I traveled. Suddenly there I was meeting Saul Bellow, and I was overenthusiastic. I said, "Oh, oh, you're Saul Bellow, I've wanted to meet you," and he ran from the room. Very afraid. I was quite ashamed of my exuberance, and then sometime, a year later, reading *Henderson the Rain King* over again, at three in the morning, I wrote Saul Bellow a fan letter about Henderson, saying that he was a monster of despair, that I understood his position because Henderson was the one who had ruined life, who had blown up the frogs, made a mess out of everything. I drove to the mailbox then and there! The next morning I wrote him a letter of apology.

Saul Bellow wrote me back on the back of a manuscript. He said to me, "Luckily, I have a message to you from the book I am writing [which was *Herzog*]. I have both your letters—the good one which was written that night at three A.M. and then the contrite one, the next day. One's best things are always followed by apoplectic, apologetic seizure. Monster of despair could be *Henderson's* subtitle." The message that he had encircled went this way, "With one long breath caught and held in his chest, he fought his sadness over his solitary life. Don't cry you idiot, live or die, but don't poison everything." And in circling that and in sending it to me, Saul Bellow had given me a message about my whole life. That I didn't want to poison the world, that I didn't want to be the killer; I wanted to be the one who gave birth, who encouraged things to grow and to flower, not the poisoner. So I stuck that message up over my desk and it was a kind of hidden message. You don't know what these messages mean to you, yet you stick them up over your desk or remember them or write them down and put them in your wallet. One day I was reading a quote from Rimbaud that said, "Anne, Anne, flee on your donkey," and I typed it out because it had my name in it and because I wanted to flee. I put it in my wallet, went to see my doctor, and at that point was committed to a hospital for about the seventh or eighth time. In the hospital, I started to write the poem, "Flee on Your Donkey," as though the message had come to me at just the right moment. Well, this was true with Bellow's quote from his book. I kept it over my desk, and when I went to Europe, I pasted it in the front of my manuscript. I kept it there as a quotation with which to preface my book. It must have just hit me one day that *Live or Die* was a damn good title for the book I was working on. And that's what it was all about, what all those poems were about. You say there's a tension there and a structure, but it was an unconscious tension and an unconscious structure that I didn't know was going on when I was doing it.

INTERVIEWER: Once you knew the title of the book, did you count up the "live" poems and count up the "die" poems and then write any more poems because of an imbalance?

SEXTON: No, no, that's far too rigid. You can't write a poem because of an imbalance. After that I wrote "Little Girl, My Stringbean, My Lovely Woman." Then I wrote a play, then "A Little Uncomplicated Hymn" and other poems. Some were negative, and some were positive. At this time I knew that I was trying to get a book together. I had more than enough for a book, but I knew I hadn't written out the live-or-die question. I hadn't written the poem "Live." This was bothering me because it wasn't coming to me. Instead of that, "Cripples and Other Stories" and "The Addict" were appearing, and I knew that I wasn't finishing the book, that I hadn't come to the cycle, I hadn't given a reason. There's nothing I could do about this and then suddenly, our dog was pregnant. I was supposed to kill all the puppies when they came; instead, I let them live, and I realized that if I let *them* live, that I could let *me* live, too, that after all I wasn't a killer, that the poison just didn't take.

INTERVIEWER: Although you received a European traveling fellowship from the American Academy of Arts and Letters, there are, to date, very few poems published about your European experience. Why?

SEXTON: First of all, poems aren't postcards to send home. Secondly I went to Europe with a purpose as well as with a grant. My great-aunt, who was really my best childhood friend, had sent letters home from Europe the three years that she lived there. I had written about this in a poem called "Some Foreign Letters." I had her letters with me as I left for Europe, and I was going to walk her walks and go to her places, live her life over again, and write letters back to her. The two poems that I did write about Europe mention the letters. In "Crossing the Atlantic," I mention that I have read my grandmother's letters and my mother's letters. I had swallowed their words like Dickens, thinking of Dickens's journals in America. The second poem, "Walking in Paris," was written about my great-aunt, how she used to walk fourteen or fifteen miles a day in Paris, and I call her Nana. Some critics have thought I meant Zola's Nana, but I didn't any more than I meant the Nana in *Peter Pan.* However, the letters were stolen from my car in Belgium. When I lost the letters in Brussels, that was the end of that kind of poem that I had gone over there to write.

INTERVIEWER: You were to go abroad for a year, but you only stayed two months. Do you want to comment on that?

SEXTON: Two and a half months. I got sick over there; I lost my sense of self. I had, as my psychiatrist said, "a leaky ego" and I had to come home. I was in the hospital for a while, and then I returned to my normal life. I had to come home because I need my husband and my therapist and my children to tell me who I am. I remember, I was talking with Elizabeth Hardwick on the phone and saying, "Oh, I feel so guilty. I couldn't get along without my husband. It's a terrible thing, really, a modern woman should be able to do it." Although I may be misquoting her, I may have remembered it the way I needed to hear it, she said to me, "If I were in Paris without my husband, I'd hide in a hotel room all day." And I said, "Well, think of Mary McCarthy." And Elizabeth Hardwick said, "Mary McCarthy, she's never been without a man for a day in her life."

INTERVIEWER: From 1964 to 1965, you held a Ford Foundation grant in playwriting and worked at Boston's Charles Street Playhouse. How did you feel writing something that had to be staged?

SEXTON: I felt great! I used to pace up and down the living room shouting out the lines, and what do they call it . . . for walking around the stage . . . *blocking* out the play as I would go along.

INTERVIEWER: Was the play [*Mercy Street*] ever performed?*

SEXTON: There were little working performances at the Charles Street Playhouse when we had time. It was pretty busy there. Now and then they would play out a scene for me, and then I would rewrite it and send it in to the director special delivery. He would call me up the next morning and say, "It's not right," and then I would work on it again, send it to him that evening, and then the next morning, he'd call, and so on it went. I found that I had one whole character in the play who was unnecessary because, as they acted it, the director had that person be quiet and say nothing. I realized that that dialogue was totally unnecessary, so I cut out that character.

INTERVIEWER: Did you find that the themes in your poetry overlapped into your play? Was your play an extension of your poetry?

SEXTON: Yes. Completely. The play was about a girl shuffling between her psychiatrist and a priest. It was the priest I cut out, realizing that she really wasn't having a dialogue with him at all. The play was about all the subjects that my poems are about— my mother, my great-aunt, my father, and the girl who wants to

*Editor's note: *Mercy Street* was eventually produced at New York's American Place Theater in 1969.

kill herself. A little bit about her husband, but not much. The play is really a morality play. The second act takes place after death.

INTERVIEWER: Many of your poems are dramatic narratives. Because you're accustomed to handling a plot, was it easy for you to switch from verse to scene writing?

SEXTON: I don't see the difference. In both cases, the character is confronting himself and his destiny. I didn't know I was writing scenes; I thought I was writing about people. In another context—helping Maxine Kumin with her novel—I gave her a bit of advice. I told her, "Fuck structure and grab your characters by the time balls." Each one of us sits in our time; we're born, live and die. She was thinking this and that, and I was telling her to get inside her characters' lives—which she finally did.

INTERVIEWER: What were your feelings when you received the Pulitzer Prize for Poetry for *Live or Die* in 1967?

SEXTON: Of course, I was delighted. It had been a bad time for me. I had a broken hip, and I was just starting to get well, still crippled, but functioning a little bit. After I received the prize, it gave me added incentive to write more. In the months following, I managed to write a poem, "Eighteen Days Without You," in fourteen days—an eighteen-section poem. I was inspired by the recognition that the Pulitzer gave me, even though I was aware that it didn't mean all that much. After all, they have to give a Pulitzer Prize every year, and I was just one in a long line.

INTERVIEWER: Do you write a spate of poems at one time, or are you disciplined by a writing schedule?

SEXTON: Well, I'm very dissatisfied with the amount I write. My first book—although it took three years to complete—was really written in one year. Sometimes ten poems were written in two weeks. When I was going at that rate, I found that I could really work well. Now I tend to become dissatisfied with the fact that I write poems so slowly, that they come to me so slowly. When they come, I write them; when they don't come, I don't. There's certainly no disciplined writing schedule except for the fact that when a poem comes a person must be disciplined and ready, flexing his muscles. That is, they burst forth, and you must put everything else aside. Ideally it doesn't matter what it is unless your husband has double pneumonia, or the child breaks his leg. Otherwise, you don't tear yourself away from the typewriter until you must sleep.

INTERVIEWER: Do the responsibilities of wife and mother interfere with your writing?

SEXTON: Well, when my children were younger, they interfered all the time. It was just my stubbornness that let me get through with it at all, because here were these young children saying, "Momma, Momma," and there I was getting the images, structuring the poem. Now my children are older and creep around the house saying, "Shh, Mother is writing a poem." But then again, as I was writing the poem, "Eighteen Days Without You"—the last poem in *Love Poems*—my husband said to me, "I can't stand it any longer, you haven't been with me for days." That poem originally was "Twenty-one Days Without You" and it became "Eighteen Days" because he had cut into the inspiration; he demanded my presence back again, into his life, and I couldn't take that much from him.

INTERVIEWER: When writing, what part of the poem is the prickliest part?

SEXTON: Punctuation, sometimes. The punctuating can change the whole meaning, and my life is full of little dots and dashes. Therefore, I have to let the editors help me punctuate. And, probably the rhythm. It's the thing I have to work hardest to get in the beginning—the feeling, the voice of the poem, and how it will come across, how it will feel to the reader, how it feels to me as it comes out. Images are probably the most important part of the poem. First of all, you want to tell a story, but images are what are going to shore it up and get to the heart of the matter—but I don't have to work too hard for the images—they have to come—if they're not coming, I'm not even writing a poem, it's pointless. So I work hardest to get the rhythm, because each poem should have its own rhythm, its own structure. Each poem has its own life, each one is different.

INTERVIEWER: How do you decide a length of line? Does it have something to do with the way it looks on a page as well as how many beats there are to a line?

SEXTON: How it looks on a page. I don't give a damn about the beats in a line, unless I want them and need them. These are just tricks that you use when you need them. It's a very simple thing to write with rhyme and with rhythmic beat—those things anyone can do nowadays; everyone is quite accomplished at that. The point, the hard thing, is to get the true voice of the poem, to make each poem an individual thing, give it the stamp of your own voice, and at the same time to make it singular.

INTERVIEWER: Do you ever find yourself saying, "Oh, yes, I've explored that in another poem," and discarding a poem?

SEXTON: No, because I might want to explore it in a new way . . . I might have a new realization, a new truth about it. Recently I noticed in "Flee on Your Donkey" that I had used some of the same facts in *To Bedlam and Part Way Back*, but I hadn't realized them in their total ugliness. I'd hidden from them. This time was really raw and really ugly and it was all involved with my own madness. It was all like a great involuted web, and I presented it the way it really was.

INTERVIEWER: Do you revise a great deal?

SEXTON: Constantly.

INTERVIEWER: Do you have any ritual which gets you set for writing?

SEXTON: I might, if I felt the poem come on, put on a certain record, sometimes the "Bachianas Brasileiras," by Villa-

Lobos. I wrote to that for about three or four years. It's my magic tune.

INTERVIEWER: Is there any time of day, any particular mood that is better for writing?

SEXTON: No. Those moments before a poem comes, when the heightened awareness comes over you, and you realize a poem is buried there somewhere, you prepare yourself. I run around, you know, kind of skipping around the house, marvelous elation. It's as though I could fly, almost, and I get very tense before I've told the truth—hard. Then I sit down at the desk and get going with it.

INTERVIEWER: What is the quality of feeling when you're writing?

SEXTON: Well, it's a beautiful feeling, even if it's hard work. When I'm writing, I know I'm doing the thing I was born to do.

INTERVIEWER: Do you have any standard by which you judge whether to let an image remain in a poem, or be cut?

SEXTON: It's done with my unconscious. May it do me no ill.

INTERVIEWER: You've said, "When I'm working away on a poem, I hunt for the truth . . . It might be a poetic truth, and not just a factual one." Can you comment on that?

SEXTON: Many of my poems are true, line by line, altering a few facts to get the story at its heart. In "The Double Image," the poem about my mother's death from cancer and the loss of my daughter, I don't mention that I had another child. Each poem has its own truth. Furthermore, in that poem, I only say that I was hospitalized twice, when in fact, I was hospitalized five times in that span of time. But then, poetic truth is not necessarily autobiographical. It is truth that goes beyond the immediate self, another life. I don't adhere to literal facts all the time; I make them up whenever needed. Concrete examples give a verisimilitude. I want the reader to feel, Yes, yes, that's the way it is. I want them to feel as if they were touching me. I would alter any word, attitude, image, or persona for the sake of a poem. As Yeats said, "I have lived many lives, I have been a slave and a prince. Many a beloved has sat upon my knee, and I have sat upon the knee of many a beloved. Everything that has been shall be again."

INTERVIEWER: There Yeats is talking about reincarnation.

SEXTON: So am I. It's a little mad, but I believe I am many people. When I am writing a poem, I feel I am the person who should have written it. Many times I assume these guises; I attack it the way a novelist might. Sometimes I become someone else, and when I do, I believe, even in moments when I'm not writing the poem, that I am that person. When I wrote about the farmer's wife, I lived in my mind in Illinois; when I had the illegitimate child, I nursed it—in my mind—and gave it back and traded life. When I gave my lover back to his wife, in my mind, I grieved and saw how ethereal and unnecessary I had been. When I was Christ, I felt like Christ. My arms hurt, I desperately wanted to pull them in off the Cross. When I was taken down off the Cross and buried alive, I sought solutions; I hoped they were Christian solutions.

INTERVIEWER: What prompted you to write "In the Deep Museum," which recounts what Christ could have felt if he were still alive in the tomb? What led you to even deal with such a subject?

SEXTON: I'm not sure. I think it was an unconscious thing. I think I had a kind of feeling Christ was speaking to me and telling me to write that story . . . the story he hadn't written. I thought to myself, This would be the most awful death. The Cross, the Crucifixion, which I so deeply believe in, has almost become trite, and that there was a more humble death that he might have had to seek for love's sake, because his love was the greatest thing about him—not his death.

INTERVIEWER: Are you a believing nonbeliever? Your poems, such as "The Division of Parts" and "With Mercy for the

Greedy," suggest you would like to believe, indeed struggle to believe, but can't.

SEXTON: Yes. I fight my own impulse. There is a hard-core part of me that believes, and there's this little critic in me that believes nothing. Some people think I'm a lapsed Catholic.

INTERVIEWER: What was your early religious training?

SEXTON: Half-assed Protestant. My Nana came from a Protestant background with a very stern patriarchal father who had twelve children. He often traveled in Europe, and when he came back and brought nude statues into his house, the minister came to call and said, "You can't come to church if you keep these nude statues." So he said, "All right, I'll never come again." Every Sunday morning he read the Bible to his twelve children for two hours, and they had to sit up straight and perfect. He never went to church again.

INTERVIEWER: Where do you get the "juice" for your religious poetry?

SEXTON: I found, when I was bringing up my children, that I could answer questions about sex easily. But I had a very hard time with the questions about God and death. It isn't resolved in my mind to this day.

INTERVIEWER: Are you saying, then, that questions from your children are what prompted you to think about these poems—that doesn't sound quite right.

SEXTON: It isn't. I have visions—sometimes ritualized visions—that come to me of God, or of Christ, or of the saints, and I feel that I can touch them almost . . . that they are part of me. It's the same "Everything that has been shall be again." It's reincarnation, speaking with another voice . . . or else with the Devil. If you want to know the truth, the leaves talk to me every June.

INTERVIEWER: How long do your visions last? What are they like?

SEXTON: That's impossible to describe. They could last for

six months, six minutes, or six hours. I feel very much in touch with things after I've had a vision. It's somewhat like the beginning of writing a poem; the whole world is very sharp and well defined, and I'm intensely alive, like I've been shot full of electric volts.

INTERVIEWER: Do you try to communicate this to other people when you feel it?

SEXTON: Only through the poems, no other way. I refuse to talk about it, which is why I'm having a hard time now.

INTERVIEWER: Is there any real difference between a religious vision and a vision when you're mad?

SEXTON: Sometimes, when you're mad, the vision—I don't call them visions, really—when you're mad, they're silly and out of place, whereas if it's a so-called mystical experience, you've put everything in its proper place. I've never talked about my religious experiences with anyone, not a psychiatrist, not a friend, not a priest, not anyone. I've kept it very much to myself—and I find this very difficult, and I'd just as soon leave it, if you please.

INTERVIEWER: A poem like "The Division of Parts" has direct reference to your mother's dying. Did those excruciating experiences of watching someone close to you disintegrate from cancer force you to confront your own belief in God or religion?

SEXTON: Yes, I think so. The dying are slowly being rocked away from us and wrapped up into death, that eternal place. And one looks for answers and is faced with demons and visions. Then one comes up with God. I don't mean the ritualized Protestant God, who is such a goody-goody . . . but the martyred saints, the crucified man . . .

INTERVIEWER: Are you saying that when confronted with the ultimate question, death, that your comfort comes, even though watered down, from the myths and fables of religion?

SEXTON: No myth or fable ever gave me any solace, but my

own inner contact with the heroes of the fables, as you put it, my very closeness to Christ. In one poem about the Virgin Mary, "For the Year of the Insane," I believed that I was talking to Mary, that her lips were upon my lips; it's almost physical . . . as in many of my poems. I become that person.

INTERVIEWER: But is it the fact in your life of someone you know dying that forces you into a vision?

SEXTON: No, I think it's my own madness.

INTERVIEWER: Are you more lucid, in the sense of understanding life, when you are mad?

SEXTON: Yes.

INTERVIEWER: Why do you think that's so?

SEXTON: Pure gift.

INTERVIEWER: I asked you, are you a believing disbeliever. When something happens like a death, are you pushed over the brink of disbelieving into believing?

SEXTON: For a while, but it can happen without a death. There are little deaths in life, too—in your own life—and at that point, sometimes you are in touch with strange things, otherworldly things.

INTERVIEWER: You have received a great deal of fan mail from Jesuits and other clergy. Do any of them interpret what you write as blasphemy?

SEXTON: No. They find my work very religious, and take my books on retreats, and teach my poems in classes.

INTERVIEWER: Why do you feel that most of your critics ignore this strain of religious experience in your poetry?

SEXTON: I think they tackle the obvious things without delving deeper. They are more shocked by the other, whereas I think in time to come people will be more shocked by my mystical poetry than by my so-called confessional poetry.

INTERVIEWER: Perhaps your critics, in time to come, will associate the suffering in your confessional poetry with the kind of sufferers you take on in your religious poetry.

SEXTON: You've summed it up perfectly. Thank you for saying that. That ragged Christ, that sufferer, performed the greatest act of confession, and I mean with his body. And I try to do that with words.

INTERVIEWER: Many of your poems deal with memories of suffering. Very few of them deal with memories that are happy ones. Why do you feel driven to write more about pain?

SEXTON: That's not true about my last book, which deals with joy. I think I've dealt with unhappy themes because I've lived them. If I haven't lived them, I've invented them.

INTERVIEWER: But surely there were also happy moments, joyous, euphoric moments in those times as well.

SEXTON: Pain engraves a deeper memory.

INTERVIEWER: Are there any poems you wouldn't read in public?

SEXTON: No. As a matter of fact, I sing "Cripples and Other Stories" with my combo to a Nashville rhythm.

INTERVIEWER: What is your combo?

SEXTON: It's called "Her Kind"—after one of my poems. One of my students started putting my poems to music—he's a guitarist, and then we got an organist, a flutist, and a drummer. We call our music "Chamber Rock." We've been working on it and giving performances for about a year. It opens up my poems in a new way by involving them in the sound of rock music, letting my words open up to sound that can be actually heard, giving a new dimension. And it's quite exciting for me to hear them that way.

INTERVIEWER: Do you enjoy giving a reading?

SEXTON: It takes three weeks out of your life. A week before it happens, the nervousness begins, and it builds up to the night of the reading when the poet in you changes into a performer. Readings take so much out of you because they are a reliving of the experience—that is, they are happening all over again. I am an actress in my own autobiographical play. Then there is the love. . . . When there is a coupling of the audience and myself, when they are really with me, and the Muse is with me, I'm not coming alone.

INTERVIEWER: Can you ever imagine America as a place where thousands of fans flock to a stadium to hear a poet, as they do in Russia?

SEXTON: Someday, perhaps. But our poets seem to be losing touch. People flock to Bob Dylan, Janis Joplin, the Beatles— these are the popular poets of the English-speaking world. But I don't worry about popularity; I'm too busy.

INTERVIEWER: At first your poetry was a therapeutic device. Why do you write now?

SEXTON: I write because I'm driven to—it's my bag. Though after every book, I think there'll never be another one. That's the end of that. Good-bye, good-bye.

INTERVIEWER: And what advice would you give to a young poet?

SEXTON: Be careful who your critics are. Be specific. Tell almost the whole story. Put your ear close down to your soul and listen hard.

INTERVIEWER: Louis Simpson criticized your poetry, saying, "A poem titled 'Menstruation at Forty' was the straw that broke this camel's back." Is it only male critics who balk at your use of the biological facts of womanhood?

SEXTON: I haven't added up all the critics and put them on different teams. I haven't noticed the gender of the critic especially. I talk of the life-death cycle of the body. Well, women tell time by the body. They are like clocks. They are always fastened to the earth, listening for its small animal noises. Sexuality is one of the most normal parts of life. True, I get a little uptight when Norman Mailer writes that he screws a woman anally. I like Allen Ginsberg very much, and when he writes about the ugly vagina, I feel awful. That kind of thing doesn't appeal to me. So I have my limitations, too. Homosexuality is all right with me. Sappho was beautiful. But when someone hates another person's body and somehow violates it—that's the kind of thing I mind.

INTERVIEWER: What do you feel is the purpose of poetry?

SEXTON: As Kafka said about prose, "A book should serve as the ax for the frozen sea within us." And that's what I want from a poem. A poem should serve as the ax for the frozen sea within us.

INTERVIEWER: How would you apply the Kafka quote to your new book, *Love Poems*?

SEXTON: Well, have you ever seen a sixteen-year-old fall in love? The ax for the frozen sea becomes embedded in her. Or have you ever seen a woman get to be forty and never have any love in her life? What happens to her when she falls in love? The ax for the frozen sea.

INTERVIEWER: Some people wonder how you can write about yourself, completely ignoring the great issues of the times, like the Vietnam war or the civil rights crisis.

SEXTON: People have to find out who they are before they can confront national issues. The fact that I seldom write about public issues in no way reflects my personal opinion. I am a pacifist. I sign petitions, etc. However, I am not a polemicist. "The Fire Bombers"—that's a new poem—is about wanton destruction, not about Vietnam, specifically; when Robert Kennedy was killed, I wrote about an assassin. I write about human emotions; I write about interior events, not historical ones. In one of my love poems, I say that my lover is unloading bodies from Vietnam. If that poem is read in a hundred years, people will have to look up the war in Vietnam. They will have mixed it up with the Korean or God knows what else. One hopes it will be history very soon. Of course, I may change. I could use the specifics of the war for a backdrop against which to reveal experience, and it would be just as valid as the details I am known by. As for the civil rights issue, I mentioned that casually in a poem, but I don't go into it. I think it's a major issue. I think many of my poems about the individual who is dispossessed, who must play slave, who cries "Freedom now," "Power now," are about the human experience of being black in this world. A black emotion can be a white emotion. It is a crisis for the individual as well as the nation. I think I've been writing black poems all along, wearing my white mask. I'm always the victim . . . but no longer!

—BARBARA KEVLES

1968

TONI MORRISON

⬥⬥⬥✦⬥⬥⬥

Toni Morrison (born Chloe Anthony Wofford in 1931) was raised in Lorain, Ohio, a steel town on the banks of Lake Erie. She received a B.A. from Howard University and an M.A. in English from Cornell, where her thesis explored the theme of suicide in the works of Faulkner and Woolf. In 1955 she began teaching at Texas Southern University, but soon returned to Howard to take up an instructor's position in the English department. She remained at Howard for seven years, teaching, writing and bringing her stories to a regular but informal writers' workshop. Her first novel, *The Bluest Eye*, appeared in 1969, four years after Morrison left Howard for an editorship at Random House. It was followed in 1971 by *Sula*, a National Book Award nominee. At that point, Morrison says, she was still uncomfortable identifying herself as a novelist. She remained both editor and writer until 1977, when the success of *Song of Solomon*, her third novel, allowed her make a "genuine commitment" to writing.

In the eighties, despite a return to teaching, Morrison produced *Dreaming Emmett*, an unpublished play; *Tar Baby*, a *New York Times* best-seller; and *Beloved*, which received a Pulitzer Prize. In

1989 she joined the faculty of Princeton University. *Jazz,* her sixth novel, and *Playing in the Dark,* a collection of essays, both appeared in 1992. A year later, citing the "visionary force and poetic import" of her novels, the Swedish Academy awarded her the Nobel Prize for literature.

American; it could be Catholic, it could be Midwestern I'm those things too,

and they are all important

INTERVIEWER

Why do you think people ask, "Why don't you write something that we can

understand?" Do you threaten them by not writing in the typical western,

linear, chronological way?

MORRISON

I don't think that they mean that ~~When they say,~~ "Are you ever going to write

a book about white people?" ~~they think that~~ that's a kind of a compliment

They're saying, "You write well enough, I would even let you write about me "

I ~~couldn't~~ say that to anybody else I mean, could I ~~go~~ up to Andre Gide and

say, "Yes, but when are you going to get serious and start writing about black

people?" I don't think he would know how to answer that question Just as I

don't He would say, "What?" "I will if I want" or "Who are you?" What is

behind that question is, there's the center, which is ~~you~~, and then there are

these regional blacks or Asians, sort of marginal people That question can

only be asked from the center. Bill Moyers asked me that when-are-you-going-

to-write-about question on television. I just said, "Well, maybe one day   "

but I couldn't say to him, you know, you can only ask that question from the

center. The center of the world! I mean he's a white male He's asking a

marginal person, "When are you going to get to the center? When are you going

to write about white people?" ~~But I can't say, "Leo Tolstoy, when are you~~

~~gonna write about black people?"~~ I can't say, "Bill, why are you asking me

that question? The point is that he's ~~complimenting~~; he's saying, "You write

A page from the corrected draft of
Toni Morrison's Writers-at-Work interview.

TONI MORRISON

Toni Morrison detests being called a "poetic writer." She seems to think that the attention that has been paid to the lyricism of her work marginalizes her talent and denies her stories their power and resonance. As one of the few novelists whose work is both popular and critically acclaimed, she can afford the luxury of choosing what praise to accept. But she does not reject all classifications, and, in fact, embraces the title "black woman writer." Her ability to transform individuals into forces and idiosyncrasies into inevitabilities has led some critics to call her the "D. H. Lawrence of the black psyche." She is also a master of the public novel, examining the relationships between the races and sexes and the struggle between civilization and nature, while at the same time combining myth and the fantastic with a deep political sensitivity.

We talked with Morrison one summer Sunday afternoon on the lush campus of Princeton University. The interview took place in her office, which is decorated with a large Helen Frankenthaler print, pen-and-ink drawings an architect did of all the houses that appear in her work, photographs, a few framed book-jacket covers and an apology note to her from Hemingway—a forgery meant as a joke. On her desk is a blue glass teacup emblazoned with the likeness of Shirley Temple filled with the number two pencils that she uses to write her first drafts. Jade plants sit in a window and a few more potted *plants hang above. A coffeemaker and cups are at the ready. Despite the high ceilings, the big desk and the high-backed black rocking chairs, the room had the warm feeling of a kitchen, maybe because talking to Morrison about writing is the intimate kind of conversation that often seems to happen in kitchens; or perhaps it was the fact that as our energy started flagging she magically produced mugs of cranberry juice. We felt that she had allowed us to enter into a sanctuary, and that, however subtly, she was completely in control of the situation.*

Outside, high canopies of oak leaves filtered the sunlight, dappling her white office with pools of yellowy light. Morrison sat behind her big desk, which, despite her apologies for the "disorder," appeared well organized. Stacks of books and piles of paper resided on a painted bench set against the wall. She is smaller than one might imagine, and her hair, gray and silver, is woven into thin steel-colored braids that hang just at shoulder length. Occasionally during the interview Morrison let her sonorous, deep voice break into rumbling laughter and punctuated certain statements with a flat smack of her hand on the desktop. At a moment's notice she can switch from raging about violence in the United States to gleefully skewering the hosts of the trash TV talk shows through which she confesses to channel-surfing sometimes, late in the afternoon, if her work is done.

INTERVIEWER: You have said that you begin to write before dawn. Did this habit begin for practical reasons, or was the early morning an especially fruitful time for you?

MORRISON: Writing before dawn began as a necessity—I had small children when I first began to write, and I needed to use the time before they said, "Mama"—and that was always around five in the morning. Many years later, after I stopped working at Random House, I just stayed at home for a couple of years. I discovered things about myself I had never thought about before. At first I didn't know when I wanted to eat, because I had always eaten when it was lunchtime or dinnertime or breakfast time. Work and the children had driven all of my habits. . . . I didn't know the weekday sounds of my own house; it all made me feel a little giddy.

I was involved in writing *Beloved* at that time—this was in 1983—and eventually I realized that I was clearer-headed, more confident and generally more intelligent in the morning. The habit of getting up early, which I had formed when the children were young, now became my choice. I am not very bright or very witty or very inventive after the sun goes down.

Recently I was talking to a writer who described something she did whenever she moved to her writing table. I don't remember exactly what the gesture was—there is something on her desk that she touches before she hits the computer keyboard—but we began to talk about little rituals that one goes through before beginning to write. I, at first, thought I didn't have a ritual, but then I remembered that I always get up and make a cup of coffee while it is still dark—it must be dark—and then I drink the coffee and watch the light come. And she said, Well, that's a ritual. And I realized that for me this ritual comprises my preparation to enter a space that I can only call nonsecular. . . . Writers all devise ways to approach that place where they expect to make the contact, where they become the conduit, or where they engage in this mysterious process. For me, light is the signal in the transition. It's not being *in* the light, it's being there *before it arrives.* It enables me, in some sense.

I tell my students one of the most important things they need to know is when they are their best, creatively. They need to ask themselves, What does the ideal room look like? Is there music? Is there silence? Is there chaos outside or is there serenity outside? What do I need in order to release my imagination?

INTERVIEWER: What about your writing routine?

MORRISON: I have an ideal writing routine that I've never experienced, which is to have, say, nine uninterrupted days when I wouldn't have to leave the house or take phone calls. And to have the space: a space where I have huge tables. I end up with this much space [she indicates a small square spot on her desk] everywhere I am, and I can't beat my way out of it. I am reminded of that tiny desk that Emily Dickinson wrote on, and I chuckle when I think, Sweet thing, there she was. But that is all any of us have—just this small space and no matter what the filing system or how often you clear it out, life, documents, letters, requests, invitations, invoices just keep going back in. I am not able to write regularly. I have never been able to do that—mostly because I have always had a nine-to-five job. I had to write either in between those hours, hurriedly, or spend a lot of weekend and predawn time.

INTERVIEWER: Could you write after work?

MORRISON: That was difficult. I've tried to overcome not having orderly spaces by substituting compulsion for discipline, so that when something is urgently there, urgently seen or understood, or the metaphor was powerful enough, then I would move everything aside and write for sustained periods of time. I'm talking to you about getting the first draft.

INTERVIEWER: You have to do it straight through?

MORRISON: I do. I don't think it's a law.

INTERVIEWER: Could you write on the bottom of a shoe while riding on a train like Robert Frost? Could you write on an airplane?

MORRISON: Sometimes something that I was having some trouble with falls into place, a word sequence, say, so I've written on scraps of paper, in hotels on hotel stationery, in automobiles. If it arrives you know. If you know it really has come, then you have to put it down.

INTERVIEWER: What is the physical act of writing like for you?

MORRISON: I write with a pencil.

INTERVIEWER: Would you ever work on a word processor?

MORRISON: Oh I do that also, but that is much later when everything is put together. I type that into a computer, and then

I begin to revise. But everything I write for the first time is written with a pencil, maybe a ballpoint if I don't have a pencil. I'm not picky, but my preference is for yellow legal pads and a nice number two pencil.

INTERVIEWER: Dixon Ticonderoga number two soft?

MORRISON: Exactly. I remember once trying to use a tape recorder, but it doesn't work.

INTERVIEWER: Did you actually dictate a story into the machine?

MORRISON: Not the whole thing, but just a bit. For instance, when two or three sentences seemed to fall into place, I thought I would carry a tape recorder in the car, particularly when I was working at Random House going back and forth every day. It occurred to me that I could just record it. It was a disaster. I don't trust my writing that is not written, although I work very hard in subsequent revisions to remove the writerliness from it, to give it a combination of lyrical, standard and colloquial language. To pull all these things together into something that I think is much more alive, and representative. But I don't trust something that occurs to me, and then is spoken and transferred immediately to the page.

INTERVIEWER: Do you ever read your work out loud while you are working on it?

MORRISON: Not until it's published. I don't trust a performance. I could get a response that might make me think it was successful when it wasn't at all. The difficulty for me in writing—*among* the difficulties—is to write language that can work quietly on a page for a reader who doesn't hear anything. Now for that, one has to work very carefully with what is *in between* the words. What is not said. Which is measure, which is rhythm and so on. So, it is what you don't write that frequently gives what you do write its power.

INTERVIEWER: How many times would you say you have to write a paragraph over to reach this standard?

MORRISON: Well, those that need reworking I do as long as I can. I mean I've revised six times, seven times, thirteen times. But there's a line between revision and fretting, just working it to death. It is important to know when you are fretting it; when you are fretting it because it is not working, it needs to be scrapped.

INTERVIEWER: Do you ever go back over what has been published and wish you had fretted more over something?

MORRISON: A lot. Everything.

INTERVIEWER: Do you ever rework passages that have already been published before reading them to an audience?

MORRISON: I don't change it for the audience, but I know what it ought to be and isn't. After twenty-some years you can figure it out; I know more about it now than I did then. It is not so much that it would have been different or even better; it is just that, taken into context with what I was trying to effect, or what consequence I wanted it to have on the reader, years later the picture is clearer to me.

INTERVIEWER: How do you think being an editor for twenty years affected you as a writer?

MORRISON: I am not sure. It lessened my awe of the publishing industry. I understood the adversarial relationship that sometimes exists between writers and publishers, but I learned how important, how critical an editor was, which I don't think I would have known before.

INTERVIEWER: Are there editors who are helpful critically?

MORRISON: Oh yes. The good ones make all the difference. It is like a priest or a psychiatrist; if you get the wrong one, then you are better off alone. But there are editors so rare and so important that they are worth searching for, and you always know when you have one.

INTERVIEWER: Who was the most instrumental editor you've ever worked with?

MORRISON: I had a very good editor, superlative for me—

Bob Gottlieb. What made him good for me was a number of things: knowing what not to touch; asking all the questions you probably would have asked yourself had there been the time. Good editors are really the third eye. Cool. Dispassionate. They don't love you or your work; for me that is what is valuable—not compliments. Sometimes it's uncanny: the editor puts his or her finger on exactly the place the writer knows is weak but just couldn't do any better at the time. Or perhaps the writer thought it might fly, but wasn't sure. Good editors identify that place, and sometimes make suggestions. Some suggestions are not useful because you can't explain everything to an editor about what you are trying to do. I couldn't possibly explain all of those things to an editor, because what I do has to work on so many levels. But within the relationship if there is some trust, some willingness to listen, remarkable things can happen. I read books all the time that I know would have profited from not a copy editor but somebody just talking through it. And it is important to get a great editor at a certain time, because if you don't have one in the beginning, you almost can't have one later. If you work well without an editor, and your books are well received for five or ten years, and then you write another one, which is successful but not very good, why should you then listen to an editor?

INTERVIEWER: You have told students that they should think of the process of revision as one of the major satisfactions of writing. Do you get more pleasure out of writing the first draft, or in the actual revision of the work?

MORRISON: They are different. I am profoundly excited by thinking up or having the idea in the first place . . . before I begin to write.

INTERVIEWER: Does it come in a flash?

MORRISON: No, it's a sustained thing I have to play with. I always start out with an idea, even a boring idea, that becomes a question I don't have any answers to. Specifically, since I began the *Beloved* trilogy, the last part of which I'm working on now, I have been wondering why women who are twenty, thirty years younger than I am are no happier than women who are my age and older. What on earth is that about, when there are so many more things that they can do, so many more choices? *All right*, so this is an embarrassment of riches, but so what. Why is everybody so miserable?

INTERVIEWER: Do you write to figure out exactly how you feel about a subject?

MORRISON: No, I know how I *feel*. My feelings are the result of prejudices and convictions like everybody else's. But I am interested in the complexity, the vulnerability of an idea. It is not: "This is what I believe," because that would not be a book, just a tract. A book is: "This may be what I believe, but suppose I am wrong . . . what could it be?" Or, "I don't know what it is, but I am interested in finding out what it might mean to me, as well as to other people."

INTERVIEWER: Did you know as a child you wanted to be a writer?

MORRISON: No. I wanted to be a reader. I thought everything that needed to be written had already been written or would be. I only wrote the first book because I thought it wasn't there, and I wanted to read it when I got through. I am a pretty good reader. I love it. It is what I do, really. So, if I can read it, that is the highest compliment I can think of. People say, "I write for myself," and it sounds so awful and so narcissistic, but in a sense if you know how to read your own work—that is, with the necessary critical distance—it makes you a better writer and editor. When I teach creative writing, I always speak about how you have to learn how to read your work; I don't mean enjoy it because you wrote it. I mean, go away from it, and read it as though it is the first time you've ever seen it. Critique it that way. Don't get all involved in your thrilling sentences and all that. . . .

INTERVIEWER: Do you have your audience in mind when you sit down to write?

MORRISON: Only me. If I come to a place where I am unsure, I have the characters to go to for reassurance. By that time they are friendly enough to tell me if the rendition of their lives is authentic or not. But there are so many things only I can tell. After all, this is my work. I have to take full responsibility for doing it right as well as doing it wrong. Doing it wrong isn't bad, but doing it wrong and thinking you've done it right is. I remember spending a whole summer writing something I was very impressed with, but couldn't get back to until winter. I went back confident that those fifty pages were really first-rate, but when I read them, each page of the fifty was terrible. It was really ill-conceived. I knew that I could do it over, but I just couldn't get over the fact that I thought it was so good at the time. And that is scary because then you think it means you don't know.

INTERVIEWER: What about it was so bad?

MORRISON: It was pompous. Pompous and unappetizing.

INTERVIEWER: I read that you started writing after your divorce as a way of beating back the loneliness. Was that true, and do you write for different reasons now?

MORRISON: Sort of. Sounds simpler than it was. I don't know if I was writing for that reason or some other reason, or one that I don't even suspect. I do know that I don't like it here if I don't have something to write.

INTERVIEWER: Here, meaning where?

MORRISON: Meaning out in the world. It is not possible for me to be unaware of the incredible violence, the willful ignorance, the hunger for other people's pain. I'm always conscious of that though I am less aware of it under certain circumstances—good friends at dinner, other books. Teaching makes a big difference, but that is not enough. Teaching could make me into someone who is complacent, unaware, rather than part of the solution. So what makes me feel as though I belong here, out in this world, is not the teacher, not the mother, not the lover but what goes on in my mind when I am writing. Then I belong here, and then all of the things that are disparate and irreconcilable can be useful. I can do the traditional things that writers always say they do, which is to make order out of chaos. Even if you are reproducing the disorder, you are sovereign at that point. Struggling through the work is extremely important—more important to me than publishing it.

INTERVIEWER: If you didn't do this. Then the chaos would—

MORRISON: Then I would be part of the chaos.

INTERVIEWER: Wouldn't the answer to that be either to lecture about the chaos or to be in politics?

MORRISON: If I had a gift for it. All I can do is read books and write books, and edit books and critique books. I don't think that I could show up on a regular basis as a politician. I would lose interest. I don't have the resources for it, the gift. There are people who can organize other people, and I cannot. I'd just get bored.

INTERVIEWER: When did it become clear to you that your gift was to be a writer?

MORRISON: It was very late. I always thought I was probably adept, because people used to say so, but their criteria might not have been mine. So, I wasn't interested in what they said. It meant nothing. It was by the time I was writing *Song of Solomon*, the third book, that I began to think that this was the central part of my life. Not to say that other women haven't said it all along, but for a woman to say "I am a writer" is difficult.

INTERVIEWER: Why?

MORRISON: Well, it isn't so difficult *anymore*, but it certainly was for me, and for women of my generation or my class or my race. I don't know that all those things are folded into it, but the point is you're moving yourself out of the gender role. You are not saying, "I am a mother, I am a wife." Or, if you're in the labor market, "I am a teacher, I am an editor." But when you move to "writer," what is that supposed to mean? Is that a job? Is this the way you make your living? It's an intervention into terrain that you are not familiar with—where you have no provenance. At the time I certainly didn't personally know any other women writers who were successful; it looked very much like a male preserve. So you sort of hope you're going to be a little minor person around the edges. It's almost as if you needed permission to write. When I read women's biographies and autobiographies, even accounts of how they got started writing, almost every one of them had a little anecdote which told about the moment someone gave them permission to do it. A mother, a husband, a teacher . . . somebody said, "Okay, go ahead—you can do it." Which is not to say that men have never needed that; frequently when they are very young, a mentor says, "You're good," and they take off. The entitlement was something they could take for granted. I couldn't. It was all very strange. So, even though I knew that writing was central to my life, that it was where my mind was, where I was most delighted and most challenged, I couldn't say it. If someone asked me, "What do you do?" I wouldn't say, "Oh I'm a writer." I'd say, "I'm an editor, or a teacher." Because when you meet people and go to lunch, if they say "What do you do?" and you say, "I'm a writer," they have to think about that, and then they ask, "What have you written?" Then they have to either like it, or not like it. People feel obliged to like or not like and say so. It is perfectly all right to hate my work. It really is. I have close friends whose work I loathe.

INTERVIEWER: Did you feel you had to write in private?

MORRISON: Oh yes, I wanted to make it a private thing. I wanted to own it myself. Because once you say it, then other people become involved. As a matter of fact, while I was at Random House I never said I was a writer.

INTERVIEWER: Why not?

MORRISON: Oh, it would have been awful. First of all they didn't hire me to do that. They didn't hire me to be one of *them.* Secondly, I think they would have fired me.

INTERVIEWER: Really?

MORRISON: Sure. There were no in-house editors who wrote fiction. Ed Doctorow quit. There was nobody else—no real buying, negotiating editor in trade who was also publishing her own novels.

INTERVIEWER: Did the fact that you were a woman have anything to do with it?

MORRISON: That I didn't think about too much. I was so busy. I only know that I will never again trust my life, my future, to the whims of men, in companies or out. Never again will their judgment have anything to do with what I think I can do. That was the wonderful liberation of being divorced and having children. I did not mind failure, ever, but I minded thinking that someone male knew better. Before that, all the men I knew *did* know better, they really did. My father and teachers were smart people who knew better. Then I came across a smart person who was very important to me who *didn't* know better.

INTERVIEWER: Was this your husband?

MORRISON: Yes. He knew better about his life, but not about mine. I had to stop and say, let me start again and see what it is like to be a grown-up. I decided to leave home, to take my children with me, to go into publishing and see what I could do. I was prepared for that not to work either, but I wanted to see what it was like to be a grown-up.

INTERVIEWER: Can you talk about that moment at Random House when they suddenly realized that they had a writer in their midst?

MORRISON: I published a book called *The Bluest Eye.* I didn't tell them about it. They didn't know until they read the review in *The New York Times.* It was published by Holt. Somebody had told this young guy there that I was writing something, and he had said in a very offhand way, If you ever complete something send it to me. So I did. A lot of black men were writing in 1968, 1969, and he bought it, thinking that there was a growing interest in what black people were writing, and that this book of mine would also sell. He was wrong. What was selling was, "Let me tell you how powerful I am and how horrible you are," or some version of that. For whatever reasons, he took a small risk. He didn't pay me much, so it didn't matter if the book sold or not. It got a really horrible review in *The New York Times Book Review* on Sunday and then got a very good daily review.

INTERVIEWER: You mentioned getting permission to write. Who gave it to you?

MORRISON: No one. What I needed permission to do was to succeed at it. I never signed a contract until the book was finished because I didn't want it to be homework. A contract meant somebody was waiting for it, that I *had* to do it, and they could ask me about it. They could get up in my face, and I don't like that. By not signing a contract, I do it, and if I want you to see it, I'll let you see it. It has to do with self-esteem. I am sure for years you have heard writers constructing illusions of freedom, anything in order to have the illusion that it is all mine, and only I can do it. I remember introducing Eudora Welty and saying that nobody could have written those stories but her, meaning that I have a feeling about most books that at some point somebody would have written them *anyway*. But then there are some writers without whom certain stories would never have been written. I don't mean the subject matter or the narrative but just the way in which they did it—their slant on it is truly unique.

INTERVIEWER: Who are some of them?

MORRISON: Hemingway is in that category, Flannery O'Connor. Faulkner, Fitzgerald . . .

INTERVIEWER: Haven't you been critical of the way these authors depicted blacks?

MORRISON: No! Me, critical? I have been revealing how white writers imagine black people, and some of them are brilliant at it. Faulkner was brilliant at it. Hemingway did it poorly in places and brilliantly elsewhere.

INTERVIEWER: How so?

MORRISON: In not using black characters, but using the aesthetic of blacks as anarchy, as sexual license, as deviance. In his last book, *The Garden of Eden*, Hemingway's heroine is getting blacker and blacker. The woman who is going mad tells her husband, "I want to be your little African Queen." The novel gets its charge that way: "Her white white hair and her black, black skin" . . . almost like a Man Ray photograph. Mark Twain talked about racial ideology in the most powerful, eloquent and instructive way I have ever read. Edgar Allan Poe did not. He loved white supremacy and the planter class, and he wanted to be a gentleman, and he endorsed all of that. He didn't contest it, or critique it. What is exciting about American literature is that business of how writers say things under, beneath and around their stories. Think of *Pudd'nhead Wilson* and all these inversions of what race is, how sometimes nobody can tell, or the thrill of discovery? Faulkner in *Absalom, Absalom!* spends the entire book tracing race, and you can't find it. No one can see it, even the character who *is* black can't see it. I did this lecture for my students that took me forever, which was tracking all the moments of withheld, partial or disinformation, when a racial fact or clue *sort* of comes out but doesn't quite arrive. I just wanted to chart it. I listed its appearance, disguise and disappearance on every page, I mean every phrase! Everything, and I delivered this thing to my class. They all fell asleep! But I was so fascinated, technically. Do you know how hard it is to withhold that kind of information but hinting, pointing all of the time? And then to reveal it in order to say that it is *not* the point anyway? It is technically just astonishing. As a reader you have been forced to hunt for a drop of black blood that means everything and nothing. The insanity of racism. So the structure is the argument. Not what this one says, or that one says . . . it is the *structure* of the book, and you are there hunting this black thing that is nowhere to be found, and yet makes all the difference. No one has done anything quite like that ever. So, when I critique, what I am saying is, I don't care if Faulkner is a racist or not; I don't personally care, but I am fascinated by what it means to write like this.

INTERVIEWER: What about black writers . . . how do they write in a world dominated by and informed by their relationship to a white culture?

MORRISON: By trying to alter language, simply to free it up, not to repress it or confine it, but to open it up. Tease it. Blast its racist straitjacket. I wrote a story entitled "Recitatif," in which there are two little girls in an orphanage, one white and one black. But the reader doesn't know which is white and which is black. I use class codes, but no racial codes.

INTERVIEWER: Is this meant to confuse the reader?

MORRISON: Well, yes. But to provoke and enlighten. I did that as a lark. What was exciting was to be forced as a writer not to be lazy and rely on obvious codes. Soon as I say, "Black woman . . ." I can rest on or provoke predictable responses, but if I leave it out then I have to talk about her in a complicated way—as a person.

INTERVIEWER: Why wouldn't you want to say, "The black woman came out of the store?"

MORRISON: Well, you can, but it has to be important that she is black.

INTERVIEWER: What about *The Confessions of Nat Turner?*

MORRISON: Well, here we have a very self-conscious character who says things like, "I looked at my black hand." Or "I woke up and I felt black." It is very much on Bill Styron's mind.

He feels charged in Nat Turner's skin . . . in this place that feels exotic to him. So it reads exotically to us, that's all.

INTERVIEWER: There was a tremendous outcry at that time from people who felt that Styron didn't have a right to write about Nat Turner.

MORRISON: He has a right to write about whatever he wants. To suggest otherwise is outrageous. What they should have criticized, and some of them did, was Styron's suggestion that Nat Turner hated black people. In the book Turner expresses his revulsion over and over again . . . he's so distant from blacks, so superior. So the fundamental question is why would anybody follow him? What kind of leader is this who has a fundamentally racist contempt that seems unreal to any black person reading it? Any white leader would have some interest and identification with the people he was asking to die. That was what these critics meant when they said Nat Turner speaks like a white man. That racial distance is strong and clear in that book.

INTERVIEWER: You must have read a lot of slave narratives for *Beloved.*

MORRISON: I wouldn't read them for information because I knew that they had to be authenticated by white patrons, that they couldn't say everything they wanted to say because they couldn't alienate their audience; they had to be quiet about certain things. They were going to be as good as they could be under the circumstances and as revelatory, but they never say how terrible it was. They would just say, "Well, you know, it was really awful, but let's abolish slavery so life can go on." Their narratives had to be very understated. So while I looked at the documents and felt *familiar* with slavery and overwhelmed by it, I wanted it to be truly *felt.* I wanted to translate the historical into the personal. I spent a long time trying to figure out what it was about slavery that made it so repugnant, so personal, so indifferent, so intimate and yet so public.

In reading some of the documents I noticed frequent references to something that was never properly described—*the bit*. This thing was put into the mouth of slaves to punish them and shut them up without preventing them from working. I spent a long time trying to find out what it looked like. I kept reading statements like, "I put the bit on Jenny," or, as Equiano says, "I went into a kitchen" and I saw a woman standing at the stove, and she had a brake (b r a k e, he spells it) "in her mouth," and I said, "What is that?" and somebody told me what it was, and then I said, "I never saw anything so awful in all my life." But I really couldn't image the thing—did it look like a horse's bit or what?

Eventually I did find some sketches in one book in this country, which was the record of a man's torture of his wife. In South America, Brazil, places like that, they kept such mementos. But while I was searching, something else occurred to me—namely, that this bit, this item, this personalized type of torture, was a direct descendant of the inquisition. And I realized that of course you can't buy this stuff. You can't send away for a mail-order bit for your slave. Sears doesn't carry them. So you have to make it. You have to go out in the backyard and put some stuff together and construct it and then affix it to a person. So the whole process had a very personal quality for the person who made it, as well as for the person who wore it. Then I realized that describing it would never be helpful: that the reader didn't need to *see* it so much as *feel* what it was like. I realized that it was important to imagine the bit as an active instrument, rather than simply as a curio or an historical fact. And in the same way I wanted to show the reader what slavery *felt* like, rather than how it looked.

There's a passage in which Paul D. says to Sethe, "I've never told anybody about it, I've sung about it sometimes." He tries to tell her what wearing the bit was like, but he ends up talking about a rooster that he swears smiled at him when he wore it—

he felt cheapened and lessened and that he would never be worth as much as a rooster sitting on a tub in the sunlight. I make other references to the desire to spit, to sucking iron and so on; but it seemed to me that describing what it *looked* like would distract the reader from what I wanted him or her to experience, which was what it *felt* like. The kind of information you can find between the lines of history. It sort of falls off the page, or it's a glance and a reference. It's right there in the intersection where an institution becomes personal, where the historical becomes people with names.

INTERVIEWER: When you create a character is it completely created out of your own imagination?

MORRISON: I never use anyone I know. In *The Bluest Eye* I think I used some gestures and dialogue of my mother in certain places, and a little geography. I've never done that since. I really am very conscientious about that. It's never based on anyone. I don't do what many writers do.

INTERVIEWER: Why is that?

MORRISON: There is this feeling that artists have—photographers more than other people, and writers—that they are acting like a succubus . . . this process of taking from something that's alive and using it for one's own purposes. You can do it with trees, butterflies or human beings. Making a little life for oneself by scavenging other people's lives is a big question, and it does have moral and ethical implications.

In fiction, I feel the most intelligent, and the most free, and the most excited, when my characters are fully invented people. That's part of the excitement. If they're based on somebody else, in a funny way it's an infringement of a copyright. That person *owns* his life, has a patent on it. It shouldn't be available for fiction.

INTERVIEWER: Do you ever feel like your characters are getting away from you, out of your control?

MORRISON: I take control of them. They are very carefully

imagined. I feel as though I know all there is to know about them, even things I don't write—like how they part their hair. They are like ghosts. They have nothing on their minds but themselves and aren't interested in anything but themselves. So you can't let them write your book for you. I have read books in which I know that has happened—when a novelist has been totally taken over by a character. I want to say, "You can't do that. If those people could write books they would, but they can't. *You* can." So, you have to say, "Shut up. Leave me alone. I am doing this."

INTERVIEWER: Have you ever had to tell any of your characters to shut up?

MORRISON: Pilate, I did. Therefore she doesn't speak very much. She has this long conversation with the two boys, and every now and then she'll say something, but she doesn't have the dialogue the other people have. I had to do that, otherwise she was going to overwhelm everybody. She got terribly interesting; characters can do that for a little bit. I had to take it back. It's *my* book; it's not called *Pilate.*

INTERVIEWER: Pilate is such a strong character. It seems to me that the women in your books are almost always stronger and braver than the men. Why is that?

MORRISON: That isn't true, but I hear that a lot. I think that our expectations of women are very low. If women just stand up straight for thirty days, everybody goes, "Oh! How brave!" As a matter of fact, somebody wrote about Sethe, and said she was this powerful, statuesque woman who wasn't even human. But at the end of the book, she can barely turn her head. She has been zonked; she can't even feed herself. Is that tough?

INTERVIEWER: Maybe people read it that way because they thought Sethe made such a hard choice slashing Beloved's throat. Maybe they think that's being strong. Some would say that's just bad manners.

MORRISON: Well, Beloved surely didn't think it was all that

tough. She thought it was lunacy. Or, more importantly, "How do you know death is better for me? You've never died. How could you know?" But I think Paul D., Son, Stamp Paid, even Guitar, make equally difficult choices; they are principled. I do think we are too accustomed to women who don't talk back or who use the weapons of the weak.

INTERVIEWER: What are the weapons of the weak?

MORRISON: Nagging. Poison. Gossip. Sneaking around instead of confrontation.

INTERVIEWER: There have been so few novels about women who have intense friendships with other women. Why do you think that is?

MORRISON: It has been a discredited relationship. When I was writing *Sula,* I was under the impression that for a large part of the female population a woman friend was considered a secondary relationship. A man and a woman's relationship was primary. Women, your own friends, were always secondary relationships when the man was not there. Because of this, there's that whole cadre of women who don't like women and prefer men. We had to be taught to like one another. *Ms.* magazine was founded on the premise that we really have to stop complaining about one another, hating, fighting one another and joining men in their condemnation of ourselves—a typical example of what dominated people do. That is a big education. When much of the literature was like that—when you read about women together (not lesbians, or those who have formed long relationships that are covertly lesbian, like in Virginia Woolf's work), it is an overtly male view of females together. They are usually male-dominated—like some of Henry James's characters—or the women are talking about men, like Jane Austen's girlfriends . . . talking about who got married and how to get married, and are you going to lose him, and I think she wants him and so on. To have heterosexual women who are friends, who are talking only about themselves to each other, seemed to me a very radical thing when *Sula* was published in 1971 . . . but it is hardly radical now.

INTERVIEWER: It is becoming acceptable.

MORRISON: Yes, and it's going to get boring. It will be overdone, and as usual it will all run amok.

INTERVIEWER: Why do writers have such a hard time writing about sex?

MORRISON: Sex is difficult to write about because it's just not sexy enough. The only way to write about it is not to write much. Let the reader bring his own sexuality into the text. A writer I usually admire has written about sex in the most off-putting way. There is just too much information. If you start saying "the curve of . . ." you soon sound like a gynecologist. Only Joyce could get away with that. He said all those forbidden words. He said *cunt*, and that was shocking. The forbidden word can be provocative. But after a while it becomes monotonous rather than arousing. Less is always better. Some writers think that if they use dirty words they've done it. It can work for a short period and for a very young imagination, but after a while it doesn't deliver. When Sethe and Paul D. first see each other, in about half a page they get the sex out of the way, which isn't any good anyway—it's fast, and they're embarrassed about it—and then they're lying there trying to pretend they're not in that bed, that they haven't met, and then they begin to think different thoughts, which begin to merge so you can't tell who's thinking what. That merging to me is more tactically sensual than if I had tried to describe body parts.

INTERVIEWER: What about plot? Do you always know where you're going? Would you write the end before you got there?

MORRISON: When I really know what it is about, then I can write that end scene. I wrote the end of *Beloved* about a quarter of the way in. I wrote the end of *Jazz* very early and the end of *Song of Solomon* very early on. What I really want is for the plot to be *how* it happened. It is like a detective story in a sense. You know who is dead and you want to find out who did it. So, you put the salient elements up front, and the reader is hooked into wanting to know, How did that happen? Who did that and why? You are forced into having a certain kind of language that will keep the reader asking those questions. In *Jazz*, just as I did before with *The Bluest Eye*, I put the whole plot on the first page. In fact, in the first edition the plot was on the cover, so that a person in a bookstore could read the cover and know right away what the book was about, and could, if they wished, dismiss it and buy another book. This seemed a suitable technique for *Jazz* because I thought of the plot in that novel—the threesome—as the melody of the piece, and it is fine to follow a melody—to feel the satisfaction of recognizing a melody whenever the narrator returns to it. That was the real art of the enterprise for me: bumping up against that melody time and again, seeing it from another point of view, seeing it afresh each time, playing it back and forth.

When Keith Jarret plays "Ol' Man River," the delight and satisfaction is not so much in the melody itself but in recognizing it when it surfaces and when it is hidden and when it goes away completely, what is put in its place. Not so much in the original line as in all the echoes and shades and turns and pivots Jarret plays around it. I was trying to do something similar with the plot in *Jazz*. I wanted the story to be the vehicle which moved us from page one to the end, but I wanted the delight to be found in moving away from the story and coming back to it, looking around it, and through it, as though it was a prism, constantly turning.

This playful aspect of *Jazz* may well cause a great deal of dissatisfaction in readers who just want the melody, who want to know what happened, who did it and why. But the jazzlike structure wasn't a secondary thing for me—it was the raison d'être of the book. The process of trial and error by which the narrator revealed the plot was as important and exciting to me as telling the story.

INTERVIEWER: You also divulge the plot early on in *Beloved.*

MORRISON: It seemed important to me that the action in *Beloved*—the fact of infanticide—be immediately known, but deferred, unseen. I wanted to give the reader all the information and the consequences surrounding the act, while avoiding engorging myself or the reader with the violence itself. I remember writing the sentence where Sethe cuts the throat of the child very, very late in the process of writing the book. I remember getting up from the table and walking outside for a long time—walking around the yard and coming back and revising it a little bit and going back out and in and rewriting the sentence over and over again. . . . Each time I fixed that sentence so that it was exactly right, or so I thought, but then I would be unable to sit there and would have to go away and come back. I thought that the act itself had to be not only buried but also understated, because if the language was going to compete with the violence itself it would be obscene or pornographic.

INTERVIEWER: Style is obviously very important to you. Can you talk about this in relation to *Jazz?*

MORRISON: With *Jazz,* I wanted to convey the sense that a musician conveys—that he has more but he's not gonna give it to you. It's an exercise in restraint, a holding back—not because it's not there, or because one had exhausted it, but because of the riches, and because it can be done again. That sense of knowing when to stop is a learned thing, and I didn't always have it. It was probably not until after I wrote *Song of Solomon* that I got to feeling secure enough to experience what it meant to be thrifty with images and language and so on. I was very conscious in writing *Jazz* of trying to blend that which is contrived and artificial with improvisation. I thought of myself as like the jazz musician: someone who practices and practices and practices in order to be able to invent and to make his art look effortless and graceful. I was always conscious of the constructed aspect of the writing process, and that art appears natural and elegant only as a result of constant practice and awareness of its formal structures. You must practice thrift in order to achieve that luxurious quality of wastefulness—that sense that you have enough to waste, that you are holding back—without actually wasting anything. You shouldn't overgratify, you should never satiate. I've always felt that that peculiar sense of hunger at the end of a piece of art—a yearning for more—is really very, very powerful. But there is at the same time a kind of contentment, knowing that at some other time there will indeed be more because the artist is endlessly inventive.

INTERVIEWER: Were there other . . . ingredients, structural entities?

MORRISON: Well, it seems to me that migration was a major event in the cultural history of this country. Now, I'm being very speculative about all of this—I guess that's why I write novels—but it seems to me something modern and new happened after the Civil War. Of course, a number of things changed, but the era was most clearly marked by the disowning and dispossession of ex-slaves. These ex-slaves were sometimes taken into their local labor markets, but they often tried to escape their problems by migrating to the city. I was fascinated by the thought of what the city must have meant to them, these second- and third-generation ex-slaves, to rural people living there in their own number. The city must have seemed so exciting and wonderful, so much the place to be.

I was interested in how the city worked. How classes and groups and nationalities had the security of numbers within their own turfs and territories, but also felt the thrill of knowing that there were other turfs and other territories, and felt the real glamour and excitement of being in this throng. I was interested in how music changed in this country. Spirituals and gospel and blues represented one kind of response to slavery— they gave voice to the yearning for escape, in code, literally on the underground railroad.

I was also concerned with personal life. How did people love one another? What did they think was free? At that time, when the ex-slaves were moving into the city, running away from something that was constricting and killing them and dispossessing them over and over and over again, they were in a very limiting environment. But when you listen to their music—the beginnings of jazz—you realized that they are talking about something else. They are talking about love, about loss. But there is such grandeur, such satisfaction in those lyrics . . . they're never happy—somebody's always leaving—but they're not whining. It's as though the whole tragedy of choosing somebody, risking love, risking emotion, risking sensuality, and then losing it all didn't matter, since it was their choice. Exercising choice in who you love was a major, major thing. And the music reinforced the idea of love as a space where one could negotiate freedom.

Obviously, jazz was considered—as all new music is—to be devil music; too sensual and provocative, and so on. But for some black people jazz meant claiming their own bodies. You can imagine what that must have meant for people whose bodies had been owned, who had been slaves as children, or who remembered their parents' being slaves. Blues and jazz represented ownership of one's own emotions. So of course it is excessive and overdone: tragedy in jazz is relished, almost as though a happy ending would take away some of its glamour, its flair. Now advertisers use jazz on television to communicate authenticity and modernity; to say "Trust me," and to say "hip."

These days the city still retains the quality of excitement it had in the jazz age—only now we associate that excitement with a different kind of danger. We chant and scream and act alarmed about the homeless; we say we want our streets back, but it is from our awareness of homelessness and our employment of strategies to deal with it that we get our sense of the urban. Feeling as though we have the armor, the shields, the moxie, the strength, the toughness and the smarts to be engaged and survive encounters with the unpredictable, the alien, the strange and the violent is an intrinsic part of what it means to live in the city. When people "complain" about homelessness they are actually bragging about it: "New York has more homeless than San Francisco"—"No, no, no, San Francisco has more homeless"—"No, you haven't been to Detroit." We are almost competitive about our endurance, which I think is one of the reasons why we accept homelessness so easily.

INTERVIEWER: So the city freed the ex-slaves from their history?

MORRISON: In part, yes. The city was seductive to them because it promised forgetfulness. It offered the possibility of freedom—freedom, as you put it, from history. But although history should not become a straitjacket, which overwhelms and binds, neither should it be forgotten. One must critique it, test it, confront it and understand it in order to achieve a freedom that is more than license, to achieve true, adult agency. If you penetrate the seduction of the city, then it becomes possible to confront your own history—to forget what ought to be forgotten and use what is useful—such true agency is made possible.

INTERVIEWER: How do visual images influence your work?

MORRISON: I was having some difficulty describing a scene in *Song of Solomon* . . . of a man running away from some obligations and himself. I used an Edvard Munch painting almost literally. He is walking, and there is nobody on his side of the street. Everybody is on the other side.

INTERVIEWER: *Song of Solomon* is such a painted book in comparison with some of your others like *Beloved*, which is sepia-toned.

MORRISON: Part of that has to do with the visual images that I got being aware that in historical terms women, black people in general, were very attracted to very bright-colored clothing. Most people are frightened by color anyway.

INTERVIEWER: Why?

MORRISON: They just are. In this culture quiet colors are considered elegant. Civilized Western people wouldn't buy bloodred sheets or dishes. There may be something more to it than what I am suggesting. But the slave population had no access even to what color there was, because they wore slave clothes, hand-me-downs, work clothes made out of burlap and sacking. For them a colored dress would be luxurious; it wouldn't matter whether it was rich or poor cloth . . . just to have a red or a yellow dress. I stripped *Beloved* of color so that there are only the small moments when Sethe runs amok buying ribbons and bows, enjoying herself the way children enjoy that kind of color. The whole business of color was why slavery was able to last such a long time. It wasn't as though you had a class of convicts who could dress themselves up and pass themselves off. No, these were people marked because of their skin color, as well as other features. So color is a signifying mark. Baby Suggs dreams of color, and says, "Bring me a little lavender. . . ." It is a kind of luxury. We are so inundated with color and visuals. I just wanted to pull it back so that one could feel that hunger and that delight. I couldn't do that if I had made it the painterly book *Song of Solomon* was.

INTERVIEWER: Is that what you are referring to when you speak about needing to find a controlling image?

MORRISON: Sometimes, yes. There are three or four in *Song of Solomon,* I knew that I wanted it to be painterly, and I wanted the opening to be red, white and blue. I also knew that in some sense he would have to "fly." In *Song of Solomon* it was the first time that I had written about a man who was the central, the driving engine of the narrative; I was a little unsure about my ability to feel comfortable inside him. I could always look at him and write from the outside, but those would have been just perceptions. I had to be able not only to look at him but to feel how it really must have felt. So in trying to think about this, the image in my mind was a train. All the previous books have been women-centered, and they have been pretty much in the neighborhood and in the yard; this was going to move out. So, I had this feeling about a train . . . sort of revving up, then moving out as he does, and then it sort of highballs at the end; it speeds up, but it doesn't brake, it just highballs and leaves you sort of suspended. So that image controlled the structure for me, although that is not something I articulate or even make reference to; it only matters that it works for me. Other books look like spirals, like *Sula*.

INTERVIEWER: How would you describe the controlling image of *Jazz*?

MORRISON: *Jazz* was very complicated because I wanted to re-represent two contradictory things—artifice and improvisation, where you have an artwork, planned, thought through, but at the same time appears invented, like jazz. I thought of the image being a book. Physically a book, but at the same time it is writing itself. Imagining itself. Talking. Aware of what it is doing. It watches itself think and imagine. That seemed to me to be a combination of artifice and improvisation—where you practice and plan in order to invent. Also the willingness to fail, to be wrong, because jazz is performance. In a performance you make mistakes, and you don't have the luxury of revision that a writer has; you have to make something out of a mistake, and if you do it well enough it will take you to another place where you never would have gone had you not made that error. So, you have to be able to risk making that error in performance. Dancers do it all the time, as well as jazz musicians. *Jazz* predicts its own story. Sometimes it is wrong because of faulty vision. It simply did not imagine those characters well enough, admits it was wrong, and the characters talk back the way jazz musicians do. It has to listen to the characters it has invented, and then learn something from them. It was the most intricate thing I had done, though I wanted to tell a very simple story about people who do not know that they are living in the jazz age, and to never use the word.

INTERVIEWER: One way to achieve this structurally is to have several voices speaking throughout each book. Why do you do this?

MORRISON: It's important not to have a totalizing view. In American literature we have been so totalized—as though there is only one version. We are not one indistinguishable block of people who always behave the same way.

INTERVIEWER: Is that what you mean by "totalized"?

MORRISON: Yes. A definitive or an authoritarian view from somebody else or someone speaking for us. No singularity and no diversity. I try to give some credibility to all sorts of voices, each of which is profoundly different. Because what strikes me about African-American culture *is* its variety. In so much of contemporary music everybody sounds alike. But when you think about black music, you think about the difference between Duke Ellington and Sidney Bechet or Satchmo or Miles Davis. They don't sound anything alike, but you know that they are all black performers, because of whatever that quality is that makes you realize, "Oh yes, this is part of something called the African-American music tradition." There is no black woman popular singer, jazz singer, blues singer who sounds like any other. Billie Holiday does not sound like Aretha, doesn't sound like Nina, doesn't sound like Sarah, doesn't sound like any of them. They are really powerfully different. And they will tell you that they couldn't possibly have made it as singers if they sounded like somebody else. If someone comes along sounding like Ella Fitzgerald, they will say, "Oh we have one of those . . ." It's interesting to me how those women have this very distinct, unmistakable image. I would like to write like that. I would like to write novels that were unmistakably mine, but nevertheless fit first into African-American traditions and second of all, this whole thing called literature.

INTERVIEWER: First African-American?

MORRISON: Yes.

INTERVIEWER: . . . rather than the whole of literature?

MORRISON: Oh yes.

INTERVIEWER: Why?

MORRISON: It's richer. It has more complex sources. It pulls from something that's closer to the edge, it's much more modern. It has a human future.

INTERVIEWER: Wouldn't you rather be known as a great exponent of literature rather than as an African-American writer?

MORRISON: It's very important to me that my work be African-American; if it assimilates into a different or larger pool, so much the better. But I shouldn't be *asked* to do that. Joyce is not asked to do that. Tolstoy is not. I mean, they can all be Russian, French, Irish or Catholic, they write out of where they come from, and I do too. It just so happens that that space for me is African-American; it could be Catholic, it could be Midwestern. I'm those things too, and they are all important.

INTERVIEWER: Why do you think people ask, "Why don't you write something that we can understand?" Do you threaten them by not writing in the typical Western, linear, chronological way?

MORRISON: I don't think that they mean that. I think they mean, Are you ever going to write a book about white people? For them perhaps that's a kind of a compliment. They're saying, "You write well enough, I would even let you write about me." They couldn't say that to anybody else. I mean, could I have gone up to André Gide and said, "Yes, but when are you going to get serious and start writing about black people?" I don't think he would know how to answer that question. Just as I don't. He would say, "What?" "I will if I want to" or "Who are you?" What is behind that question is, there's the center, which is white, and then there are these regional blacks or Asians, or any sort of marginal people. That question can only be asked from the center. Bill Moyers asked me that when-are-you-going-to-write-about question on television. I just said, "Well, maybe one day . . ." but I couldn't say to him, you know, you can only ask that question from the center. The center of the world! I mean he's a white male. He's asking a marginal person, "When are you going to get to the center? When are you going to write about white people?" I can't say, "Bill, why are you asking me that question?" or "As long as that question seems reasonable is as long as I won't, can't." The point is that he's patronizing; he's saying, "You write well enough. You could come on into the center if you wanted to. You don't have to stay out there on the margins." And I'm saying, "Yeah, well, I'm gonna stay out here on the margin, and let the center look for me."

Maybe it's a false claim, but not fully. I'm sure it was true for the ones we think of as giants now. Joyce is a good example. He moved here and there, but he wrote about Ireland wherever he was, didn't care where he was. I am sure people said to him, "Why . . . ?" Maybe the French asked, "When you gonna write about Paris?"

INTERVIEWER: What do you appreciate most in Joyce?

MORRISON: It is amazing how certain kinds of irony and humor travel. Sometimes Joyce is hilarious. I read *Finnegans Wake* after graduate school, and I had the great good fortune of reading it without any help. I don't know if I read it right, but it was hilarious! I laughed constantly! I didn't know what was going on for whole blocks but it didn't matter because I wasn't going to be graded on it. I think the reason why everyone still has so much fun with Shakespeare is because he didn't have any literary critic. He was just doing it; and there were no reviews except for people throwing stuff on stage. He could just do it.

INTERVIEWER: Do you think if he had been reviewed he would have worked less?

MORRISON: Oh, if he'd cared about it, he'd have been very self-conscious. That's a hard attitude to maintain, to pretend you don't care, pretend you don't read.

INTERVIEWER: Do you read your reviews?

MORRISON: I read everything.

INTERVIEWER: Really? You look deadly serious.

MORRISON: I read everything written about me that I see.

INTERVIEWER: Why is that?

MORRISON: I have to know what's going on!

INTERVIEWER: You want to see how you're coming across?

MORRISON: No, no. It's not about me or my work, it's about what is going on. I have to get a sense, particularly of what's going on with women's work, or African-American work, contemporary work. I teach a literature course. So I read any information that's going to help me teach.

INTERVIEWER: Are you ever really surprised when they compare you to the magic realists, such as Gabriel García Márquez?

MORRISON: Yes, I used to be. It doesn't mean anything to me. Schools are only important to me when I'm teaching literature. It doesn't mean anything to me when I'm sitting here with a big pile of blank yellow paper . . . what do I say? I'm a magic realist? Each subject matter demands its own form, you know.

INTERVIEWER: Why do you teach undergraduates?

MORRISON: Here at Princeton, they really do value undergraduates, which is nice because a lot of universities value only the graduate school or the professional research schools. I like Princeton's notion. I would have loved that for my own children. I don't like freshman and sophomores being treated as the staging ground or the playground or the canvas on which graduate students learn how to teach. They need the best instruction. I've always thought the public schools needed to study the best literature. I always taught *Oedipus Rex* to all kinds of what they used to call remedial or development classes. The reason those kids are in those classes is that they're bored to death; so you can't give them boring things. You have to give them the best there is to engage them.

INTERVIEWER: One of your sons is a musician. Were you ever musical, did you ever play the piano?

MORRISON: No, but I come from a family of highly skilled musicians. Highly skilled, meaning most of them couldn't read music but they could play everything that they heard . . . instantly. They sent us, my sister and me, to music lessons. They were sending me off to learn how to do something that they could do naturally. I thought I was deficient, retarded. They didn't explain that perhaps it's more important that you learn how to *read* music . . . that it's a good thing, not a bad thing. I thought we were sort of lame people going off to learn how to walk, while, you know, they all just stood up and did it naturally.

INTERVIEWER: Do you think there is an education for becoming a writer? Reading perhaps?

MORRISON: That has only limited value.

INTERVIEWER: Travel the world? Take courses in sociology, history?

MORRISON: Or stay home . . . I don't think they have to go anywhere.

INTERVIEWER: Some people say, "Oh I can't write a book until I've lived my life, until I've had experiences."

MORRISON: That may be—maybe they can't. But look at the people who never went anywhere and just thought it up. Thomas Mann. I guess he took a few little trips. . . . I think you either have or you acquire this sort of imagination. Sometimes you do need a stimulus. But I myself don't ever go anywhere for stimulation. I don't want to go anywhere. If I could just sit in one spot I would be happy. I don't trust the ones who say I have to go do something before I can write. You see, I don't write autobiographically. First of all, I'm not interested in real-life people as subjects for fiction—including myself. If I write about somebody who's a historical figure like Margaret Garner, I really don't know anything about her. What I knew came from reading two interviews with her. They said, Isn't this extraordinary. Here's a woman who escaped into Cincinnati from the horrors of slavery and was not crazy. Though she'd killed her child, she was not foaming at the mouth. She was very calm, she said, "I'd do it again." That was more than enough to fire my imagination.

INTERVIEWER: She was sort of a *cause célèbre?*

MORRISON: She was. Her real life was much more awful than it's rendered in the novel, but if I had known all there was to know about her I never would have written it. It would have been finished, there would have been no place in there for me. It would be like a recipe already cooked. There you are. You're already this person. Why should I get to steal from you? I don't like that. What I really love is the process of invention. To have characters move from the curl all the way to a full-fledged person, that's interesting.

INTERVIEWER: Do you ever write out of anger or any other emotion?

MORRISON: No. Anger is a very intense but tiny emotion, you know. It doesn't last. It doesn't produce anything. It's not creative . . . at least not for me. I mean these books take at least three years!

INTERVIEWER: That is a long time to be angry.

MORRISON: Yes. I don't trust that stuff anyway. I don't like those little quick emotions, like, "I'm lonely, *ohhh*, God. . . ." I don't like those emotions as fuel. I mean, I have them, but—

INTERVIEWER: —they're not a good muse?

MORRISON: No, and if it's not your brain thinking cold, cold thoughts, which you can dress in any kind of mood, then it's nothing. It has to be a cold, cold thought. I mean cold, or cool at least. Your brain. That's all there is.

—ELISSA SCHAPPELL
WITH ADDITIONAL MATERIAL
FROM CLAUDIA BRODSKY LACOUR

1993

SUSAN SONTAG

Susan Sontag was born in 1933 in New York City and grew up in Arizona and, later, Southern California. She graduated from high school at fifteen, attended Berkeley for a year, graduated from the University of Chicago (1951) and received two M.A.'s from Harvard, one in English (1954) and one in philosophy (1955). In 1950 she married Philip Rieff, with whom she had a son, the writer David Rieff; the marriage lasted nine years. Since 1957, when she spent a year in France, Sontag has often lived abroad, though New York City has generally served as her base. In the early sixties she taught philosophy and the history of religion at various universities, but since then has eschewed academic life. She has won many awards and fellowships, including the National Book Critics Circle Award for *On Photography* (1977), and a five-year MacArthur Fellowship.

Sontag has published fifteen books, including the novels *The Benefactor* (1963), *Death Kit* (1967) and *The Volcano Lover* (1992), a collection of short stories, *I, etcetera* (1978) and three collections of essays: *Against Interpretation* (1966), *Styles of Radical Will* (1969) and *Under the Sign of Saturn* (1980). *A Susan Sontag Reader* appeared in 1982. *Illness as Metaphor* (1978) and its companion volume, *AIDS and Its Metaphors* (1989), anatomize the putative uses of metaphors for tuberculosis, cancer and AIDS in our culture. Her latest work is a play employing elements from the life of Alice James entitled *Alice in Bed* (1993). Sontag has also written and directed four films—*Duet for Cannibals* (1969), *Brother Carl* (1971), *Promised Lands* (1974) and *Unguided Tour* (1983)—and edited and introduced writings by Antonin Artaud (1976), Roland Barthes (1981) and, most recently, Danilo Kiš (1995), as well as written prefaces to books by Robert Walser (1982), Marina Tsvetayeva (1983), Machado de Assis (1990) and Juan Rulfo (1995), among others.

A manuscript page from an early draft
of Susan Sontag's The Volcano Lover.

SUSAN SONTAG

Susan Sontag lives in a sparsely furnished five-room apartment on the top floor of a building in Chelsea on the west side of Manhattan. Books—as many as fifteen thousand—and papers are everywhere. A lifetime could be spent browsing through the books on art and architecture, theater and dance, philosophy and psychiatry, the history of medicine and the history of religion, photography and opera and so on. The various European literatures—French, German, Italian, Spanish, Russian, etc., as well as hundreds of books of Japanese literature and books on Japan—are arranged by language in a loosely chronological way. So is American literature as well as English literature, which runs from Beowulf to, say, James Fenton. Sontag is an inveterate clipper, and the books are filled with scraps of paper ("Each book is marked and filleted," she says), the bookcases festooned with notes scrawled with the names of additional things to read.

Sontag usually writes by hand on a low marble table in the living room. Small theme notebooks are filled with notes for her novel in progress, In America. An old book on Chopin sits atop a history of table manners. The room is lit by a lovely Fortuny lamp, or a replica of one. Piranesi prints decorate the wall (architectural prints are one of her passions).

Everything in Sontag's apartment testifies to the range of her interests, but *it is the work itself, like her conversation, that demonstrates the passionate nature of her commitments. She is eager to follow a subject wherever it leads, as far as it will go—and beyond. What she has said about Roland Barthes is true about her as well: "It was not a question of knowledge . . . but of alertness, a fastidious transcription of what* could *be thought about something, once it swam into the stream of attention."*

Sontag was interviewed in her Manhattan apartment on three blisteringly hot days in July 1994. She had been traveling back and forth to Sarajevo, and it was gracious of her to set aside time for the interview. Sontag is a prodigious talker—candid, informal, learned, ardent—and each day at a wooden kitchen table held forth for seven- and eight-hour stretches. The kitchen is a mixed-use room, but the fax machine and the photocopier were silent; the telephone seldom rang. The conversation ranged over a vast array of subjects— later the texts would be scoured and revised—but always returned to the pleasures and distinctions of literature. Sontag is interested in all things concerning writing—from the mechanism of the process to the high nature of the calling. She has many missions, but foremost among them is the vocation of the writer.

INTERVIEWER: When did you begin writing?

SONTAG: I'm not sure. But I know I was self-publishing when I was about nine: I started a four-page monthly newspaper, which I hectographed (a very primitive method of duplication) in about twenty copies and sold for five cents to the neighbors. The paper, which I kept going for several years, was filled with imitations of things I was reading. There were stories, poems and two plays that I remember, one inspired by Čapek's *R.U.R.*, the other by Edna St. Vincent Millay's *Aria de Capo*. And accounts of battles—Midway, Stalingrad and so on; remember, this was 1942, 1943, 1944—dutifully condensed from articles in real newspapers.

INTERVIEWER: We've had to postpone this interview several times because of your frequent trips to Sarajevo which, you've told me, have been one of the most compelling experiences of your life. I was thinking how war recurs in your work and life.

SONTAG: It does. I made two trips to North Vietnam under American bombardment, the first of which I recounted in "Trip to Hanoi," and when the Yom Kippur War started in 1973 I went to Israel to shoot a film, *Promised Lands*, on the front lines. Bosnia is actually my third war.

INTERVIEWER: There's the denunciation of military meta phors in *Illness as Metaphor*. And the narrative climax of *The Volcano Lover*, a horrifying evocation of the viciousness of war. And when I asked you to contribute to a book I was editing, *Transforming Vision: Writers on Art*, the work you chose to write about was Goya's *The Disasters of War*.

SONTAG: I suppose it could seem odd to travel to a war, and not just in one's imagination—even if I do come from a family of travelers. My father, who was a fur trader in northern China, died there during the Japanese invasion—I was five. I remember hearing about "world war" in September 1939, entering elementary school, where my best friend in the class was a Spanish Civil War refugee. I remember panicking on December 7, 1941. And one of the first pieces of language I ever pondered over was "for the duration"—as in "there's no butter for the duration." I recall savoring the oddity, and the optimism, of that phrase.

INTERVIEWER: In "Writing Itself," on Roland Barthes, you express surprise that Barthes, whose father was killed in one of the battles of the First World War (Barthes was an infant) and who, as a young man himself, lived through the Second World War—the Occupation—never once mentions the word *war* in any of his writings. But your work seems haunted by war.

SONTAG: I could answer that a writer is someone who pays attention to the world.

INTERVIEWER: You once wrote of *Promised Lands*: "My subject is war, and anything about any war that does not show the appalling concreteness of destruction and death is a dangerous lie."

SONTAG: That prescriptive voice rather makes me cringe. But . . . yes.

INTERVIEWER: Are you writing about the siege of Sarajevo?

SONTAG: No. I mean, not yet, and probably not for a long time. And almost certainly not in the form of an essay or report. David Rieff, who is my son, and who started going to Sarajevo before I did, has published such an essay-report, a book called Slaughterhouse—and one book in the family on the Bosnian genocide is enough. So I'm not spending time in Sarajevo to write about it. For the moment it's enough for me just to be there as much as I can: to witness, to lament, to offer a model of noncomplicity, to pitch in. The duties of a human being, one who believes in right action, not of a writer.

INTERVIEWER: Did you always want to be a writer?

SONTAG: I read the biography of Madame Curie by her daughter, Eve Curie, when I was about six, so at first I thought I was going to be a chemist. Then for a long time, most of my childhood, I wanted to be a physician. But literature swamped me. What I really wanted was every kind of life, and the writer's life seemed the most inclusive.

INTERVIEWER: Did you have any role models as a writer?

SONTAG: Of course I thought I was Jo in Little Women. But I didn't want to write what Jo wrote. Then in Martin Eden I found a writer-protagonist with whose writing I could identify, so then I wanted to be Martin Eden—minus, of course, the dreary fate Jack London gives him. I saw myself as, I guess I was, a heroic autodidact. I looked forward to the struggle of the writing life. I thought of being a writer as a heroic vocation.

INTERVIEWER: Any other models?

SONTAG: Later, when I was thirteen, I read the journals of André Gide, which described a life of great privilege and relentless avidity.

INTERVIEWER: Do you remember when you started reading?

SONTAG: When I was three, I'm told. Anyway, I remember reading real books—biographies, travel books—when I was about six. And then free fall into Poe and Shakespeare and Dickens and the Brontës and Victor Hugo and Schopenhauer and Pater, and so on. I got through my childhood in a delirium of literary exaltations.

INTERVIEWER: You must have been very different from other children.

SONTAG: Was I? I was good at dissembling, too. I didn't think that much about myself, I was so glad to be on to something better. But I so wanted to be elsewhere. And reading produced its blissful, confirming alienations. Because of reading—and music—my daily experience was of living in a world of people who didn't give a hoot about the intensities to which I had pledged myself. I felt as if I were from another planet—a fantasy borrowed from the innocent comic books of that era, to which I was also addicted. And of course I didn't really have much sense of how I was seen by others. Actually, I never thought people were thinking of me at all. I do remember—I was about four—a scene in a park, hearing my Irish nanny saying to another giant in a starched white uniform, "Susan is very high-strung," and thinking, "That's an interesting word. Is it true?"

INTERVIEWER: Tell me something about your education.

SONTAG: All in public schools, quite a number of them, each one more lowering than the one before. But I was lucky to have started school before the era of the child psychologists. Since I could read and write, I was immediately put into the third grade, and later I was skipped another semester, so I was graduated from high school—North Hollywood High School—when I was still fifteen. After that, I had a splendid education at Berkeley, then in the so-called Hutchins College of the University of Chicago, and then as a graduate student in philosophy at Harvard and Oxford. I was a student for most of the 1950s and I never had a teacher from whom I didn't learn. But at Chicago, the most important of my universities, there were not just teachers I admired but three to whose influence I gratefully submitted: Kenneth Burke, Richard McKeon and Leo Strauss.

INTERVIEWER: What was Burke like as a teacher?

SONTAG: Completely inside his own enthralling way of unpacking a text. He spent almost a year with the class reading Conrad's *Victory* word by word, image by image. It was from Burke that I learned how to read. I still read the way he taught me. He took some interest in me. I had already read some of his books before he was my teacher in Humanities III; remember, he wasn't well known then and he'd never met an undergraduate who had read him while still in high school. He gave me a copy of his novel, *Towards a Better Life*, and told me stories about sharing an apartment in Greenwich Village in the 1920s with Hart Crane and Djuna Barnes—you can imagine what that did to me. He was the first person I met who had written books that I owned. (I except an audience I was roped into with Thomas Mann when I was fourteen years old, which I recounted in a story called "Pilgrimage.") Writers were as remote to me as movie stars.

INTERVIEWER: You had your B.A. from the University of Chicago at eighteen. Did you know by then you would become a writer?

SONTAG: Yes, but I still went to graduate school. It never occurred to me that I could support myself as a writer. I was a grateful, militant student. I thought I would be happy teaching, and I was. Of course, I had been careful to prepare myself to teach not literature but philosophy and the history of religion.

INTERVIEWER: But you taught only through your twenties, and have refused countless invitations to return to university teaching. Is this because you came to feel that being an academic and being a creative writer are incompatible?

SONTAG: Yes. Worse than incompatible. I've seen academic life destroy the best writers of my generation.

INTERVIEWER: Do you mind being called an intellectual?

SONTAG: Well, one never likes to be called anything. And the word makes more sense to me as an adjective than as a noun, though, even so, I suppose there will always be a presumption of graceless oddity—especially if one is a woman. Which makes me even more committed to my polemics against the ruling anti-intellectual clichés: heart versus head, feeling versus intellect, and so forth.

INTERVIEWER: Do you think of yourself as a feminist?

SONTAG: That's one of the few labels I'm content with. But even so . . . is it a noun? I doubt it.

INTERVIEWER: What women writers have been important to you?

SONTAG: Many. Sei Shōnagon, Austen, George Eliot, Dickinson, Woolf, Tsvetayeva, Akhmatova, Elizabeth Bishop, Elizabeth Hardwick . . . the list is much longer than that. Because women are, culturally speaking, a minority, with my minority consciousness I always rejoice in the achievement of women. With my writer's consciousness, I rejoice in any writer I can admire, women writers no more or less than men.

INTERVIEWER: Whatever the models of a literary vocation that inspired you as a child, I have the impression that your adult idea of a literary vocation is more European than American.

SONTAG: I'm not so sure. I think it's my own private brand. But what is true is that living in the second half of the twentieth century, I could indulge my Europhile tastes without actually expatriating myself, while still spending a lot of my adult life in Europe. That's been my way of being an American. As Gertrude Stein remarked, "What good are roots if you can't take them with you?" One might say that's very Jewish, but it's also very American.

INTERVIEWER: Your third novel, The Volcano Lover, seems to me a very American book, even though the story it tells takes place in eighteenth-century Europe.

SONTAG: It is. Nobody but an American would have written *The Volcano Lover.*

INTERVIEWER: And *The Volcano Lover*'s subtitle: "A Romance." That's a reference to Hawthorne, right?

SONTAG: Exactly. I was thinking of what Hawthorne says in the preface to *The House of Seven Gables:* "When a writer calls his work a romance, it need hardly be observed that he wishes to claim a certain latitude, both as to its fashion and material, which he would not have felt himself entitled to assume had he been writing a novel." My imagination is very marked by nineteenth-century American literature—first by Poe, whom I read at a precocious age and whose mixture of speculativeness, fantasy and gloominess enthralled me. Poe's stories still inhabit my head. Then by Hawthorne and Melville. I love Melville's obsessiveness. *Clarel, Moby-Dick.* And *Pierre*—another novel about the terrible thwarting of a heroic solitary writer.

INTERVIEWER: Your first book was a novel, *The Benefactor.* Since then you've written essays, travel narratives, stories, plays, as well as two more novels. Have you ever started something in one form and then changed it to another?

SONTAG: No. From the beginning I always know what something is going to be: every impulse to write is born of an idea of form, for me. To begin I have to have the shape, the architecture. I can't say it better than Nabokov did: "The pattern of the thing precedes the thing."

INTERVIEWER: How fluent are you as a writer?

SONTAG: I wrote *The Benefactor* quickly, almost effortlessly, on weekends and during two summers (I was teaching in the Department of Religion at Columbia College); I thought I was telling a pleasurably sinister story that illustrated the fortune of certain heretical religious ideas that go by the name of Gnosticism. The early essays came easily, too. But writing is an activity that in my experience doesn't get easier with practice. On the contrary.

INTERVIEWER: How does something get started for you?

SONTAG: It starts with sentences, with phrases, and then I know something is being transmitted. Often it's an opening line. But sometimes I hear the closing line, instead.

INTERVIEWER: How do you actually write?

SONTAG: I write with a felt-tip pen, or sometimes a pencil, on yellow or white legal pads, that fetish of American writers. I like the slowness of writing by hand. Then I type it up and scrawl all over that. And keep on retyping it, each time making corrections both by hand and directly on the typewriter, until I don't see how to make it any better. Up to five years ago, that was it. Since then there is a computer in my life. After the second or third draft it goes into the computer, so I don't retype the whole manuscript anymore, but continue to revise by hand on a succession of hard-copy drafts from the computer.

INTERVIEWER: Is there anything that helps you get started writing?

SONTAG: Reading—which is rarely related to what I'm writing, or hoping to write. I read a lot of art history, architectural history, musicology, academic books on many subjects. And poetry. Getting started is partly stalling, stalling by way of reading and of listening to music, which energizes me and also makes me restless. Feeling guilty about *not* writing.

INTERVIEWER: Do you write every day?

SONTAG: No. I write in spurts. I write when I have to because the pressure builds up and I feel enough confidence that something has matured in my head and I can write it down. But once something is really under way, I don't want to do anything else. I don't go out, much of the time I forget to eat, I sleep very little. It's a very undisciplined way of working and makes me not very prolific. But I'm too interested in many other things.

INTERVIEWER: Yeats said famously that one must choose between the life and the work. Do you think that is true?

SONTAG: As you know, he actually said that one must choose between perfection of the life and perfection of the work. Well, writing *is* a life—a very peculiar one. Of course, if by life you mean life with other people, Yeats's dictum is true. Writing requires huge amounts of solitude. What I've done to soften the harshness of that choice is that I don't write all the time. I like to go out—which includes traveling; I can't write when I travel. I like to talk. I like to listen. I like to look and to watch. Maybe I have an Attention Surplus Disorder. The easiest thing in the world for me is to pay attention.

INTERVIEWER: Do you revise as you go along or do you wait until you have an entire draft and then revise the whole thing?

SONTAG: I revise as I go along. And that's quite a pleasurable task. I don't get impatient and I'm willing to go over and over something until it works. It's beginnings that are hard. I always begin with a great sense of dread and trepidation. Nietzsche says that the decision to start writing is like leaping into a cold lake. Only when I'm about a third of the way can I tell if it's good enough. Then I have my cards, and I can play my hand.

INTERVIEWER: Is there a difference between writing fiction and writing essays?

SONTAG: Writing essays has always been laborious. They go through many drafts, and the end result may bear little relation to the first draft: often I completely change my mind in the course of writing an essay. Fiction comes much easier, in the sense that the first draft contains the essentials—tone, lexicon, velocity, passions—of what I eventually end up with.

INTERVIEWER: Do you regret anything you've written?

SONTAG: Nothing in its entirety except two theater chronicles I did in the mid-1960s for *Partisan Review,* and unfortunately included in the first collection of essays, *Against Interpretation*—I'm not suited for that kind of pugnacious, impressionistic task. Obviously, I don't agree with everything in the early essays. I've changed, and I know more. And the cultural context which inspired them has altogether changed. But there would be no point in modifying them now. I think I would like to take a blue pencil to the first two novels, though.

INTERVIEWER: *The Benefactor,* which you wrote in your late twenties, is narrated in the voice of a Frenchman in his sixties. Did you find it easy to impersonate someone so different from yourself?

SONTAG: Easier than writing about myself. But writing is impersonation. Even when I write about events in my own life, as I did in "Pilgrimage" and "Project for a Trip to China," it's not really me. But I admit that, with *The Benefactor,* the difference was as broad as I could make it. I wasn't celibate, I wasn't a recluse, I wasn't a man, I wasn't elderly, I wasn't French.

INTERVIEWER: But the novel seems very influenced by French literature.

SONTAG: Is it? It seems many people think that it was influenced by the *nouveau roman.* But I don't agree. There were ironic allusions to two French books, hardly contemporary ones: Descartes's *Meditations* and Voltaire's *Candide.* But those weren't influences. If there was an influence on *The Benefactor,* though one I wasn't at all conscious of at the time, it was Kenneth Burke's *Towards a Better Life.* I reread Burke's novel recently, after many decades (I may never have reread it since he gave me a copy when I was sixteen), and discovered in its programmatic preface what seems like a model for *The Benefactor.* The novel as sequence of arias and fictive moralizing. The coquetry of a protagonist—Burke dared to call his the novel's hero—so ingeniously self-absorbed that no reader could be tempted to identify with him.

INTERVIEWER: Your second novel, *Death Kit,* is quite different from *The Benefactor.*

SONTAG: *Death Kit* invites identification with its miserable protagonist. I was in the lamenting mood—it's written in the shadow of the Vietnam war. It's a book of grief, veils and all.

INTERVIEWER: Hardly a new emotion in your work. Wasn't your first published story entitled "Man with a Pain?"

SONTAG: Juvenilia. You won't find it in *I, etcetera.*

INTERVIEWER: How did you come to write those theater chronicles for *Partisan Review?*

SONTAG: Well, you have to understand that the literary world then was defined by so-called small magazines—hard to imagine because it's so different now. My sense of literary vocation had been shaped by reading literary magazines—*Kenyon Review, Sewanee Review, The Hudson Review, Partisan Review*—at the end of the 1940s, while still in high school in Southern California. By the time I came to New York in 1960, those magazines still existed. But it was already the end of an era. Of course, I couldn't have known that. My highest ambition had been and still was to publish in one of these magazines, where five thousand people would read me. That seemed to me very heaven.

Soon after I moved to New York, I saw William Phillips at a party and got up my nerve to go over and ask him, "How does one get to write for *Partisan Review?*" He answered, "You come down to the magazine and I give you a book to review on spec." I was there the next day. And he gave me a novel. Not one I was interested in, but I wrote something decent, and the review was printed. And so the door was opened. But then there was some inappropriate fantasy, which I tried to squelch, that I was going to be "the new Mary McCarthy"—as Phillips made plain to me by asking me to do a theater chronicle. "You know, Mary used to do it," he said. I told him I didn't want to write theater reviews. He insisted. And so, much against my better judgment (I certainly had no desire to be the new Mary McCarthy, a writer who'd never mattered to me), I did turn out two of them. I reviewed plays by Arthur Miller and James Baldwin and Edward Albee and said they were bad and tried to be witty and hated myself for doing it. After the second round I told Phillips I couldn't go on.

INTERVIEWER: But you did go on and write those famous essays, some of which were published in *Partisan Review.*

SONTAG: Yes, but those subjects were all of my own choosing. I've hardly ever written anything on commission. I am not at all interested in writing about work I don't admire. And even among what I've admired, by and large I've written only about things I felt were neglected or relatively unknown. I am not a critic, which is something else than an essayist; I thought of my essays as cultural work. They were written out of a sense of what *needed* to be written.

I was assuming that a principal task of art was to strengthen the adversarial consciousness. And that led me to reach for relatively eccentric work. I took for granted that the liberal consensus about culture—I was and am a great admirer of Lionel Trilling—would stay in place, that the traditional canon of great books could not be threatened by work that was more transgressive or playful. But taste has become so debauched in the thirty years I've been writing that now simply to defend the idea of seriousness has become an adversarial act. Just to be serious or to care about things in an ardent, disinterested way is becoming incomprehensible to most people. Perhaps only those who were born in the 1930s—and maybe a few stragglers—are going to understand what it means to talk about art as opposed to art projects. Or artists as opposed to celebrities. As you see, I'm chock-full of indignation about the barbarism and relentless vacuity of this culture. How tedious always to be indignant.

INTERVIEWER: Is it old-fashioned to think that the purpose of literature is to educate us about life?

SONTAG: Well, it does educate us about life. I wouldn't be the person I am, I wouldn't understand what I understand, were it not for certain books. I'm thinking of the great question of nineteenth-century Russian literature: how should one live? A novel worth reading is an education of the heart. It enlarges your sense of human possibility, of what human nature is, of what happens in the world. It's a creator of inwardness.

INTERVIEWER: Do writing an essay and writing a piece of fiction come from different parts of yourself?

SONTAG: Yes. The essay is a constrained form. Fiction is freedom. Freedom to tell stories and freedom to be discursive, too. But essayistic discursiveness, in the context of fiction, has an entirely different meaning. It is always voiced.

INTERVIEWER: It seems as if you have pretty much stopped writing essays.

SONTAG: I have. And most of the essays I've succumbed to writing in the past fifteen years are requiems or tributes. The essays on Canetti, Barthes and Benjamin are about elements in their work and sensibility that I feel close to: Canetti's cult of admiration and hatred of cruelty, Barthes's version of the aesthete's sensibility, Benjamin's poetics of melancholy. I was very aware that there's much to be said about them which I didn't say.

INTERVIEWER: Yes, I can see that those essays are disguised self-portraits. But weren't you doing much the same thing in early essays, including some of those in *Against Interpretation*?

SONTAG: I suppose it can't be helped that it all hangs together. Still, something else was going on in the essays that went into the last collection, *Under the Sign of Saturn*. I was having a kind of slow-motion, asymptomatic nervous breakdown writing essays. I was so full of feeling and ideas and fantasies that I was still trying to cram into the essay mode. In other words, I'd come to the end of what the essay form could do for me. Maybe the essays on Benjamin, Canetti and Barthes were self-portraits, but they were also really fictions. My volcano lover, the Cavaliere, is the fully realized fictional form of what I'd been trying to say, in an impacted way, in the essay-portraits of Canetti and Benjamin.

INTERVIEWER: Writing fiction, is your experience one of inventing or figuring out a plot?

SONTAG: Oddly enough, the plot is what seems to come all of a piece—like a gift. It's very mysterious. Something I hear or see or read conjures up a whole story in all its concreteness: scenes, characters, landscapes, catastrophes. With *Death Kit*, it was hearing someone utter the childhood nickname of a mutual friend named Richard—just the hearing of the name: Diddy. With *The Volcano Lover*, it was browsing in a print shop near the British Museum and coming across some images of volcanic landscapes that turned out to be from Sir William Hamilton's *Phlegraei. Campi* For the new novel, it was reading something in Kafka's diaries, a favorite book, so I must have already read this paragraph, which may be an account of a dream, more than once. Reading it this time the story of a whole novel, like a movie I'd seen, leaped into my head.

INTERVIEWER: The whole story?

SONTAG: Yes, the whole story. The plot. But what the story can carry or accumulate—*that* I discover in the writing. If *The Volcano Lover* starts in a flea market and ends with Eleonora's beyond-the-grave monologue, it isn't as if I knew before I started writing all the implications of that journey, which goes from an ironic, down-market vignette of a collector on the prowl to Eleonora's moral wide-shot view of the whole story that the reader has experienced. Ending with Eleonora, and her denunciation of the protagonists, is as far as you can get from the point of view with which the novel starts.

INTERVIEWER: At the beginning of your legendary essay "Notes on Camp," which appeared in 1964, you wrote that your attitude was one of "deep sympathy modified by revulsion." This seems a typical attitude of yours: both yes and no to camp. Both yes and no to photography. Both yes and no to narrative . . .

SONTAG: It isn't that I like it and I don't like it: that's too simple. Or, if you will, it isn't "both yes and no." It's "this but also
that." I'd love to settle in on a strong feeling or reaction. But,
having seen whatever I see, my mind keeps on going and I
see something else. It's that I quickly see the limitations of
whatever I say or whatever judgment I make about anything.
There's a wonderful remark of Henry James: "Nothing is my
last word on anything." There's always more to be said, more to
be felt.

INTERVIEWER: I think most people might imagine that you
bring some theoretical agenda to fiction—if not as a writer of
novels, at least as a reader of them.

SONTAG: But I don't. I need to care about and be touched by
what I read. I can't care about a book that has nothing to contribute to the wisdom project. And I'm a sucker for a fancy
prose style. To put it less giddily, my model for prose is poet's
prose: many of the writers I most admire were poets when
young or could have been poets. Nothing theoretical in all that.
In fact, my taste is irrepressibly catholic. I shouldn't care to be
prevented from doting on Dreiser's *Jennie Gerhardt* and Didion's
Democracy, Glenway Wescott's *The Pilgrim Hawk* and Donald
Barthelme's *The Dead Father.*

INTERVIEWER: You're mentioning a number of contemporaries you admire. Would you also say you've been influenced by
them?

SONTAG: Whenever I avow to being influenced, I'm never
sure I'm telling the truth. But here goes. I think I learned a lot
about punctuation and speed from Donald Barthelme, about
adjectives and sentence rhythms from Elizabeth Hardwick. I
don't know if I learned from Nabokov and Thomas Bernhard,
but their incomparable books help me keep my standards for
myself as severe as they ought to be. And Godard—Godard has
been a major nourishment to my sensibility and therefore, inevitably, to my writing. And I've certainly learned something as

a writer from the way Schnabel plays Beethoven, Glenn Gould plays Bach, and Mitsuko Uchida plays Mozart.

INTERVIEWER: Do you read the reviews of your work?

SONTAG: No. Not even those I'm told are entirely favorable. All reviews upset me. But friends give me a certain thumbs-up, thumbs-down sense of what they are.

INTERVIEWER: After *Death Kit* you didn't write much for a few years.

SONTAG: I'd been very active in the antiwar movement since 1964, when it couldn't yet be called a movement. And that took up more and more time. I got depressed. I waited. I read. I lived in Europe. I fell in love. My admirations evolved. I made some movies. I had a crisis of confidence of how to write because I've always thought that a book should be something necessary, and that each book by me should be better than the one before. Punishing standards, but I'm quite loyal to them.

INTERVIEWER: How did you come to write *On Photography*?

SONTAG: I was having lunch with Barbara Epstein of *The New York Review of Books* in early 1972 and going on about the Diane Arbus show at the Museum of Modern Art, which I'd just seen, and she said, "Why don't you write a piece about the show?" I thought that maybe I could. And then when I began writing it I thought that it should start with a few paragraphs about photography in general and then move to Arbus. And soon there was a lot more than a few paragraphs, and I couldn't extricate myself. The essays multiplied—I felt often like the hapless sorcerer's apprentice—and they got harder and harder to write, I mean, to get right. But I'm stubborn—I was on the third essay before I managed to place some paragraphs about Arbus and the show—and, feeling I'd committed myself, wouldn't give up. It took five years to write the six essays that make up *On Photography*.

INTERVIEWER: But you told me that you wrote your next book, *Illness as Metaphor*, very fast.

SONTAG: Well, it's shorter. One long essay, the nonfiction equivalent of a novella. And being ill—while writing it I was a cancer patient with a gloomy prognosis—was certainly very focusing. It gave me energy to think I was writing a book that would be helpful to other cancer patients and those close to them.

INTERVIEWER: All along you'd been writing stories . . .

SONTAG: Revving up for a novel.

INTERVIEWER: Soon after finishing *The Volcano Lover* you started another novel. Does that mean that you're more drawn to longer, rather than shorter, forms of fiction?

SONTAG: Yes. There are a few of my stories which I like a lot—from *I, etcetera*, "Debriefing" and "Unguided Tour," and "The Way We Live Now," which I wrote in 1987. But I feel more drawn to polyphonic narratives, which need to be long— or longish.

INTERVIEWER: How much time did it take you to write *The Volcano Lover*?

SONTAG: From the first sentence of the first draft to the galleys, two and a half years. For me that's fast.

INTERVIEWER: Where were you?

SONTAG: I started *The Volcano Lover* in September 1989 in Berlin, where I had gone to hang out thinking that I was going to a place that was both very isolated and the Berkeley of Central Europe. Although only two months after I arrived Berlin had started to become a very different place, it still retained its main advantages for me: I wasn't in my apartment in New York, with all my books, and I wasn't in the place that I was writing about either. That sort of double distancing works very well for me.

About half of *The Volcano Lover* was written between late 1989 and the end of 1990 in Berlin. The second half was written in my apartment in New York, except for two chapters that I wrote in a hotel room in Milan (a two-week escapade) and another chapter which I wrote in the Mayflower Hotel in New York. That was the Cavaliere's deathbed interior monologue, which I thought I had to write in one go, in complete isolation, and knew—I don't know how I knew—that I could do in three days. So I left my apartment and checked into the hotel with my typewriter and legal-sized pads and felt-tip pens, and ordered up BLTs until I was done.

INTERVIEWER: Did you write the novel in sequence?

SONTAG: Yes. I write chapter by chapter and I don't go on to the next chapter until the one I'm working on is in final form. That was frustrating at first because from the beginning I knew much of what I wanted the characters to say in the final monologues, but I feared that if I wrote them early on I wouldn't be able to go back to the middle. I was also afraid that maybe by the time I got to it I would have forgotten some of the ideas or no longer be connected to those feelings. The first chapter, which is about fourteen typewritten pages, took me four months to write. The last five chapters, some one hundred typewritten pages, took me two weeks.

INTERVIEWER: How much of the book did you have in mind before you started?

SONTAG: I had the title; I can't write something unless I already know its title. I had the dedication; I knew I would dedicate it to my son. I had the *Così fan tutte* epigraph. And of course I had the story in some sense, and the span of the book. And what was most helpful, I had a very strong idea of a structure. I took it from a piece of music, Hindemith's *The Four Temperaments*—a work I know very well, since it's the music of one of Balanchine's most sublime ballets, which I've seen countless times. The Hindemith starts with a triple prologue, three very short pieces. Then come four movements: melancholic, sanguinic, phlegmatic, choleric. In that order. I knew I was going to have a triple prologue and then four sections or parts corresponding to the four temperaments—though I saw no reason to belabor the idea by actually labeling Parts I to IV "melancholic," "sanguinic," etc. I knew all of that, plus the novel's last sentence: "Damn them all." Of course, I didn't know who was going to utter it. In a sense, the whole work of writing the novel consisted of making something that would justify that sentence.

INTERVIEWER: That sounds like a lot to know before beginning.

SONTAG: Yes, but for all that I knew about it, I still didn't understand all that it could be. I started off thinking that *The Volcano Lover* was the story of the volcano lover, Sir William Hamilton, the man I call the Cavaliere; that the book would stay centered on him. And I was going to develop the character of the self-effacing first Lady Hamilton, Catherine, at the expense of the story of his second wife, which everyone knows. I knew her story and the relation with Nelson had to figure in the novel, but I intended to keep it in the background. The triple prologue and Part I, with its many variations on the theme of melancholy (or depression, as we call it)—the melancholy of the collector, the ecstatic sublimation of that melancholy—all that went as planned. Part I never leaves the Cavaliere. But then, when I started Part II—which was to have variations on the theme of blood, from the sanguinic Emma, this person bursting with energy and vitality, to the literal blood of the Neapolitan revolution—Emma kidnapped the book. And that permitted the novel to open out (the chapters got longer and longer) into a furor of storytelling and of reflections about justice, war and cruelty. That was the end of the main narrative, told in the third person. The rest of the novel was to be in the first person. A very short Part III: the Cavaliere—delirious, "phlegmatic"—enacts, in words, his dying. That went exactly as I'd imagined it, but then I was back in the Cavaliere-centered world of Part I. There were more surprises for me when I came to write the monologues of Part IV, "choleric": women, angry women, speaking from beyond the grave.

INTERVIEWER: Why beyond the grave?

SONTAG: A supplementary fiction, making it more plausible that they are speaking with such insistent, heartfelt, heartbreaking truthfulness. My equivalent of the unmediated, acutely rueful directness of an operatic aria. And how could I resist the challenge of ending each monologue with the character describing her own death?

INTERVIEWER: Were they always going to be all women?

SONTAG: Yes, definitely. I always knew the book would end with women's voices, the voices of some of the women characters in the book, who would finally have their say.

INTERVIEWER: And give the woman's point of view.

SONTAG: Well, you're assuming that there is a woman's, or female, point of view. I don't. Your question reminds me that, whatever their numbers, women are always regarded, are culturally constructed, as a minority. It's to minorities that we impute having a unitary point of view. Lord, what do women want? etc. Had I ended the novel with the voices of four men, no one would suppose I was giving the male point of view; the differences among the four voices would be too striking. These women are as different from each other as any of four men characters in the novel I might have chosen. Each retells the story (or part of it) already known to the reader from her own point of view. Each has a truth to tell.

INTERVIEWER: Do they have anything in common?

SONTAG: Of course. They all know, in different ways, that the world is run by men. So, with respect to the great public events that have touched their lives, they have the insight of the disenfranchised to contribute. But they don't speak only about public events.

INTERVIEWER: Did you know who the women would be?

SONTAG: I knew pretty soon that the first three beyond-the-grave monologues would be by Catherine, Emma's mother and Emma. But I was already in the middle of writing Part II, Chapter 6 and boning up on the Neapolitan Revolution of 1799, before I found the speaker of the fourth and last monologue: Eleonora de Fonseca Pimentel, who makes a brief appearance toward the end of that chapter, the narrative climax of the novel. And, finding her, I finally understood the unwrapped gift of that last line, which I'd heard in my head before I'd even started writing—that hers would be the voice that had the right to utter it. The events, public and private, of her life, as well as her atrocious death, follow the historical record, but her principles—her ethical ardor—are the novelist's invention. While I'd felt sympathy for the characters in *The Benefactor* and *Death Kit,* what I feel for the characters in *The Volcano Lover* is love (I had to borrow a stage villain, Scarpia, to have one character in *The Volcano Lover* I didn't love). But I can live with their becoming small at the end. I mean, it *is* the end of the novel. I was thinking in cinematic terms as I did throughout Part II, Chapter 6. Remember how so many French films of the early 1960s ended with the camera in long shot starting to pull back, and the character moving further and further into the rear of the pictured space, becoming smaller and smaller as the credits start to roll. Seen in the ethical wide shot that Eleonora de Fonseca Pimentel provides, Nelson and the Cavaliere and Emma should be judged as harshly as she judges them. Although they do end badly in one way or another, they are extremely privileged, they're still winners—except for poor Emma, and even she has quite a ride for a while. The last word should be given to someone who speaks for victims.

INTERVIEWER: There are so many voices—stories and substories.

SONTAG: Until the late 1980s most of what I did in fiction was going on inside a single consciousness, whether it was actually in the first person like *The Benefactor* or nominally in the third person like *Death Kit*. Until *The Volcano Lover*, I wasn't able to give myself permission to tell a story, a real story, as opposed to the adventures of somebody's consciousness. The key was this structure that I borrowed from the Hindemith composition. I'd had the idea for a long time that my third novel was going to have the title *The Anatomy of Melancholy*. But I was resisting it—I don't mean fiction, but *that* novel, whose story hadn't yet been given to me. But it's obvious to me now that I didn't really want to write it. I mean a book written under the aegis of that title, which is just another way of saying "under the sign of Saturn." Most of my work had projected only one of the old temperaments: melancholy. I didn't want to write just about melancholy. The musical structure, with its arbitrary order, freed me. Now I could do all four.

With *The Volcano Lover* the door opened and I have a wider entry. That's the great struggle, for more access and more expressiveness, isn't it? You don't—I'm adapting a phrase of Philip Larkin—write the novels you really want to write. But I think I'm coming closer.

INTERVIEWER: It seems as if some of your essayistic impulses are also part of the novel's form.

SONTAG: I suppose it's true that if you strung together all the passages about collecting in *The Volcano Lover* you'd have a discontinuous, aphoristic essay that might well stand on its own. Still, the degree of essayistic speculation in *The Volcano Lover* seems restrained if compared with a central tradition of the European novel. Think of Balzac and Tolstoy and Proust, who go on for pages and pages that could really be excerpted as essays. Or *The Magic Mountain*, perhaps the thinkiest great novel of all. But speculation, rumination, direct address to the reader are entirely indigenous to the novel form. The novel is a big boat. It's not so much that I was able to salvage the banished essayist in myself. It's that the essayist in me was only part of the novelist I've finally given myself permission to be.

INTERVIEWER: Did you have to do a lot of research?

SONTAG: You mean reading? Yes, some. The me who is a self-defrocked academic found that part of writing a novel set in the past very pleasurable.

INTERVIEWER: Why set a novel in the past?

SONTAG: To escape the inhibitions connected with my sense of the contemporary, my sense of how degraded and debased the way we live and feel and think is now. The past is bigger than the present. Of course, the present is always there, too. The narrating voice of *The Volcano Lover* is very much of the late twentieth century, driven by late-twentieth-century concerns. It was never my idea to write a "you are there" historical novel, even while it was a matter of honor to make the historical substance of the novel as dense and accurate as I could. It felt even more spacious that way. But having decided to give myself one more romp in the past—with *In America*, the novel I'm writing now—I'm not sure it will work out the same way this time.

INTERVIEWER: When is it set?

SONTAG: From the mid-1870s almost to the end of the nineteenth century. And, like *The Volcano Lover*, it's based on a real story, that of a celebrated Polish actress and her entourage who left Poland and went to Southern California to create a utopian community. The attitudes of my principal characters are wonderfully exotic to me—Victorian, if you will. But the America they arrive in is not so exotic, though I'd thought that to set a book in late-nineteenth century America would feel almost as remote as late-eighteenth-century Naples and London. It's not. There is an astonishing continuity of cultural attitudes in our country. I never cease to be surprised that the America Tocqueville observed in the early 1830s is, in most respects, recognizably the America of the end of the twentieth century—even though the demographic and ethnographic composition of the country has totally changed. It's as if you had changed both the blade and handle of a knife and it is still the same knife.

INTERVIEWER: Your play, *Alice in Bed*, is also about a late-nineteenth-century sensibility.

SONTAG: Yes—Alice James plus the nineteenth century's most famous Alice, Lewis Carroll's. I was directing a production of Pirandello's *As You Desire Me* in Italy, and one day Adriana Asti, who played the lead, said to me—dare I say it?—playfully: "Please write a play for me. And remember, I have to be onstage all the time." And then Alice James, thwarted writer and professional invalid, fell into my head, and I made up the play on the spot and told it to Adriana. But I didn't write it for another ten years.

INTERVIEWER: Are you going to write more plays? You've always been very involved with theater.

SONTAG: Yes. I hear voices. That's why I like to write plays. And I've lived in the world of theater artists for much of my life. When I was very young, acting was the only way I knew how to insert myself into what happens on a stage: starting at ten, I was taken on for some kiddie roles in Broadway plays put on by a community theater (this was in Tucson); I was active in student theater—Sophocles, Shakespeare—at the University of Chicago; and in my early twenties did a bit of summer stock. Then I stopped. I'd much rather direct plays (though not my own). And make films (I hope to make better ones than the four I wrote and directed in Sweden, Israel and Italy in the 1970s and early 1980s). And direct operas, which I haven't done yet. I'm very drawn to opera—the art form that most regularly and predictably produces ecstasy (at least in this opera lover). Opera is one of the inspirations of *The Volcano Lover*: stories from operas and operatic emotions.

INTERVIEWER: Does literature produce ecstasy?

SONTAG: Sure, but less reliably than music and dance: literature has more on its mind. One must be strict with books. I want to read only what I'll want to reread—the definition of a book worth reading once.

INTERVIEWER: Do you ever go back and reread your work?

SONTAG: Except to check translations, no. Definitely no. I'm not curious. I'm not attached to the work I've already done. Also, perhaps I don't want to see how it's all the same. Maybe I'm always reluctant to reread anything I wrote more than ten years ago because it would destroy my illusion of endless new beginnings. That's the most American part of me: I feel that it's always a new start.

INTERVIEWER: But your work is so diverse.

SONTAG: Well it's supposed to be diverse, though of course there is a unity of temperament, of preoccupation—certain predicaments, certain emotions that recur: ardor and melancholy. And an obsessive concern with human cruelty, whether cruelty in personal relations or the cruelty of war.

INTERVIEWER: Do you think your best work is still to come?

SONTAG: I hope so. Or . . . yes.

INTERVIEWER: Do you think much about the audience for your books?

SONTAG: Don't dare. Don't want to. But, anyway, I don't write because there's an audience. I write because there is literature.

—EDWARD HIRSCH

JOAN DIDION

Novelist, essayist and screenwriter Joan Didion was born in 1936 in Sacramento, California. In 1956, when she was a senior at the University of California at Berkeley, her essay on the architect William Wilson Wurster won *Vogue* magazine's Prix de Paris, as a consequence of which she accepted a position on the magazine's editorial staff and moved to New York. She contributed to *Vogue*, *Mademoiselle* and *The National Review* in her early professional years and went on to be a columnist for *The Saturday Evening Post*, *Esquire* and *Life*. Though now best known as a journalist and regular contributor to *The New Yorker* and *The New York Review of Books*, Didion's reputation as a writer was established with the 1964 publication of her first novel, *Run River*.

From the outset of her career she has consistently alternated between the forms of fiction and nonfiction, and has also collaborated on numerous screenplays with her husband, John Gregory Dunne, whom she married in 1964. Didion's seminal second book, *Slouching Towards Bethlehem* (1968), collects her essays on California in the sixties, most of which were originally published in *The Saturday Evening Post*. Her next two works were novels: *Play It As It Lays* (1970) and *A Book of Common Prayer*

(1977). Another collection of essays, *The White Album* (1979), and a work of nonfiction, *Salvador* (1982), preceded her fourth novel, *Democracy* (1984). Didion's most recent books are the nonfiction work *Miami* (1987), *After Henry* (1992), an essay collection, and *The Last Thing He Wanted* (1996), her fifth novel. Even as her writing has fluctuated between fiction and nonfiction, Didion's life has alternated between the coasts. "Goodbye to All That" (in *Slouching Towards Bethlehem*) is Didion's coming to terms with leaving New York for California after a short visit east extended itself into an eight-year sojourn. At present she and Dunne once again live on the Upper East Side of New York City. Didion is a member of the American Institute of Arts and Letters and the American Academy of Arts and Sciences.

JOAN DIDION

It is usual for the interviewer to write this paragraph about the circumstances in which the interview was conducted, but the interviewer in this case, Linda Kuehl, died not long after the tapes were transcribed. Linda and I talked on August 18 and August 24, 1977, from about ten in the morning until early afternoon. Both interviews took place in the living room of my husband's and my house on the ocean north of Los Angeles, a house we no longer own. The walls in that room were white. The floors were of terracotta tile, very highly polished. The glare off the sea was so pronounced in that room that corners of it seemed, by contrast, extremely dark, and everyone who sat in the room tended to gravitate toward these dark corners. Over the years the room had in fact evolved to the point where the only comfortable chairs were in the dark, away from the windows. I mention this because I remember my fears about being interviewed, one of which was that I would be construed as the kind of loon who had maybe 300 degrees of sea view and kept all the chairs in a kind of sooty nook behind the fireplace. Linda's intelligence dispelled these fears immediately. Her interest in and acuity about the technical act of writing made me relaxed and even enthusiastic about talking, which I rarely am. As a matter of fact, this enthusiasm for talking technically makes me seem to myself, as I read over the transcript, a kind of ap-

"I can't seem to tell what you do get the real points for,"
Charlotte said. "I mean I seem to miss getting them."

"So what.

"So what. So I guess I'll stick around here a while."

And when his plane was cleared to leave she had walked out
to the gate with him and he had said again don't you want to see
Marin and she had said I don't have to see Marin because I have
Marin in my mind and Marin has me in her mind and they closed the
gate and that was the last time Leonard Douglas ever saw Charlotte alive.
The last time I ever saw Charlotte was the night two weeks later
when she pinned the gardenia on my dress and dabbed the Gres perfume
on my wrists like a child helping her mother dress for a party.

VICKY: — SPACE BREAK —

¶ The last time I ever saw Charlotte alive
was the night two weeks later when I left
for New Orleans.

¶ When she pinned her gardenia on my
dress.

¶ When she dabbed her Gres perfume on
my wrists.

¶ Like a child helping her mother dress
for a party.

A manuscript page from Joan Didion's novel
A Book of Common Prayer.

prentice plumber of fiction, a Cluny Brown at the writer's trade, but there we were.

J.D.

INTERVIEWER: You have said that writing is a hostile act; I have always wanted to ask you why.

DIDION: It's hostile in that you're trying to make somebody see something the way you see it, trying to impose your idea, your picture. It's hostile to try to wrench around someone else's mind that way. Quite often you want to tell somebody your dream, your nightmare. Well, nobody wants to hear about someone else's dream, good or bad; nobody wants to walk around with it. The writer is always tricking the reader into listening to the dream.

INTERVIEWER: Are you conscious of the reader as you write? Do you write listening to the reader listening to you?

DIDION: Obviously I listen to a reader, but the only reader I hear is me. I am always writing to myself. So very possibly I'm committing an aggressive and hostile act toward myself.

INTERVIEWER: So when you ask, as you do in many nonfiction pieces, "Do you get the point?" you are really asking if you *yourself* get the point.

DIDION: Yes. Once in a while, when I first started to write pieces, I would try to write to a reader other than myself. I always failed. I would freeze up.

INTERVIEWER: When did you know you wanted to write?

DIDION: I wrote stories from the time I was a little girl, but I didn't want to be a writer. I wanted to be an actress. I didn't realize then that it's the same impulse. It's make-believe. It's performance. The only difference being that a writer can do it all alone. I was struck a few years ago when a friend of ours—an actress—was having dinner here with us and a couple of other writers. It suddenly occurred to me that she was the only person in the room who couldn't plan what she was going to do. She had to wait for someone to ask her, which is a strange way to live.

INTERVIEWER: Did you ever have a writing teacher?

DIDION: Mark Schorer was teaching at Berkeley when I was an undergraduate there, and he helped me. I don't mean he helped me with sentences, or paragraphs—nobody has time for that with student papers; I mean that he gave me a sense of what writing was about, what it was for.

INTERVIEWER: Did any writer influence you more than others?

DIDION: I always say Hemingway, because he taught me how sentences worked. When I was fifteen or sixteen I would type out his stories to learn how the sentences worked. I taught myself to type at the same time. A few years ago when I was teaching a course at Berkeley I reread *A Farewell to Arms* and fell right back into those sentences. I mean they're perfect sentences. Very direct sentences, smooth rivers, clear water over granite, no sinkholes.

INTERVIEWER: You've called Henry James an influence.

DIDION: He wrote perfect sentences too, but very indirect, very complicated. Sentences *with* sinkholes. You could drown in them. I wouldn't dare to write one. I'm not even sure I'd dare to read James again. I loved those novels so much that I was paralyzed by them for a long time. All those possibilities. All that perfectly reconciled style. It made me afraid to put words down.

INTERVIEWER: I wonder if some of your nonfiction pieces aren't shaped as a single Jamesian sentence.

DIDION: That would be the ideal, wouldn't it. An entire piece—eight, ten, twenty pages—strung on a single sentence. Actually, the sentences in my nonfiction are far more complicated than the sentences in my fiction. More clauses. More semicolons. I don't seem to hear that many clauses when I'm writing a novel.

INTERVIEWER: You have said that once you have your first sentence you've got your piece. That's what Hemingway said. All he needed was his first sentence and he had his short story.

DIDION: What's so hard about that first sentence is that you're stuck with it. Everything else is going to flow out of that sentence. And by the time you've laid down the first *two* sentences, your options are all gone.

INTERVIEWER: The first is the gesture, the second is the commitment.

DIDION: Yes, and the last sentence in a piece is another adventure. It should open the piece up. It should make you go back and start reading from page one. That's how it *should* be, but it doesn't always work. I think of writing anything at all as a kind of high-wire act. The minute you start putting words on paper you're eliminating possibilities. Unless you're Henry James.

INTERVIEWER: I wonder if your ethic—what you call your "harsh Protestant ethic"—doesn't close things up for you, doesn't hinder your struggle to keep all the possibilities open.

DIDION: I suppose that's part of the dynamic. I start a book and I want to make it perfect, want it to turn every color, want it to *be the world.* Ten pages in, I've already blown it, limited it, made it less, marred it. That's very discouraging. I hate the book at that point. After a while I arrive at an accommodation: well, it's not the ideal, it's not the perfect object I wanted to make, but maybe—if I go ahead and finish it anyway—I can get it right next time. Maybe I can have another chance.

INTERVIEWER: Have any women writers been strong influences?

DIDION: I think only in the sense of being models for a life, not for a style. I think that the Brontës probably encouraged my own delusions of theatricality. Something about George Eliot attracted me a great deal. I think I was not temperamentally attuned to either Jane Austen or Virginia Woolf.

INTERVIEWER: What are the disadvantages, if any, of being a woman writer?

DIDION: When I was starting to write—in the late fifties, early sixties—there was a kind of social tradition in which male novelists could operate. Hard drinkers, bad livers. Wives, wars, big fish, Africa, Paris, no second acts. A man who wrote novels had a role in the world, and he could play that role and do whatever he wanted behind it. A woman who wrote novels had no particular role. Women who wrote novels were quite often perceived as invalids. Carson McCullers, Jane Bowles. Flannery O'Connor, of course. Novels by women tended to be described, even by their publishers, as sensitive. I'm not sure this is so true anymore, but it certainly was at the time, and I didn't much like it. I dealt with it the same way I deal with everything. I just tended my own garden, didn't pay much attention, behaved—I suppose—deviously. I mean I didn't actually let too many people know what I was doing.

INTERVIEWER: Advantages?

DIDION: The advantages would probably be precisely the same as the disadvantages. A certain amount of resistance is good for anybody. It keeps you awake.

INTERVIEWER: Can you tell simply from the style of writing, or the sensibility, if the author is a woman?

DIDION: Well, if style is character—and I believe it is—then obviously your sexual identity is going to show up in your style. I don't want to differentiate between style and sensibility, by the way. Again, your style *is* your sensibility. But this whole question of sexual identity is very tricky. If I were to read, cold, something by Anaïs Nin, I would probably say that it was written by a man trying to write as a woman. I feel the same way about Colette, and yet both those women are generally regarded as intensely "feminine" writers. I don't seem to recognize "feminine." On the other hand, *Victory* seems to me a profoundly female novel. So does *Nostromo,* so does *The Secret Agent.*

INTERVIEWER: Do you find it easy to write in depth about the opposite sex?

DIDION: *Run River* was partly from a man's point of view. Everett McClellan. I don't remember those parts as being any harder than the other parts. A lot of people thought Everett was "shadowy," though. He's the most distinct person in the book to me. I loved him. I loved Lily and Martha but I loved Everett more.

INTERVIEWER: Was *Run River* your first novel? It seems so finished for a first that I thought you might have shelved earlier ones.

DIDION: I've put away nonfiction things, but I've never put away a novel. I might throw out forty pages and write forty new ones, but it's all part of the same novel. I wrote the first half of *Run River* at night over a period of years. I was working at *Vogue* during the day, and at night I would work on these scenes for a novel. In no particular sequence. When I finished a scene I would tape the pages together and pin the long strips of pages on the wall of my apartment. Maybe I wouldn't touch it for a month or two, then I'd pick a scene off the wall and rewrite it. When I had about a hundred and fifty pages done I showed them to twelve publishers, all of whom passed. The thirteenth, Ivan Obolensky, gave me an advance, and with that thousand dollars or whatever it was I took a two-month leave of absence and wrote the last half of the book. That's why the last half is better than the first half. I kept trying to run the first half through again, but it was intractable. It was set. I'd worked on it for too many years in too many moods. Not that the last half is perfect. It's smoother, it moves faster, but there are a great many unresolved problems. I didn't know how to do anything at all. I had wanted *Run River* to be very complicated chronologically, to somehow have the past and present operating simultaneously, but I wasn't accomplished enough to do that with any clarity. Everybody who read it said it wasn't working.

So I straightened it out. Present time to flashback to present time. Very straight. I had no option, because I didn't know how to do it the other way. I just wasn't good enough.

INTERVIEWER: Did you or Jonathan Cape put the comma in the title of the English edition?

DIDION: It comes back to me that Cape put the comma in and Obolensky left the comma out, but it wasn't of very much interest to me because I hated it both ways. The working title was *In the Night Season,* which Obolensky didn't like. Actually, the working title during the first half was *Harvest Home,* which everybody dismissed out of hand as uncommercial, although later there was a big commercial book by Thomas Tyron called exactly that. Again, I was not very sure of myself then, or I never would have changed the title.

INTERVIEWER: Was the book autobiographical? I ask this for the obvious reason that first novels often are.

DIDION: It wasn't except that it took place in Sacramento. A lot of people there seemed to think that I had somehow maligned them and their families, but it was just a made-up story. The central incident came from a little one-inch story in *The New York Times* about a trial in the Carolinas. Someone was on trial for killing the foreman on his farm, that's all there was. I think I really put the novel in Sacramento because I was homesick. I wanted to remember the weather and the rivers.

INTERVIEWER: The heat on the rivers?

DIDION: The heat. I think that's the way the whole thing began. There's a lot of landscape which I never would have described if I hadn't been homesick. If I hadn't wanted to remember. The impulse was nostalgia. It's not an uncommon impulse among writers. I noticed it when I was reading *From Here to Eternity* in Honolulu just after James Jones died. I could see exactly that kind of nostalgia, that yearning for a place, overriding all narrative considerations. The incredible amount of description. When Prewitt tries to get from the part of town where he's been wounded out to Alma's house, every street is named. Every street is described. You could take that passage and draw a map of Honolulu. None of those descriptions have any narrative meaning. They're just remembering. Obsessive remembering. I could see the impulse.

INTERVIEWER: But doesn't the impulse of nostalgia produce the eloquence in *Run River*?

DIDION: It's got a lot of sloppy stuff. Extraneous stuff. Words that don't work. Awkwardness. Scenes that should have been brought up, scenes that should have been played down. But then *Play It As It Lays* has a lot of sloppy stuff. I haven't reread *Common Prayer*, but I'm sure that does too.

INTERVIEWER: How did you come to terms with point of view in *Play It As It Lays*? Did you ever question your authority to do it in both first and third person?

DIDION: I wanted to make it all first person, but I wasn't good enough to maintain at first. There were tricks I didn't know. So I began playing with a close third person, just to get something down. By a "close third" I mean not an omniscient third but a third very close to the mind of the character. Suddenly one night I realized that I had some first person and some third person and that I was going to have to go with both, or just not write a book at all. I was scared. Actually, I don't mind the way it worked out. The juxtaposition of first and third turned out to be very useful toward the ending, when I wanted to accelerate the whole thing. I don't think I'd do it again, but it was a solution to that particular set of problems. There's a point when you go with what you've got. Or you don't go.

INTERVIEWER: How long, in all, did *Play It As It Lays* take to write?

DIDION: I made notes and wrote pages over several years, but the actual physical writing—sitting down at the typewriter and working every day until it was finished—took me from January until November 1969. Then of course I had to run it through again—I never know quite what I'm doing when I'm writing a novel, and the actual line of it doesn't emerge until I'm finishing. Before I ran it through again I showed it to John and then I sent it to Henry Robbins, who was my editor then at Farrar, Straus. It was quite rough, with places marked "chapter to come." Henry was unalarmed by my working that way, and he and John and I sat down one night in New York and talked, for about an hour before dinner, about what it needed doing. We all knew what it needed. We all agreed. After that I took a couple of weeks and ran it through. It was just typing and pulling the line through.

INTERVIEWER: What do you mean exactly by "pulling through"?

DIDION: For example, I didn't know that BZ was an important character in *Play It As It Lays* until the last few weeks I was working on it. So those places I marked "chapter to come" were largely places where I was going to go back and pull BZ through, hit him harder, prepare for the way it finally went.

INTERVIEWER: How did you feel about BZ's suicide at the end?

DIDION: I didn't realize until after I'd written it that it was essentially the same ending as *Run River.* The women let the men commit suicide.

INTERVIEWER: I read that *Play It As It Lays* crystallized for you when you were sitting in the lobby of the Riviera Hotel in Las Vegas and saw a girl walk through.

DIDION: I had thought Maria lived in New York. Maybe she was a model. Anyway, she was getting a divorce, going through grief. When I saw this actress in the Riviera Hotel, it occurred to me that Maria could be an actress. In California.

INTERVIEWER: Was she always Maria Wyeth?

DIDION: She didn't even have a name. Sometimes I'll be fifty, sixty pages into something and I'll still be calling a character "X." I don't have a very clear idea of who the characters are until they start talking. Then I start to love them. By the time I finish the book, I love them so much that I want to stay with them. I don't want to leave them ever.

INTERVIEWER: Do your characters talk to you?

DIDION: After a while. In a way. When I started *Common Prayer*, all I knew about Charlotte was that she was a nervous talker and told pointless stories. A distracted kind of voice. Then one day I was writing the Christmas party at the American embassy, and I had Charlotte telling these bizarre anecdotes with no point while Victor Strasser-Mendana keeps trying to find out who she is, what she's doing in Boca Grande, who her husband is, what her husband does. And suddenly Charlotte says, "He runs guns. I wish they had caviar." Well, when I heard Charlotte say this, I had a very clear fix on who she was. I went back and rewrote some early stuff.

INTERVIEWER: Did you reshuffle a lot and, if so, how? Did you use pins or tape or what?

DIDION: Toward the beginning of a novel I'll write a lot of sections that lead me nowhere. So I'll abandon them, pin them on a board with the idea of picking them up later. Quite early in *Common Prayer* I wrote a part about Charlotte Douglas going to airports, a couple of pages that I liked but couldn't seem to find a place for. I kept picking this part up and putting it in different places, but it kept stopping the narrative; it was wrong everywhere, but I was determined to use it. Finally I think I put it in the middle of the book. Sometimes you can get away with things in the middle of a book. The first hundred pages are very tricky, the first forty pages especially. You have to make sure you have the characters you want. That's really the most complicated part.

INTERVIEWER: Strategy would seem to be far more complicated in *Common Prayer* than in *Play It As It Lays* because it had so much more plot.

DIDION: *Common Prayer* had a lot of plot and an awful lot of places and weather. I wanted a dense texture, and so I kept throwing stuff into it, making promises. For example, I promised a revolution. Finally, when I got within twenty pages of the end, I realized I still hadn't delivered this revolution. I had a lot of threads, and I'd overlooked this one. So then I had to go back and lay in the preparation for the revolution. Putting in that revolution was like setting in a sleeve. Do you know what I mean? Do you sew? I mean I had to work that revolution in on the bias, had to ease out the wrinkles with my fingers.

INTERVIEWER: So the process of writing the novel is for you the process of discovering the precise novel that you want to write.

DIDION: Exactly. At the beginning I don't have anything at all, don't have any people, any weather, any story. All I have is a technical sense of what I want to do. For example, I want sometime to write a very long novel, eight hundred pages. I want to write an eight-hundred-page novel precisely *because* I think a novel should be read at one sitting. If you read a novel over a period of days or weeks the threads get lost, the suspension breaks. So the problem is to write an eight-hundred-page novel in which all the filaments are so strong that nothing breaks or gets forgotten ever. I wonder if García Márquez didn't do that in *The Autumn of the Patriarch.* I don't want to read it because I'm afraid he might have done it, but I did look at it, and it seems to be written in a single paragraph. *One paragraph.* The whole novel. I love that idea.

INTERVIEWER: Do you have any writing rituals?

DIDION: The most important is that I need an hour alone before dinner, with a drink, to go over what I've done that day. I can't do it late in the afternoon because I'm too close to it. Also, the drink helps. It removes me from the pages. So I spend this hour taking things out and putting other things in. Then I start the next day by redoing all of what I did the day before, following these evening notes. When I'm really working I don't like to go out or have anybody to dinner, because then I lose the hour. If I don't have the hour, and start the next day with just some bad pages and nowhere to go, I'm in low spirits. Another thing I need to do, when I'm near the end of the book, is sleep in the same room with it. That's one reason I go home to Sacramento to finish things. Somehow the book doesn't leave you when you're asleep right next to it. In Sacramento nobody cares if I appear or not. I can just get up and start typing.

INTERVIEWER: What's the main difference between the process of fiction and the process of nonfiction?

DIDION: The element of discovery takes place, in nonfiction, not during the writing but during the research. This makes writing a piece very tedious. You already know what it's about.

INTERVIEWER: Are the subject of pieces determined by editors or are you free to go your own way?

DIDION: I make them up. They reflect what I want to do at the time, where I want to be. When I worked for *Life* I did a great many Honolulu pieces—probably more than *Life* might have wanted—because that's where I wanted to be then. Last night I finished a piece for *Esquire* about the California Water Project. I had always wanted to see the room where they control the water, where they turn it on and off all over the state, and I also wanted to see my mother and father. The water and my mother and father were all in Sacramento, so I went to Sacramento. I like to do pieces because it forces me to make appointments and see people, but I never wanted to be a journalist or reporter. If I were doing a story and it turned into a big breaking story, all kinds of teams flying in from papers and magazines and the networks, I'd probably think of something else to do.

INTERVIEWER: You've said that when you were an editor at *Vogue*, Allene Talmey showed you how verbs worked.

DIDION: Every day I would go into her office with eight lines of copy or a caption or something. She would sit there and mark it up with a pencil and get very angry about extra words, about verbs not working. Nobody has time to do that except on a magazine like *Vogue*. Nobody, no teacher. I've taught and I've tried to do it, but I didn't have that much time and neither did the students. In an eight-line caption everything had to work, every word, every comma. It would end up being a *Vogue* caption, but on its own terms it had to work perfectly.

INTERVIEWER: You say you treasure privacy, that "being left alone and leaving others alone is regarded by members of my family as the highest form of human endeavor." How does this mesh with writing personal essays, particularly the first column you did for *Life* where you felt it imperative to inform the reader that you were at the Royal Hawaiian Hotel in lieu of getting a divorce?

DIDION: I don't know. I could say that I was writing to myself, and of course I was, but it's a little more complicated than that. I mean the fact that eleven million people were going to see that page didn't exactly escape my attention. There's a lot of mystery to me about writing and performing and showing off in general. I know a singer who throws up every time she has to go onstage. But she still goes on.

INTERVIEWER: How did the "fragility of Joan Didion" myth start?

DIDION: Because I'm small, I suppose, and because I don't talk a great deal to people I don't know. Most of my sentences drift off, don't end. It's a habit I've fallen into. I don't deal well with people. I would think that this appearance of not being very much in touch was probably one of the reasons I started writing.

INTERVIEWER: Do you think some reviewers and readers have mistaken you for your characters?

DIDION: There was a certain tendency to read *Play It As It Lays* as an autobiographical novel, I suppose because I lived out here and looked skinny in photographs and nobody knew anything else about me. Actually, the only thing Maria and I have in common is an occasional inflection, which I picked up from her—not vice versa—when I was writing the book. I like Maria a lot. Maria was very strong, very tough.

INTERVIEWER: That's where I have difficulty with what so many critics have said about your women. Your women hardly seem fragile to me.

DIDION: Did you read Diane Johnson's review of *Common Prayer* in *The New York Review of Books*? She suggested that the women were strong to the point of being figures in a romance, that they were romantic heroines rather than actual women in actual situations. I think that's probably true. I think I write romances.

INTERVIEWER: I'd like to ask you about things that recur in your work. There's the line about "dirty tulips" on Park Avenue in a short story and in a piece. Or how about the large, square emerald ring that Lily wears in *Run River* and Charlotte wears in *Common Prayer*?

DIDION: Does Lily wear one too? Maybe she does. I've always wanted one, but I'd never buy one. For one thing emeralds—when you look at them closely—are always disappointing. The green is never blue enough. Ideally, if the green were blue enough you could look into an emerald for the rest of your life. Sometimes I think about Katherine Anne Porter's emeralds, sometimes I wonder if they're blue enough. I hadn't planned that emerald in *Common Prayer* to recur the way it does. It was just something I thought Charlotte might have, but as I went along the emerald got very useful. I kept taking that emerald one step further. By the end of the novel the emerald is almost the narrative. I had a good time with that emerald.

INTERVIEWER: What about the death of a parent, which seems to recur as a motif?

DIDION: You know how doctors who work with children get

the children to tell stories? And they figure out from the stories what's frightening the child, what's worrying the child, what the child thinks? Well, a novel is just a story. You work things out in the stories you tell.

INTERVIEWER: And the abortion or loss of a child?

DIDION: The death of children worries me all the time. It's on my mind. Even *I* know that, and I usually don't know what's on my mind. On the whole, I don't want to think too much about why I write what I write. If I know what I'm doing I don't do it, I can't do it. The abortion in *Play It As It Lays* didn't occur to me until I'd written quite a bit of the book. The book needed an active moment, a moment at which things changed for Maria, a moment in which—this was very, very important—Maria was center stage for a number of pages. Not at a party reacting to somebody else. Not just thinking about her lot in life, either. A long section in which she was the main player. The abortion was a narrative strategy.

INTERVIEWER: Was it a narrative strategy in *Run River*?

DIDION: Actually, it was the excuse for a digression, into landscape. Lily has an abortion in San Francisco and then she comes home on the Greyhound bus. I always think of the Greyhound bus and not the abortion. The bus part is very detailed about the look of the towns. It's something I wrote in New York; you can tell I was homesick.

INTERVIEWER: How about the freeways that reappear?

DIDION: Actually, I don't drive on the freeway. I'm afraid to. I freeze at the top of the entrance, at the instant when you have to let go and join it. Occasionally I *do* get on the freeway—usually because I'm shamed into it—and it's such an extraordinary experience that it sticks in my mind. So I use it.

INTERVIEWER: And the white space at the corner of Sunset and La Brea in Hollywood? You mention it in some piece and then in *Play It As It Lays.*

DIDION: I've never analyzed it, but one line of poetry I always have in mind is the line from *Four Quartets:* "at the still point of the turning world." I tend to move toward still points. I think of the equator as a still point. I suppose that's why I put Boca Grande on the equator.

INTERVIEWER: A narrative strategy.

DIDION: Well, this whole question of how you work out the narrative is very mysterious. It's a good deal more arbitrary than most people who don't do it would ever believe. When I started *Play It As It Lays* I gave Maria a child, a daughter, Kate, who was in kindergarten. I remember writing a passage in which Kate came home from school and showed Maria a lot of drawings, orange and blue crayon drawings, and when Maria asked her what they were, Kate said, "Pools on fire." You can see I wasn't having too much success writing this child. So I put her in a hospital. You never meet her. Now, it turned out to have a great deal of importance—Kate's being in the hospital is a very large element in *Play It As It Lays*—but it began because I couldn't write a child, no other reason. Again, in *Common Prayer,* Marin bombs the Transamerica Building because I *needed* her to. I needed a crisis in Charlotte's life. Well, at this very moment, right now, I can't think of the Transamerica Building without thinking of Marin and her pipe bomb and her gold bracelet, but it was all very arbitrary in the beginning.

INTERVIEWER: What misapprehensions, illusions and so forth have you had to struggle against in your life? In a commencement address you once said there were many.

DIDION: All kinds. I was one of those children who tended to perceive the world in terms of things read about it. I began with a literary idea of experience, and I still don't know where all the lies are. For example, it may not be true that people who try to fly always burst into flames and fall. That may not be true at all. In fact people *do fly,* and land safely. But I don't really believe that. I still see Icarus. I don't seem to have a set of physical facts at my disposal, don't seem to understand how things really work. I just have an *idea* of how they work, which is always trouble. As Henry James told us.

INTERVIEWER: You seem to live your life on the edge, or, at least, on the literary idea of the edge.

DIDION: Again, it's a literary idea, and it derives from what engaged me imaginatively as a child. I can recall disapproving of the golden mean, always thinking there was more to be learned from the dark journey. The dark journey engaged me more. I once had in mind a very light novel, all surface, all conversations and memories and recollections of some people in Honolulu who were getting along fine, one or two misapprehensions about the past notwithstanding. Well, I'm working on that book now, but it's not running that way at all. Not at all.

INTERVIEWER: It always turns into danger and apocalypse.

DIDION: Well, I grew up in a dangerous landscape. I think people are more affected than they know by landscapes and weather. Sacramento was a very extreme place. It was very flat, flatter than most people can imagine, and I still favor flat horizons. The weather in Sacramento was as extreme as the landscape. There were two rivers, and these rivers would flood in the winter and run dry in the summer. Winter was cold rain and tulle fog. Summer was 100 degrees, 105 degrees, 110 degrees. Those extremes affect the way you deal with the world. It so happens that if you're a writer the extremes show up. They don't if you sell insurance.

—LINDA KUEHL

1978

JOYCE CAROL OATES

Joyce Carol Oates was born on June 16, 1938, to a working-class Irish family in the town of Lockport in rural Erie County, New York. Oates, who became interested in writing as a child, wrote a novel each term while she was in college at Syracuse University and won a *Mademoiselle* magazine college fiction award. In 1961, she earned a master's degree at the University of Wisconsin. She accompanied her husband, Raymond J. Smith, a college professor, to Texas, but soon abandoned her plans to pursue a doctorate in order to concentrate on her fiction. Oates's first short-story collection, *By the North Gate*, was published in 1963 and her first novel, *With Shuddering Fall*, the following year; a second collection of stories, *Upon the Sweeping Flood*, came out in 1965.

Oates has maintained an uncanny literary pace throughout her career, publishing at least one book per year. Of the some seventy novels, collections of poetry and short stories Oates has written since 1963, several have received the highest prizes in their fields. *Them* won the 1970 National Book Award for fiction; *A Garden of Earthly Delights* (1970) and *Expensive People* (1969) were nominated for the National Book Award; and

What I Lived For (1994) was nominated for the Pulitzer Prize and the PEN/Faulkner Award for Fiction. Other notable works include the short-story collections *Where Are You Going, Where Have You Been?: Stories of Young America* (1974) and *Heat and Other Stories* (1991) and the novels *Do with Me What You Will* (1973), *You Must Remember This* (1987) and *Black Water* (1992).

Oates has been a Guggenheim Fellow, a recipient of the O'Henry Special Award for Continuing Achievement and a National Endowment for the Arts grantee and is a member of the American Academy and Institute of Arts and Letters. She is the Roger S. Berlind Distinguished Professor in the Humanities at Princeton University.

JOYCE CAROL OATES

Joyce Carol Oates is the rarest of commodities, an author modest about her work, though there is such a quantity of it that she has three publishers—one for fiction, one for poetry and a "small press" for more experimental work, limited editions, and books her other publishers simply cannot schedule. And despite the added demands of teaching, she continues to devote much energy to The Ontario Review, *a literary quarterly that her husband edits and for which she serves as a contributing editor.*

Ms. Oates is striking-looking and slender, with dark hair and large, inquiring eyes. She is highly attractive but not photogenic; no photo has ever done justice to her appearance, which conveys grace and high intelligence. If her manner is taken for aloofness—as it sometimes has been—it is, in fact, a shyness that the publication of thirty-three books, the production of three plays, and the winning of the National Book Award has not displaced.

This interview began at her Windsor home in the summer of 1976 before she and her husband moved to Princeton. When interviewed, her speaking voice was, as always, soft and reflective. One receives the impression that she never speaks in anything but perfectly formed sentences. Ms. Oates answered all questions openly while curled with her Persian cats upon a sofa. (She is a confirmed cat lover and recently took in two more kittens at the Princeton house.)

xx other customers in <u>Rinaldi's</u> to overhear. Voice shrill, laughter shrill. Must guard against excitement. ...A true gift, such women possess; "artistic arrangement of life" a phrase I think I read somewhere. Can't remember. She wants to understand me but will not inwade me like the others. Sunshine: her hair. (Though it is brown, not very unusual. But always clean.) Sunshine: dispelling of demons. Intimacy always a danger. Intimacy/hell/intimacy/hell. Could possibly make love to her thinking of XXXXXXXXXXXXX or (say) the boy with the kinky reddish hair on the bicycle...but sickening to think of. What if. What if an attack of laughter. Hysterical gig-gling. And. Afterward. Such shame, disgust. She would not laugh of course but might be wounded for life: cannot exaggerate the dangers of intimacy, on my side or hers. The Secret between us. My secret, not hers. Our friendship--nearly a year now-- on my footing, never hers. Can't deny what others have known before me, the pleasure of secrecy, taking of risks.

--With XXXXXXXXXXX etc. last night, unable to wake this morning till after ten; already at work; sick headache, dryness of mouth, throat. But no fever. Temperature normal. XXXXXXXXXXXXXXX so bitter, speaks of having been blackmailed by some idiot, but (in my opinion) it all happened years ago, not connected with his position here in town. Teaches juniors, seniors. Advises Drama Club. Tenure. I'm envious of him & impatient with his continual bitterness. Rehashing of past. What's the point of it? Of course, he is over forty (how much over forty is his secret) and I am a decade younger, x maybe fifteen years younger. Will never turn into that. Hag's face, lines around mouth, eyes. Grotesque moustache: trying to be 25 years old & misses by a x mile.... Yet my pen-and-ink portrait of him is endearing. Delighted, that it should please even him. & did not mind the CA$H. Of course I am talented & of course misused at the agency but refuse to be bitter like the others. XXXXXXXXXXX lavish, flattery and money. I deserve both but don't expect everyone to recognize me...in no hurry...can't demand fame overnight. Would I want fame anyway???? Maybe not. With XXXXXXXXXXXX's hundred dollars bought her that $35 book of Toulouse-Lautrec's work, dear Henri, perhaps should not have risked x it with her but genuinely thought she would like it. Did not think, as usual. She seemed grateful enough, thanking me, surprised, said she'd received only a few cards from home & a predictable present from her mother, certainly did not expect anything ffom me--"But aren't you saving for a trip to Europe"--remembers so much about me, amazing--so sweet--unlike XXXXXXXXXXX who calls me by the names of strangers and is vile. His image with me till early afternoon, tried to vomit in the first-floor lavatory where no one from the office might ~~stomach~~ drop in, dry heaving gasps, not so easy to do on an empty ~~stomach~~ Mind over matter?????? Not with "Farrell van Buren"!

--A complete day xxxx wasted. Idiotic trendy "collage" for MacKenzie's Diary, if you please. Cherubs, grinning teenagers, trophies. An "avant-garde" look to it. Haha. Looking forward to lay-out for the Hilton & Trader Vic's, at least some precedent to work from <u>and resist</u>. ...Could send out my Invisible Soldiers to hack up a few of these bastards, smart-assed paunchy hags bossing me around. Someday things will be different. (Of course

---

A manuscript page from a short story by Joyce Carol Oates.

Talk continued during a stroll by the banks of the Detroit River where she confessed to having sat for hours, watching the horizon and the boats, and dreaming her characters into existence. She sets these dreams physically onto paper on a writing table in her study, which faces the river.

Additional questions were asked in New York during the 1976 Christmas season, when Ms. Oates and her husband attended a seminar on her work which was part of that year's Modern Language Association convention. Many of the questions in this interview were answered via correspondence. She felt that only by writing out her replies could she say precisely what she wished to, without possibility of misunderstanding or misquotation.

INTERVIEWER: We may as well get this one over with first: you're frequently charged with producing too much.

OATES: Productivity is a relative matter. And it's really insignificant: what is ultimately important is a writer's strongest books. It may be the case that we all must write many books in order to achieve a few lasting ones—just as a young writer or poet might have to write hundreds of poems before writing his first significant one. Each book as it is written, however, is a completely absorbing experience, and feels always as if it were *the* work I was born to write. Afterward, of course, as the years pass, it's possible to become more detached, more critical.

I really don't know what to say. I note and can to some extent sympathize with the objurgatory tone of certain critics, who feel that I write too much because, quite wrongly, they believe they ought to have read most of my books before attempting to criticize a recently published one. (At least I *think* that's why they react a bit irritably.) Yet each book is a world unto itself and must stand alone, and it should not matter whether a book is a writer's first, or tenth, or fiftieth.

INTERVIEWER: About your critics—do you read them, usually? Have you ever learned anything from a book review or an essay on your work?

OATES: Sometimes I read reviews, and without exception I will read critical essays that are sent to me. The critical essays are interesting on their own terms. Of course, it's a pleasure simply to discover that someone has read and responded to one's work; being understood, and being praised, is beyond expectation most of the time. . . . The average review is a quickly written piece not meant to be definitive. So it would be misguided for a writer to read such reviews attentively. All writers without exception find themselves clapperclawed from time to time; I think the experience (provided one survives it) is wonderfully liberating: after the first death there is no other. . . . A writer who has published as many books as I have has developed, of necessity, a hide like a rhino's, while inside there dwells a frail, hopeful butterfly of a spirit.

INTERVIEWER: Returning to the matter of your "productivity": have you ever dictated into a machine?

OATES: No, oddly enough I've written my last several novels in longhand first. I had an enormous, rather frightening stack of pages and notes for *The Assassins*, probably eight hundred pages—or was it closer to a thousand? It alarms me to remember. *Childwold* needed to be written in longhand, of course. And now everything finds its initial expression in longhand and the typewriter has become a rather alien thing—a thing of formality and impersonality. My first novels were all written on a typewriter: first draft straight through, then revisions, then final draft. But I can't do that any longer.

The thought of dictating into a machine doesn't appeal to me at all. Henry James's later works would have been better had he resisted that curious sort of self-indulgence, dictating to a secretary. The roaming garrulousness of ordinary speech is usually corrected when it's transcribed into written prose.

INTERVIEWER: Do you ever worry—considering the vast body of your work—if you haven't written a particular scene before, or had characters say the same lines?

OATES: Evidently, there are writers (John Cheever, Mavis Gallant come immediately to mind) who never reread their work, and there are others who reread constantly. I suspect I am somewhere in the middle. If I thought I *had* written a scene before, or written the same lines before, I would simply look it up.

INTERVIEWER: What kind of work schedule do you follow?

OATES: I haven't any formal schedule, but I love to write in the morning, before breakfast. Sometimes the writing goes so smoothly that I don't take a break for many hours—and consequently have breakfast at two or three in the afternoon on good days. On school days, days that I teach, I usually write for an hour or forty-five minutes in the morning, before my first class. But I don't have any formal schedule, and at the moment I am feeling rather melancholy, or derailed, or simply lost, because I completed a novel some weeks ago and haven't begun another . . . except in scattered, stray notes.

INTERVIEWER: Do you find emotional stability is necessary in order to write? Or can you get to work whatever your state of mind? Is your mood reflected in what you write? How do you describe that perfect state in which you can write from early morning into the afternoon?

OATES: One must be pitiless about this matter of "mood." In a sense, the writing will *create* the mood. If art is, as I believe it to be, a genuinely transcendental function—a means by which we rise out of limited, parochial states of mind—then it should not matter very much what states of mind or emotion we are in. Generally I've found this to be true: I have forced myself to begin writing when I've been utterly exhausted, when I've felt my soul as thin as a playing card, when nothing has seemed worth enduring for another five minutes . . . and somehow the activity of writing changes everything. Or appears to do so. Joyce said of the underlying structure of *Ulysses*—the Odyssean parallel and parody—that he really didn't care whether it was plausible so long as it served as a bridge to get his "soldiers" across. Once they were across, what does it matter if the bridge collapses? One might say the same thing about the use of one's self as a means for the writing to get written. Once the soldiers are across the stream . . .

INTERVIEWER: What does happen when you finish a novel? Is the next project one that has been waiting in line? Or is the choice more spontaneous?

OATES: When I complete a novel I set it aside, and begin work on short stories, and eventually another long work. When I complete *that* novel I return to the earlier novel and rewrite much of it. In the meantime the second novel lies in a desk drawer. Sometimes I work on two novels simultaneously, though one usually forces the other into the background. The rhythm of writing, revising, writing, revising, et cetera, seems to suit me. I am inclined to think that as I grow older I will come to be infatuated with the art of revision, and there may come a time when I will dread giving up a novel at all. My next novel, *Unholy Loves*, was written around the time of *Childwold*, for instance, and revised after the completion of that novel, and again revised this past spring and summer. My reputation for writing quickly and effortlessly notwithstanding, I am strongly in favor of intelligent, even fastidious revision, which is, or certainly should be, an art in itself.

INTERVIEWER: Do you keep a diary?

OATES: I began keeping a formal journal several years ago. It resembles a sort of ongoing letter to myself, mainly about literary matters. What interests me in the process of my own experience is the wide range of my feelings. For instance, after I finish a novel I tend to think of the experience of having written it as being largely pleasant and challenging. But in fact (for I keep careful records) the experience is various: I do suffer temporary bouts of frustration and inertia and depression. There are pages in recent novels that I've rewritten as many as seventeen times, and a story, "The Widows," which I revised both before and after publication in *The Hudson Review*, and then revised slightly again before I included it in my next collection of stories—a fastidiousness that could go on into infinity.

Afterward, however, I simply forget. My feelings crystallize (or are mythologized) into something much less complex. All of us who keep journals do so for different reasons, I suppose, but we must have in common a fascination with the surprising patterns that emerge over the years a sort of arabesque in which certain elements appear and reappear, like the designs in a well-wrought novel. The voice of my journal is very much like the one I find myself using in these replies to you: the voice in which I think or meditate when I'm not writing fiction.

INTERVIEWER: Besides writing and teaching, what daily special activities are important to you? Travel, jogging, music? I hear you're an excellent pianist?

OATES: We travel a great deal, usually by car. We've driven slowly across the continent several times, and we've explored the South and New England and of course New York State with loving thoroughness. As a pianist I've defined myself as an "enthusiastic amateur," which is about the most merciful thing that can be said. I like to draw, I like to listen to music, and I spend an inordinate amount of time doing nothing. I don't even think it can be called daydreaming.

I also enjoy that much-maligned occupation of housewifery, but hardly dare say so, things being what they are today. I like to cook, to tend plants, to garden (minimally), to do simple domestic things, to stroll around shopping malls and observe the qualities of people, overhearing snatches of conversations, noting people's appearances, their clothes, and so forth. Walking and driving a car are part of my life as a writer, really. I can't imagine myself apart from these activities.

INTERVIEWER: Despite critical and financial success, you continue to teach. Why?

OATES: I teach a full load at the University of Windsor,

which means three courses. One is creative writing, one is the graduate seminar (in the Modern Period), the third is an oversized (115 students) undergraduate course that is lively and stimulating but really too swollen to be satisfying to me. There is, generally, a closeness between students and faculty at Windsor that is very rewarding, however. Anyone who teaches knows that you don't *really* experience a text until you've taught it, in loving detail, with an intelligent and responsive class. At the present time I'm going through Joyce's work with nine graduate students and each seminar meeting is very exciting (and draining) and I can't think, frankly, of anything else I would rather do.

INTERVIEWER: It is a sometimes publicized fact that your professor-husband does not read most of your work. Is there any practical reason for this?

OATES: Ray has such a busy life of his own, preparing classes, editing *The Ontario Review* and so forth, that he really hasn't time to read my work. I do, occasionally, show him reviews, and he makes brief comments on them. I would have liked, I think, to have established an easygoing relationship with some other writers, but somehow that never came about. Two or three of us at Windsor do read one another's poems, but criticism as such is minimal. I've never been able to respond very fully to criticism, frankly, because I've usually been absorbed in another work by the time the criticism is available to me. Also, critics sometimes appear to be addressing themselves to works other than those I remember writing.

INTERVIEWER: Do you feel in any way an expatriate or an exile, living in Canada?

OATES: We are certainly exiles of a sort. But we would be, I think, exiles if we lived in Detroit as well. Fortunately, Windsor is really an international, cosmopolitan community, and our Canadian colleagues are not intensely and narrowly nationalistic.

But I wonder—doesn't everyone feel rather exiled? When I return home to Millerport, New York, and visit nearby Lockport, the extraordinary changes that have taken place make me feel like a stranger; the mere passage of time makes us all exiles. The situation is a comic one, perhaps, since it affirms the power of the evolving community over the individual, but I think we tend to feel it as tragic. Windsor is a relatively stable community, and my husband and I have come to feel, oddly, more at home here than we probably would anywhere else.

INTERVIEWER: Have you ever consciously changed your lifestyle to help your work as a writer?

OATES: Not really. My nature is orderly and observant and scrupulous, and deeply introverted, so life wherever I attempt it turns out to be claustral. Live like the bourgeois, Flaubert suggested, but I was living like that long before I came across Flaubert's remark.

INTERVIEWER: You wrote *Do with Me What You Will* during your year living in London. While there you met many writers such as Doris Lessing, Margaret Drabble, Colin Wilson, Iris Murdoch—writers you respect, as your reviews of their work indicate. Would you make any observations on the role of the writer in society in England versus that which you experience here?

OATES: The English novelist is almost without exception an observer of society. (I suppose I mean "society" in its most immediate, limited sense.) Apart from writers like Lawrence (who doesn't seem altogether *English*, in fact) there hasn't been an intense interest in subjectivity, in the psychology of living, breathing human beings. Of course, there have been marvelous novels. And there *is* Doris Lessing, who writes books that can no longer be categorized: fictional parable, autobiography, allegory . . . ? And John Fowles. And Iris Murdoch.

But there is a feel to the American novel that is radically different. We are willing to risk being called "formless" by people whose ideas of form are rigidly limited, and we are wilder, more exploratory, more ambitious, perhaps less easily shamed, less easily discouraged. The intellectual life as such we tend to keep out of our novels, fearing the sort of highly readable but ultimately disappointing cerebral quality of Huxley's work . . . or, on a somewhat lower level, C. P. Snow's.

INTERVIEWER: The English edition of *Wonderland* has a different ending from the American. Why? Do you often rewrite published work?

OATES: I was forced to rewrite the ending of that particular novel because it struck me that the first ending was not the correct one. I have not rewritten any other published work (except of course for short stories, which sometimes get rewritten before inclusion in a book) and don't intend to if I can possibly help it.

INTERVIEWER: You've written novels on highly specialized fields, such as brain surgery. How do you research such backgrounds?

OATES: A great deal of reading, mainly. Some years ago I developed a few odd symptoms that necessitated my seeing a doctor, and since there was for a time talk of my being sent to a neurologist, I nervously and superstitiously began reading the relevant journals. What I came upon so chilled me that I must have gotten well as a result. . . .

INTERVIEWER: In addition to the novel about medicine, you've written one each on law, politics, religion, spectator sports: Are you consciously filling out a "program" of novels about American life?

OATES: Not really consciously. The great concern with "medicine" really grew out of an experience of some duration that brought me into contact with certain thoughts of mortality: of hospitals, illnesses, doctors, the world of death and dying and our human defenses against such phenomena. (A member of my family to whom I was very close died rather slowly of cancer.) I attempted to deal with my own very inchoate feelings about these matters by dramatizing what I saw to be contemporary responses to "mortality." My effort to wed myself with a fictional character and our synthesis in turn with a larger, almost allegorical condition resulted in a novel that was difficult to write and also, I suspect, difficult to read.

A concern with law seemed to spring naturally out of the thinking many of us were doing in the sixties: What is the relationship between "law" and civilization, what hope has civilization without "law," and yet what hope has civilization *with* law as it has developed in our tradition? More personal matters blended with the larger issues of "crime" and "guilt," so that I felt I was able to transcend a purely private and purely local drama that might have had emotional significance for me, but very little beyond that; quite by accident I found myself writing about a woman conditioned to be unnaturally "passive" in a world of hearty masculine combat—an issue that became topical even as the novel *Do with Me What You Will* was published, and is topical still, to some extent.

The "political" novel, *The Assassins,* grew out of two experiences I had some years ago, at high-level conferences involving politicians, academic specialists, lawyers, and a scattering—no, hardly that—of literary people. (I won't be more specific at the moment.) A certain vertiginous fascination with work which I noted in my own nature I was able to objectify (and, I think, exaggerate) in terms of the various characters' fanaticism involving their own "work"—most obviously in Andrew Petrie's obsession with "transforming the consciousness of America." *The Assassins* is about megalomania and its inevitable consequences, and it seemed necessary that the assassins be involved in politics, given the peculiar conditions of our era.

The new "religious" novel, *Son of the Morning,* is rather painfully autobiographical, in part; but only in part. The religion it explores is not institutional but rather subjective, intensely personal, so as a novel it is perhaps not like the earlier three I have mentioned, or the racing novel, *With Shuddering Fall.* Rather, *Son of the Morning* is a novel that begins with wide ambitions and ends very, very humbly.

INTERVIEWER: Somewhere in print you called *The Assassins* the favorite of your novels. It received very mixed reviews. I've often thought that book was misread. For instance, I think the "martyr" in that novel arranged for his own assassination, true? And that his wife was never really attacked outside the country house; she never left it. Her maiming was all confined within her head.

OATES: What a fine surprise! You read the scene exactly as it was meant to be read. Even well-intentioned reviewers missed the point; so far as I know, only two or three people read Yvonne's scene as I had intended it to be read. Yet the hallucinatory nature of the "dismemberment" scene is explicit. And Andrew Petrie did, of course, arrange for his own assassination, as the novel makes clear in its concluding pages.

The novel has been misread, of course, partly because it's rather long and I think reviewers, who are usually pressed for time, simply treated it in a perfunctory way. I'm not certain that it is my favorite novel. But it is, or was, my most ambitious. It involved a great deal of effort, the collating of passages (and memories) that differ from or contradict one another. One becomes attached to such perverse, maddening ugly ducklings, but I can't really blame reviewers for being impatient with the novel. As my novels grow in complexity they please me more and please the "literary world" hardly at all—a sad situation, but not a paralyzing one.

INTERVIEWER: It's not merely a matter of complexity. One feels that your fiction has become more and more urgent, more subjective and less concerned with the outward details of this world—especially in *Childwold.* Was that novel a deliberate attempt to write a "poetic novel"? Or is it a long poem?

OATES: I don't see that *Childwold* is not concerned with the outward details of the world. In fact, it's made up almost entirely of visual details—of the natural world, of the farm the Bartletts own, and of the small city they gravitate to. But you are right, certainly, in suggesting that it is a "poetic novel." I had wanted to create a prose poem in the form of a novel, or a novel in the form of a prose poem: the exciting thing for me was to deal with the tension that arose between the image-centered structure of poetry and the narrative-centered and linear structure of the interplay of persons that constitutes a novel. In other words, poetry focuses upon the image, the particular thing, or emotion, or feeling, while prose fiction focuses upon motion through time and space. The one impulse is toward stasis, the other toward movement. Between the two impulses there arose a certain tension that made the writing of the novel quite challenging. I suppose it is an experimental work, but I shy away from thinking of my work in those terms: it seems to me there is a certain self-consciousness about anyone who sets himself up as an "experimental" writer. All writing is experimental.

But experimentation for its own sake doesn't much interest me; it seems to belong to the early sixties, when Dadaism was being rediscovered. In a sense we are all post-*Wake* writers and it's Joyce, and only Joyce, who casts a long terrifying shadow. . . . The problem is that virtuoso writing appeals to the intellect and tends to leave one's emotions untouched. When I read aloud to my students the last few pages of *Finnegans Wake*, and come to that glorious, and heartbreaking, final section ("But you're changing, acoolsha, you're changing from me, I can feel"), I think I'm able to communicate the almost overwhelmingly beautiful emotion behind it, and the experience certainly leaves *me* shaken, but it would be foolish to think that the average reader, even the average intelligent reader, would be willing to labor at the *Wake*, through those hundreds of dense pages, in order to attain an emotional and spiritual sense of the work's wholeness, as well as its genius. Joyce's *Ulysses* appeals to me more: that graceful synthesis of the "naturalistic" and the "symbolic" suits my temperament also. . . . I try to write books that can be read in one way by a literal-minded reader, and in quite another way by a reader alert to symbolic abbreviation and parodistic elements. And yet, it's the same book—or nearly. A trompe l'oeil, a work of "as if."

INTERVIEWER: Very little has been made of the humor in your work, the parody. Some of your books, like *Expensive People, The Hungry Ghosts,* and parts of *Wonderland,* seem almost Pinteresque in their absurd humor. Is Pinter an influence? Do you consider yourself a comedic writer?

OATES: There's been humor of a sort in my writing from the first; but it's understated, or deadpan. Pinter has never struck me as very funny. Doesn't he really write tragedy?

I liked Ionesco at one time. And Kafka. And Dickens (from whom Kafka learned certain effects, though he uses them, of course, for different ends). I respond to English satire, as I mentioned earlier. Absurdist or "dark" or "black" or whatever: what isn't tragic belongs to the comic spirit. The novel is nourished by both and swallows both up greedily.

INTERVIEWER: What have you learned from Kafka?

OATES: To make a jest of the horror. To take myself less seriously.

INTERVIEWER: John Updike has been accused of a lack of violence in his work. You're often accused of portraying too much. What is the function of violence in your work?

OATES: Given the number of pages I have written, and the "violent" incidents dispersed throughout them, I rather doubt that I am a violent writer in any meaningful sense of the word. Certainly, the violence is minimal in a novel like *them,* which purported to be a naturalistic work set in Detroit in the sixties; real life is much more chaotic.

INTERVIEWER: Which of your books gave you the greatest trouble to write? And which gave the greatest pleasure or pride?

OATES: Both *Wonderland* and *The Assassins* were difficult to write. *Expensive People* was the least difficult. I am personally very fond of *Childwold*, since it represents, in a kind of diffracted way, a complete world made of memory and imagination, a blending together of different times. It always surprises me that other people find that novel admirable because, to me, it seems very private . . . the sort of thing a writer can do only once.

Aside from that, *Do with Me What You Will* gives me a fair amount of pleasure, and of course, I am closest to the novel I finished most recently, *Son of the Morning*. (In general, I think we are always fondest of the books we've just completed, aren't we? For obvious reasons.) But then I think of Jules and Maureen and Loretta of *them* and I wonder if perhaps that isn't my favorite novel, after all.

INTERVIEWER: For whom do you write—yourself, your friends, your "public"? Do you imagine an ideal reader for your work?

OATES: Well, there are certain stories, like those in *The Hungry Ghosts*, which I have written for an academic community and, in some cases, for specific people. But in general the writing writes itself—I mean a character determines his or her "voice" and I must follow along. Had I my own way the first section of *The Assassins* would be much abbreviated. But it was impossible to shut Hugh Petrie up once he got going and, long and painful and unwieldy as his section is, it's nevertheless been shortened. The problem with creating such highly conscious and intuitive characters is that they tend to perceive the contours of the literary landscape in which they dwell and, like Kasch of *Childwold*, try to guide or even to take over the direction of the narrative. Hugh did not want to die, and so his section went on and on, and it isn't an exaggeration to say that I felt real dismay in dealing with him.

Son of the Morning is a first-person narration by a man who is addressing himself throughout to God. Hence the whole novel is a prayer. Hence the ideal reader is, then, God. Everyone else, myself included, is secondary.

INTERVIEWER: Do you consider yourself religious? Do you feel there is a firm religious basis to your work?

OATES: I wish I knew how to answer this. Having completed a novel that is saturated with what Jung calls the God-experience, I find that I know less than ever about myself and my own beliefs. I have beliefs, of course, like everyone—but I don't always believe in them. Faith comes and goes. God diffracts into a bewildering plenitude of elements—the environment, love, friends and family, career, profession, "fate," biochemical harmony or disharmony, whether the sky is slate-gray or a bright mesmerizing blue. These elements then coalesce again into something seemingly unified. But it's a human predilection, isn't it?—our tendency to see, and to wish to see, what we've projected outward upon the universe from our own souls? I hope to continue to write about religious experience, but at the moment I feel quite drained, quite depleted. And as baffled as ever.

INTERVIEWER: You mention Jung. Is Freud also an influence? Laing?

OATES: Freud I have always found rather limited and biased; Jung and Laing I've read only in recent years. As an undergraduate at Syracuse University I discovered Nietzsche, and it may be the Nietzschean influence (which is certainly far more provocative than Freud's) that characterizes some of my work. I don't really know, consciously. For me, stories usually begin—or began, since I write so few of them now—out of some magical association between characters and their settings. There are some stories (I won't say which ones) which evolved almost entirely out of their settings, usually rural.

INTERVIEWER: Your earliest stories and novels seem influenced by Faulkner and by Flannery O'Connor. Are these influences you acknowledge? Are there others?

OATES: I've been reading for so many years, and my influences must be so vast—it would be very difficult to answer. An influence I rarely mention is Thoreau, whom I read at a very impressionable age (my early teens), and Henry James, O'Connor and Faulkner certainly, Katherine Anne Porter, and Dostoyevsky. An odd mixture.

INTERVIEWER: The title *Wonderland,* and frequent other allusions in your work, point toward a knowledge of, if not an affinity for, Lewis Carroll. What is the connection, and is it an important one?

OATES: Lewis Carroll's *Alice in Wonderland* and *Through the Looking Glass* were my very first books. Carroll's wonderful blend of illogic and humor and horror and justice has always appealed to me, and I had a marvelous time teaching the books last year in my undergraduate course.

INTERVIEWER: Was there anything you were particularly afraid of as a child?

OATES: Like most children, I was probably afraid of a variety of things. The unknown? The possibility of those queer fortuitous metamorphoses that seem to overtake certain of Carroll's characters? Physical pain? Getting lost? . . . My proclivity for the irreverent and the nonsensical was either inspired by Carroll or confirmed by him. I was always, and continue to be, an essentially mischievous child. This is one of my best-kept secrets.

INTERVIEWER: You began writing at a very early age. Was it encouraged by your family? Was yours a family of artistic ambitions?

OATES: In later years my parents have become "artistic," but when they were younger, and their children were younger, they had no time for anything much except work. I was always encouraged by my parents, my grandmother, and my teachers to be creative. I can't remember when I first began to tell stories—

by drawing, it was then—but I must have been very young. It was an instinct I followed quite naturally.

INTERVIEWER: Much of your work is set in the 1930s, a period during which you were merely an infant at best. Why is that decade so important to your work or vision?

OATES: Since I was born in 1938, the decade is of great significance to me. This was the world of my parents, who were young adults at the time, the world I was born into. The thirties seem in an odd way still "living" to me, partly in terms of my parents' and grandparents' memories, and partly in terms of its treatment in books and films. But the twenties are too remote—lost to me entirely! I simply haven't had the imaginative power to get that far back.

I identify very closely with my parents in ways I can't satisfactorily explain. The lives they lived before I was born seem somehow accessible to me. Not directly, of course, but imaginatively. A memory belonging to my mother or father seems almost to "belong" to me. In studying old photographs I am struck sometimes by a sense of my being contemporary with my parents—as if I'd known them when they were, let's say, only teenagers. Is this odd? I wonder. I rather suspect others share in their family's experiences and memories without knowing quite how.

INTERVIEWER: When we were undergraduates together at Syracuse, you already were something of a legend. It was rumored you'd finish a novel, turn it over, and immediately begin writing another on the back side. When both sides were covered, you'd throw it all out, and reach for clean paper. Was it at Syracuse you first became aware you were going to be a writer?

OATES: I began writing in high school, consciously training myself by writing novel after novel and always throwing them out when I completed them. I remember a three-hundred-page book of interrelated stories that must have been modeled on Hemingway's *In Our Time* (I hadn't yet read *Dubliners*), though the subject matter was much more romantic than Hemingway's. I remember a bloated, trifurcated novel that had as its vague model *The Sound and the Fury.* . . . Fortunately, these experiments were thrown away and I haven't remembered them until this moment.

Syracuse was a very exciting place academically and intellectually for me. I doubt that I missed more than half a dozen classes in my four years there, and none of them in English.

INTERVIEWER: I remember you were in a sorority. It is incredible to contemplate you as a "sorority girl."

OATES: My experience in a sorority wasn't disastrous, but merely despairing. (I tried to resign but found out that upon joining I had signed some sort of legal contract.) However, I did make some close friends in the sorority, so the experience wasn't a total loss. I would never do it again, certainly. In fact, it's one of the three or four things in my entire life I would never do again.

INTERVIEWER: Why was life in a Syracuse sorority so despairing? Have you written about it?

OATES: The racial and religious bigotry; the asininity of "secret ceremonies"; the moronic emphasis upon "activities" totally unrelated to—in fact antithetical to—intellectual exploration; the bullying of the presumably weak by the presumably strong; the deliberate pursuit of an attractive "image" for the group as a whole, no matter how cynical the individuals might have been; the aping of the worst American traits— boosterism, God-fearingism, smug ignorance, a craven worship of conformity; the sheer *mess* of the place once one got beyond the downstairs. . . . I tried to escape in my junior year, but a connection between sororities and the Dean of Women and the university-housing office made escape all but impossible, and it seemed that, in my freshman naïveté, I had actually signed some sort of contract that had "legal" status . . . all of which quite cowed me. I remember a powdered and perfumed alum explaining the sorority's exclusion of Jews and blacks: "You see, we have conferences at the Lake Placid Club, and wouldn't it be a shame if *all* our members couldn't attend. . . . Why, it would be embarrassing for them, wouldn't it?"

I was valedictorian of my class, the class of 1960. I fantasized beginning my address by saying, "I managed to do well academically at Syracuse despite the concerted efforts of my sorority to prevent me. . . ."

I haven't written about it, and never will. It's simply too stupid and trivial a subject. To even *care* about such adolescent nonsense one would have to have the sensitivity of a John O'Hara, who seems to have taken it all seriously.

INTERVIEWER: I recall you won the poetry contest at Syracuse in your senior year. But your books of poetry appeared relatively later than your fiction. Were you always writing poetry?

OATES: No, I really began to write poetry later. The poetry still comes with difficulty, I must admit. Tiny lyric asides, droll wry enigmatic statements: They aren't easy, are they? I'm assembling a book which I think will be my last—of poems, I mean. No one wants to read a novelist's poetry. It's enough—too much, in fact—to deal with the novels. Strangely enough, my fellow poets have been magnanimous indeed in accepting me as a poet. I would not have been surprised had they ignored me, but, in fact, they've been wonderfully supportive and encouraging. Which contradicts the general notion that poets are highly competitive and jealous of one another's accomplishments. . . .

INTERVIEWER: You say no one wants to read a novelist's poetry. What about Robert Penn Warren? John Updike? Erica Jong? I suppose Allen Tate and James Dickey are poets who happened to write novels. . . .

OATES: I suppose I was thinking only of hypothetical reactions to my own poetry. Robert Penn Warren aside, however, there *is* a tendency on the part of critics to want very much to categorize writers. Hence one is either a writer of prose or of poetry. If Lawrence hadn't written those novels he would have been far more readily acclaimed as one of the greatest poets in the language. As it is, however, his poetry has been neglected. (At least until recently.)

INTERVIEWER: *By the North Gate*, your first book, is a collection of short stories, and you continue to publish them. Is the short story your greatest love? Do you hold with the old adage that it is more difficult to write a good story than a novel?

OATES: Brief subjects require brief treatments. There is *nothing* so difficult as a novel, as anyone knows who has attempted one; a short story is bliss to write set beside a novel of even ordinary proportions.

But in recent years I haven't been writing much short fiction. I don't quite know why. All my energies seem to be drawn into longer works. It's probably the case that my period of greatest productivity is behind me, and I'm becoming more interested in focusing upon a single work, usually a novel, and trying to "perfect" it section by section and page by page.

INTERVIEWER: Nevertheless, you've published more short stories, perhaps, than any other serious writer in America today. I remember that when you chose the twenty-one stories to compose *The Wheel of Love*, you picked from some ninety which had been in magazines the two years since your previous collection. What will become of the seventy or so stories you didn't include in that collection? Were some added to later collections? Will you ever get back and pick up uncollected work?

OATES: If I'm serious about a story, I preserve it in book form; otherwise I intend it to be forgotten. This is true of course for poems and reviews and essays as well. I went back and selected a number of stories that for thematic reasons were not included in *The Wheel of Love*, and put them into a collection called *The Seduction and Other Stories*. Each of the story collections is organized around a central theme and is meant to be read as a whole—the arrangement of the stories being a rigorous one, not at all haphazard.

INTERVIEWER: You don't drink. Have you tried any consciousness-expanding drugs?

OATES: No. Even tea (because of caffeine) is too strong for me. I must have been born with a rather sensitive constitution.

INTERVIEWER: Earlier you mentioned Hugh Petrie in *The Assassins.* He is but one of many deranged characters in your books. Have you known any genuine madmen?

OATES: Unfortunately, I have been acquainted with a small number of persons who might be considered mentally disturbed. And others, strangers, are sometimes drawn my way; I don't know why.

Last week when I went to the university, I wasn't allowed to teach my large lecture class because, during the night, one of my graduate students had received a telephone call from a very angry, distraught man who announced that he intended to kill me. So I had to spend several hours sequestered away with the head of our department and the head of security at the university and two special investigators from the Windsor City Police. The situation was more embarrassing than disturbing. It's the first time anyone has so explicitly and publicly threatened my life—there have been sly, indirect threats made in the past, which I've known enough not to take seriously.

(The man who called my student is a stranger to us all, not even a resident of Windsor. I have no idea why he's so angry with me. But does a disturbed person really need a reason . . . ?)

INTERVIEWER: How about the less threatening, but nonetheless hurtful, reactions of friends and relatives—any reactions to conscious or unconscious portraits in your work?

OATES: My parents (and I, as a child) appear very briefly in *Wonderland,* glimpsed by the harassed young hero on his way to, or from, Buffalo. Otherwise there are no portraits of family or relatives in my writing. My mother and father both respond (rather touchingly at times) to the setting of my stories and novels, which they recognize. But since there is nothing of a personal nature in the writing, I have not experienced any difficulties along those lines.

INTERVIEWER: Aside from the singular incident at the university, what are the disadvantages of being famous?

OATES: I'm not aware of being famous, especially here in Windsor, where the two major bookstores, Coles', don't even stock my books. The number of people who are "aware" of me, let alone who read my writing, is very small. Consequently I enjoy a certain degree of invisibility and anonymity at the university, which I might not have at an American university—which is one of the reasons I am so much at home here.

INTERVIEWER: Are you aware of any personal limitations?

OATES: Shyness has prevented me from doing many things; also the amount of work and responsibility here at Windsor.

INTERVIEWER: Do you feel you have any conspicuous or secret flaw as a writer?

OATES: My most conspicuous flaw is . . . well, it's so conspicuous that anyone could discern it. And my secret flaw is happily secret.

INTERVIEWER: What are the advantages of being a woman writer?

OATES: Advantages! Too many to enumerate, probably. Since, being a woman, I can't be taken altogether *seriously* by the sort of male critics who rank writers 1, 2, 3 in the public press, I am free, I suppose, to do as I like. I haven't much sense of, or interest in, competition; I can't even grasp what Hemingway and the epigonic Mailer mean by battling it out with the other talent in the ring. A work of art has never, to my knowledge, displaced another work of art. The living are no more in competition with the dead than they are with the living. . . . Being a woman allows me a certain invisibility. Like Ellison's *Invisible Man*. (My long journal, which must be several hundred pages by now, has the title *Invisible Woman.* Because a woman, being so mechanically judged by her appearance, has the advantage of hiding within it—of being absolutely whatever she knows herself to be, in contrast with what others imagine her to be. I feel no connection at all with my physical appearance and have often wondered whether this was a freedom any man—writer or not—might enjoy.)

INTERVIEWER: Do you find it difficult to write from the point of view of the male?

OATES: Absolutely not. I am as sympathetic with any of my male characters as I am with any of my female characters. In many respects I am closest in temperament to certain of my male characters—Nathan Vickery of *Son of the Morning,* for instance—and feel an absolute kinship with them. The Kingdom of God *is* within.

INTERVIEWER: Can you tell the sex of a writer from the prose?

OATES: Never.

INTERVIEWER: What male writers have been especially effective, do you think, in their depiction of women?

OATES: Tolstoy, Lawrence, Shakespeare, Flaubert . . . Very few, really. But then very few women have been effective in their depiction of men.

INTERVIEWER: Do you enjoy writing?

OATES: I do enjoy writing, yes. A great deal. And I feel somewhat at a loss, aimless and foolishly sentimental, and disconnected, when I've finished one work and haven't yet become absorbed in another. All of us who write work out of a conviction that we are participating in some sort of communal activity. Whether my role is writing, or reading and responding, might not be very important. I take seriously Flaubert's statement that we must love one another in our art as the mystics love one another in God. By honoring one another's creation we honor something that deeply connects us all, and goes beyond us.

Of course, writing is only one activity out of a vast number of activities that constitute our lives. It seems to be the one that some of us have concentrated on, as if we were fated for it. Since I have a great deal of faith in the processes and the wisdom of the unconscious, and have learned from experience to take lightly the judgments of the ego and its inevitable doubts, I never find myself constrained to answer such questions. Life is energy, and energy is creativity. And even when we as individuals pass on, the energy is retained in the work of art, locked in it and awaiting release if only someone will take the time and the care to unlock it. . . .

—ROBERT PHILLIPS

1978

Notes on Contributors

Edwina Burness (interview with P. L. Travers) was born in Edinburgh and now lives in the countryside near London. She reviews for the *Times Educational Supplement*, contributes to the *Spectator* and *Harper's and Queen*, and teaches part-time at London University.

Marion Capron (interview with Dorothy Parker) is a former member of the editorial staff of *The Paris Review* and worked for the public relations office of Barnard College in New York City. She lives in Florida.

Madeleine Gobeil (interview with Simone de Beauvoir) is a graduate of McGill University, Montreal. She first met Simone de Beauvoir while a student in Paris in 1958.

Jerry Griswold (interview with P. L. Travers) is the author of *Audacious Kids: America's Favorite Children's Books* and *The Children's Books of Randall Jarrell*. He teaches at San Diego State University.

Donald Hall (interview with Marianne Moore) is the author of twenty-two books of prose, four plays and twelve books of poetry, including *The Old Life* (1996). He has been the recipient of numerous awards, fellowships and honors, including the 1990 Frost Medal from the Poetry Society of America for *Old and New Poems*, and the 1994 Ruth Lilly Poetry Prize from the American Council for the Arts. Hall is the poet laureate of New Hampshire.

Edward Hirsch (interview with Susan Sontag) teaches at the University of Houston and is the author of four books of poems: *For the Sleepwalkers, Wild Gratitude, The Night Parade* and *Earthly Measures.*

Jannika Hurwitt (interview with Nadine Gordimer) is a freelance writer. Her work has been published in *The Paris Review, The Village Voice, SoHo Weekly News* and *Yankee Magazine.*

Barbara Kevles (interview with Anne Sexton) is a charter contributing editor to *Working Woman* and a past contributing editor to *American Health,* and has written for leading national publications including: *The Atlantic, Esquire, New York, The New York Times, Mademoiselle, Glamour, Cosmopolitan, Good Housekeeping, Redbook, Ladies' Home Journal, People, Harper's Bazaar,* and *The Village Voice.*

Linda Kuehl (interviews with Eudora Welty and Joan Didion) was an authority on jazz and published book reviews and interviews in *The New York Times Book Review, Saturday Review* and *Playboy.* She was at work on a biography of Billie Holiday when she died in 1977, at the age of thirty-eight.

Claudia Brodsky Lacour (interview with Toni Morrison) is a professor at Princeton University.

George Plimpton (interview with Maya Angelou) is the editor of *The Paris Review.* His most recent book is *The X Factor.*

Robert Phillips (interview with Joyce Carol Oates) is a professor of English and the director of the creative writing program at the University of Houston and a contributing editor of *The Paris Review.* His work has appeared in *The New Yorker, The Hudson Review* and *Partisan Review.* His most recent collection of poetry is *Breakdown Lane.*

Elissa Schappell (interview with Toni Morrison) is an advisory editor of *The Paris Review* and the book columnist for *Vanity Fair.*

Her fiction has appeared in *Bomb, Interview* and *The Ark/angel Review*. She lives in New York City with her husband and daughter.

Elisabeth Sifton (interview with Mary McCarthy) is senior vice president of Farrar, Straus & Giroux and publisher of Hill and Wang. A graduate of Radcliffe College, she became an editor at the Viking Press in 1968 and was named its editor in chief in 1980. Her own imprint, Elizabeth Sifton Books, won the Carey Thomas Award for Creative Publishing in 1986. She has worked with John Ashbery, Robertson Davies, William Gaddis, Allan Gurganus and Peter Matthiessen, among many other authors. Ms. Sifton is married to the historian Fritz Stern.

Elizabeth Spires (interview with Elizabeth Bishop) is the author of four collections of poetry: *Globe, Swan's Island, Annonciade* and *Worldling* and a book of riddles for children, *With One White Wing*. She has been a Guggenheim Fellow and holds a Distinguished Chair for Achievement at Goucher College in Baltimore, where she lives.

Barbara Thompson (interview with Katherine Anne Porter) has had her short stories published in the Pushcart Prize anthologies VII and IX and *Shenandoah Anthology: From the First 35 Years*. Her interview with Peter Taylor appeared in *The Paris Review* in 1987.

Marina Warner (interview with Rebecca West) is the author of a collection of short stories, *The Mermaids in the Basement*; four novels, most recently, *Indigo: The Lost Father*; and volumes of history and scholarly criticism, including *Joan of Arc* and *From the Beast to the Blonde*. She is a visiting professor of women's studies at the University of Ulster.

Photo Credits

About the Type

This book was set in Centaur, a typeface designed by the American typographer Bruce Rogers in 1929. Centaur was a typeface that Rogers adapted from the fifteenth-century type of Nicholas Jenson and modified in 1948 for a cutting by the Monotype Corporation.